The Moving Text

The Moving Text

*Interdisciplinary Perspectives on
David Brown and the Bible*

Edited by
Garrick V. Allen,
Christopher R. Brewer
and
Dennis F. Kinlaw III

scm press

© Garrick V. Allen, Christopher R. Brewer and Dennis F. Kinlaw III 2018

Published in 2018 by SCM Press
Editorial office
3rd Floor, Invicta House,
108–114 Golden Lane,
London EC1Y 0TG, UK
www.scmpress.co.uk

SCM Press is an imprint of Hymns Ancient & Modern Ltd
(a registered charity)

Hymns Ancient & Modern® is a registered trademark of
Hymns Ancient & Modern Ltd
13A Hellesdon Park Road, Norwich,
Norfolk NR6 5DR, UK

All rights reserved. No part of this publication may be reproduced,
stored in a retrieval system, or transmitted,
in any form or by any means, electronic, mechanical,
photocopying or otherwise, without the prior permission of
the publisher, SCM Press.

The Author has asserted his right under the Copyright, Designs and
Patents Act 1988 to be identified as the Author of this Work

British Library Cataloguing in Publication data

A catalogue record for this book is available
from the British Library

978 0 334 05526 6

Typeset by Regent Typesetting Ltd
Printed and bound by
CPI Group (UK) Ltd

Contents

Editor's Introduction   ix
    Christopher R. Brewer

Part 1: The Biblical Text

1. Text and Tradition: David Brown and New Testament Textual Criticism   3
    Garrick V. Allen
2. From the Magi to Pilate's Wife: David Brown, Tradition and the Reception of Matthew's Text   17
    Ian Boxall
3. Memory, Remembrance and Imagination in the Formation of Redemptive Tradition: Reflecting on the Gospel of John with David Brown   37
    Stephen C. Barton
4. Moving Texts and Mirror Neurons: David Brown and Eleonore Stump on Biblical Interpretation   51
    Robert MacSwain

Part 2: The Visual Imagination

5. Paradise Reclaimed: Kerry James Marshall and Chris Ofili in the Garden of Eden   73
    Taylor Worley
6. Re-visions of Sacrifice: Abraham in Art and Interfaith Dialogue   91
    Aaron Rosen
7. 'Surely the Lord is in this Place': Jacob's Ladder in Painting, Contemporary Sculpture and Installation Art   107
    Christopher R. Brewer

8 Understanding John's Visions: Unlocking the Insights of
   Revelation's Visual History   122
      Natasha O'Hear
9 The Stained Glass *Biblia Pauperum* Windows of Steinfeld
   Abbey: Monastic Spirituality, Salvation History and the
   Theological Imagination   143
      William P. Hyland

Part 3: The Literary Imagination

10 David Brown and the Virgin Mary: A Literary Perspective 163
      Thomas Rist
11 Intertextuality, Tradition and Finding Theology in
   Unexpected Places: Reading *Frankenstein* with the Help of
   David Brown   177
      Jon Greenaway
12 The Forms of Faith in Contemporary American Fiction   195
      Dennis F. Kinlaw III

The Moving Text: A Reply   207
   David Brown

Appendix: The Moving Text in the Life of the Church

Introduction   233
   Garrick V. Allen, Christopher R. Brewer and Dennis F.
   Kinlaw III
The Ladder Between Heaven and Earth: John 1.43–51   234
   David Brown
Rachel and Leah: Genesis 29.15–28   237
   David Brown
Food offered to Idols and Idolatry in Word and Image:
Revelation 2.12–17   240
   David Brown
Emotion and the Tears of Peter: Mark 8.31–38   245
   David Brown

Bibliography   248
Index of Scripture References   267
Index of Names and Subjects   269

Contributors

Garrick V. Allen is Lecturer in New Testament at Dublin City University (Republic of Ireland), and research associate of the Department of Ancient Languages, University of Pretoria (South Africa).

Stephen C. Barton is Honorary Fellow in the Department of Theology and Religion at Durham University, and was formerly Reader in New Testament in the same department. He is also Honorary Research Fellow in the Department of Religions and Theology at Manchester University.

Ian Boxall is Associate Professor of New Testament in the School of Theology and Religious Studies at The Catholic University of America (USA).

Christopher R. Brewer is a Program Officer of the Templeton Religion Trust in Nassau (The Bahamas).

David Brown is Wardlaw Professor Emeritus of Theology, Aesthetics and Culture at St Mary's College, University of St Andrews. He was elected a Fellow of the British Academy in 2002 and of the Royal Society of Edinburgh in 2012.

Jon Greenaway is Associate Lecturer in English and Film at Manchester Metropolitan University.

William P. Hyland is Lecturer in Church History at St Mary's College, University of St Andrews.

Dennis F. Kinlaw III is Assistant Professor of English and member of the Honors College at Houston Baptist University (USA).

Robert MacSwain is Associate Professor of Theology at the School of Theology of the University of the South (USA).

Natasha O'Hear is Honorary Lecturer at St Mary's College, University of St Andrews.

Thomas Rist is Senior Lecturer in the Department of English at the University of Aberdeen.

Aaron Rosen is Professor of Religious Thought at Rocky Mountain College (USA) and Visiting Professor of Theology at King's College London.

Taylor Worley is Associate Professor of Faith and Culture at Trinity International University (USA).

Editor's Introduction

CHRISTOPHER R. BREWER

'Disciplinarity and interdisciplinarity positively reinforce each other.'[1] David Brown (b. 1948) is an Anglican priest and theologian whose work is a prime example of this claim. Brown has written and edited a number of volumes, and this in addition to more than 50 essays.[2] These books and essays address a wide variety of themes, including theology, philosophy and the arts, but also biblical studies.[3] Brown's work, however, is rarely engaged in any meaningful way by biblical scholars.[4] For his part, Brown demonstrates a significant knowledge of currents in biblical scholarship and uses this information as evidence for his broader arguments, but the conversation has more or less moved in one direction. In an effort to reverse the flow, the editors of this volume organized a colloquium – held on 22 June 2015 at St Mary's College, University of St Andrews – for biblical and interdisciplinary scholars interested in engaging Brown's work, and more specifically his 1999 monograph, *Tradition and Imagination: Revelation and Change*.[5] Madhavi Nevader, Stephen Barton, Garrick V. Allen, Jon Greenaway and Dennis F. Kinlaw III presented papers, followed by a response from Brown himself.

In his review of Brown's *Discipleship and Imagination* (2000), John Macquarrie concluded: 'This book, together with the earlier volume, is a profound study ... To do it justice would require not a review but a point-by-point commentary.'[6] We do not yet have a point-by-point commentary, but with the 2012 publication of a volume of essays responding to Brown's five Oxford University Press volumes (including the two just named),[7] a more general Festschrift just published,[8] and this volume of essays from the St Andrews colloquium, we have what amounts to a substantial down payment on the more exhaustive commentary. It may, in the end, come piecemeal, but what cannot be denied is the expansive, profound and generative nature of Brown's work, which crosses disciplinary boundaries and invites further exploration.[9] Along these lines, and with reference to biblical studies, James Barr wrote:

I think that David Brown's work is quite magnificent ... I do not say that biblical theology *must* ally itself with an approach like his; I do suggest that it should see in it a possibility for its own development. It remains possible that biblical theologians will want to keep free from any sort of alliance with doctrinal theology of any kind; I only suggest that in doing so they might first of all make themselves aware of what this line of theological thinking, closely interlinked with biblical exegesis, actually provides. And from its distinctly Christian position, its understanding approach towards Judaism (and Islam) and to Greek religion (and thus in principle to the history of religion) ought to be significant, even if only as a pointer in a direction along which one may go.[10]

If Brown's work is a pointer – a trail marker, if you will – then this volume is a map that directs readers to the trailhead. The introduction thus begins with a brief discussion of David Brown and the Bible before turning to the work of what might be called Brown's allies and then to a brief introduction to the contents of the volume itself.

David Brown and the Bible

Brown begins, more generally, with an interactionist God,[11] as well as an accompanying twin commitment to divine generosity and human freedom. These commitments may, at first glance, seem irrelevant to, or in any case a good distance from, biblical studies, having instead more to do with philosophical theology, but for Brown the ongoing nature of God's involvement with humanity has everything to do with the Bible. As he wrote in the Preface to *The Divine Trinity*: 'It was through reading John Henry Newman ... on development of doctrine within the Church that I gradually came to appreciate that the same approach must also be rigorously applied to the Bible.'[12] The motivation for this application of Newman's insight has to do with biblical criticism, and more specifically, the fallibility of the Bible. Put simply: Brown argues that stress on divine respect for human freedom is the only plausible way to maintain the notion of an interactionist God while acknowledging the fallibility of Scripture.[13] Against conservatives, who seek 'to retain the old model of inspiration', and also against radical critics, who 'tend to move the locus of authority to divine acts in history', Brown argues for revision of the concept of revelation in light of religious experience.[14] Revelation is, according to Brown's incarnational logic,[15] historically situated and culturally conditioned. It is, in other words, an interactionist, kenotic,[16] sensitive/adaptive, progressive/developmental theory of revelation as divine dialogue,[17] an address adapted to specific situations that because of human freedom and its limitations may also regress as well as advance.

Given that Brown emphasizes the conditioned character of all thought (including Scripture and revelation), it should come as no surprise that he thinks the Bible fallible, but for him this means potential for development. He explains: 'Close attention to original context can uncover open trajectories as it were, pressure points that almost demand further development.'[18] I will return to this idea in a moment, and more specifically the related concepts of triggers and criteria, but the point to be made here is that while some would think fallibility a sign of weakness, perhaps even grounds for rejecting the faith, it is for Brown part and parcel of the divine dialogue that constitutes *living* faith. Brown explains:

> [Dialogue] suggests, on the one hand, accommodation to one's interlocutor – expressing oneself at a level at which he can understand and, on the other hand, some contribution from that interlocutor, some explication of the point which he believes the dialogue to have reached, which will then in turn elicit a further response and so on. Or, putting it another way, the notion of dialogue fully acknowledges that God's communication with man takes place in very specific contexts with certain things already assumed at each stage, an already existing canon of assumptions, as it were, – a canon that has shaped the community's conception of God, and thus inevitably shapes both the present experient's response to a particular experience and also what it is possible for God to put into that particular experience by way of content.[19]

Fallibility is, from Brown's perspective, to be preferred, and this for logical as well as moral reasons.[20] To be more specific, the logical reason is that God works with existing thought patterns, and so reveals within a tradition of understanding that is developed over time. The moral reason, on the other hand, has to do with human freedom, as Brown explains:

> For it might be that God deliberately refrains from ever imposing a particular viewpoint on a recipient, but always wishes that it should become, as it were, internalised or, putting it another way, experienced as the recipient's own insight.[21]

In any case, fallibility means openness to change, and this development occurs when 'triggers' (i.e. external stimuli, beyond Scripture) lead to reinterpretation. Brown thus concludes: 'What we therefore seem to have is a community of faith in continual process of change as fresh contexts trigger fresh handlings of inherited traditions.'[22] This process of change no doubt raises the question of criteria (i.e. which changes are legitimate and on what basis?), and though Brown has identified nine types of criteria,[23] critics have continued to press the issue.[24] This is not the place to adjudicate, and more work certainly needs to be done by Brown and others to address this issue; but surely, as Brown has noted, 'we must not use that as an excuse for not facing the more complex reality which we find'.[25] In any case, what the reader should take away from the discussion of Brown and the Bible thus far is that Brown accepts the findings of biblical criticism, and more specifically the fallibility of the Bible, but thinks fallibility not only acceptable but also preferable in light of his developmental theory of revelation which, together with fallibility, maintains divine interactionism and human freedom.

At this point several things should be noted. First, Brown rejects any sharp distinction between natural and revealed theology, emphasizing the role of reason as well as the wider context of religious experience in any adequate account of revealed theology.[26] Second, he distinguishes revelation from the canon of Scripture.[27] Third, he expands the notion of canon to include not only the biblical canon but also the canon of interpretation. Fourth, he relocates revelation to the act of interpretation. Tradition (i.e. interpretation) is thus, for Brown, potentially revelatory and, I might add, imaginatively mediated. He thus speaks of tradition as 'the motor that sustains revelation both within Scripture and beyond'[28] and, additionally, suggests that 'the truth of imaginative "fit"' may well be preferable to the criterion of 'literal fact'.[29] It is for this reason that Brown speaks of 'Art as revelation'[30] and, elsewhere, 'Artists as Theologians';[31] that is, because ongoing imaginative mediation is, from Brown's perspective, more than reception or illustration but, instead and more significantly, has the potential to innovate and reinvigorate. Going further, Brown argues that these later developments might even correct or 'critique' the scriptural text.[32] All of this is part of what Brown calls 'the moving text', which spans scriptural and interpretative canons; that is, 'a shifting real text whose actual content at any particular moment could only be determined by careful analysis of its social setting'.[33]

Brown's attention to a given text's social setting may, at first glance, seem to privilege history – that is, insofar as he wishes to draw attention to the text's intervening history – and this is in one sense true,[34] but he ultimately gives priority to questions of meaning and significance rather than history or canon. As he explains:

> Neither history nor canon can be allowed to function as final arbiters, since more fundamental are questions of significance. What we need to consider is whether theologically or spiritually the new versions of a story or a new use to which it is put had something valuable to say in its new context, and so perhaps also to us today.[35]

Brown is, in other words, concerned with relevance, or as he puts it, 'spiritual significance'. As he explains in the introduction to his first collection of sermons:

> when I became a priest, I determined that – no matter how difficult it should prove – I would attempt to integrate fully these two areas of my life: study and pulpit. To my delight this seemed to enable me to communicate the good news of Jesus Christ *more* effectively, not less. But this should not have surprised me, for the biblical writers themselves had thought spiritual significance more important than a literal recording of events ... Through acknowledging this, the text ceased to be a burden upon me; instead it insisted that I too spoke of God's power of healing and renewal for my own day.[36]

And so we have come full circle, back to an interactionist God who is involved in an ongoing dialogue with humanity through 'the moving text'.

Brown speaks also of 'an open tradition that is willing to learn from approaches beyond the narrow compass of the Christian community itself',[37] and this 'open tradition' is more or less synonymous with his notion of 'the moving text', albeit framed in terms of 'tradition' rather than 'text'. The point here is that tradition is more indefinite than definite, supple rather than static or unchanging. And while innovation may well come from within the tradition itself, change might just as easily come from external stimuli, including other religions.[38] Brown explains:

> The Christian story has thus acquired new insights not merely through recovery of neglected aspects of its past but also through external stimuli necessitating fresh thought and with it rather different imaginative appropriations of the Christian message from what the primitive community would have envisaged.[39]

This notion of 'an open tradition' might be compared and contrasted with Howard E. Root's 'constellations', William Desmond's discussion of 'open wholeness' (aka 'a more "open" reading of Hegel') or Lieven Boeve's articulation of the 'open narrative'.[40] That said, comparison with any of these thinkers would take us further from biblical studies, where there are plenty of comparisons to be made.

David Brown and his Allies

While Brown's notion of 'the moving text' may at first glance appear extreme, there are a number of scholars – biblical as well as theological – who have advanced similar notions, and though not all interact with Brown, they nevertheless display a certain 'family resemblance'. David Parker, for example, has argued from the perspective of biblical studies that 'Scripture is Tradition'; that is, 'part of the early tradition ... transmitted to us only by tradition'.[41] Brown would, I think, in principle agree,[42] but in addition to 'the moving text' within the scriptural canon, he speaks also of 'the moving text' beyond 'the canon' (i.e. 'the canon of interpretation'), itself revelatory. More fully, Brown explains:

> To my mind it is thus a delusion to suppose that the Church, having acquired a fixed canon, thereby lost the pattern of development which characterized the earlier community. The canon of interpretation continued to develop, even if this ceased to be by the simple creation of wholly new texts. Sometimes this involved creative mistranslation; sometimes a new grid being imposed upon an existing story; sometimes lacunae being filled and thus indirectly an almost wholly new story generated. Sometimes even what is constitutive of this real canon is not written text at all but a narrative controlled by visual image ... The real narrative text that controls the Christian imagination of today is not the various biblical stories as such, but an amalgam created over the centuries, and in particular more often than not mediated through nativity plays, art and hymns rather than the details of the biblical narratives.[43]

This idea that the real canon is not a written text at all goes beyond Parker, who – though he argues that, in one sense, 'there is no such thing as the New Testament'[44] – maintains the notion of a 'living text',[45] rather than something beyond the textual (e.g. Brown's interpretative canon). In any case, this gets beyond the idea of a static text accompanied by reception history of which Brown is critical. For Brown, there is only 'the moving text' within and beyond the canon, and that beyond is better described, according to Brown (who cites the work of Paul M. Joyce and Diana Lipton on Lamentations as being exemplary in this regard), as 'reception exegesis'.[46] In other words, according to Brown, too much of the currently fashionable investigation of reception history confines itself to an account of what has happened across the centuries rather than sympathetic engagement with the reasons for the changes and their potential to speak as relevant exegesis for the community of faith then and perhaps also now.

Drawing more explicitly on Brown, Benjamin D. Sommer has advocated a 'participatory theory of revelation' ('participatory theology') characterized by 'dialogue between God and Israel'.[47] He explains:

> Many biblical texts that describe the giving of Torah move simultaneously and without contradiction in two directions: they anchor the authority of Jewish law and lore in the revelation at Sinai, but they also destabilize that authority by teaching that we cannot be sure how, exactly, the specific rules found in the Pentateuch relate to God's self-disclosure ... These biblical texts suggest that revelation involved active contributions by both God and Israel; revelation was collaborative and participatory.[48]

Going further, he writes:

> that the participatory theology of revelation implies that the very category of scripture is a chimera, and that the participatory theology resituates – and, surprisingly, resuscitates – the Bible as a work of tradition. This approach implies that for Judaism there really is no such thing as scripture; there is only tradition, which begins with and includes the Pentateuch, the Prophets, and the Writings.[49]

We find fascinating this notion that what Brown refers to as 'the moving text' – and Sommer as 'participatory revelation' – might well 'resuscitate' the Bible, and the essays in this volume are intended to explore this idea. The point, in any case, is that neither Brown nor Sommer mean to disparage the Bible. Rather, in seeking to acknowledge the findings of higher criticism, they are trying, in Brown's words, 'to extricate it from a burden which ... it cannot possibly bear'.[50] With this context in mind, I turn now to the contents of the volume.

The Moving Text: An Overview of its Contents

Part 1 of this volume draws Brown into the orbit of biblical scholars with essays ranging from New Testament textual criticism to hermeneutics. In 'Text and Tradition: David Brown and New Testament Textual Criticism', Garrick V. Allen argues that textual critics are not only interested in 'establishing an "original" or "authoritative" text', but also, and perhaps more so, in textual variation (i.e. development within Scripture itself). Given that Brown wants to push Newman's insight back into Scripture, Allen thinks him an excellent dialogue partner for the New Testament textual critic. Allen thus seeks, on the one hand, to reinforce and extend Brown's argument and, on the other, to draw upon and present Brown as a 'ready-made' resource for textual scholars. Ian Boxall's chapter, 'From the Magi to Pilate's Wife: David Brown, Tradition and the Reception of Matthew's Text', begins with Brown's discussion of the Magi, but – as an extension of Brown's commitment to 'Learning from Pagans'[51] – considers receptions of the story of Pilate's wife. Boxall argues that these receptions are a prime example of positive enrichment. In another chapter focused on the Gospels, 'Memory, Remembrance and Imagination in the Formation of Redemptive Tradition: Reflecting on the Gospel of John with David Brown', Stephen C. Barton offers a sympathetic summary of Brown's project before arguing that more attention might be paid to the role of memory and remembrance in John 2.13–22. Shifting from the Bible to biblical interpretation, Robert MacSwain's chapter, 'Moving Texts and Mirror Neurons: David Brown and Eleonore Stump on Biblical Interpretation', compares Brown's approach with that of Eleonore Stump and, more specifically, considers their respective interpretations of Abraham, Job and Mary Magdalene/Mary of Bethany.

Part 2 engages, interrogates and extends Brown's work with reference to a wide range of visual art, all the while mindful of the larger argument and its implications for biblical studies. In 'Paradise Reclaimed: Kerry James Marshall and Chris Ofili in the Garden of Eden', Taylor Worley considers the paintings of Marshall and Ofili – two in particular – as part of what Brown calls 'the interpretative canon', and argues that these two painters, whose work embodies a 'black aesthetic', offer a necessary, corrective reading of Genesis 1—2. Aaron Rosen's chapter, 'Re-visions of Sacrifice: Abraham and Interfaith Dialogue', interrogates Brown's reading of Genesis 22 and highlights potential trajectories for dialogue. In yet another chapter on the book of Genesis, '"Surely the Lord is in this Place': Jacob's Ladder in Painting, Contemporary Sculpture and Installation Art', I argue that Jacob's ladder is a great example of art – and more specifically, contemporary sculpture and installation art – raising not only semantic but also metaphysical questions in ways perhaps more engaging than Scripture itself. Natasha O'Hear's chapter, 'Understanding John's Visions: Unlocking the Insights of Revelation's Visual History', seeks to challenge – and in so doing extend – Brown's consideration of the reception history of Revelation. More specifically, O'Hear examines the visionary experience behind the text, and some images of Revelation's Beasts. Moving on from scriptural to interpretative canon, William P. Hyland's chapter, 'The Stained Glass *Biblia Pauperum* Windows of Steinfeld Abbey: Monastic Spirituality, Salvation History and the Theological Imagination', considers the fascinating history of the cloister windows from the former Premonstratensian abbey

EDITOR'S INTRODUCTION

of Steinfeld. Hyland raises the question of context and the experience of the sacred in relation to Brown's conception of 'the moving text'.

Part 3 turns the page, so to speak, and explores the ways narratives outside of Scripture serve to develop and enrich our understanding and experience of the narratives within Scripture. In 'David Brown and the Virgin Mary: A Literary Perspective', Thomas Rist questions Brown's subjugation of literature to religion and, focusing on literary depictions of Mary, seeks to offer a helpful corrective. Jon Greenaway's chapter, 'Intertextuality, Tradition and Finding Theology in Unexpected Places: Reading *Frankenstein* with the Help of David Brown', takes the reader from Rist's early modern survey to a particular Gothic novel: Mary Shelley's *Frankenstein*. Seeking to apply Brown's work to his own area of specialization (i.e. the Gothic) – and more specifically, to read *Frankenstein* as part of 'the moving text' – Greenaway explores issues of value, worth and personhood in an effort to highlight the theological relevance of the Gothic. Dennis F. Kinlaw III then draws us firmly into the present with his consideration of contemporary American fiction, and more specifically the work of David Foster Wallace.[52] The volume concludes with a reply and – in the Appendix – four sermons from Brown himself. These sermons are intended to illustrate how Brown's approach might be put into practice.

Mostly sympathetic, even if critical, the essays in this volume are constructive insofar as they seek to make the case for interdisciplinarity, and more specifically for a more thorough consideration of Brown's contribution to biblical studies. Our hope is that they will serve as points of contact, footholds for students and scholars alike as they seek out and read 'the moving text'.

Notes

1 David Soskice, 'Foreword', in *Crossing Paths: Interdisciplinary Institutions, Careers, Education and Applications* (London: The British Academy, 2016), 6. Online: www.britac.ac.uk/sites/default/files/Crossing%20Paths%20-%20Full%20Report.pdf; accessed 30 April 2017.

2 Some of these essays have been republished, alongside several new ones, in two volumes: David Brown, *God in a Single Vision: Integrating Philosophy and Theology*, ed. Christopher R. Brewer and Robert MacSwain (London and New York: Routledge, 2016); idem, *Divine Generosity and Human Creativity: Theology through Symbol, Painting and Architecture*, ed. Christopher R. Brewer and Robert MacSwain (London and New York: Routledge, 2017).

3 See, for example, David Brown, *The Divine Trinity* (London: Duckworth; La Salle, IL: Open Court, 1985), 52–98; idem, *Invitation to Theology* (Oxford: Blackwell, 1989), 12–14, 42–89, 106–7, 144–5; idem, 'Did Revelation Cease?', in *Reason and the Christian Religion: Essays in Honour of Richard Swinburne*, ed. Alan G. Padgett

(Oxford: Clarendon, 1994), 121–41; *idem, The Word to Set You Free: Living Faith and Biblical Criticism* (London: SPCK, 1995); *idem, Tradition and Imagination: Revelation and Change* (Oxford: Oxford University Press, 1999), *passim*; *idem, Discipleship and Imagination: Christian Tradition and Truth* (Oxford: Oxford University Press, 2000), *passim*; *idem*, 'Sinai in Art and Architecture', in *The Significance of Sinai: Traditions about Sinai and Divine Revelation in Judaism and Christianity*, ed. George J. Brooke, Hindy Najman and Loren T. Stuckenbruck (Leiden and Boston, MA: Brill, 2008), 313–31; *idem, Divine Humanity: Kenosis and the Construction of Christian Theology* (Waco, TX: Baylor University Press, 2011), 4–14; *idem, God in a Single Vision*, ed. Brewer and MacSwain, 61–85; *idem*, 'The Bible and Wider Culture: Animals as a Test Case', in *In the Fullness of Time: Essays on Christology, Creation, and Eschatology in Honor of Richard Bauckham*, ed. Daniel M. Gurtner, Grant Macaskill and Jonathan T. Pennington (Grand Rapids, MI: Eerdmans, 2016), 65–81; *idem, Divine Generosity and Human Creativity*, ed. Brewer and MacSwain, 81–7.

4 Notable exceptions include James Barr, *The Concept of Biblical Theology: An Old Testament Perspective* (Minneapolis, MN: Augsburg Fortress, 1999), 586–604; James D. G. Dunn, *New Testament Theology: An Introduction* (Nashville, TN: Abingdon, 2009), 158; and Benjamin D. Sommer, *Revelation and Authority: Sinai in Jewish Scripture and Tradition*, The Anchor Yale Bible Reference Library (New Haven, CT and London: Yale University Press, 2015), 103, and 403–4 for a complete listing. For reflections on the Bible in pastoral practice with reference to Brown, see Gordon Oliver, *Holy Bible, Human Bible: Questions Pastoral Practice Must Ask* (Grand Rapids, MI: Eerdmans, 2006), 97–8.

5 The editors are grateful to the Centre for Academic, Professional and Organisational Development at the University of St Andrews for a CAPOD Professional Development Grant, and also to Professor Mark Elliot, then Head of School, for a matching grant from St Mary's College, University of St Andrews.

6 John Macquarrie, review of David Brown, 'Discipleship and Imagination: Christian Tradition and Truth', *Journal of Theological Studies* 52.2 (2001), 982.

7 Robert MacSwain and Taylor Worley (eds), *Theology, Aesthetics, and Culture: Responses to the Work of David Brown* (Oxford: Oxford University Press, 2012). For a concise introduction to Brown's five OUP volumes, see Robert MacSwain, 'Introduction: Theology, Aesthetics, and Culture', in *Theology, Aesthetics, and Culture*, ed. MacSwain and Worley, 1–10.

8 Christopher R. Brewer (ed.), *Christian Theology and the Transformation of Natural Religion: From Incarnation to Sacramentality – Essays in Honour of David Brown* (Leuven: Peeters, 2018).

9 See also David James Stewart, 'The Fulfillment of a Polanyian Vision of Heuristic Theology: David Brown's Reframing of Revelation, Tradition, and Imagination', *Tradition & Discovery: The Polanyi Society Periodical* 41.3 (2015), 4–19.

10 Barr, *The Concept of Biblical Theology*, 603.

11 For discussion of Brown's view, which he originally described as interventionist, and then later interactionist, see Brown, *The Divine Trinity*, x, xv, 4–5, 53–4, 101, 140–1, 236–7, 239, 255–6; *idem*, 'Wittgenstein Against the "Wittgensteinians": A Reply to Kenneth Surin on *The Divine Trinity*', *Modern Theology* 2 (1986), 264; *idem*, 'God and Symbolic Action', in *Scripture, Metaphysics, and Poetry: Austin Farrer's* The Glass of Vision *with Critical Commentary*, ed. Robert MacSwain (Farnham: Ashgate, 2013), 134; *idem, Tradition and Imagination*, 277.

12 Brown, *The Divine Trinity*; cf. *idem, Choices: Ethics and the Christian* (Oxford: Blackwell, 1983), 34. See also *idem, Tradition and Imagination*, 62.

13 See Brown, 'God and Symbolic Action', in *Scripture, Metaphysics, and Poetry*, ed. MacSwain, 136; cf. Sommer, *Revelation and Authority*, 186–7, 235–9, 248.

14 Brown, *The Divine Trinity*, xii; cf. Sommer, ch. 1: 'Artifact or Scripture?', in *Revelation and Authority*, 11–26.

15 Brown explains: '[T]he incarnation involved a more radical kenosis than Christianity has assumed throughout most of its history, with Jesus very much conditioned by the culture of which he was part. But if this was true at the point of God's deepest disclosure and involvement with humanity, then *a fortiori* one would expect matters to proceed similarly elsewhere in revelation, and this is in fact what we find as we study the origin of the various biblical ideas. Revelation was thus a matter of God taking seriously our historical situatedness, our dependence on our own particular environment and setting, rather than attempting to override it.' Brown, *Tradition and Imagination*, 7–8. See also ibid., 109; *idem*, *God in a Single Vision*, ed. Brewer and MacSwain, 64–5.

16 For discussion of the kenotic model, see Brown, *The Divine Trinity*, 219–71; David Brown, *Divine Humanity: Kenosis Explored and Defended* (London: SCM Press; with an alternate subtitle – *Kenosis and the Construction of a Christian Theology* – Waco, TX: Baylor University Press, 2011); *idem*, 'Incarnational Models Revisited', in *God in a Single Vision*, ed. Brewer and MacSwain, 92–106.

17 Brown writes: '[R]evelation is a process whereby God progressively unveils the truth about himself and his purposes to a community of believers, but always in such a manner that their freedom of response is respected.' Brown, *The Divine Trinity*, 70. See also *idem*, *God in a Single Vision*, ed. Brewer and MacSwain, 61–2.

18 Brown, *Tradition and Imagination*, 54.

19 Brown, *The Divine Trinity*, 70.

20 For discussion, see ibid., 71–4.

21 Ibid., 72.

22 Brown, *Tradition and Imagination*, 57. Going further, Brown writes: 'The reason why narratives retain their power in different circumstances is because readers either give new prominence to hitherto neglected aspects of the text or because they resolve to tell the story in a new way.' Ibid.

23 Brown, *Discipleship and Imagination*, 389–405.

24 Brown mentions this criticism in *God and Enchantment of Place: Reclaiming Human Experience* (Oxford: Oxford University Press, 2004), 3. For additional discussion, see Christopher R. Brewer, 'Editor's Introduction', in *Divine Generosity and Human Creativity*, ed. Brewer and MacSwain, viii–ix; and for what is probably the most comprehensive response on this point to date (even though it has primarily to do with Brown's writings on music), see Gavin Hopps, 'Popular Music and Spilt Religion: A Window onto the Infinite', in David Brown and Gavin Hopps, *The Extravagance of Music* (New York: Palgrave Macmillan, forthcoming).

25 Brown, *Tradition and Imagination*, 127.

26 Brown, *The Divine Trinity*, 61, 77–86; cf. *idem*, *God in a Single Vision*, ed. Brewer and MacSwain, 3; cf. James Barr, *Biblical Faith and Natural Theology: The Gifford Lectures for 1991 Delivered in the University of Edinburgh* (Oxford: Clarendon, 1993), 103, 115, 121–2, 136–7, 144–5, 195–8, 200; *idem*, *Bible and Interpretation: The Collected Essays of James Barr*, vol. 1: Interpretation and Theology, ed. John Barton (Oxford: Oxford University Press, 2013), 411–80.

27 Brown, *The Divine Trinity*, 61, 74–7.

28 Brown, *Tradition and Imagination*, 1.

29 Ibid., 7. See also Brown, *The Divine Trinity*, 103–5; *idem*, *Discipleship and Imagination*, 402–3.

30 Brown, *Tradition and Imagination*, 322–64.

31 Brown, *Divine Generosity and Human Creativity*, ed. Brewer and MacSwain, 99–149.

32 Brown, *Tradition and Imagination*, 1, 5. Important to note is that this process of critique works in both directions (ibid., 1, 51), and also that progress is not inevitable

(ibid., 207). See also David Brown, 'Human Sacrifice and Two Imaginative Worlds, Aztec and Christian: Finding God in Evil', in *Sacrifice and Modern Thought*, ed. Julia Meszaros and Johannes Zachhuber (Oxford: Oxford University Press, 2013), 180, n. 1. Making an important clarification, Brown there notes: 'That is, undermine the predominance of texts, even if still brought under some more fundamental scriptural principle.' Ibid.

33 Brown, *Tradition and Imagination*, 127.

34 I say 'in one sense' as Brown does, in fact, wish to draw attention to 'the intervening history'. He explains: 'Present-day Christianity, it seems to me, will go badly wrong, if it attempts an unmediated dialogue with the biblical text rather than recognizing also the intervening history that has helped shape its present perception of the text's meaning.' Ibid., 2. See also ibid., 117.

35 Ibid., 208.

36 Brown, *The Word to Set You Free*, ix–x.

37 Brown, *Tradition and Imagination*, 7.

38 Ibid., 106ff.

39 Ibid., 8.

40 Howard E. Root, *Theological Radicalism and Tradition: 'The Limits of Radicalism' with Appendices*, ed. Christopher R. Brewer (London and New York: Routledge, 2018), 65–71; William Desmond, *Art and the Absolute: A Study of Hegel's Aesthetics*, SUNY Series in Hegelian Studies (Albany, NY: State University of New York Press, 1986), xix; Lieven Boeve, *Interrupting Tradition: An Essay on Christian Faith in a Postmodern Context*, Louvain Theological and Pastoral Monographs 30 (Leuven: Peeters, 2003). For discussion of Root and Desmond along these lines, see Christopher R. Brewer, 'Rolling with Release into the Future: William Desmond's Donation to a Natural Theology of the Arts', in *William Desmond and Contemporary Theology*, ed. Christopher Ben Simpson and Brendan Thomas Sammon (Notre Dame, IN: University of Notre Dame Press, 2017), 217–37.

41 David Parker, 'Scripture is Tradition', *Theology* 94.757 (1991), 17.

42 That said, Brown has been critical of Parker's 'exaggeration'. Brown, *Tradition and Imagination*, 301–2.

43 Ibid., 123–4.

44 Parker, 'Scripture is Tradition', 16.

45 D. C. Parker, *The Living Text of the Gospels* (Cambridge: Cambridge University Press, 1997). For further reflection on the relationship between Brown and Parker, see Garrick V. Allen's chapter in this volume.

46 Brown, *God in a Single Vision*, ed. Brewer and MacSwain, 82.

47 Sommer, *Revelation and Authority*, 2.

48 Ibid., 1.

49 Ibid., 8; cf. Parker, 'Scripture is Tradition', 16.

50 Brown, *Tradition and Imagination*, 1.

51 David Brown, 'The Glory of God Revealed in Art and Music: Learning from Pagans', in *Celebrating Creation: Affirming Catholicism and the Revelation of God's Glory*, ed. Mark Chapman (London: Darton, Longman & Todd, 2004), 43–56; republished as *idem*, 'Learning from Pagans', in *Divine Generosity and Human Creativity*, ed. Brewer and MacSwain, 37–48.

52 I am grateful to my co-editors, and also to David Brown, Robert MacSwain and Ben Sommer, for feedback on an earlier version of this introduction.

PART I

The Biblical Text

I

Text and Tradition: David Brown and New Testament Textual Criticism

GARRICK V. ALLEN

In popular perception, New Testament textual criticism belongs to the realm of the überspecialist, practitioners with access to secret knowledge, worshipping at clandestine altars in the recesses of medieval university buildings. They strain by candlelight to use worn copies of Tischendorf's *editio octava critica maior* and hoary copies of Westcott and Hort as objects of cultic reverence, combing tattered apparatuses like Babylonian shamen practising extispicy. The fruit of the occult-like activities for NT scholarship – when considered relevant at all – is the creation of the hand edition, usually the Nestle-Aland prepared by the Institut für Neutestamentliche Textforschung in Münster (28th edn, 2012). 'Thank goodness for lower criticism', they say with relief, 'and that we are spared from this labour that produced a trustworthy, unproblematic, and authoritative critical edition from which we can get on to the important businesses of history, exegesis, and perhaps even theology.'

This portrait of the textual critic, while an obvious exaggeration on many fronts, points nonetheless to a misconception of the discipline: that it is interested only in establishing an 'original' or 'authoritative' text (a task that is more or less complete), not the historical, social and religious scruples that influenced the transmission of texts; that the discipline is primarily concerned with the small-scale refinement of adequate editions. In fact, textual scholars are more and more interested in what textual variation and the shape of textual culture tell us about tradents (i.e. the people who produced manuscripts), and the development of Christian tradition.[1] The presentation of the text in its manuscripts has come to the fore and textual variation is no longer viewed as a reality to be lamented and corrected.[2]

Although not the only source of tradition, the Bible played a central role in the development of doctrine and thought, as David Brown himself has argued in *Tradition and Imagination*. Textual scholars are continuing to discover and describe the ways that Scripture – a randomly preserved sample of ancient texts found in mostly late-antique and medieval documents that encompass parts of Christian sacred works containing various wordings, paratexts and forms – is tradition.[3]

This contribution analyses the ways that the Greek manuscripts and their wordings of the NT are both shaped by and a product of tradition by bringing the current major project of NT textual criticism, the *Editio Critica Maior* (ECM), into conversation with the work of David Brown. On the one hand, Brown's insights into the development of tradition provide perceptive assistance into how the textual traditions and the physical *realia* of the NT function as mediators of tradition. On the other, the way that many scholars conceive of the task of textual criticism, as something more than hypothesizing or reconstructing the text as it left an author's hand, provides another example that supports Brown's overarching argument that tradition not only works alongside Scripture but critiques it, sometimes leading to developments in texts and forms. The place to begin such a discussion is with a brief rehearsal of Brown's work on Scripture and tradition as it is relevant to the ECM project that focuses on the Apocalypse currently underway in Wuppertal.[4] Following this prefatory discussion, which time-travels back to the late 1990s by placing David Brown into conversation with David Parker's deceptively thin volume *The Living Text of the Gospels*, I briefly examine some examples of places in the NT's textual history where the continuing development of tradition left its mark on the wording of scriptural works and where paratexts – the allographic products of tradition – shape the understanding of a particular passage. First, let us turn to the ECM.

Tradition, Imagination and the Editio Critica Maior

The ECM, the brainchild of Kurt Aland,[5] was devised to address a need that arose from the fact that the most accurate (Tischendorf 1869, 1872²) and complete (von Soden 1913) critical apparatuses were outdated with recent discoveries and complied in different editions.[6] The ECM was designed to describe the fullness of the textual data derived from Greek, versional and patristic witnesses to the NT in an accurate and consistent manner through the first Christian millennium. This data would, in turn, implicitly trace the narrative embedded in the text of the NT that provides evidence for how it was conceived of, used and changed over time.[7] In addition to its stated goals, the ECM fills out the story of the text with as much data as is possible and/or palatable. To date, only the Catholic Epistles and Acts of the Apostles have appeared,[8] and the other portions of the NT are in various stages of completion. Based on the unique textual histories of the various NT works, the workflow of each project must necessarily be tailored to the existing evidence. At the Institut für Septuaginta- und biblische Textforschung at the Kirchliche Hochschule in Wuppertal, the ECM of the Apocalypse (i.e. the book of Revelation) is in production and it is helpful here to briefly describe the stages of the project and its intended goals in order to understand clearly how Brown's very different theological programme might inform and influence how we conceptualize the value and uses of the ECM in the context of Christian tradition and theological studies broadly conceived.[9]

The groundwork for the ECM project consisted of assembling microfilm and photographs of all NT Greek manuscripts, a task that was 90 per cent complete in 1970,[10] and more recently in their digitization in the New Testament Virtual Manuscript Room.[11] This task is mostly complete for Revelation, owing to the fact that the Apocalypse has no lectionary witnesses and relatively few Greek manuscripts in comparison to other NT works.[12] Next, the texts of the collected witnesses were initially tested at 180 different variation units (paired down to 123 *Teststellen*) to determine Revelation's internal textual affiliations and to see which text families might be discerned among material based on the numerous variants preserved.[13] Although there is no clear majority text for Revelation, two traditions – the Andrew text related to Revelation's most prevalent commentary tradition and the Koine group (a text associated with the Byzantine period) – dominate the extant attestation. As such, many late manuscripts that belong to these groups (especially the Koine text, which is more unified in its wording than the Andrew text) and which clearly have derivative texts have been set aside, leaving around 110 manuscripts for the next stage of the project.[14]

The task of phase two of the project (2014–17) is to transcribe selected manuscripts from the digitized photographs, noting numerous features including variant readings, line and column divisions, varieties of marginalia, punctuation, corrections, *nomina sacra*, the division of sense contours, capitals, colophons, rubrications and artwork.[15] The transcriptions will be electronically published and collated with the data from patristic citations and the early versions (Latin, Sahidic, Syriac and Ethiopic) to create an initial apparatus.

In the third phase of the project (2017–20) the material will be submitted to analysis using the Coherence-Based Genealogical Method (CBGM), a stemmatic method for evaluating and plotting the textual genetics of the tradition in an effort to create the oldest attainable text in each variation unit.[16] This method creates text-flow diagrams that illustrate the reading of a given variation unit from which all others arose based on the omnibus of editorial decisions, creating an eclectic text supported by the philological skills of the editor. This process is followed in the next phase (2020–3) with the finalization of the main text and the organization of the apparatus. The edition will be published in both paper and electronic forms.

In sum, the ECM provides, on the one hand, a reliable, accurate and consistent critical edition for exegetes, historians, translators, students and theologians; on the other (and this is perhaps the key point), it implicitly describes of the book of Revelation as a fluid product of Christian tradition. In addition to emphasizing the variation of Revelation's wording, the transcription of manuscripts provides fresh insight into the influence of textual presentation on the reading of particular manuscripts. Put simply, the ECM points out the fact that the distinction between Scripture and tradition is untenable – the shape of the text and its format is shaped by interpretative traditions embedded within the life of the Church and behaviours of production. The project's consideration of the graphic medium upon which our scriptural texts are inscribed through the transcription of paratexts (even though the CBGM is a purely textual tool) shows that the critical texts found in modern editions implicitly uphold a false dichotomy between a supposedly rigid scriptural text (marred by only a handful of variants) and a supposedly uncontrolled interpretative tradition (located in an endless network of media and cultures). The ECM rethinks the cultural machinery of the critical edition in light of the vast available textual data and changes in technology. This new machinery is a point of tension where the domains of Scripture and tradition converge; as Parker has argued, Scripture is tradition. The question remains, however, of how textual scholars might describe this dialectic relationship of Scripture as tradition that the ECM throws into relief. This is where David Brown becomes a fruitful dialogue partner.[17]

Brown's perspective that tradition can be revelatory is instructive for considering how the transmission of scriptural works functions as a conduit for tradition along with the texts they transmit. Can the documents that transmit the NT, with their varying presentations of their texts and numerous variants, function as points (sources?) of revelation? If so, the theological consequences are dramatic for how we conceive of the function of a critical edition; it becomes not only a reconstruction of the earliest recoverable text, but a guide to breadth of the traditions pertaining to a work. A project like the ECM, then, coheres well with Brown's articulation of the revelatory nature of interpretation, offering access to unappreciated information for theologians: 'traditions of reading continue to maintain their imaginative power not by staying the same but by being open to the transforming power of influences beyond themselves'.[18] Editions highlight the internal variation within an ancient work's copies. This variation, often the result of technological changes and other practical considerations (script, scribal habits, word division, traditions of accentuation, etc.), continues to transform and renew encounters with its ancient text. A critical edition provides a point of access to these changes, and the publication of a fully integrated electronic critical edition is only the latest phase in the development of scriptural media, one that completes the circle from papyrus scroll to electronic scroll. If this is true not only for the wording of the texts that people read, but also for the objects on which the texts were inscribed, then a critical edition like the ECM should guide users through the narratives of change and evolutions of traditions embedded in scriptural documents themselves. And it does. Therefore we can take Brown's following statement a step further:

> For, though the tendency remains to think of sacred canons as static, this is true only in the trivial sense of the words on the page, not of the interpretation to which they have been subject nor, significantly, even the grid or shape of their assumed narrative.[19]

The detailed re-evaluation of NT manuscripts inherent to the ECM project shows that not even the words of Scripture, at least until the advent of the printing press (and even then only in a pedantic sense), were static. Textual criticism and the appreciation of material culture allows us to take Brown's observation about interpretation and apply it to the object of interpretation itself.

My argument thus far is supported by the recent work of David Parker, which Brown does acknowledge, although he is somewhat dismissive.[20] The title of Parker's introduction to textual criticism, *An Introduction to the New Testament Manuscripts and their Texts*,[21] highlights the important distinction between the interaction of text, artefact and tradition. Additionally, the fluidity of NT texts is highlighted by Parker in another influential work, *The Living Text of the Gospels*, in which he cautions exegetes and theologians against the assumption that the text they use is the original text of the author, in effect arguing that our scriptural texts are the products of tradition.[22] Parker notes: 'the tradition flows on – and the manuscripts are just points in it'.[23] And more explicitly:

> the character of manuscript copying meant that there was a continuing interplay between Scripture – the text copied – and the tradition – the person engaged in the process of copying in and for the church ... [the Gospels] convey part of the early tradition, and are transmitted to us only by tradition. In fact, Scripture is tradition.[24]

The controlled fluidity of the NT's text and the consequences of material culture on the formation of tradition are now being emphasized thanks in large part to projects like the ECM.[25] The collection of photos and transcriptions of manuscripts in an easily accessible electronic database, and the fresh appraisal of this bounty of data has highlighted the inherent complexities of our assumptions as to what constitutes Scripture.[26] As a result, textual criticism is increasingly relevant for reception historical studies and historical theology, an entry point that enables us to mark particular instantiations of and changes to tradition – 'Textual criticism is more than an essential tool for theology. It is an essential theological tool.'[27] Even if we do decide, with Brown, that Parker has overplayed the significance of the NT's textual variation, it is undeniable that the wording of Scripture was developing alongside tradition from its earliest early stages and that the ongoing development of the physical representation of scriptural texts represents a development of tradition that has potential revelatory consequences.[28]

Nonetheless, scriptural manuscripts and Christian tradition represent two sides of the same coin. Projects like the ECM provide an interesting outlet for considering Brown's claim that tradition is revelatory and that it, at times, reshapes and even corrects the interpretation of scriptural texts. This squares with Brown's argument that the canonical text is not always the immediate object of interpretation, but that its interpretation is mediated through other traditions.[29] The choice of script, material, forms of emphasis, marginal comments and artwork, all of which represent social conventions of textual production, nonetheless inform the reading experience and provide later tradents the opportunity to extend, emphasize or challenge the power of the message already latent in a given work.[30] Scripture is more than its reconstructed earliest wording, it is also an omnibus of all of its existing exemplars and their form. I think that Brown can safely point to the work of Parker and others as a further resource for his project.[31]

Moving in the opposite direction, Brown's work shapes the perception of the scope of textual scholarship. His emphasis on tradition encourages the textual scholar to integrate the details of percentages and text-flow diagrams into a broader discussion, challenging the discipline to look at the role of text and document in the history of the Church and the ebbing and flowing tides of theological discourse. This broader awareness of the discipline brings added import to the creation of critical editions that moves beyond the *Ausgangstext* and into the realm of reception history. Textual scholarship provides a further window on to the development of tradition, and Brown's theological thinking about the revelatory nature of tradition provides the textual scholar with a framework to understand their critical task theologically; that is, built on patterns of revelation and the development of tradition first located within the scriptural text.

This thinking reframes the goal of classical textual criticism: if tradition is revelatory in any meaningful sense, the earliest textual forms are not necessarily the most important and the totality of the manuscript tradition gains a deeper significance. Scripture is not different from tradition in this regard – 'the text', Brown notes, 'becomes part of a living tradition that is constantly subject to change, and that includes change in the perceived content of biblical narratives: new insights are generated as different social conditions open up new possibilities and perspectives.'[32] I want to suggest that the text of Scripture itself and its presentation in material culture is also subject to a similar system of continuing change controlled by socially acceptable forms of text production and attitudes towards the sanctity of scriptural wording.[33] The dialogue Brown envisages between Scripture and tradition, 'part of a single, ongoing process of revelation',[34] takes place within the manuscript tradition of the NT itself. Extant exemplars provide glimpses into the 'running film', as Brown refers to it, of God's interaction with his community.[35] 'Revelation is mediated to the community of faith through a continuous stream of developing tradition',[36] including the development of the shape of scriptural texts and their manuscripts. This reality accosts the text critic whose aim is to reconstruct an 'original' text, a task that turns 'a movie into a single snapshot', Parker notes (using the same metaphor as Brown).[37] Searching for the earliest text is not without value, but it should not be a singular goal. Briefly, a few examples related to the Apocalypse uncovered in the process of the production of the ECM support the assertion that the manuscript tradition is (at least) a locus for better understanding the development of tradition in regard to Scripture.

First, the book of Revelation is distinctive in that a large number of its manuscripts consist of texts transmitted with commentaries, mostly those of Andrew of Caesarea (536–614), but also earlier traditions traced to Oecumenius (465–538) and the later, more poorly attested commentary of Arethas (c.860).[38] Josef Schmid has located at least 80 manuscripts that contain the Andrew commentary, sometimes in abbreviated forms, accounting for over one third of the work's manuscript record. Additionally, many other manuscripts bear the somewhat expanded text of the Andrew tradition and some of its paratextual features (*kephalaia* and *logoi*), even though the commentary itself is not present (e.g. GA 35 88 205 209 632).[39] Usually, the commentary is interspersed among the text where the lemma (i.e. the scriptural text) is followed by commentary and so forth. Most often the different portions are distinguished from each other (e.g. 2028 2058), but occasionally they were copied in a formally indistinguishable manner, where the boundary between commentary and text is not immediately obvious (e.g. 2062). Additionally, in some manuscripts, the text of the commentary created a literal frame around the scriptural text on which it commented called a *Rahmenkommentar* or frame commentary. GA 82 (Paris, B.N. gr. 237) is a beautiful tenth- or eleventh-century exemplar of this phenomenon that provides some insights into the relationship between Scripture and tradition within this manuscript.[40]

In GA 82's presentation of the text, the scriptural text reserves pride of place as its own unit at the centre of the manuscript, copied in a somewhat larger and more careful hand, complete with artistic emphases (e.g. *Initiale*) at certain points. While the surrounding script of the commentary is smaller and its text abbreviated, its location around the text speaks to its function: it provides a controlling interpretative perimeter. In this instance, influential metatextual traditions literally frame the reading experience: text is inseparable from tradition, a tradition that aids readers in understanding the text located at the visual centre of the artefact. In this case, a second layer of tradition forcefully influences the text's interpretation: commentary. Artefactual evidence visually describes the relationship of tradition and Scripture – in this case, the two work hand in hand to create meaning.

A reader's experience with this manuscript would be fundamentally influenced by the interpretative traditions preserved in the margins of the work. This is especially true since markings within the central text draw the reader's attention to segments in the margin. For example, in Revelation 16.17, a verse that describes the pouring of the seventh bowl and its catastrophic outcome, a prominent scribal mark brackets the first letter in the start of the verse. This mark draws the reader's attention to the upper left corner of the page, where the identical mark initiates a section of Andrew commentary (the start of *kephalaion* 52) on 16.17–21. The Andrew commentary connects the 'flashes of lightning, voices, and thunders' (16.18) to the theophany at Sinai (Exod. 19.16–19) and argues that the great earthquake is 'an alteration of all things in existence'. This interpretation offers an overtly, but somewhat obvious eschatological interpretation of the seventh bowl. Although there is no evidence that this tradition somehow influenced the wording of the lemmatic text,[41] the physical framing of the scriptural text by the Andrew comment controls and, conversely, opens up the reading experience in a way and solidifies its own particular interpretation. This situation is not unique to the Apocalypse, but the relationship of the Andrew tradition to the text and reception history of Revelation cannot be overstated, and there is much work to be done on the relationship between lemma, commentary and interpretation in particular manuscripts.[42]

Another example of the interplay between tradition and Scripture in the artefactual evidence is found in artwork located in some manuscripts of the Apocalypse. Brown notes that 'the riot of imagery in the book of Revelation is one major reason why for so many Christians today it remains a closed book'.⁴³ While an accurate portrayal of modern sensibilities, in some locations Revelation's visual aspect was an integral part of its representation even within some Greek manuscripts. While unusual in the history of the Apocalypse, a grouping of fifteenth- and sixteenth-century manuscripts (2028 2044 2054 2083) contain images associated with Revelation's cosmic antagonists in 12.3; 13.1, 11; 17.1–3. Three of these manuscripts were produced in the workshop of Andreas Darmarios.⁴⁴ These manuscripts too contain the Andrew commentary tradition in the more usual formation of lemma interrupted by comment, and the segments are clearly distinguished by various formal modes of emphasis. The images in these manuscripts also provide some visual commentary on the text: most obviously a visual map of Revelation's cosmic antagonists. Take the image of the whore seated atop the seven-headed, ten-horned beast (Rev. 17.1–3) in 2083 (Leiden, Univ. Bibl., Voss. Gr. Fol. 48). This image follows barely over one line of text (the end of 17.3), covering a large expanse of the folio, followed by the Andrew commentary that addresses the identity of this woman.⁴⁵

The placement of this image here was planned; she is not a marginal notation working around the empty space of a page but an integral and planned part of the commentary. She stands as a mediating figure between text and commentary, a visual bridge from Scripture to tradition, graphically mediating their relationship. The selective placement of images in this manuscript also functions to highlight the segments of text and commentary associated with them. The artistic features encourage the reader to dwell on the images, and the commentary that follows them provides a framework within which to understand their referent. The placement of these images also engenders an imaginative and visual reading of a very imaginative and visual text.

Moreover, the correlation of the image of the ten-horned beast with the others in the mini-cycle highlights the similarities of each of the antagonists described in the text. For example, the beast that the whore rides is markedly similar to the great red dragon described in Revelation 12.3–4. The similarities in the visual representations of these texts indicates that the artist intuited a connection between them. The dragon in Revelation 12 – 'the ancient serpent, who is call the devil and satan, the deceiver of the whole world' (12.9) – is the same power that supports Rome symbolized by the whore of Babylon. The images in this series of manuscripts function as interpreters of the texts that tend to blur in the final ten chapters of Revelation, assisting the reader to distinguish between the beasts, while at the same time capturing their similarities. In these exemplars visual exegesis (the cycle of images) and textual exegesis (Andrew commentary) are powerful mediators of meaning that become inextricable from the scriptural text itself.

Conclusions: David Brown and the Bible

Brown's work shows an intense interest in and mastery of scriptural texts, along with a panoply of other texts, religions and disciplines. His use of biblical studies points to the theological 'next step' that Biblicists are often reluctant to take; he ought to be lauded for taking seriously critical biblical scholarship when it comes to his brand of theological engagement and even preaching.[46] His engagement with biblical studies in and of itself is not revolutionary, but his drawing out of the consequences for hermeneutical questions is precisely where he takes the logical next move, suggesting that:

> Where both modern and ancient hermeneutics to my mind err is thus in not taking with sufficient seriousness the conditioned character of all human thought, and therefore the necessity for tradition to keep meanings alive not simply by preserving them but by allowing their constant adaptation as ... the trajectories from the past meet fresh triggers in new situations and thereby help generate new meanings.[47]

Brown has integrated theology, philosophy and biblical studies in a way that is healthy for biblical studies as whole, a discipline that tends towards internalization.[48] This model of interdisciplinary engagement serves as an example textual scholars should aim to emulate to the degree that they are able. (Few in either discipline, especially myself, are as capable as Brown.) Numerous other examples of Brown's engagement with the Bible would lead to similar conclusions, including his discussion of the rewriting of the infancy narrative in Christian tradition,[49] his overview of Jewish literature of the Second Temple period as a potential medium of revelation[50] and his insistence on the fact that the continual rewriting and reforming of scriptural stories in antiquity (e.g. the *Akedah* and Joseph novella) are evidence of a desire to maintain their relevance.[51]

My argument here has been twofold. On the one hand, I have attempted to demonstrate that some of the patterns of development that Brown perceives in tradition – both within and beyond the scriptural text – are also to be found in the textual and artefactual history of the NT itself. Brown could go further back into the details of the text and manuscripts if he dares. This observation supports the broad contours of Brown's project and, at least preliminarily, posits that the artefacts of the scriptural tradition might well function as a reservoir of revelation (among other sources), although I am not yet confident how this might be measured or articulated. I leave this to more theologically adept minds.

On the other hand, I wanted to show that Brown's observations help textual scholars on two fronts. First, they move textual critics beyond the detail of the editing process to consider the ramifications of manuscripts and their readings for theology and Christian tradition. This is something that many already do, but Brown's approach provides a ready-made way to continue down this path. Second, and most importantly, Brown's work aids the textual scholar in conceiving of Scripture as part of the broader stream of Christian tradition. It is an eminent and perhaps foundational facet of this tradition, but it is also a product of tradition that changes with developments external to itself. Although not expressly articulated in its goals, the ECM to my mind represents the best in the continuing search for the NT – its main text does not claim to be 'the New Testament in the original Greek' or other such titles employed in the history of printed editions, but it remains a map that orientates the reader to explore the scriptural tradition collected in the apparatus.

Notes

1 This trend is best exemplified in a number of studies that use textual and bibliographic data to reconstruct the social and theological history of early Christianity as it relates to textual production, books and reading. See e.g. Harry Y. Gamble, *Books and Readers in the Early Church: A History of Early Christian Texts* (London: Yale University Press, 1995); D. C. Parker, *The Living Text of the Gospels* (Cambridge: Cambridge University Press, 1997); Kim Haines-Eitzen, *Guardians of Letters: Literacy, Power, and the Transmitters of Early Christian Literature* (Oxford: Oxford University Press, 2000).

2 For example, in commenting on the freedom with which the wording of Codex Bezae (05) is formulated, Parker playfully indicates the source of this interest: 'One may well feel ambivalent about this freedom. As textual critics, we can only deplore it (except as a source of absorbing activity). Humanly and theologically, there seems something admirable in this willingness to seek out the authentic spirit at the expense of the letter.' D. C. Parker, *Codex Bezae: An Early Christian Manuscript and its Text* (Cambridge: Cambridge University Press, 1992), 258.

3 In his aptly titled article, D. C. Parker makes a similar argument. 'Scripture is Tradition', *Theology* 94.757 (1991), 11–17.

4 Other institutes are also involved in producing other fascicles of the project, including the INTF in Münster and the Institute for Textual Scholarship and Electronic Editing in Birmingham.

5 See K. Aland, 'Novi Testamenti Graeci Editio Critica Maior: Der Gegenwärtige Stand der Arbeit an einer neuen grossen kritischen Ausgabe des Neuen Testamentes', *NTS* 16 (1970), 163–77.

6 On the outdatedness of editions, see D. C. Parker, *Textual Scholarship and the Making of the New Testament* (Oxford: Oxford University Press, 2012), 106–13.

7 'Perhaps a page of critical apparatus', David Parker notes, 'does not seem what one might expect a story to be like, but for those prepared to read and to learn, that is precisely what it is.' Ibid., 123. Elsewhere Parker states that 'rather than a theological desert, the textual critic's playground, that is to say the critical apparatus, will turn out to be a garden of delights.' D. C. Parker, 'Textual Criticism and Theology', *Expository Times* 118.12 (2007), 589.

8 B. Aland et al. (eds), *Novum Testamentum Graecum: Editio Critica Maior VI/1-2 Catholic Letters*, 2nd edn (Stuttgart: Deutsche Bibelgesellschaft, 2013); H. Strutwolf et al. (eds), *Novum Testamentum Graecum: Editio Critica Maior III The Acts of the Apostles* (Stuttgart: Deutsche Bibelgesellschaft, 2017).

9 See Parker, *Textual Scholarship*, 104-24 for the general contours of the production of the ECM as a whole. See also U. Schmid, with assistance from M. Karrer, 'Die neue Edition der Johannesapokalypse: Ein Arbeitsbericht', in *Zur Edition Critica Maior der Johannesapokalypse*, ANTF 47, ed. M. Sigismund, M. Karrer and U. Schmid (Leiden: Brill, 2015), 3-14 for a report on the progress of the first two years of the project and, more recently, Marcus Sigismund, 'Die neue Edition der Johannesapokalypse: Stand der Arbeiten', in *Studien zum Text der Apokalypse II* (ANTF 50; ed. M. Sigismund and D. Müller; Berlin: De Gruyter, 2017), 3-15.

10 Aland, 'Novi Testamenti', 166.

11 Online: www.ntvmr.uni-muenster.de; accessed 2 September 2017.

12 Only *c*.307, according to Markus Lembke, of which 288 are minuscules. 'Beobachtungen zu den Handschriften der Apokalypse des Johannes', in *Die Johannesoffenbarung: Ihr Text und ihre Auslegung*, ABG 38, ed. M. Labahn and M. Karrer (Leipzig: Evangelische Verlagsanstalt, 2012), 19-69, esp. 20-1. Compare this with the *c*.600 manuscripts for the Catholic Letters and Acts, *c*.800 for the Pauline letters and over 1,700 for the Gospels.

13 For more on the selection of *Teststellen*, see Lembke, 'Beobachtungen', 30-47 and Markus Lembke et al. (eds), *Text und Textwert der griechischen Handschriften des Neuen Testaments VI. Die Apokalypse: Teststellenkollation und Auswertungen* (ANTF 49; Berlin: De Gruyter, 2017), 83*-103*.

14 See Lembke et al., *Text und Textwert*, 142*-43*.

15 Illuminated manuscripts and artistic representations of the Apocalypse are most often – but not always – associated with the Latin tradition and, later, vernacular versions, especially German. See Lucas Cranach and Albrecht Dürer as influential examples. See also the recent work of Natasha F. H. O'Hear, *Contrasting Images of the Book of Revelation in Late Medieval and Early Modern Art: A Case Study in Visual Exegesis* (Oxford: Oxford University Press, 2011). On artwork in the Greek manuscripts, see Garrick V. Allen, 'Image, Memory, and Allusion in the Textual History of the Apocalypse: GA 2028 and Visual Exegesis', in *Studien zum Text der Apokalypse II*, ANTF 50, ed. M. Sigismund and D. Müller (Berlin: De Gruyter, 2017), 435-54.

16 See Tommy Wasserman and Peter J. Gurry, *A New Approach to Textual Criticism: An Introduction to the Coherence-Based Genealogical Method* (Atlanta, GA: SBL Press, 2017); Gerd Mink, 'Contamination, Coherence, and Coincidence in Textual Transmission: The Coherence-Based Genealogical Method (CBGM) as a Complement and Corrective to Existing Approaches', in *The Textual History of the Greek New Testament: Changing Views in Contemporary Research*, TCS 8, ed. K. Wachtel and M. W. Holmes (Atlanta, GA: SBL Press, 2011), 141-216; *idem*, 'Eine umfassende Genealogie der neutestamentlichen Überlieferung', *NTS* 39 (1993), 481-99; Klaus Wachtel, 'The Coherence-Based Genealogical Method: A New Way to Reconstruct the Text of the Greek New Testament', in *Editing the Bible: Assessing the Task Past and Present*, ed. J. S. Kloppenborg and J. H. Newman (Atlanta, GA: SBL Press, 2012), 123-38.

17 For an incisive summary and critique of *Tradition and Imagination*, see William J. Abraham, 'Scripture, Tradition, and Revelation: An Appreciative Critique of David Brown', in *Theology, Aesthetics, and Culture: Responses to the Work of David Brown*, ed. Robert MacSwain and Taylor Worley (Oxford: Oxford University Press, 2012), 13-28. See also James Barr, *The Concept of Biblical Theology: An Old Testament Perspective* (London: SCM Press, 1999), 586-604.

18 David Brown, *Tradition and Imagination: Revelation and Change* (Oxford: Oxford University Press, 1999), 11-12.

19 Ibid., 31 and also 208–9. See also, however, 61–2, 74, where Brown seems to set off the fluidity of tradition against the fixed nature of Scripture. Projects like the ECM point out once again the myth of Scripture as a fixed entity, either in wording or form.

20 Ibid., 301–2. However, it seems to me that Brown's appraisal of the development of tradition in Judaism and Christianity, the 'scriptural pilgrimage' as he refers to it (*Tradition and Imagination*, 222–34, 268–71), particularly his assertion that triggers within the text itself already suggest various avenues of interpretation, squares nicely with Parker's notion of the 'living text'. Brown's 'moving text' and Parker's 'living text' make for natural conversation partners.

21 D. C. Parker, *An Introduction to New Testament Manuscripts and their Texts* (Cambridge: Cambridge University Press, 2008).

22 Parker, *The Living Text of the Gospels*, esp. 7.

23 Parker, 'Scripture is Tradition', 12.

24 Ibid., 15, 17.

25 I use the word 'controlled' here because I do not mean to argue that the transmission of the text of the NT is uninhibited or whimsical, but that the fluidity within the tradition is organized around particular historically contextualized textual interpretations, changes in book technology and developments in the scribal craft.

26 Cf. Parker, *The Living Text of the Gospels*, 93.

27 Ibid., 94.

28 Frances Young's work on exegesis in the patristic sources has emphasized this fact as well, suggesting that the change of medium from roll to codex might have corresponded to the early Christian predilection for the orality of the scriptural text over its inscribed form, although I am not yet convinced by her assertion. *Biblical Exegesis and the Formation of Christian Culture* (Cambridge: Cambridge University Press, 1997), 10–16. Additionally, Bart D. Ehrman has argued that theologically crucial texts were changed in antiquity in an effort to support an emerging orthodox tradition. *The Orthodox Corruption of Scripture: The Effect of Early Christological Controversies on the Text of the New Testament* (Oxford: Oxford University Press, 1993). This is a direct argument for the active intervention of tradents in the scriptural text.

29 By this I mean that interpretations of scriptural texts are never *de novo* creations but mediated through the interpreter's past experiences with the text and knowledge of other circulating interpretive traditions. See Brown, *Tradition and Imagination*, 121–7.

30 Cf. Brown's take on the development on the infancy narratives in *Tradition and Imagination*, 97.

31 The recent work of Martin Karrer as it pertains to the Apocalypse is also helpful in this regard. See especially 'Der Text der Johannesoffenbarung – Varianten und Theologie', *Neotestamentica* 42.2 (2009), 373–98; idem, 'The Angels of the Congregations in Revelation – Textual History and Interpretation', *Journal of Early Christian History* 1.1 (2011), 57–84; idem, 'Der Text der Johannesapokalypse', in *Die Johannesapokalypse: Kontexte – Konzepte – Rezeption*, WUNT 287, ed. J. Frey, J. A. Kelhoffer and F. Tóth (Tübingen: Mohr Siebeck, 2012), 43–78.

32 Brown, *Tradition and Imagination*, 107–8.

33 This is a point Brown also acknowledges: 'Whether we change the meaning or, as with those scribes, change the written text, what we have is once more what Part Two described as a "moving text", one which of necessity changes as new perceptions arise.' Brown, *Tradition and Imagination*, 301.

34 Ibid., 111.

35 Ibid., 134, cf. 210–11.

36 Ibid., 169.

37 Parker, 'Textual Criticism and Theology', 586.

38 For the latter two traditions, see Marc de Groote, *Oecumenii Commentarius in Apocalypsin* (TEG 8; Leuven: Peeters, 1999). GA 2329 also preserves a somewhat

strange commentary tradition only attested in this manuscript that seems to be a conglomeration of patristic traditions of the Apocalypse. See P. Tzamalikos, *An Ancient Commentary on the Book of Revelation: A Critical Edition of the* Scholia in Apocalypsin (Cambridge: Cambridge University Press, 2013); and Garrick V. Allen, 'The Reception of Scripture and Exegetical Resources in the *Scholia in Apocalypsin* (GA 2351)', in *Commentaries, Catenae and Biblical Tradition*, ed. H. A. G. Houghton (Piscataway, NJ: Gorgias, 2016), 141–63.

39 See Parker, *New Testament Manuscripts*, 238–40 for a summary, and J. Schmid, *Studien zur Geschichte des griechischen Apokalypse-Textes*, 3 vols (Munich: Karl Zink, 1955).

40 For further, see W. H. P. Hatch, *Facsimiles and Descriptions of Minuscule Manuscripts of the New Testament* (Cambridge, MA: Harvard University Press, 1951), 94–5; Schmid, *Studien*, 1.74–5; M. L. Agati, *La Minuscola 'Bouletée'*, LA 9,1 (Vatican City: Scuola Vaticana di Paleografica, Diplomatica e Archivistica, 1992), 272–3. The other works in this manuscript (Praxapostolos and Pauline letters) also have frame commentaries, but I focus here on Revelation.

41 The description of the angelic in the commentary as coming from heaven (οὐρανόθεν) does correspond to a variant in 16.17 witnessed in the Andrews tradition and other manuscripts: ναου] ουρανου 051* 1854 M^A. Additionally, the scriptural text associated with the Andrew commentary includes a number of expansions, especially in Revelation 1.2.

42 See E. S. Constantinou, *Guiding to a Blessed End: Andrew of Caesarea and his Apocalypse Commentary in the Ancient Church* (Washington, DC: The Catholic University Press of America, 2013), 288–97.

43 Brown, *Tradition and Imagination*, 283.

44 I have written more fully on these manuscripts elsewhere, in Allen, 'Image, Memory, and Allusion'. Cf. also Schmid, *Studien*, 1.13–15 and Otto Kresten, 'Der Schreiber und Handschrifthändler Andreas Darmarios', *Mariahilfer Gymnasium, Jahresbericht* (1967), 6–11 for more on Darmarios.

45 See E. S. Constantinou (ed.), *Andrew of Caesarea: Commentary on the Apocalypse*, Fathers of the Church 123 (Washington, DC: Catholic University of America Press, 2011), 181–2.

46 See David Brown, *The Word to Set You Free: Living Faith and Biblical Criticism* (London: SPCK, 1995).

47 Brown, *Tradition and Imagination*, 60–72, here 72.

48 See also Robert MacSwain's similar comments on Brown's *The Divine Trinity* (London: Duckworth, 1985) in his 'Introduction: Theology, Aesthetics, and Culture', in *Theology, Aesthetics, and Culture: Responses to the Work of David Brown*, ed. Robert MacSwain and Taylor Worley (Oxford: Oxford University Press, 2012), 1.

49 Brown, *Tradition and Imagination*, 76–105.

50 Ibid., 113–21.

51 Ibid., 174, 207.

2

From the Magi to Pilate's Wife: David Brown, Tradition and the Reception of Matthew's Text

IAN BOXALL

David Brown's treatment of tradition in his 1999 monograph *Tradition and Imagination*, understood dynamically as 'the motor that sustains revelation both within Scripture and beyond',[1] is of significant interest for the field of biblical studies. Although Brown approaches his task from within the field of systematic theology, there is a natural synergy between his interests in how a text is creatively reworked in response to later Christian self-perception, and the growing interest among biblical scholars in reception history and *Wirkungsgeschichte* or the 'history of effects'.[2]

Brown's treatment of the developing traditions about the Magi (Matt. 2.1–12) well illustrates what he calls 'the hermeneutics of Pentecost and crib', whereby texts and traditions come to mean new things in response to changed circumstances. This is a process at work already within the biblical canon itself.[3] Thus, for Brown, the Fourth Evangelist takes significant 'liberties' in his treatment of Pentecost – the Spirit being handed over already at the cross (John 19.30) and being breathed out by the risen Christ at Easter (John 20.22; cf. Gen. 2.7) – thus providing a biblical model for tradition's subsequent 'imaginative reappropriation of the past', understood as integral to that dynamic process by which the Spirit-Paraclete leads the disciples 'into all truth' (John 16.13).[4] For Brown, truth should not be restricted to historical truths, narrowly defined, but incorporates what he calls 'truths of the imagination', which might be historically untrue yet have the capacity to convey theological truth more effectively than the former. This presents a much more positive assessment of the role of the imagination in understanding texts than is normally found among biblical critics.[5]

One of Brown's key examples comes from Matthew's infancy narrative (Matt. 1—2), which is itself the fruit of imaginative retelling,[6] continuing apace in its subsequent post-biblical reception. His brief presentation of the development of Matthew's Magi narrative reveals how the focus shifted from the past defeat of pagan magic to reflection on their universality – no longer merely 'from the east' – and contemporary significance in a world that now incorporated Christian rulers. In the process, the Magi became very different from what the evangelist probably intended: now understood as kings in their own right rather than legates of an eastern ruler.[7] But this imaginative rewriting of their story, drawing on influences from surrounding culture, far from being detrimental to the Matthean narrative, was essential for ensuring the ongoing power of the story to critique and not simply to support worldly power.

If Matthew's concerns about the Magi 'from the east', namely, that they exemplify the potential of non-Jewish figures to recognize the truth about the child, have been best preserved across the centuries by transforming these eastern priest-magicians into a motley crew of kings originating also from other points of the compass (and even eventually from different continents), what of those positive Gentile characters in Matthew's story who literally come 'from the west'? The promise of many coming 'from east and west' to 'eat with Abraham and Isaac and Jacob in the kingdom of heaven' (Matt. 8.11)[8] is made to a Roman centurion who must have travelled from the west to Capernaum in Jewish Galilee. But the focus of this chapter is on another visitor 'from the west', the wife of the Roman governor Pontius Pilate, whose subsequent reception, if not as rich and colourful as that of the Magi, certainly exemplifies the same kind of dynamic examined by David Brown in *Tradition and Imagination*. Her story too has been the subject of diverse imaginative retellings. These respond in different ways to significant gaps in the Gospel narrative: for example, the question of her prior knowledge of Jesus and his teaching, the specific content and origin of her dream and the impact of this episode in her personal biography and that of her husband. They also reflect the changed circumstances in which her story is being recounted: to predominantly Gentile-Christian audiences for whom this Gentile woman has particular significance.

Pilate's Wife's Dream (Matt. 27.19)

Pilate's wife makes just one, tantalizingly brief appearance in the pages of Matthew's Gospel, in a verse Joachim Gnilka describes as an 'intermezzo' interrupting the action of the Roman trial of Jesus.[9] The source for this brief interlude is probably popular Christian folklore, of a kind that will eventually produce full-scale apocryphal acts and novellas.[10] In its present Matthean context, it functions both to provide narrative time for the authorities to turn the crowd in favour of Barabbas (27.20) and to prepare for Pilate's hand-washing and declaration of Jesus' innocence (27.24).[11]

> While he was sitting on the judgment seat, his wife sent word to him, 'Have nothing to do with that innocent man, for today I have suffered a great deal because of a dream about him.' [Καθημένου δὲ αὐτοῦ ἐπὶ τοῦ βήματος ἀπέστειλεν πρὸς αὐτὸν ἡ γυνὴ αὐτοῦ λέγουσα· Μηδὲν σοὶ καὶ τῷ δικαίῳ ἐκείνῳ, πολλὰ γὰρ ἔπαθον σήμερον κατ' ὄναρ δι' αὐτόν.] (Matt. 27.19)

Yet as Donald Senior notes, the significance of this verse cannot be reduced to either narrative time-filler or preparation for Pilate's subsequent action.[12] The function of dreams elsewhere in Matthew (1.20; 2.12, 13, 19) suggests that this dream too is a mode of divine communication, containing both counsel and warning.[13] Its insertion at this point in the narrative, when the leaders are about to call for Barabbas' release, creates 'a dramatic parallel between the two sets of intercessors: Pilate's wife pleads for Jesus – the Jewish hierarchy pleads for Barabbas'.[14]

Senior's observations are largely reflected in the treatment of this verse in modern critical commentaries. Such treatment tends to be brief, given her briefest of appearances in Matthew's text.[15] Most commentators connect Pilate's wife with the Jewish Joseph and the Gentile Magi through the motif of divine revelation 'in a dream' (κατ' ὄναρ, a phrase unique to Matthew in the New Testament). A few complement the obvious Old Testament parallels (the dreams of the patriarchs Jacob and Joseph)[16] with Greco-Roman ones, especially the dream of Julius Caesar's wife, Calpurnia, received on the night before Caesar was assassinated (Dio Cassius 44.17.1; Suetonius, *Julius* 81.1, 3; Appian, *B. Civ.* 2.16 [115]).[17] Indeed, Florence Gillman has even proposed that in its pre-Matthean origins, the legend about Pilate's wife was directly influenced by the Calpurnia story.[18]

There is also widespread agreement among modern exegetes that Pilate's wife is a positive figure in the narrative: a Gentile contrasted positively with the Jewish leadership for recognizing Jesus as a 'just' or 'righteous' man (see Matt. 1.19; 3.15; 5.6 etc.; though there is less unanimity over the comparative assessment of her husband Pilate).[19] Intratextual connections are also made between her and other marginal yet positive characters in Matthew's narrative: for example, the centurion whose faith is praised by Jesus (8.5–13) or the Canaanite woman (15.21–28). Alternatively, parallels are drawn between Pilate's wife and other influential Roman women in classical literature, notably Poppaea the wife of the emperor Nero, who according to Josephus was a 'God-fearer' or 'pious' (θεοσεβής) and interceded with her husband on behalf of the Jews (*Ant.* 20.195; see *Life* 16).[20]

Both these motifs – Pilate's wife as a positive Gentile character and her dream as an example of divine revelation – are well attested, as we shall see, in the earlier reception history of this passage. However, a close reading of Matthew 27.19, rich as it is in distinctive Matthean vocabulary,[21] suggests further possibilities rarely noted by recent critical scholars, but which have left their mark in the more imaginative retellings of her story across the centuries. First, Matthew relates how Pilate's wife 'sent to' (ἀπέστειλεν πρὸς) her husband. That this is a positive action on her part is suggested by the fact that, of the 22 usages of the verb in Matthew, eight refer to an action of Jesus or the Son of Man (8.31; 10.5, 16; 13.41; 21.1; 23.34, 37; 24.31), and nine of God or a God-like character in the parables (10.40; 11.10; 15.24; 20.2; 21.34, 36, 37; 22.3, 4).[22] Moreover, the only other occurrence of ἀποστέλλω πρὸς refers to Christ sending prophets, wise men and scribes (23.34–35), a positive act of warning that receives a negative response, including killing and crucifixion, and the shedding of the blood of 'Abel the righteous' (there are obvious verbal links with the current passage).[23]

Second, Pilate's wife has 'suffered a great deal' on account of Christ (πολλὰ γὰρ ἔπαθον ... δι' αὐτόν). The occasional commentator therefore places her in the company of the disciples in Matthew, who are called to suffer on account of Christ's name (10.16–23; 24.9–22).[24] What is rarely noted, however, is that although Jesus warns his disciples in two discourses that they will endure hardships on his behalf (e.g. being handed over, flogged, hated on account of his name), in neither of these passages is the verb πάσχω used. The verb only occurs three times in Matthew, two of them (16.21; 17.12) describing the suffering of Jesus as Son of Man.[25] Moreover, the first of these, part of the first passion prediction taken over from Mark, closely parallels the report of Pilate's wife: the Son of Man is to suffer many things (καὶ πολλὰ παθεῖν).[26] Thus the text allows the possibility that she is conformed more perfectly to Christ through participation in his passion.

These two features open up for Pilate's wife a particular affinity to Christ and his disciples, which is all the more significant given her Gentile status. Yet the brevity of the biblical reference leaves much more to be said. What was the nature of her suffering on Christ's account? Was her dream the sole source of her knowledge of Christ, or is there a previous story of familiarity with his message or even personal encounter? What were the consequences of her report to her husband, both immediate and long term? The remainder of this chapter will explore how the Christian imagination engaged these questions, creatively reworking her story for new circumstances. In particular, it will focus on four aspects of this verse's subsequent reception history. In a manner very similar to the reception history of the Magi (transformed into kings who come to represent all the nations of the known world), we will consider the significance of Pilate's wife as a righteous Gentile and type of the Gentile church. This will be followed by a consideration of how the ambiguity inherent in Matthew's version of the Roman trial is exploited: if Pilate's wife functions as a foil in the narrative, to whom is she a foil? To her husband or to the Jewish authorities? Finally, consideration will be given to a significant 'wrong turn' in the reception of Pilate's wife in the west, albeit one arguably rooted in another ambiguity in the text, which is a striking illustration of the extent to which cultural contexts and theological assumptions regularly steer interpretation in particular directions. But we will begin with an instinct to bring Pilate's wife out of the shadows, by giving this nameless character a name.

Naming the Nameless

History has long forgotten the actual name of Pontius Pilate's wife.[27] No classical text survives that identifies the spouse of the Roman governor of Judea, nor is her personal identity of interest to the first evangelist. Matthew presents her as one of a number of women who are identified, albeit for different reasons, by their relationship to their husband: 'the wife of Uriah' (1.6); Mary 'your wife' (1.20; 'his wife', 1.24); 'Herodias, his brother Philip's wife' (14.3); the wife of the unforgiving servant ('his wife', 18.25); the wife married in turn to the seven brothers (literally 'his wife', 22.24, 25: 'whose wife?' 22.28).

However, her lack of personal name belies the significance accorded to her by Matthew as a righteous Gentile who receives divine revelation and does what Christ does. Unsurprisingly, therefore, as her story develops in the early Christian imagination, she acquires a name. The naming of unnamed characters from the gospel story is a common feature of Christian tradition, as their personal biographies are imaginatively expanded to reflect their growing significance as witnesses to Christ. Thus the penitent thief of Luke 23.40–43 acquires the name Dismas or Dysmas (e.g. *Acts of Pilate* 9.4), and the soldier with the lance (John 19.34) is known to posterity as Longinus (e.g. *Acts of Pilate* 16.7). The Magi come to be known by a variety of names. Most common in the west are Caspar, Melchior and Balthazar. Ephrem the Syrian knows them as Hormizdadh, king of Persia, Yazdegerd, king of Saba, and Perozadh, king of Sheba, while the Syrian *Book of Adam and Eve* has the names Hor, Basantor and Karsudas.[28]

The name of Pilate's wife is relatively stable in the reception history in both east and west. It is attested in some versions of the apocryphal *Acts of Pilate*, otherwise referred to as the *Acta Pilati* or *Gesta Pilati* (the latter title specifically referring to the Latin text), part of the *Gospel of Nicodemus* (generally dated to the fifth or sixth century, though possibly containing earlier Pilate traditions).[29] Although late and fictional, and therefore generally dismissed as useless for critical scholarship, the *Acts of Pilate* are valuable as evidence for ways early readers of Matthew responded imaginatively to the significant gaps in Matthew's text. In certain Greek manuscripts (*Acta Pilati* B. IV.4 in Tischendorf's Greek recension B) she is named Prokla, and in many Latin manuscripts (the Latin family A), Procula.[30] The name Procla is also attested in the *Paradosis Pilati*, an apocryphal text of probable eastern provenance,[31] and Procula is her standard designation in western literature.

A rare exception is the twelfth-century Syrian theologian Dionysius bar-Salibi, who claims that her name was Longina. This may well be the result of confusion with the Roman soldier Longinus.[32] Eventually her name is extended to Claudia Procula, though – regular claims to the contrary notwithstanding – probably not until the *Chronicle of Pseudo-Dexter*, published in 1619.[33] This then leads to her identification with the Roman Christian called Claudia mentioned at 2 Timothy 4.21, strengthening the view that she converted to Christianity as a result of her dream. In some cases it heightens her social status and political influence, connecting her with the Julio-Claudian imperial family.

Her acquisition of a name brings her further out of the shadows and allows her to discover her own voice and biography. Although rarely depicted in Christian art, she has left a prominent mark on literature, from Langland's fourteenth-century *Piers Plowman* to a string of poems, novels and short stories in the modern period. Perhaps best known is Gertrud von le Fort's 1970 novel *Die Frau des Pilatus*,[34] in which Claudia Procula's 'suffering' consists in dreaming of a large multitude, across the centuries, praying the words of the Nicene Creed: 'Suffered under Pontius Pilate, was crucified, died and was buried.' At the end of von le Fort's novel, back in Rome, Pilate's wife begins attending Christian assemblies in secret and is eventually martyred (a baptism of blood, prior to actual baptism). She also features as a character in her own right in film and stage productions, from Cecil B. DeMille's 1927 *The King of Kings* to Mel Gibson's 2004 *The Passion of the Christ* (although she failed to survive the editor's cut in Monty Python's *Life of Brian*, while in Tim Rice and Andrew Lloyd-Webber's musical *Jesus Christ Superstar* she is entirely upstaged by her husband, who becomes the recipient of the dream).

Righteous Gentile and Christian Saint

If many modern commentators place Pilate's wife in the company of other Gentile characters in Matthew who respond positively to Jesus (e.g. the Magi, the centurion in Capernaum, the Canaanite woman; Matt. 2.1–12; 8.5–13; 15.21–28), their instinct is well rooted in the early reception of this passage. In his commentary on Matthew, Origen believes that God 'desired to convert Pilate's wife in a dream'.[35] The justification for this he finds in taking seriously Matthew's statement that she suffered much 'on account of' Christ. Similarly, in the fourth century, Hilary of Poitiers describes her as 'faithful' (*fidelis*), and presents her as an image (*species*) of the pagans, 'who, already believing, summoned her husband and an unbelieving people to faith in Christ'.[36] In other words, Hilary ascribes to Pilate's wife a representative role similar to that widely recognized for the faithful centurion of Capernaum and the Canaanite woman. Even more striking is Augustine's typological reading in one of his sermons, in which he juxtaposes her story with the story of Eden, presenting Pilate's wife in the role of the New Eve more typically ascribed to Mary: 'In the beginning of the world the wife leads the husband to death, in the Passion she leads him on to salvation [*In nativitate mundi uxor ducit virum ad mortem; in passione Christi uxor provocat ad salutem*].'[37]

This sample of patristic comments exemplifies the early instinct to interpret the figure of Pilate's wife in a positive sense, and in some cases in a representative role. But how is this Matthean truth best preserved? One option is through imaginative embellishment of her story in apocryphal acts and other popular Christian literature.[38] One of the most influential imaginative elaborations is found in the *Acts of Pilate* 2. The author has just described how the Roman standards in Pilate's praetorium bowed down in worship to Jesus (indicative of a developed Christology in which Christ's universal lordship is acknowledged even by inanimate symbols of Roman power):

> When Pilate saw this he was afraid, and tried to rise from the judgement-seat. And while he was still thinking of rising up, his wife sent to him saying, 'Have nothing to do with this righteous man. For I have suffered many things because of him by night.' And Pilate summoned all the Jews, and stood up and said to them, 'You know my wife is pious [θεοσεβής][39] and prefers to practise Judaism with you.' They answered him, 'Yes, we know it.' Pilate said to them, 'See, my wife sent to me saying, "Have nothing to do with this righteous man. For I have suffered many things because of him by night."' The Jews answered Pilate, 'Did we not tell you that he is a sorcerer? Behold, he has sent a dream to your wife.' (*Acts of Pilate* 2.1)[40]

Three features of this apocryphal expansion are noteworthy. First, the *Acts of Pilate* addresses a particular ambiguity in Matthew's text concerning the timing of this premonition. Matthew states rather vaguely that she has suffered many things 'today' as a result of her dream, which could mean concurrently with Pilate's interrogation of Jesus. The *Acts of Pilate*, by locating the suffering, and by implication her dream, during the night, places the various events in a plausible narrative sequence. Second, this passage provides early evidence for the theory, occasionally proposed by modern scholars,[41] that the story should be read in light of Greco-Roman parallels such as Poppaea interceding with Nero on behalf of the Jews, or Calpurnia's terrifying dream on the night prior to Caesar's assassination. In particular, Pilate's statement that his wife was θεοσεβής, 'pious' or a 'God-fearer', and an adherent of the Jewish religion, directly parallels Josephus' description of Poppaea. This presentation of Pilate's wife as living a Jewish life suggests that the *Acts of Pilate* is the product of Judeo-Christian circles,[42] albeit circles in which a definite breach with the synagogue has taken place. Hence this pious woman, held up as an exemplar of Jewish practice, is contrasted with 'the Jews', who attribute her dream to Jesus' role as sorcerer. A similar interpretation is found in an Irish version of the scene: 'The Jews responded by saying to Pilate: "We have told you, Pilate, that man is devilish, and now his evil-doing is manifest, for he sent a demon as a tempter to harm your wife."'[43]

A third dimension of this passage provides a definitive answer to another textual ambiguity, concerning the precise effect of his wife's dream on Pilate's subsequent action. The *Acts of Pilate* presents it as a converting experience, Pilate even repeating his wife's message publicly to 'all the Jews'. Hence the *Acts* concludes with a statement of Pilate's grief on hearing of the events of the crucifixion, thus interpreting his handwashing as a genuine expression of his innocence in Jesus' death (*Acts of Pilate* 11; in some Greek and Latin versions we read that both Pilate and his wife 'were deeply grieved, and they neither ate nor drank on that day').[44]

An alternative route for preserving Matthew's positive portrayal of Pilate's wife was liturgical and hagiographical. Here western and eastern Christianity take different paths. Despite the positive assessments of western theologians such as Hilary and Augustine, western Christians did not recognize this representative Gentile as a saint in her own right. Matters are very different in the east. St Prokla is celebrated by Eastern Orthodox Christians on 27 October. In the Coptic and Ethiopian Orthodox Churches, both she and Pilate have been canonized, and their common feast day falls on 25 June. One Ethiopian liturgical text emphasizes their shared innocence:

Salutation to Pilate who washed his hands
so he himself was pure of the blood of Christ
and salutation to Procula, his wife,
who sent him the message: Do not condemn Him
because that man is pure and just.[45]

Foil to Pilate, or to the Jewish Authorities?

The Coptic and Ethiopian decision to canonize both is rather more controversial than the route taken by churches of the Byzantine tradition, given the ambiguity just noted concerning the characterization of Pilate in Matthew 27. Recent scholarly interest in narrative characterization highlights this difficulty. How is Matthew's audience to respond to the juxtaposition of Pilate's wife's dream and Pilate washing his hands? Are they juxtaposed so as to present both as positive role models, foils to the Jewish leadership? Or is she contrasted positively with her husband?

Those who prioritize Matthew's distinctive redactional additions to Mark's account of the Roman trial – also the suicide of Judas and Pilate washing his hands – regard all three characters as foils to the Jewish authorities, promoting Jesus' innocence and underscoring the guilt of his own people. Robert Gundry is willing to find the portrayal of Pilate the Christian already present in Matthew's story.[46] Although less persuaded that the narrative excuses the Roman authorities, Davies and Allison nonetheless interpret the primary thrust of the narrative to set Gentile voices (Pilate and his wife) against the Jewish voices calling for Jesus to be crucified.[47]

By contrast, other recent scholars claim that Matthew's text draws a wedge between Pilate's wife and her husband, the former positively portrayed and the latter negatively: cynically performing a Jewish rite of handwashing yet ignoring his wife's pleas by handing Jesus over to be crucified.[48] Callie Callon draws on the oft-cited parallel to Nero's wife Poppaea to read Matthew's depiction of Pilate in a more negative light. If, for Matthew, Pilate's wife is another Poppaea, then Pilate is being cast as another Nero, known to Matthew's original audiences as first imperial persecutor of Christians. Moreover, according to Callon they would almost certainly share the common knowledge that Pilate was notoriously anti-Judean, and therefore his performance of a Jewish ritual of handwashing (see Deut. 21.1–9) would have been understood as an offensive anomaly rather than a genuine attempt to disclaim responsibility for Jesus' death.[49]

Patristic authors also read the Gospel portrayal of Pontius Pilate in strikingly different ways. Certainly there is some patristic support for the step subsequently made by Coptic and Ethiopian Christians in honouring him as a saint. In his *Apology*, Tertullian claims that Pilate became a Christian by conviction, though apparently after the crucifixion, and seems to know the apocryphal correspondence between Pilate and the Emperor Tiberius on the subject of Jesus (Tertullian, *Apol.* 21). It is in Tertullian's interests to present Pilate in such a positive light, given that his *Apology* is aimed at disabusing Roman authorities of the idea that Christians deserved suspicion. But this view is not unique to Tertullian among early commentators. For Hilary of Poitiers, both Pilate and his wife prefigure the conversion of the Gentiles and their acceptance of baptism:

> Because she herself had suffered much for Christ, she invited her husband to the same glory of a future hope. And so Pilate washed his hands and bore witness to the Jews that he was innocent of the Lord's blood. While the Jews have accepted upon themselves and their children the crime of shedding the Lord's blood, the pagans, by washing themselves, are daily passing over to a confession of faith.[50]

The fact that Pilate's wife suffers *pro Christo* has a positive effect on her husband. Similarly, Jerome interprets the confession of both Pilate and his wife that Jesus is righteous as the 'testimony of the Gentile people'.[51] This positive assessment may well be indicative of the very different cultural contexts of these commentators from that of Matthew's first audiences: the more the Gospel of Matthew is read by Gentile Christians as a Gentile text, the greater the wedge drawn between the Gentile governor and his wife on the one hand, and the Jewish authorities and crowds on the other. In early Christian fiction, Pilate is even presented as a Christian martyr. In the *Paradosis Pilati*, probably of eastern provenance, Pilate declares his innocence before the Emperor Tiberius in Rome, declaring 'the multitude of the Jews' to be guilty of Christ's blood. Pilate is nonetheless beheaded at Caesar's behest, his death presented by the text in martyrological terms. His dying words are a prayer for divine pardon for himself and for his wife, whose dream is presented as an act of prophecy:

> Lord, do not destroy me with the wicked Hebrews, for had it not been because of the nation of the lawless Jews, I would not have raised my hand against you, because they plotted a revolt against me. You know that I acted in ignorance. Therefore do not destroy me because of this sin, but pardon me, Lord, and your servant Procla, who stands with me in this hour of my death, whom you taught to prophesy that you must be nailed to the cross. Do not condemn her also because of my sin, but pardon us and number us among your righteous ones.[52]

Pilate's prayer is answered by a confirming heavenly voice, and an angel of the Lord receives Pilate's head. Procla, witnessing the angel, joyfully dies and is buried alongside her husband.

On the other hand, there are plenty of patristic authors who dissent from this positive assessment of Pilate. John Chrysostom, in a homily on Matthew 27, raises the possibility that Pilate's wife received the dream rather than her husband because she was 'more worthy', and wonders why Pilate was not more reluctant to 'participate' in Christ's death, even if only out of a feeling of sympathy towards his wife.[53] Ambrose of Milan is even more severe, concluding that, because Pilate failed to heed his wife's warning, he is a judge who condemns the innocent.[54] Negative traditions also abound, particularly into the Middle Ages, concerning Pilate's subsequent banishment and sinister events surrounding his death. In the medieval *Mors Pilati*, the emperor has Pilate's corpse bound to a block of stone and cast into the Tiber, provoking activity in the river from evil spirits. His body was then removed from the Tiber, taken to Vienne in Gaul and thrown into the Rhône, where the same thing happened. Finally his body was sunk in a lake, surrounded by mountains.[55] Such negative assessments of her husband enable the story of Pilate's wife to function as critique of political power, even in contexts in which political authority was at least ostensibly Christian.

The vast majority of the surviving receptions of this passage are from men. Rare women's voices tend to highlight the failures of Pilate, contrasting him negatively with the fidelity of his wife. Aemilia Lanyer (1569–1645), in her 1611 poem on Christ's passion, 'Salve Deus Rex Judaeorum', makes extensive use of the voice of Pilate's wife in what one scholar has called 'a lengthy "apologie," or defense and explanation, for Eve'.[56] By contrast with the male players in the story, who variously betray, deny and condemn Jesus, Pilate's wife recounts the story of his passion sympathetically, and appeals to her husband 'to beg her Saviours life' (line 752). Not even Pilate can absolve himself by the act of hand-washing:

> Washing thy hands, thy conscience cannot cleare,
> But to all worlds this staine must needs appeare. (lines 935–6)[57]

An alternative imaginative reading of Matthew's text, the possibility of a wedge between Pilate and his wife not only over Christ but at the heart of their marriage, is the subject of Charlotte Brontë's poem 'Pilate's Wife's Dream'.[58] Brontë has expanded Matthew's single verse into a poetic monologue of 26 stanzas. Wakened from her dream, Pilate's wife looks out and sees Christ's cross being constructed:

> Dreams, then, are true – for thus my vision ran;
> Surely some oracle has been with me,
> The gods have chosen me to reveal their plan,
> To warn an unjust judge of destiny:
> I, slumbering, heard and saw; awake I know,
> Christ's coming death, and Pilate's life of woe.[59]

Her suffering is clearly directed towards Christ; she is unable to pray or mourn for her husband:

> How can I love, or mourn, or pity him?
> I, who so long my fettered hands have wrung;
> I, who for grief have wept my eye-sight dim;
> Because, while life for me was bright and young,
> He robbed my youth – he quenched my life's fair ray –
> He crushed my mind, and did my freedom slay.[60]

The poem conveys a profound and poignant sense of a wife trapped in a 'stifling marriage'.[61]

Diabolical Intervention?

These negative portrayals of Pilate reflect an ambiguity regarding his character in the Gospel passion narratives, including Matthew's. By contrast, for the most part the positive interpretation of Pilate's wife and her dream has been remarkably stable. Yet even here there is a gap in the Matthean text, which opens the possibility to an alternative view. Although elsewhere in Matthew dreams are presented rhetorically as reliable sources of divine revelation, in each of these cases the content of the dream is made explicit (Matt. 1.20–21; 2.12, 13, 20). Moreover, the divine origin of the dreams received by Joseph and the Magi is clarified, either by reference to an 'angel of the Lord' (Matt. 1.20; 2.13, 19) or by the verb 'warned' (2.12, 22). By contrast, Pilate's wife's dream is not revealed in a dream narrative but alluded to in a secondary report.[62] Readers of Matthew 27 learn only that Pilate's wife has suffered greatly because of her dream, with no explanation of the content of her dream, its origin or the nature of her suffering.

It is precisely these questions that emerge in one final aspect of the reception of Pilate's wife to be considered, which is arguably the most controversial: the possibility that her dream has a different origin from the dreams of Joseph and the eastern Magi. Interest in dreams as modes of communication, their source and their interpretation, is a dimension of human experience where patristic and medieval commentators are probably significantly closer to the world view of the evangelist Matthew than most modern commentators. Admittedly, the majority of older exegetes – such as Ambrose, John Chrysostom, Bruno of Segni, Christian of Stavelot, Erasmus and Calvin – have in common with their modern counterparts the general presumption that Pilate's wife's dream is indeed a vehicle of divine revelation. Yet they are often keen to provide greater precision about this.

One particular example, reflecting an increasingly developed Christology, is the claim that Christ himself is the originator of the dream, providing evidence for his divinity. Ephrem the Syrian poses the following rhetorical question in a sermon on the Transfiguration: 'And if he wasn't God, who frightened the wife of Pilate with a dream?'[63] For Theophylact, an eleventh-century exegete from Ochrid in Bulgaria, Christ even orchestrates these events while standing before her husband: 'O, how miraculous! While being judged by Pilate, Christ caused his wife to suffer a fright.'[64]

However, my main interest is in a minority reading – albeit one that will become highly significant in popular circles in the west – that attributes the dream not to divine invention but to diabolical activity. Already in the *Acts of Pilate* the possibility was raised that the dream was the result of Jesus being a sorcerer, though the implied reader of the *Acts* is clearly to reject this interpretation given that it is found on the lips of 'the Jews'.

But some receptions positively promote the alternative claim that the source of the dream was in fact the devil. The driving force behind this alternative interpretation seems to be theological and soteriological: the consequences of Pilate preventing Christ's crucifixion and thereby blocking the means of humanity's salvation. The earliest reference to this seems to be a passage in the pseudonymous letter of Ignatius of Antioch to the Philippians (*Phil.* 4), dated to the late fourth century,[65] and it is regularly repeated by a string of medieval exegetes through to the Reformation.[66] Most surprising for modern commentators is the capacity for this negative reading to stand side by side with the positive view of Pilate's wife as a symbol of the Gentiles in the same medieval commentaries, such as the important medieval *Glossa ordinaria*.[67]

This interpretation has also proved remarkably resilient in drama and literature. It is attested in the ninth-century Old Saxon poem *The Heliand*, and William Langland's *Piers Plowman* (18.300–310),[68] and found its way via translations of the *Gospel of Nicodemus* and the *Golden Legend*, as well as verse narratives of the passion such as the *Passion des jongleurs* (vv. 1198–257),[69] into the dramatic tradition. In the medieval Cornish *Passio Christi* (one of three plays in the Cornish

Ordinalia), Lucifer sends Beelzebub to threaten Pilate's wife with the following words:

> Greetings and salutations, great lady! To be brief, send a messenger to Pilate, warning him that if the innocent prisoner is destroyed, unsparing vengeance will be exacted from you and from your children, as will shortly become only too clear.[70]

In so doing, Beelzebub reveals the truth about Jesus, namely that he is the Christ, the Son of God.

In the York Cycle, dependent on the fourteenth-century *Stanzaic Gospel of Nicodemus*, the demonic origin of the dream has extended to the transformation of Pilate's wife into a wholly negative character. Procula is now a sorceress, a second Eve (though of a very different kind from that posited by Augustine), while Pilate is a tortured and complex character, torn between his wife's negative influence and the positive influence of his beadle.[71] Why this tradition should have been so popular is uncertain; however, in her discussion of the York Cycle, Kimberly Fonzo makes a strong case that the transformation of Procula reflects male suspicion of female spirituality: 'a would-be visionary who has been tricked by the devil and must be properly examined or simply ignored lest she damn all of humanity through her own folly'.[72] In other words, external factors are the driving force behind the preservation, if not the origins of this marginal interpretation.

In *Tradition and Imagination*, David Brown explored how the biblical narrative was imaginatively developed, and often improved, in order to reflect developing understanding of the significance of Jesus. Although the negative assessment of Pilate's wife's dream, particularly in its dramatic form in the York Cycle, can hardly be said to be an 'improvement' on the text, it is nonetheless driven by a positive concern to preserve another, arguably more dominant concern of Matthew's: the salvific character of Christ's death as achieving the forgiveness of sins (see e.g. Matt. 26.28). The more central a role the crucifixion has theologically, the greater the tendency to underscore how Pilate's wife's dream represents a potential threat to the plan of salvation, even though this moves the story sharply away from Matthew's probable intention concerning the dreamer herself.

Conclusion

This survey of receptions of the story of Pilate's wife has sought to illustrate, at least in relation to one brief and tantalizingly incomplete biblical reference (Matt. 27.19), David Brown's contention that the biblical text is not the final word. We have encountered significant imaginative developments in the text, taking as their springboard Matthew's silence about the extent of Pilate's wife's prior knowledge of Jesus, the nature of her dream, the meaning of her suffering 'on account of him' and the fruit borne in her later life, and that of her husband, by her positive acknowledgement of Christ's righteousness.

Each of these receptions can be shown to respond to specific dimensions of the text, thereby conveying different kinds of truths from the purely historical. If we can see beyond the evidently fictional and embellished character of texts like the *Acts of Pilate*, for example, we might be able to appreciate how such imaginative fiction is a way of preserving the text's positive portrayal of Pilate's wife as a Gentile who sees, through divine revelation, the truth about Jesus. By painting her as another Poppaea, a god-fearing pagan, giving her a name and imagining her wider story, her representative role in the Gospel is underscored. This parallels the transformation of Matthew's Magi from the east into three kings from different continents, which ensured their ongoing significance as representatives of all the nations. Nor is this use of the imagination absent from some of the questions asked about Pilate's wife in recent critical commentaries. The *Acts of Pilate* may be a particularly advanced form of imaginative exegesis, but it differs from its modern counterparts by degree rather than kind.

Another example is Pilate's wife's eventual canonization by certain eastern churches. The development of her cult is arguably rooted in her reported statement in Matthew that she 'suffered many things' on account of Christ. Whether this statement is construed as a statement of her pre-passion attachment to Jesus, or anticipates her future role as post-Easter convert, it offers an explanation of her eventual path to sainthood. The Matthean terminology makes possible a reading whereby this Gentile noblewoman is associated with Christ's own disciples and even with Christ himself.

Moreover, as in the case of the Magi, certain trajectories taken by her story could arguably represent an 'advance' on the biblical text. Later receptions – most notably in Lanyer and Brontë – that give this female character a more prominent role are one such instance. Although positively portrayed, in Matthew's text Pilate's wife remains firmly offstage and, like Mary in Matthew's infancy narrative, has no direct speaking part.[73] This may well reflect the evangelist's own androcentric assumptions. Changed cultural circumstances allow her, and those she represents, a more central role and a more robust speaking voice. Such moves will eventually feed into the work of modern commentators who seek to bring her in from the margins entirely.[74]

In a sermon on the Epiphany (*Serm.* 201.2), Augustine references Matthew's story of the centurion's servant – and Jesus' promise of many coming from east and west (Matt. 8.11) – to draw a striking parallel between the Magi in the infancy narrative and Pontius Pilate in the passion narrative:

> The Magi came from the East, Pilate came from the West. They accordingly witnessed to Him at His birth, he at His death, that they might sit down with Abraham, &c., not as their descendants in the flesh, but as grafted into them by faith.[75]

But might not that honour of coming 'from the west' belong more appropriately to Pilate's wife? She seems to be presented unambiguously, despite the wrong turn in certain strands of western reception, as a righteous Gentile. She, like the Magi, receives revelation in a dream. She, like Jesus, suffers greatly and shares with the disciples the privilege of facing hardships on account of his name. If many will come from east and west to recline with Abraham, Isaac and Jacob in the kingdom of the heavens, then the woman we now know as Claudia Procula should surely have a prominent place among them.

Notes

1 David Brown, *Tradition and Imagination: Revelation and Change* (Oxford: Oxford University Press, 1999), 1.

2 See e.g. Ulrich Luz, *Matthew in History: Interpretation, Influence, and Effects* (Minneapolis, MN: Fortress Press, 1994); David P. Parris, *Reception Theory and Biblical Hermeneutics*, Princeton Theological Monograph Series (Eugene, OR: Pickwick, 2009); Emma England and William John Lyons (eds), *Reception History and Biblical Studies: Theory and Practice*, Scriptural Traces: Critical Perspectives on the Reception and Influence of the Bible 9 (London: Bloomsbury, 2015).

3 Few biblical scholars would disagree with the latter point, even if they have not worked out its potentially radical implications: see William J. Abraham, 'Scripture, Tradition and Revelation: An Appreciative Critique of David Brown', in *Theology, Aesthetics, and Culture: Responses to the Work of David Brown*, ed. Robert MacSwain and Taylor Worley (Oxford: Oxford University Press, 2012), 13–28.

4 Brown, *Tradition and Imagination*, 60–5.

5 There is a certain irony here, given that in practice historical critics have regularly relied on the imagination to reconstruct plausible historical origins for Gospel texts: e.g. Raymond E. Brown, *The Community of the Beloved Disciple* (London: Geoffrey

Chapman, 1979). On imaginatively conceived 'truths of history' in historical criticism, see Ian Boxall, *Patmos in the Reception History of the Apocalypse* (Oxford: Oxford University Press, 2013), 224-6.

6 See especially Raymond E. Brown, *The Birth of the Messiah*, new updated edn (London: Geoffrey Chapman, 1993), 45-232.

7 On how Matthew's first audiences are likely to have understood the Magi, see Mark A. Powell, 'The Magi as Kings: An Adventure in Reader-Response Criticism', *Catholic Biblical Quarterly* 62.3 (2000), 459-80.

8 Unless otherwise stated, all biblical quotations are taken from the NRSV, Anglicized Edition.

9 Joachim Gnilka, *Das Matthäusevangelium II. Teil*, F (Basel: Herder, 1988), 456: 'Ein Intermezzo unterbricht den Handlungsablauf.'

10 Florence M. Gillman, 'The Wife of Pilate (Matthew 27:19)', *Louvain Studies* 17.2-3 (1992), 152-65; Raymond E. Brown, *The Death of the Messiah: From Gethsemane to the Grave* (New York: Doubleday, 1994), 755; W. D. Davies and Dale C. Allison, *A Critical and Exegetical Commentary on the Gospel according to Saint Matthew*, vol. 3 (Edinburgh: T&T Clark, 1997) 578-9.

11 Wolfgang Trilling, *Das Wahre Israel: Studien zur Theologie des Matthäusevangeliums* (Leipzig: St Benno-Verlag, 1959), 50.

12 Donald P. Senior, *The Passion Narrative According to Matthew*, BETL XXIX (Leuven: Leuven University Press, 1975), 246-8.

13 On dreams, see e.g. Robert Gnuse, 'Dream Genre in the Matthean Infancy Narratives', *Novum Testamentum* 32.2 (1990), 97-120; Derek S. Dodson, 'Dreams, the Ancient Novels, and the Gospel of Matthew: An Intertextual Study', *Perspectives in Religious Studies* 29.1 (2002), 39-52; William J. Subash, *The Dreams of Matthew 1:18−2:23 Tradition, Form, and Theological Investigation* (New York: Lang, 2012).

14 Senior, *The Passion Narrative According to Matthew*, 247.

15 More surprising is her relative neglect in critical studies attentive to women's voices: e.g. Amy Jill Levine and Marianne Blickenstaff (eds), *A Feminist Companion to Matthew*, Feminist Companion to the New Testament and Early Christian Writings 1 (Sheffield: Sheffield Academic Press, 2001), 50-1, 108; Stuart L. Love, *Jesus and Marginal Women: The Gospel of Matthew in Social-Scientific Perspective* (Cambridge: James Clarke, 2009), 162, 184.

16 On the possible influence of traditions about Joseph and Potiphar's wife, see J. Duncan M. Derrett, '"Have Nothing to Do With That Just Man!" (Matt. 27, 19). Haggadah and the Account of the Passion', *Downside Review* 97.329 (1979), 308-15.

17 E.g. Brown, *Death of the Messiah*, 803-7; Davies and Allison, *Matthew*, vol. 3, 587.

18 Gillman, 'The Wife of Pilate', 163-4.

19 E.g. Daniel J. Harrington, *The Gospel of Matthew*, Sacra Pagina 1 (Collegeville, MN: Liturgical Press, 1992), 389; Robert H. Gundry, *Matthew: A Commentary on his Handbook for a Mixed Church under Persecution*, 2nd edn (Grand Rapids, MI: Eerdmans, 1994), 562; Brown, *Death of the Messiah*, 805; Warren Carter, *Matthew and the Margins* (Maryknoll, NY: Orbis, 2000), 526; Rudolf Schnackenburg, *The Gospel of Matthew* (Grand Rapids, MI: Eerdmans, 2002), 284; Ulrich Luz, *Matthew 21−28*, Hermeneia (Minneapolis, MN: Fortress Press, 2005), 498.

20 For other Gentile women interceding for Jews, see Josephus, *War* 2.314 (Bernice); *Ant.* 12.204 (Cleopatra); *Ant.* 20.135 (Agrippina).

21 For Luz (*Matthew 21−28*, 493), v. 19 is 'clearly redactional', even if it is 'conceivable' that Matthew is utilizing a 'pre-Matthean church tradition'; for Senior (*Passion Narrative*, 246), it is a 'mixture of undeniable Matthean words and common synoptic or traditional vocabulary'.

22 The other occurrences refer to Herod (2.16), people sending word about Jesus

(14.35), the owner of the donkey and colt (21.3), the Pharisees (22.16) and Pilate's wife (27.19).

23 See John Nolland, *The Gospel of Matthew*, NIGTC (Grand Rapids, MI: Eerdmans, 2005), 1172.

24 See e.g. Dorothy Jean Weaver, '"Thus You Will Know Them By Their Fruits": The Roman Characters of the Gospel of Matthew', in *The Gospel of Matthew in its Roman Imperial Context*, ed. John Riches and David C. Sim (New York: T&T Clark, 2005), 107–27 (reference is to 120); also Dorothy Jean Weaver, '"Wherever this Good News is Proclaimed": Women and God in the Gospel of Matthew', *Interpretation* 64.4 (2010), 390–401 (reference is to 400).

25 The third example describes the suffering of the epileptic boy at 17.15.

26 Nolland, *Gospel of Matthew*, 1172; he also references the mother of the seven sons who suffers in her anguish on their behalf at 4 Maccabees 15.22 (though he contrasts this with Pilate's wife's sufferings, which are 'limited to those of a bad dream').

27 Roland Kany, 'Die Frau des Pilatus und ihr Name: Ein Kapitel aus der Geschichte neutestamentlicher Wissenschaft', *ZNW* 86.2 (1995), 104–10.

28 J. C. Marsh-Edwards, 'The Magi in Tradition and Art', *Irish Ecclesiastical Record* series 5 (1956), 85: 6.

29 J. K. Elliott (ed.), *The Apocryphal New Testament* (Oxford: Clarendon, 1993), 164–6; also M. Geerard, *Clavis apocryphorum Novi Testamenti*, CCCA 62 (Turnhout: Brepols, 1992), 43–6. On the complex reception of the *Gospel of Nicodemus* and its textual diversity in the west, see Zbigniew Izydorczyk (ed.), *The Medieval Gospel of Nicodemus: Texts, Intertexts, and Contexts in Western Europe*, Medieval and Renaissance Texts and Studies 158 (Tempe, AZ: Arizona State University, 1997).

30 Constantine von Tischendorf (ed.), *Evangelia Apocrypha* (Hildesheim: Georg Olms, 1966), 296, 343. It has been proposed, e.g. by H. E. G. Paulus, that *nomine Procula* is due to a transcription error, the Latin original – of which the Greek is a translation – reading *procul posita*: see Kany, 'Die Frau des Pilatus', 106–7.

31 *Paradosis Pilati* 9; Elliott, *Apocryphal New Testament*, 210–11.

32 Anne-Catherine Baudoin, 'La femme de Pilate dans les *Actes de Pilate*, recension grecque A (II, 1)', *Apocrypha* 21 (2010), 133–49 (reference is to 145).

33 *Claudia Procula uxor Pilati admonita per somnium in Christum credit, et salutem consequitur*: PL 31:69–70. The claim is sometimes made that she is called Claudia Procula in Nicephorus Kallistos Xanthopoulos, *H.E.* I.30 = PG 145:720, though the text reads only 'Prokla'; see Kany, 'Die Frau des Pilatus', 106.

34 Gertrud von le Fort, *The Wife of Pilate and Other Stories*, trans. M. J. Miller (San Francisco, CA: Ignatius Press, 2015).

35 Origen, *Commentary on Matthew* 122; Manlio Simonetti (ed.), *Matthew 14–28*, Ancient Christian Commentary on Scripture: New Testament 1b (Downers Grove, IL: InterVarsity Press, 2002), 280.

36 Hilary of Poitiers, *Commentary on Matthew*, trans. D. H. Williams, Fathers of the Church 125 (Washington, DC: Catholic University of America Press, 2012), 287.

37 Augustine, *Sermo* 150.4 = PL 39:2038; English translation from Cornelius à Lapide, *The Great Commentary*, vol. 3, trans. Thomas W. Mossman, 4th edn, Catholic Standard Library (London: John Hodges, 1890), 264.

38 An apocryphal letter of Pilate to Herod claims that his wife accompanied Longinus to Jesus' tomb (see Montague R. James, *The Apocryphal New Testament* (Oxford: Oxford University Press, 1966), 155), while a passage in the Slavonic version of Josephus' *War* (inserted after *War* 2.174) has Jesus healing her as she lay dying.

39 Clough translates as 'a worshiper of God': W. O. Clough (ed.), *Gesta Pilati; or the Reports, Letters and Acts of Pontius Pilate* (Indianapolis, IN: Robert Douglass, 1880), 107.

40 Translation from Elliott, *Apocryphal New Testament*, 172 (using Tischendorf's

Greek recension A). This passage is found also in most Latin manuscripts of the Latin families B and C, and in the Coptic, shorter Slavic, Armenian and Georgian versions: Baudoin, 'La femme de Pilate', 134.

41 E.g. Brown, *Death of the Messiah*, 806.
42 Baudoin, 'La femme de Pilate', 133, 141.
43 Máire Herbert and Martin McNamara, *Irish Biblical Apocrypha: Selected Texts in Translation* (Edinburgh: T&T Clark, 1989), 62. Rabbinic tradition also preserves the accusation that Jesus was a sorcerer who led Israel astray: *b. Sanh.* 43a. On the connection between dreams and magic in antiquity, see Derek S. Dodson, 'Dream Magic: The Dream of Pilate's Wife and the Accusation of Magic in the *Acts of Pilate*', in *Gelitten, Gestorben, Auferstanden: Passions- und Ostertraditionen im antiken Christentum*, ed. Tobias Nicklas, Andreas Merkt and Joseph Verheyden, WUNT 2/273 (Tübingen: Mohr Siebeck, 2010), 21–30.
44 Translation from Elliott, *Apocryphal New Testament*, 177.
45 E. Cerulli, *Tiberius and Pontius Pilate in Ethiopian Tradition and Poetry*, Proceedings of the British Academy, vol. LIX (London: Oxford University Press, 1973), 10.
46 Gundry, *Matthew: A Commentary*, 562.
47 Davies and Allison, *Matthew*, vol. 3, 579.
48 E.g. Augustine Stock, *The Method and Message of Matthew* (Collegeville, MN: Michael Glazier, 1994), 421; Carter, *Matthew and the Margins*, 524.
49 Callie Callon, 'Pilate the Villain: An Alternative Reading of Matthew's Portrayal of Pilate', *Biblical Theology Bulletin* 36.2 (2006), 62–71; see also Warren Carter, *Matthew and Empire: Initial Explorations* (Harrisburg, PA: Trinity, 2001), 145–68.
50 Hilary of Poitiers, *Commentary on Matthew*, 287.
51 Jerome, *Commentary on Matthew*, trans. Thomas P. Scheck, Fathers of the Church 117 (Washington, DC: Catholic University of America Press, 2008), 311. Equally positive is the assessment of Bengel: 'By this warning a great favour was shown to the governor, in preference to the Jews, who had been sufficiently warned from other sources'. John Albert Bengel, *New Testament Word Studies. Volume One: Matthew–Acts*, trans. Charlton T. Lewis and Marvien R. Vincent (Grand Rapids, MI: Kregel, 1971), 303.
52 *Paradosis Pilati* 9; translation from Elliott, *Apocryphal New Testament*, 210–11.
53 John Chrysostom, *In Matthaeum* 86.1; translation from Simonetti (ed.), *Matthew 14–28*, 280 = PG 58:764.
54 Ambrose, *Expositio evangelii secundum Lucam* 10.100–101; see Ronald H. van der Bergh, 'The Reception of Matthew 27:19b (Pilate's Wife's Dream) in the Early Church', *Journal of Early Christian History* 2.1 (2012), 70–85 (reference is to 79).
55 Elliott, *Apocryphal New Testament*, 623–4.
56 Susanne Woods (ed.), *The Poems of Aemilia Lanyer: Salve Deus Rex Judaeorum* (New York: Oxford University Press, 1993), xxxv.
57 Woods, *The Poems of Aemilia Lanyer*, 91.
58 On this see Sara L. Pearson, 'Charlotte Brontë's Poetics: A Study of 'Pilate's Wife's Dream', *Brontë Studies* 37.3 (2012), 194–207.
59 Charlotte Brontë, Emily Brontë and Anne Brontë, *Poems by Currer, Ellis, and Acton Bell* (London: Aylott & Jones, 1846), 3.
60 Brontë, Brontë and Brontë, *Poems by Currer, Ellis, and Acton Bell*, 3–4.
61 Pearson, 'Charlotte Brontë's Poetics', 205.
62 Dodson, 'Dreams, the Ancient Novels, and the Gospel of Matthew', 51.
63 van der Bergh, 'The Reception of Matthew 27:19b', 75.
64 Theophylact, *The Explanation by Blessed Theophylact Archbishop of Ochrid and Bulgaria of the Holy Gospel according to St. Matthew* (House Springs, MO: Chrysostom, 1992), 242.
65 Baudoin, 'La femme de Pilate', 148.

66 E.g. Pseudo-Bede, *In Matthaei Evangelium Expositio* 27 = PL 92:121C; Rabanus Maurus, *Comment. In Matt* 8 = PL 107:1131; Peter Comestor, *Historia Scholastica* 167 = PL 198:1628B.

67 See A. Scheidgen, *Die Gestalt des Pontius Pilatus in Legende, Bibelauslegung und Geschichtsdichtung vom Mittelalter bis in die frühe Neuzeit: Literaturgeschichte einer umstrittenen Figur*, Mikrokosmos Band 68 (Frankfurt am Main: Lang, 2002), 55.

68 On *The Heliand*, see Eric Fascher, *Das Weib des Pilatus (Matthäus 27, 19); Die Auferweckung der Heiligen (Matthäus 27, 51–53). Zwei Studien zur Geschichte der Schriftauslegung*, Hallische Monographien 20 (Halle: Max Niemeyer, 1951), 5–6.

69 On the latter text, see Richard O'Gorman, 'The *Gospel of Nicodemus* in the Vernacular Literature of Medieval France', in *The Medieval* Gospel of Nicodemus: *Texts, Intertexts, and Contexts in Western Europe*, ed. Zbigniew Izydorczyk, Medieval and Renaissance Texts and Studies 158 (Tempe, AZ: Arizona State University, 1997), 124–5.

70 Markham Harris, trans., *The Cornish Ordinalia: A Medieval Dramatic Trilogy* (Washington, DC: Catholic University of America Press, 1969), 137.

71 Kimberly Fonzo, 'Procula's Civic Body and Pilate's Masculinity Crisis in the York Cycle's "Christ Before Pilate 1: The Dream of Pilate's Wife"', *Early Theatre* 16.2 (2013), 11–32. For visual reception, see e.g. Herrad von Landsberg, *Hortus deliciarum*, fol. 143r: Die Passio Christi: Der Traum der Frau des Pilatus (the devil stands over Pilate's wife's bed as she sleeps): Scheidgen, *Die Gestalt des Pontius Pilatus*, 327.

72 Fonzo, 'Procula's Civic Body', 16.

73 Though some might consider the fact that Pilate's wife's words are reported, albeit secondhand through an intermediary, as an advance on Matthew's characterization of Jesus' mother.

74 E.g. Carter, *Matthew and the Margins*, 526; M. A. Getty-Sullivan, *Women in the New Testament* (Collegeville, MN: Liturgical Press, 2001), 130–4; Weaver, 'Thus You Will Know Them By Their Fruits', 120.

75 Translation from Lapide, *The Great Commentary*, vol. 3, 265.

3

Memory, Remembrance and Imagination in the Formation of Redemptive Tradition: Reflecting on the Gospel of John with David Brown*

STEPHEN C. BARTON

Put briefly, I take the central argument of David Brown's *Tradition and Imagination*, presented as it is with clarity and erudition, to be as follows. First, any sharp distinction between Scripture and Christian tradition is historically and theologically ill-conceived. Second, and related, Scripture is itself tradition, the result of a demonstrable 'traditioning' process.[1] In terms both of the history of its formation and of the history of its reception, it is not at all a static deposit; rather, it is a 'moving text'. Third, as the imaginative development of incarnational faith in and for changing circumstances, Christian tradition is at least as much revelation as Scripture is – indeed, it is *continuing* revelation. As Brown says at the outset:

> My aim is to show that tradition, so far from being something secondary or reactionary, is the motor that sustains revelation both within Scripture and beyond. Indeed, so much is this so that Christians must disabuse themselves of the habit of contrasting biblical revelation and later tradition, and instead see the hand of God in a continuing process that encompasses both ... Present-day Christianity, it seems to me, will go badly wrong, if it attempts an unmediated dialogue with the biblical text rather than recognizing also the intervening history that has helped shape its present perception of the text's meaning.[2]

Along the way, a number of related goals are achieved. I note the following. First, Brown offers a major study, amply illustrated, of how a developing tradition works and of the role of the human imagination in that process. This allows him to offer an account not just of biblical and Christian tradition but of the developing traditions of both Judaism and Islam – indeed, of the heroic traditions in the classical sources as well. It also allows him to offer a corrective to versions of Enlightenment polemic, sometimes heard even within the Church, that are hostile to tradition, as per se reactionary and oppressive.

Second, and pre-eminently, Brown offers a major study of the role of tradition in Christian religion. This serves as a significant counterweight to Biblicist tendencies in Christian use of Scripture. Says Brown:

> A Christianity that confines God's revelatory acts to the narrow compass of Scripture, even when this is expressed in terms of the effect of that Scripture upon us in the here and now, I find less and less plausible, the more I become aware of the historical situatedness of the text.[3]

Third, and related to the preceding, the work represents a significant challenge to traditional claims made for the canon of Scripture. Canon as a literary phenomenon consisting of Old and New Testaments is accepted; but the canon of Scripture as ultimate norm against which developments in tradition are to be tested is rejected. As Brown writes:

> While not denying the right of Scripture to offer a critique of later elements in the tradition, there is also in my view an equal right of later tradition to critique Scripture, and this is what makes it inappropriate to speak of one always acting as the norm for the other. Instead, a dialogue must take place, with now one yielding, now the other ... [Scripture and tradition] ... are part of a single, ongoing process of revelation.[4]

Fourth, much needed air is given to the vital role of imagination – in particular the *hermeneutical* imagination – in bringing faith to life. This provides a warrant for serious attention to the revelatory potential of popular traditions, rituals and practices, such as those associated with the crib at Christmas – and here, by the way, one notes a certain congruence with recent work on the significance of 'ordinary theology'.[5] But attention to the role of imagination also provides a warrant for a turn to the visual arts, with their 'capacity to transmit the biblical story in ways which at times could speak more powerfully to contemporaries than the original deposit'.[6] And of course, attention to the visual arts points more broadly to the impact of stimuli on a much wider front, including stimuli from *outside* the Christian community; and this reflects what I would call a profound Christian humanism in Brown's work, evident, for instance, in his argument overall for recognition that revelation arises from 'a much wider pattern of divine disclosure'.[7]

Fifth, a nuanced account of the nature of Christian truth is achieved. Put briefly, by a balanced appropriation of the epistemological legacies of both modernity and postmodernity, due weight is given to both correspondence and coherence theories of truth. Historicity, as a criterion of truth dear to modernity (as the child of the Enlightenment), is important; but it is by no means the sole or even most important criterion in relation to the truth of faith. The kind of imaginative truth rooted and grounded in communal narratives, including that of religious communities, is also important – but not without the 'reality checks' offered by other ways of knowing. As Brown points out, in relation to truth and verification, what question is being asked is a critical *desideratum*.[8]

Sixth, the strategic choice of traditions concerning the biblical patriarchs – here Abraham, Isaac and Joseph – opens the way for significant comparisons of the interaction of tradition and imagination within and across the three great monotheisms of Christianity, Judaism and Islam, with real potential for increasing interreligious understanding. The scope for convergence between Brown's work with that of the Scriptural Reasoning project, initiated by David Ford and colleagues at Cambridge, is considerable.[9]

Seventh, the direct manner of Brown's engagement as a theologian with Scripture and biblical scholarship is salutary for a *Neutestamentler* like myself, for Brown often goes where at least some angels fear to tread. Where biblical scholars often prescind from theological appraisal and moral evaluation in favour of (say) literary analysis and historical exegesis, Brown does not hesitate to point out what he regards as limitation or error – for precisely the reason that sensitivity to limitation or error signals a recognition of the importance of the ongoing development of tradition in the light of changing historical circumstances and new knowledge.[10]

Now, this is not the place for offering quibbles on particular points. Inevitably in a work as wide-ranging and bold as Brown's, there will be ideas to contest or statements of the case that another writer would put differently. What I want to offer is more by way of a constructive suggestion as to how Brown might make his case even stronger – should he wish to revise his work for a second edition!

The Role of Memory and Remembrance: A Johannine Case Study

What strikes me as 'at most' implicit in Brown's account of Scripture, tradition and the role of the imagination is attention to the role of *memory and remembrance*.[11] There is, I believe, scope for development here in ways that would enhance Brown's project as a whole. In recent scholarship across a number of academic disciplines, the importance of memory, memorization and acts of remembrance, both individual and communal, in the formation and preservation of tradition, has been increasingly recognized.[12] Not least has this been the case in biblical studies generally and also, more specifically, in gospel and Jesus studies.[13] In what follows, what I want to offer is a case study in 'the moving text', drawing attention to the role of – or at least the role *claimed for* – memory and remembrance.

Brown makes frequent reference to the Fourth Gospel as an imaginative development of Synoptic tradition. Indeed, in his account of 'the hermeneutics of Pentecost' he remarks on a freedom in John 'that refuses to be content with what has come down from the past, and a resultant willingness to rewrite the story so that some truths may be told more effectively'.[14] And he goes on to make a more general point about tradition, as follows:

> So far, then, from tradition being the mere endorsement of the dead hand of the past, I would argue that we may use John to think anew, and thus recognize the way in which tradition can be seen as biblically constituted by the imaginative reappropriation of the past, and not its slavish copying.[15]

These points about John are well made.[16] As far as I can see, however, he overlooks a text that would be grist to his Johannine mill for the explicit evidence it gives of *tradition in process* already within Scripture, and of one of the key factors involved, namely the contribution claimed for memory and remembrance. Consideration of this and related texts will help us to see, I believe, that John's 'imaginative reappropriation' of the past is *by no means whimsical or uncontrolled* – more precisely, that the Evangelist as narrator wishes to represent his recounting of the past not only as authoritative but, even more, *as Spirit-inspired*, and that he is unique among the Gospel writers in making that explicit.

The text I have in mind is John 2.13–22, which is John's account of the so-called 'Cleansing of the Temple', an episode he combines with a version of the tradition of Jesus' sayings about the temple's destruction. Comparison between the Synoptic and Johannine traditions shows clear development, and what we might call serious imaginative play (cf. Matt. 21.10–17; Mark 11.15–19; Luke 19.45–48). Indeed, the development and play begin already with the Synoptics, as is widely recognized.[17] Here we certainly have a case of 'the moving text'.

Among Johannine developments are the following: (1) John places Jesus' temple demonstration at the outset of his public ministry,[18] not at its climax, as in the Synoptics. To put it more sharply, in a quite radical rewriting of the tradition, John up-ends the received sequence of events, as if to signal *from the beginning* of his Jesus narrative the revolutionary implications for the Jewish cult – and therefore for the Jews and Judaism – of the revelation of the One designated in the opening chapter, and with striking intensity, as the Logos, the place of God's dwelling, the Son of God, the King of Israel and the heavenly Son of Man (cf. John 1.14, 34, 49, 51).

But we can go further. Certainly John is signalling that, for the full significance of Jesus to be recognized, the story of Jesus has to be told 'backwards', as it were; that is, in the light of its ending in the glorious 'lifting up' of the Son of Man via the cross and resurrection to the Father. Indeed, it may not be going too far to suggest that he also seems to be signalling that, in the light of the death and exaltation of the Messiah, *time and narrative are relative to eternity*, in which case historical beginnings and endings – and other time markers for that matter – may be deployed in service of a larger truth, a truth John regards as revelatory and redemptive.

(2) The demonstration in the temple in Jerusalem is preceded by the sign-miracle of the turning of water into wine at the wedding feast at Cana in Galilee (John 2.1–11). This episode, unique to John, invites an implied interpretative comparison and contrast with what follows. This can be elaborated in many ways. Overall it plays its part in the moral-theological dualism – the dualism of light and darkness, life and death, salvation and judgement – that is all-pervasive in John's Gospel. Of the juxtaposed episodes, the one speaks of abundant life (all that wine!), the other of judgement; the one of spaces, times and occasions of joy, the other of spaces, times and occasions blighted by idolatry.

But it is not a case of a tradition developing by simple contrast. Both episodes carry eschatological symbolism; both convey the fulfilment in Jesus of the old order. On the one hand, we have a 'sign' (σημεῖον) that takes place 'on the third day', a wedding banquet, a reference by Jesus to his yet-to-come 'hour', the displacement of Jewish rites of purification, the provision of wine in quality and quantity beyond expectation, a mysterious bridegroom, the revelation of Jesus' 'glory' (δόξα) and the coming to believe of the disciples. On the other hand, in the temple episode we have the soteriological Passover setting (v. 13a, repeated at v. 23a), the symbolic action (clearly identified as one of the 'signs', at v. 23b), the enigmatic reference to the destruction of the temple, the references to 'raising up' and resurrection and, once again, the coming to believe of the disciples. It seems fair to suggest, then, that John's play with setting and sequence, as well as with content, reflect (what he no doubt regarded as) his Spirit-inspired freedom (cf. John 14.16–17, 26) to reinterpret the 'temple cleansing' and temple sayings traditions in the service of a deeper, eschatological truth perhaps newly understood.[19]

(3) But for present purposes, it is John's twofold interpolation into the tradition of the motif of *memory and remembrance* that is particularly striking.[20] John's narrative is in two parts. The first tells of Jesus' actions and words in the temple (vv. 13–17). This is John's version of the 'temple cleansing' tradition. The second part tells of a dialogue between Jesus and 'the Jews' as provoked by the temple incident (vv. 18–22). This is John's version of a tradition of a saying attributed to Jesus about the temple which, in the Synoptics, is *unconnected* with the temple cleansing (cf. Mark 14.58; 15.30 and par.). So in a creative interpretative act, John has brought these otherwise disparate temple traditions together.[21] The effect is stunning. Given that Jesus' action of prophetic protest in the temple is symbolic of the end of the cult (just as the turning of water into wine is symbolic of the end of Jewish purificatory rites),[22] the dialogue following offers an authoritative revelation of what is taking its place – the temple of Jesus' body (v. 21).

Equally stunning, in my opinion, is that each of the two parts thus joined together ends with a commentary that includes the phrase, ἐμνήσθησαν οἱ μαθηταὶ αὐτοῦ ὅτι ... ('his disciples remembered that ...') (vv. 17, 22). It is as if the narrator is binding the two parts of the episode together, both at the literary level and at the hermeneutical level. In the process he is rooting his creative development of the temple traditions in the post-resurrection, interpretative 'remembering' of Jesus' disciples. We are witnessing tradition in the making.

But closer analysis is warranted. Take the first part. To the pigeon-sellers Jesus says, 'Take these things away; you shall not make my Father's house a house of trade.' This is distinctive to John's version. In the Synoptics, Jesus castigates his audience for making God's house 'a den of robbers' instead of what it should be, 'a house of prayer for all the nations' (Mark 11.17 and par.). His words in the Synoptic version combine two scriptural texts, Isaiah 56.7 and Jeremiah 7.11. In John's version, however, Jesus alludes to a *different* scriptural text when he says, 'you shall not make my Father's house a house of trade' (v. 16b). The text in question is Zechariah 14.20–21, a text that 'looks forward to the day of the Lord and to God's presence in a renewed Jerusalem'[23] when the offering of sacrifices will be necessary no longer. Clearly, John's alternative scriptural text is more consistent with the thrust of the episode as a whole, which is that the old order of cult and sacrifice has been fulfilled in Jesus' body as the eschatological temple, the place where God's glory is revealed and human salvation secured.

As if in confirmation, and drawing the first part to a close, the narrator reports, 'His disciples remembered that it was written, "Zeal for thy house will consume me."' A number of comments are warranted. The mention of the disciples is, if not quite unexpected (cf. 2.11, 12), still noteworthy since, up to now, it has been all about Jesus.[24] But now they are introduced, and attention is drawn to an important role they play not only in witnessing but also in *interpreting* Jesus' actions and words – scripturally, no less![25] We are not told *when* they 'remembered' – there is an ambiguity here. It is as if past, present and future time expands or collapses in the intensity of the story John is telling. Significantly, *what* the disciples 'remember' is a scriptural text, Psalm 69.9.[26] The appeal to Scripture serves as a justification for Jesus' otherwise outrageous action: Jesus is fulfilling Scripture. Most importantly, Psalm 69.9 makes it possible to interpret Jesus' action and words in the temple as *culminating in his death* ('will *consume* me'). In other words, whereas the Synoptics make this connection by maintaining the likely historical sequence of events, with the 'temple cleansing' precipitating the judicial action against him following his final entry into Jerusalem, John makes the connection via the disciples' 'remembering' of Scripture. And the way Scripture is remembered points in the same direction, for the past tense of the verb in the original of Psalm 69.9 (LXX) is changed to the future: 'Zeal for thy house *will consume* (καταφάγεταί) me.' So the interpretative link between the temple action and Jesus' death is made secure; and, as we shall see, the second reference to the disciples remembering makes secure a link with the resurrection. Thus what we are witnessing is *the Evangelist's creative reworking of the tradition within an overall hermeneutical framework of Jesus' death and resurrection*. The signal of this hermeneutical reworking, and the guarantee of its truth, is the motif of disciple remembrance.

This brings us to the second part of the episode: the follow-up dialogue between the unbelieving Jews and Jesus, and the narrator's concluding comment (vv. 18–22). 'The Jews' show their blindness to the prophetic sign Jesus has just offered in the temple by themselves asking for a 'sign'. Jesus replies with the typically riddling comment, 'Destroy this temple, and in three days I will raise it up.' Interestingly, in the Synoptic tradition a saying about the destruction of the temple and the building of another is attributed to Jesus *by others*: false witnesses at the Sanhedrin trial (Mark 14.58) and mocking passers-by at the crucifixion (Mark 15.29). In John it is placed *on the lips of Jesus* – not surprisingly, given this Evangelist's portrayal of Jesus as the One who has power both to lay his life down and to take it up again (cf. 10.17–18). In the process, the word for 'build' or 'rebuild' is changed from οἰκοδομέω in Mark 15.29 to ἐγείρω in John (2.19), more fitting as the latter verb is for a resurrection hermeneutic.

'The Jews', as is typical of Johannine characters outside the circle of resurrection faith, misunderstand. Like Nicodemus in the very next episode (3.1–12), they interpret Jesus literally: 'It has taken forty-six years to build this temple, and will you raise it up in three days?' Amazingly, Jesus makes no reply. He has nothing to add to the climactic revelation just imparted (at v. 19). Where we might have expected a word of riposte from Jesus, what we find instead, bringing the episode to an end, is another intervention from the omniscient narrator who – in order to leave no room for doubt – informs the reader of the correct interpretation of the revelation, that Jesus 'spoke of the temple of his body [περὶ τοῦ ναοῦ τοῦ σώματος αὐτοῦ]' (v. 21).[27]

The whole episode then culminates in the second attestation of disciple remembrance: 'When therefore he was raised from the dead, *his disciples remembered that* [ἐμνήσθησαν οἱ μαθηταὶ αὐτοῦ ὅτι] he had said this; and they believed the Scripture and the word which Jesus had spoken' (v. 22). Again, several comments are in order. First, where the previous attestation of interpretative remembering has to do with Jesus' death, the second and final one has to do with Jesus' resurrection. The temple destroyed and the temple raised up is the temple of Jesus' body. Second, and related, the ambiguity earlier about when the disciples remembered is not carried over. This time, they remembered ὅτε ... ἠγέρθη ἐκ νεκρῶν ('when he was raised from the dead'). This spotlights the resurrection as the catalyst – but *how* the resurrection is the catalyst is left open (for illumination subsequently, as we shall see). Third, noteworthy is the fact that Scripture (presumably Ps. 69.9) and the saying of Jesus (presumably the saying about the destruction and raising up of the temple) are put on a par[28] as the object of the disciples' belief. In the light of the resurrection – of space, time, persons and things now conceived eschatologically – both Scripture and the sayings of Jesus *are released to speak in new ways*. Hence Jesus becomes the speaker of the psalm ('Zeal for thy house will consume *me*'); and the temple in Jerusalem becomes a figure of the body of Jesus crucified and risen.

On the basis of this case study of Jesus and the temple in John 2, it is reasonable to conclude, with Brown, that the Fourth Evangelist displays significant freedom and inspired imagination in rewriting, and therefore developing the tradition – and not just the Jesus tradition but the tradition of the Scriptures as well. What we are witnessing, I would say, is *tradition in the making*. The catalyst is resurrection faith;[29] and we have seen how Jesus' death and resurrection are the pivots around which John's rewriting of the temple traditions revolves. But John's imaginative rewriting is *not uncontrolled*, for he twice makes explicit – and he is the *only* Evangelist to do so – that his narrative has as its warrant the remembering activity of Jesus' disciples, possibly during the events (a reasonable inference from v. 17), and certainly after Jesus' resurrection (v. 22).

Christ, the Spirit and Pneumatic Remembering

It is crucial to observe that the appeal in John 2 to remembering activity is not a one-off. Rather, remembrance plays a very important part in John's creative development of the tradition overall, in the direction of a resurrection hermeneutic.[30] What is more, it is linked specifically with the eschatological Spirit (cf. 7.37–39; 14.26), as we shall see. Instead of speaking of *imaginative* rewriting, therefore, it would be more true to John, I believe, to speak of *pneumatic* rewriting – even better, *pneumatic remembering*.[31] This significant pneumatological inflection by no means distracts from the narrative-biographical form and christological focus of John since, as the Evangelist makes clear, the Spirit is '*another* Paraclete', sent by the Father in Christ's name after his resurrection (14.16). So Christ and Spirit are integrally related as both the subject matter of the text *and* its source of inspiration and authority.

That it is legitimate, with Martin Hengel, to describe John's development of the tradition as evidence of the creative imagination of a 'towering theologian'[32] is not in doubt. But it is important to stress – and I wonder if Brown goes far enough here – that John grounds what he does theologically, in his doctrine of revelation *christologically and pneumatologically conceived*. But to complete the argument, two further texts merit particular attention.[33]

First, in his creative reworking of the 'triumphal entry into Jerusalem' (12.12–19), John follows the Synoptic tradition (at Matt. 21.5) in presenting the coming of Jesus as a fulfilment of Scripture, specifically, Zechariah 9.9 (and cf. Isa. 35.4), 'Fear not, daughter of Zion; behold, your king is coming, sitting on an ass's colt!' However, uniquely among the Gospels, the Evangelist as omniscient narrator adds the following explanatory comment: 'His disciples did not understand this at first [τὸ πρῶτον]; but when Jesus was glorified [ἀλλ' ὅτε ἐδοξάσθη Ἰησοῦς], then they remembered [τότε ἐμνήσθησαν] that this had been written of him and had been done to him' (12.16).

John does here something closely analogous to what he had done earlier in his account of the temple 'cleansing' in chapter 2. Indeed, a good case can be made for positing an *inclusio* here: the temple incident (2.13–22) and the entry into Jerusalem (12.12–19) bracket Jesus' public ministry; both take place at Passover; both are related – symbolically and narratively – to Jesus' passion; both offer scriptural interpretation; and both include the tell-tale acknowledgements of post-resurrection 'remembering' by the disciples, remembering that sets Scripture and Jesus narrative side by side.[34]

With regard to 12.16, what is indubitable is that, to provide assurance of the truth of his account, including the appeal to Scripture, the

Evangelist as narrator makes an overt appeal to a process of 'remembrance' on the part of the disciples. As at 2.22, it is an appeal that distinguishes with absolute clarity between pre- and post-Easter cognition – making the point that the full truth about Jesus, and in particular the events of his life and passion, can be grasped only in the light of the resurrection and in the context of believing discipleship.

But the most significant development of the motif of disciple remembrance comes in 14.25–26, in the significant context of the Farewell Discourse:

> These things I have spoken to you while I am still with you. But the Counsellor, the Holy Spirit, whom the Father will send in my name, he will teach you all things, and bring to your remembrance [καὶ ὑπομνήσει ὑμᾶς] all that I have told you.

Here we have a key to the extraordinary creativity of the Johannine tradition, and at its heart is Spirit-inspired remembrance.[35] Such Spirit-inspired remembrance is intended to be understood as *in fundamental continuity* with respect to the past; that is, with respect to Scripture and Jesus tradition – and this will have offered assurance with regard to the truth, an assurance essential for those in the period after Jesus' departure who may have been on trial for their faith (cf. John 9),[36] or whose hearts may have been 'troubled' (cf. 14.1), or who may have felt bereft, like orphans (cf. 14.8).

But Spirit-inspired remembrance is also to be understood as *creative*. It takes Scripture and Jesus tradition and reinterprets and develops them for changing circumstances. Larry Hurtado puts the aspect of creative development incisively (and in terms that Brown, I think, would find congenial):

> GJohn is certainly a textual/literary product that, in some sense, reflects a process of authoring and editing; but it also reflects a lively experiential 'micro-culture' of inspiration and revelation, in which new insights came with forceful effects, and often occurred in circumstances that included prayerful and expectant pondering of scripture and traditional sayings of Jesus ... Indeed, I propose that the author knew very well that the historic Jesus had not actually said many of the sayings that he utters in GJohn, particularly those that reflect the exalted christological claims about Jesus' pre-existence and divine significance, and yet the author felt free to put these words on Jesus' lips. In doing so, the author believed that he was simply reflecting the true and ultimate significance of Jesus. For the author, these articulations of Jesus' divine status – although revealed by the Paraclete subsequent to Jesus – expressed truths that had always been valid.[37]

As regards what Hurtado calls the '"micro-culture" of inspiration and revelation', it is likely, not least by analogy with Paul's eschatologically orientated charismatic communities (cf. 1 Corinthians 12 and 14), or the Spirit-possessed Seer of the book of Revelation (cf. Rev. 1.10–11), that a significant role in the shaping of the Johannine tradition will have been played by Christian prophets speaking what were understood and received as words of Christ now risen and continuing to reveal saving truth – including truth about himself – from heaven (cf. John 16.7–11, 12–15).[38]

Conclusion

In a short chapter it is impossible to do justice to the rich and multi-faceted account of tradition and its development offered in *Tradition and Imagination*. What I have offered, working as a New Testament scholar, is a single case study from John's Gospel, a Gospel to which Brown himself refers as exemplifying, within Scripture itself, the creative freedom he sees as a necessary facet of living religion.

What I have shown is that the narrative account of the temple episode in John 2 brilliantly illuminates, cameo-style, the kind of process Brown demonstrates on a much wider scale. John's narrative – not least by the manner of its creative reworking of Synoptic temple texts and associated scriptural materials – displays tradition in the making. By drawing attention to the startling intrusion of references to acts of discipleship 'remembering' in the making of that tradition, I am suggesting that the role of – or claimed for – memory and remembrance could, *by analogy*, be given more attention in Brown's larger enterprise. Further, by observing the christological and pneumatological underpinnings claimed by John for his narrative as a whole, I am offering a reminder that an account of *Christian* tradition and the role of imagination in its development must be grounded theologically, not least because issues of truth and evangelical witness are at stake.

Notes

* It is a privilege to contribute to this collection stimulated by David Brown's seminal work, *Tradition and Imagination: Revelation and Change* (Oxford: Oxford University Press, 1999). As both a New Testament scholar and a priest of the Church of England, I must say how congenial I find its main thrust. The work also provokes happy memories of our time as colleagues in the Department of Theology and Religion of Durham University, where we co-chaired a series of Hermeneutical Workshops whose aim was to engage in interdisciplinary interpretation of significant biblical texts: and I note that two of these texts, the 'sacrifice' of Isaac in Genesis 22 and the cry of God-forsakenness in the Gospel passion narratives, appear as case studies in Brown's book.

1 Cf. Brown's comment, '[T]he case for a cumulative tradition appears overwhelming.' Brown, *Tradition and Imagination*, 113.

2 Ibid., 1-2.

3 Ibid., 5.

4 Ibid., 111.

5 Cf. Jeff Astley, *Ordinary Theology: Looking, Listening and Learning in Theology* (Aldershot: Ashgate, 2002).

6 Brown, *Tradition and Imagination*, 324.

7 Ibid., 60.

8 Cf. ibid., 115.

9 Cf. David F. Ford and C. C. Pecknold (eds), *The Promise of Scriptural Reasoning* (Oxford: Blackwell, 2006).

10 Cf. Brown's critique of patristic allegorizing as a way of overcoming moral and other kinds of objections to the literal sense of the biblical text, in favour of what is required of us today, namely 'full and frank acknowledgement of the limitations within the text itself: that the Bible contains that from which we may now legitimately recoil'. Brown, *Tradition and Imagination*, 69-70.

11 As evidence of what appears to be an aspect yet to be explored, I note the absence of these terms from the Index.

12 A seminal work has been that of the French sociologist Maurice Halbwachs (1877-1945), *On Collective Memory*, ed./trans. Lewis A. Coser (Chicago, IL: University of Chicago Press, 1992), on which cf. J. Fentress and C. Wickham, *Social Memory: New Perspectives on the Past* (Oxford: Blackwell, 1992). For the Late Antique and Medieval periods, see Mary Carruthers, *The Book of Memory: A Study of Memory in Medieval Culture* (Cambridge: Cambridge University Press, 1990); also Janet Coleman, *Ancient and Medieval Memories: Studies in the Reconstruction of the Past* (Cambridge: Cambridge University Press, 1992). I am especially grateful to Dr Anthony Le Donne for bibliographic advice in this field.

13 Seminal was Nils A. Dahl, 'Anamnesis: Memory and Commemoration in Early Christianity', in *Jesus in the Memory of the Early Church* (Minneapolis, MN: Augsburg, 1976), 11-29. More recent work includes James D. G. Dunn, *Jesus Remembered* (Grand Rapids, MI: Eerdmans, 2003); Doron Mendels, *Memory in Jewish, Pagan and Christian Societies of the Graeco-Roman World* (London: T&T Clark, 2004); Alan Kirk and Tom Thatcher (eds), *Memory, Tradition, and Text: Uses of the Past in Early Christianity* (Leiden: Brill, 2005); Stephen C. Barton et al. (eds), *Memory in the Bible and Antiquity* (Tübingen: Mohr Siebeck, 2007); Tom Thatcher (ed.), *Memory and Identity in Ancient Judaism and Early Christianity: A Conversation with Barry Schwartz* (Atlanta, GA: SBL Press, 2014).

14 Brown, *Tradition and Imagination*, 64.

15 Ibid., 65.

16 I suggest, however, that the qualifying adjectives in the expressions 'dead hand' and 'slavish copying' are unnecessarily provocative!

17 Cf. Morna D. Hooker, 'Traditions about the Temple in the Sayings of Jesus', *Bulletin of the John Rylands Library* 70.1 (1988), 7-20; Alexander J. M. Wedderburn, 'Jesus' Action in the Temple: A Key or a Puzzle?', *ZNW* 97.1-2 (2006), 1-22.

18 The temple action is also Jesus' first *public* act: the miracle at Cana, as C. K. Barrett observes, 'is represented as taking place privately and as known only to a few servants and to the disciples'. Barrett, *The Gospel According to John* (London: SPCK, 1978), 188.

19 Cf. Alan R. Kerr, *The Temple of Jesus' Body: The Temple Theme in the Gospel of John* (Sheffield: Sheffield Academic Press, 2002), 67-101.

20 Valuable on this aspect of John are the following: Richard Hays, 'Reading Scripture in Light of the Resurrection', in *The Art of Reading Scripture*, ed. Ellen F. Davis and Richard B. Hays (Grand Rapids, MI: Eerdmans, 2003), 216–38; Peter Stuhlmacher, 'Spiritual Remembering: John 14:26', in *The Holy Spirit and Christian Origins*, ed. Graham N. Stanton et al. (Grand Rapids, MI: Eerdmans, 2004), 55–68; Larry W. Hurtado, 'Remembering and Revelation: The Historic and Glorified Jesus in the Gospel of John', *Israel's God and Rebecca's Children: Christology and Community in Early Judaism and Christianity*, ed. David Capes et al. (Waco, TX: Baylor University Press, 2007), 195–213; Catrin H. Williams, 'Unveiling Revelation: The Spirit-Paraclete and Apocalyptic Disclosure in the Gospel of John', in *John's Gospel and Intimations of Apocalyptic*, ed. Catrin H. Williams and Christopher Rowland (London: Bloomsbury, 2013), 104–27.

21 Cf. C. K. Barrett: 'This Johannine narrative, at first sight artless and simple, is in fact a very striking example of the way in which John collects scattered synoptic material and synoptic themes, welds them into a whole, and uses them to bring out unmistakably the true meaning of the synoptic presentation of Jesus.' Barrett, *Gospel According to John*, 196.

22 For this interpretation of Jesus' actions and words in the temple, see Andrew Lincoln, *The Gospel According to St John* (London: Continuum, 2005), 137: 'It is unlikely, then that Jesus' activity is being depicted as a "cleansing of the temple" from commercial abuse. Rather, this disruption of one of the most significant feasts of the year is seen as a symbolic action that temporarily brings to a halt the sacrificial system understood to be ordained by God in the law. Within the context of John's narrative as a whole it also anticipates the end of temple sacrifices through the death of Jesus as the true Passover lamb (cf. 1.29; 19.36; also 18.34).'

23 Lincoln, *Gospel According to St John*, 138.

24 Note, for example, that 2.13b tells us that '*Jesus* went up to Jerusalem'. No mention is made of the disciples.

25 The contrast with the portrayal of the disciples as generally obtuse in Mark's Gospel is striking.

26 On the widespread use of Psalm 69 in early Christian apologetic for the suffering and death of the Messiah, see the references in Lincoln, *Gospel According to St John*, 138.

27 As Lincoln comments (*Gospel According to St John*, 140–1), 'God's presence, which previously had its special focus on earth in the Jerusalem temple, is now supremely manifested in the crucified and risen body of Jesus.'

28 If not put on a par, they are certainly brought into the closest possible association as *together* the object of belief. Hurtado ('Remembering and Revelation', 208) makes the point well: 'The remembering and the believing recognition of the import of the Scripture passage and Jesus' saying seem here to be so closely connected that they really comprise one cognitive development. Clearly, the remembering posited in this passage involved more than recollection; it also included a new perception that Jesus' actions are prefigured in, and interpreted by, Scripture, and also a new understanding of Jesus' pre-resurrection sayings and actions in light of his resurrection.'

29 Influential also, of course, will have been the dynamics and circumstances of life for Jesus-followers after his departure, on which the classic work is J. Louis Martyn, *History and Theology in the Fourth Gospel* (Nashville, TN: Abingdon, 1979). For a recent, sanguine assessment of the quest for the 'Johannine community', see Robert Kysar, 'The Whence and Whither of the Johannine Community', in *Life in Abundance: Studies in John's Gospel in Tribute to Raymond E. Brown*, ed. John R. Donahue (Collegeville, MN: Liturgical Press, 2005), 65–81. My point, however, is that it is *the resurrection* to which the text itself points as – in ways as yet unspecified – catalytic.

30 By 'resurrection hermeneutic' I mean two things. On the one hand, there is the

chronological point that the narrative's point of view is *post*-resurrection. On the other hand, there is the theological-hermeneutical point that the narrative's point of view is post-*resurrection*; that is, thoroughly eschatological.

31 Cf. Gary M. Burge, *The Anointed Community: The Holy Spirit in the Johannine Tradition* (Grand Rapids, MI: Eerdmans, 1987), 212–14.

32 Martin Hengel, *The Johannine Question*, trans. John Bowden (London: SCM Press, 1989), 96: on this 'greatest theological thinker in the earliest church alongside Paul'.

33 Also relevant for their use of the language of remembrance are 15.20; 16.4, 21.

34 Cf. Hurtado, 'Remembering and Revelation', 209.

35 Anticipation of such pneumatic inspiring, authorizing and authoring comes earlier, in John 7.39, where the prophetic-eschatological symbol of 'rivers of living water' (cf. Isa. 43.14—44.8; also Exod. 17.6; Ps. 78.16; Zech. 14.8) flowing from 'his' (most likely Jesus') belly is interpreted as follows: 'Now this he said about the Spirit, which those who believed in him were to receive; for as yet the Spirit had not been given, because Jesus was not yet glorified [οὔπω γὰρ ἦν πνεῦμα, ὅτι Ἰησοῦς οὐδέπω ἐδοξάσθη].' That this constitutes evidence of the self-understanding of the Evangelist and his circle as a post-resurrection, Spirit-inspired – or, as we might say, 'charismatic' – group is clear.

36 Cf. Andrew T. Lincoln, *Truth on Trial: The Lawsuit Motif in the Fourth Gospel* (Peabody, MA: Hendrickson, 2000).

37 Hurtado, 'Remembering and Revelation', 206–7.

38 For the phenomenon in general, cf. David E. Aune, *Prophecy in Early Christianity and the Ancient Mediterranean World* (Grand Rapids, MI: Eerdmans, 1983); also, M. Eugene Boring, *The Continuing Voice of Jesus: Christian Prophecy and the Gospel Tradition* (Louisville, KY: Westminster John Knox, 1991); Hurtado, 'Remembering and Revelation', 205–6.

4

Moving Texts and Mirror Neurons: David Brown and Eleonore Stump on Biblical Interpretation[*]

ROBERT MACSWAIN

I first encountered David Brown through the philosopher Eleonore Stump's substantial review of his book *The Divine Trinity*.[1] She began by stating that it was

> an important book which I hope will influence the direction of certain work in contemporary philosophy of religion. It is an attempt to stimulate a dialogue between philosophers of religion and biblical scholars, a dialogue I think is long overdue, in order to combine the studies of the historical basis for and philosophical credibility of Christian doctrines.[2]

She observes that, according to Brown, the Jewish and Christian Scriptures are 'a fallible record of a progressive dialogue between God and human beings in which God's nature is increasingly revealed but often enough misunderstood and misreported by Scriptural authors'.[3] After noting Brown's various arguments regarding continuing divine action, Chalcedonian and kenotic models of the Incarnation, the full Personhood of the Holy Spirit, and the social nature of Trinitarian relations, Stump registers specific points of agreement and disagreement. In one of her commendatory passages she says that Brown

> moves easily from discussions of the historical conditions surrounding the Old Testament exile of the Jews to [David] Wiggins's view on identity. He is familiar with the complexities of Patristic theology and scholastic philosophy and yet clearly is able to address contemporary

---

[*] I am grateful to Chris Brewer, David Brown, Chris Bryan and Eleonore Stump for helpful comments on earlier versions of this chapter, and to Corey Stewart-Hassman for pointing me towards Sarah Dillon's article.

theology in its own terms. And, most importantly for the overall purpose of this book, he comprehends the historical concerns of the biblical critic, but he is also familiar with the methods and the literature of current philosophy of religion. In consequence, his book is itself an example of the sort of dialogue between biblical exegetes and philosophers Brown is urging; and in my view the importance of his beginning such a dialogue far outweighs his book's flaws.[4]

Stump's review of *The Divine Trinity* appeared at a time when philosophers of religion were indeed beginning to take up this particular interdisciplinary dialogue. Focusing on Stump's contribution, in addition to some essays dealing with medieval biblical commentary,[5] she co-edited *Hermes and Athena: Biblical Exegesis and Philosophical Theology*, bringing together philosophers and New Testament scholars, to which she also contributed a chapter responding to Wayne A. Meeks.[6] A much later volume focused on the Hebrew Bible is *Divine Evil? The Moral Character of the God of Abraham*, to which Stump made three contributions.[7] And in 2010 she published *Wandering in Darkness: Narrative and the Problem of Suffering*, a massive volume dealing with both the methodology and practice of biblical exegesis in the context of a larger argument about theodicy, which I will discuss further below.[8] The dialogue between philosophers and biblical scholars that Stump saw beginning in *The Divine Trinity* has now become a lively conversation, and she has been one of the major voices promoting and contributing to it.

What then of Brown? As the current volume bears witness, 14 years after *The Divine Trinity* Brown returned to the theme and task of biblical interpretation with *Tradition and Imagination: Revelation and Change* and *Discipleship and Imagination: Christian Tradition and Truth*.[9] A trilogy on religious experience mediated through culture and the arts followed: *God and Enchantment of Place: Reclaiming Human Experience*, *God and Grace of Body: Sacrament in Ordinary*, and *God and Mystery in Words: Experience Through Metaphor and Drama*.[10] As I have written elsewhere, the five volumes inaugurated by *Tradition and Imagination*

> present many detailed arguments across a vast canvas through a sophisticated blend of philosophy, theology, biblical studies, classical studies, church history, comparative religion, comparative literature, and a wide range of other disciplines and cultural studies, particularly those related to the fine and performing arts, up to and including pop culture in its various manifestations and media. The primarily analytic and empirical approach of *The Divine Trinity* was not totally aban-

doned, but has now been thoroughly integrated into a much deeper and richer context, one that more faithfully represents the genuine complexity of the Christian tradition and which is thus more fruitful in interpreting, assessing, and defending it.[11]

Both Brown and Stump have developed their respective understandings of biblical interpretation in different ways since 1985. Neither is a professional biblical scholar as the guild defines such matters. Yet their work in this area surely deserves more attention than it has so far received. It is especially interesting to note how they independently focus on some of the same narratives – Abraham, Job, and Mary Magdalene/Mary of Bethany – and yet again with different concerns and conclusions. Brown engages with the hermeneutical philosophical tradition and traces the reception exegesis of these narratives, showing how they have been 'rewritten' through the centuries in Judaism, Christianity and Islam in order to address different contexts, mediating divine revelation in the process.[12] Stump, by contrast, situates herself in the analytic philosophical tradition, current discussions of philosophy and literature, and contemporary neuroscience, and offers original interpretations that often bear little relation to more common readings of these texts, while sometimes intentionally bracketing the question of their revelatory status. The following sections will compare Brown's *Tradition and Imagination* and *Discipleship and Imagination* with Stump's *Wandering in Darkness* to bring their respective approaches to biblical interpretation into conversation with one another.

Methodology: Hermeneutics and Neuroscience

Before comparing their interpretations of selected biblical narratives, it is illuminating to consider their divergent methodological starting points. Ever since *Continental Philosophy and Modern Theology*, published two years after *The Divine Trinity*, Brown has been identified as an analytic philosopher in dialogue with the Continental tradition.[13] It is thus not surprising that in *Tradition and Imagination* he positions himself between modernism and postmodernism;[14] and in *Discipleship and Imagination* he says that he wants to locate himself 'on both sides at once, as it were, of the modernist-postmodernist debate'.[15]

From modernism's Enlightenment inheritance Brown retrieves an insistence on 'properly researched history' that is not simply the reiteration of a communal tradition's prejudices and self-understanding, immune from external criticism or confirmation.[16] Brown rejects both extreme confidence and extreme scepticism about our knowledge of the past.

Complete historical knowledge is impossible, but 'provisional judgements' can 'make some claim to truth', and such truth-claims exhibit 'vast differences in degrees of plausibility even if these are often difficult or even impossible to quantify'.[17] Advocating 'plausibility as the norm' is Brown's Anglican epistemological *via media* between cognitive certainty and ignorance.[18] When it comes to the Jewish and Christian Scriptures this means that many canonical narratives must be judged non-historical and the theological implications faced squarely, although those implications vary greatly and are often difficult to predict in advance.[19]

From postmodernism Brown retrieves an emphasis on tradition, narrative, community, multivalence and the cultural conditioning – although not determinism – of human thought.[20] Unusually for an analytic philosopher, this leads to a critical but sympathetic conversation with Continental hermeneutics, engaging with Schleiermacher, Dilthey, Bultmann, Ricoeur and Gadamer, among others.[21] For example, Brown cites approvingly Gadamer's claim that history 'does not belong to us, but we belong to it. Long before we understand ourselves through the process of self-examination, we understand ourselves in a self-evident way in the family, society and state in which we live.'[22] However, Brown faults Gadamer for not recognizing that there are more than

> just two dialogue partners, the present community and its prejudices and the past text. For, in so far as we are aware of its history, each stage of the transmission of the tradition, including those aspects that were jettisoned, has the potential to act as a critique of our present concerns and obsessions.[23]

This emphasis on the 'staged-process' of a developing tradition where each individual stage has its own intrinsic value is important and will return in due course.[24] Equally important is Brown's conviction that seeking authorial intention and original meaning is legitimate and indeed necessary, but that such intentions and meanings are not final. Indeed, when it comes to certain biblical texts – such as Galatians 3.28 – it is appropriate that we should now interpret them in ways that differ from the authors' original intentions, just so long as we know that we are doing so.[25]

Having endorsed the modernist project of 'properly researched history', Brown also insists with postmodernism that 'non-historical' does not automatically equal 'untrue'. Metaphor and fiction can convey truth just as well as literal or historical discourse 'by conveying significance and values rather than one to one correspondence with historical fact'.[26] The truth-value of fiction and metaphor leads to perhaps Brown's most distinctive methodological/theological points, namely (i), that 'tradition, so far from being something secondary or reactionary, is the motor that sustains revelation both within Scripture and beyond'[27] and (ii), one 'of the principal ways in which God speaks to humanity is through the imagination, and, as we might have expected, the human imagination has not stood still'.[28] Despite his training in analytic philosophy with its emphasis on empiricism, logic, propositions and conceptual analysis, Brown now makes the crucial Romantic move that doctrines are in fact 'secondary and parasitic on the stories and images that give religious belief its shape and vitality'.[29] Indeed, towards the end of *Tradition and Imagination* he says that his 'most important claim' in the volume is that 'imagination is absolutely integral to the flourishing of any religion, Christianity included'.[30]

In Stump's *Wandering in Darkness* we encounter a different set of methodological assumptions, but with some interesting parallels. Even more than Brown, Stump is known for her commitment to the Anglo-American tradition of philosophy, a tradition that 'prizes lucidity, analysis, careful distinction, and rigorous argument'.[31] Without disavowing her commitment to this approach in its proper context, Stump admits that its considerable strengths can mask profound weaknesses, particularly when engaging with literary texts and personal relations. The characteristic practices of Anglo-American philosophy are – 'to use amateur but accurate neurobiological concepts' – left-brain skills, but there is 'no reason to suppose that left-brain skills alone will reveal to us all that is philosophically interesting about the world'.[32] We also need right-brain skills such as breadth of focus, the capacity to understand stories and poems as well as arguments, and an appreciation 'for that part of reality that includes the complex, nuanced thought, behavior, and relations of persons'.[33]

To employ such right-brain skills, Stump appeals to the interdisciplinary field of philosophy and literature. Stump holds that 'there are things that can be known through narrative but which cannot be known as well, if at all, through the methods of analytic philosophy'.[34] She advocates an 'antiphonal' interaction between philosophy and literature, in which a narrative 'is considered in its disorderly richness. But once it has been allowed into the discussion on its own [right-brain] terms, philosophical reflection enlightened by the narrative can proceed in its customary [left-brain] way.'[35] Stump characterizes her method in *Wandering in Darkness* as combining 'the techniques of philosophy and literary criticism in order to achieve something neither set of techniques would accomplish on its own'.[36]

Stump's approach to philosophy and literature could be applied to any narrative whatsoever, but in *Wandering in Darkness* her focus is on biblical narratives, specifically those of Job, Samson, Abraham and Mary of Bethany. Any treatment of biblical texts raises at least implicit questions regarding history and revelation, but Stump brackets those questions for this particular project. She acknowledges that her approach to these texts is not historical, and thus mostly not in dialogue with historical-critical scholarship, although she does engage with some standard treatments as a foil to her own. She is more in dialogue with literary approaches such as Robert Alter's.[37] Likewise, she says, 'for my purposes here I am treating the biblical narratives only as stories, not as history or as revelation; and nothing in this project presupposes the truth of belief in God'.[38] As her other work makes clear, questions of the historicity and revelatory character of the biblical texts are indeed important to Stump, but not in terms of the interpretations she offers in *Wandering in Darkness*.[39]

As a final piece of her methodological assumptions, Stump links narrative and the knowledge of persons and joins them under an account of so-called 'second-person experience'. Drawing on recent studies in neuroscience and cognitive psychology, Stump notes that autism consists of 'a severe impairment in the cognitive capacities necessary for ... the knowledge of persons and their mental states'.[40] Acknowledging that autism remains mysterious, Stump reports that since the 1990s a major theory has involved so-called 'mirror neurons' – that is, those that 'fire in the brain both when one does some action oneself *and also* when one sees that same action performed by someone else' – and says that it now seems that 'the mirror neuron system is the foundation for the capacity of all fully functional human beings at any age to know the mind of another person'.[41] In contemporary philosophy such knowledge is known as 'second-person experience'. The autistic lack or have difficulty with second-person experience, arguably due to a defect in their mirror-neuron system.

How does this neuroscience connect to narrative? Stump argues that genuine second-person experiences can be conveyed to others via 'second-person accounts' and that such accounts are most effective when expressed through detailed stories rather than plain expository prose.[42] A second-person account is not identical to *real* second-person experience, but it is the closest approximation to it, and Stump sees mirror neurons as the crucial explanation of this as well. Why do we respond to fiction as though it were real? Perhaps because 'when we engage with fiction, we also employ the mirror neuron system' to give us access to second-person accounts of human experience.[43] This is likewise true of the biblical narratives Stump interprets in *Wandering in Darkness*, not because they are necessarily fiction but because they are complex and profound stories regardless of their authorship or historicity.[44]

To compare the interpretative methodologies of Brown and Stump shows interesting similarities and differences. Despite their shared background in analytic philosophy, they both now appeal – although in different ways – to the power of imagination and narrative in opening crucial aspects of reality to us and granting us access to those aspects. Both are thus seeking – again in different ways – to break out of a single 'Enlightenment' approach to the biblical texts, exemplified by the dominance of historical-critical method. But the differences are perhaps more striking than the similarities. Although fully aware of the need for 'properly researched history', Brown's emphasis on the 'staged-process' of the developing biblical tradition and its interpretative history, combined with his insistence on imagination, leads to a reception exegesis approach to the biblical texts in conversation with hermeneutical theory. Moreover, his method is explicitly open to the questions of both historical accuracy and divine revelation through these texts, to the point where these questions drive his project – for example, in his view that certain biblical narratives may be non-historical but yet still 'true' and even revelatory. By contrast, and fascinatingly, Stump completely avoids any engagement with the hermeneutical tradition and its historic concern for knowing the minds of others through texts and replaces it with contemporary neuroscience. Likewise, despite her known theological commitments, in *Wandering in Darkness* she adopts a secular stance to the biblical narratives, bracketing their historicity and potentially revelatory character and treating them simply as stories that can be incorporated into a philosophical argument via her 'antiphonal' approach to philosophy and literature. That they are *biblical* stories seems largely irrelevant to this project – what matters is the specific content of their respective narratives.

Interpreting Scripture: Tradition and Originality

Although I have focused thus far on their respective methodologies, both Brown and Stump spend much more time in rich, detailed and interesting engagements with selected biblical narratives. As it happens, both offer interpretations of the stories of Abraham, Job, and Mary Magdalene/Mary of Bethany.[45] In this section I offer the barest summary of their respective readings, simply to demonstrate further similarities and differences in their practice of biblical interpretation. Readers are directed to the full and lengthy treatments in their work for the regrettably missing nuances in this section.

Abraham

As the title of this current volume indicates, Brown argues that the long and complex tradition of biblical exegesis is best described as a 'moving text'. He admits that – once the canon has been fixed – 'the words on the page do not alter', but nevertheless insists that in the interpretative process, 'content, focus and themes are so restructured ... that effectively a wholly new grid has been imposed, with what is most important often seen as hidden, as it were, in the interstices of the text'.[46] A key example is offered in the *Akedah* or 'binding' of Isaac by Abraham (Gen. 22.1–19). Brown explores the reception exegesis of this famously disturbing story in Christianity, Judaism and Islam, including within the New Testament itself. The Letter to the Hebrews, for example, 'sought to defuse the tension by giving Abraham grounds for continued trust' in the hope of raising Isaac from the dead (Heb. 11.19), and Philo takes the similar line that 'to God all things are possible'.[47] Perhaps the most influential interpretation among general readers is Kierkegaard's in *Fear and Trembling* (1843), where religious faith supersedes ethical norms. But Brown rejects Kierkegaard's reading on theological grounds, for if 'we are forced to say that God is the source of two distinct demands (the moral and the religious) that can conflict, then we seem to end up with a God divided against himself'.[48]

Brown thus lifts up an important but now largely neglected thread of Jewish and Christian tradition in which, unlike in Hebrews, Philo or Kierkegaard, the primary moral agent of the story is not Abraham but Isaac.[49] The age of Isaac is unspecified in the biblical narrative, but despite common assumptions that he was still a young boy, Josephus identifies him as an adult of 25, and the midrash *Genesis Rabbah* reckons him to be 37 based on the age of Sarah at her death.[50] The details cannot detain us, but the point is that in this thread Isaac is now seen as an adult and thus as a full participant in Abraham's test, perhaps even initiating it himself against the cavils of Ishmael. The offered sacrifice was not Abraham's but Isaac's. Thus in Judaism Isaac 'was to become the norm for life understood as self-sacrificial dedication to God',[51] and in Christianity he was even seen as a type of Christ.[52] Brown acknowledges that such readings depart from the original meaning of the text, and even from the canonical interpretation of it offered in Hebrews, but insists that the focus on self-sacrifice is morally, religiously and imaginatively superior to the sacrifice of another (however understood), and this superiority can be discerned in various paintings of the story as well as written interpretations.[53]

Stump agrees with Brown in rejecting Kierkegaard's interpretation of Genesis 22, and for similar moral/theological reasons, but she follows

Hebrews, Philo, Kierkegaard and others in identifying Abraham as the primary agent rather than Isaac. For Stump, the story is about discerning the true desires of Abraham's heart and purifying them from misdirection. Rather than surrender the desires of his heart, Abraham must learn to 'trust in the goodness of God to fulfill those desires'.[54] Stump places the binding of Isaac in the context of the entire story of Abraham's life up to this point, with detailed discussions of Abraham's encounters with God, God's promises to Abraham and Abraham's complicated relationships with Lot, Sarah, Hagar, Ishmael, Isaac and his six other sons by Keturah.[55] The gist of this narrative is that Abraham has benefited from God's blessings thus far but has also demonstrated a troubling double-mindedness when it comes to trusting God to fulfil God's promises. How can God – and we – know if Abraham now truly trusts God to keep God's promise that, through Isaac, he will have many descendants? Only through a test – and God thus tells Abraham to sacrifice Isaac.[56]

Noting that the narrative does not specify Isaac's age, Stump says that

> the only way to mark time is by the description of Isaac. He is still young enough to be diffident and deferential toward his father. On the other hand, he is old enough to carry some distance up a mountain a load of wood big enough for him to lie down on.[57]

Stump thus proposes that Isaac is an adolescent in the story, about the same age as Ishmael when he was sent out into the desert with Hagar at God's command (another but more ambiguous sacrifice). Abraham's dilemma, as Stump sees it, is whether he will trust God to provide him descendants through Isaac even if Abraham obeys God's command to perform an act that would – all things being equal – make that impossible:

> Abraham passes this test not in case he is willing to give up Isaac, as most commentators assume, but just in case he believes that, if he obeys God's command to sacrifice Isaac, he will *not* be ending Isaac's life.[58]

Stump acknowledges that, as an adolescent, Isaac could have resisted his aged father's test and thus must have cooperated in it, but the central figure whose faith is tested and commended remains Abraham.[59] Abraham passes the test, and the desires of his heart are refined, but 'what is praiseworthy about Abraham is not his readiness to kill his son in obedience to God' (à la Kierkegaard) but rather 'Abraham's willingness to believe in God's goodness, even against strong temptations to the contrary'.[60]

Job

Brown begins his chapter on Job by stating that his concern here is

> not so much with the so-called problem of evil and its more technical philosophical or theological resolution, as with religious attitudes, with how believers have chosen to face the onslaught of unmerited suffering, and in particular with what the practice of discipleship has meant in such a context.[61]

Rather than look for a 'presumed original intention' and end the discussion there, Brown is more interested in seeing how Jews and Christians have applied the narrative over the years to cope with specific situations. He thus takes a historical approach, moving from the canonical text to *The Testament of Job*, Gregory the Great, Aquinas, Calvin and Blake. He argues that 'these later and often much despised interpretations' at least sometimes 'constitute significant advances on the canonical text', and concludes that 'the Christian community today is the poorer if in its response to innocent suffering it is not allowed to build upon these rewritings of Job's story'.[62]

Turning to the canonical text, Brown first notes possible antecedents in Egyptian and Babylonian documents and observes that 'questions do not arise out of thin air, but from specific cultural contexts', such as belief or not in an afterlife.[63] God's decisive reply to Job from the whirlwind (chapters 38—41) is normally thought to provide one or more of three possible answers to Job's accusation:

> that it was intended to put an end to further debate; that it spoke of a type of God of whom such questions were inappropriate; and that a specific answer was after all given, in a particular type of reassuring experience.[64]

Brown has varying degrees of unhappiness with all three, both as answers to the perceived problem and as readings of the text, and he thus engages in a substantial survey of contemporary studies on Job supplemented with a critical engagement with Girard.[65] In regard to each proposed answer, Brown concludes that the 'final shape of the book as a whole argues for a quite different conclusion: the legitimacy of continuing exploration'.[66]

In this short chapter I cannot begin to do justice to the remainder of Brown's chapter that looks at post-canonical trajectories of interpretation in Judaism and Christianity.[67] He maintains that later tradition often improves on Job by moving the questions from an externalist to an internalist perspective, 'stimulating deeper reflection in response to such questions as these: What is it to be good? What are the proper limits of anger? and, What resources are required for one to be good?'[68] For example, in the midst of detailed and occasionally critical expositions, Brown endorses the expanded role *The Testament of Job* provides for Job's wife, Gregory the Great's internalization of Job's ethics and Aquinas's discussion of competing value systems.[69] And the chapter concludes with an analysis of William Blake's illustrations of the book of Job as 'indicative of perhaps the most important way of coming to terms with suffering in this new [i.e. post-eighteenth century] understanding of experience as no longer directly engineered by God'.[70] In the art of Blake we find:

> a much more complete integration of ethics and internalization in that the 'solution' to suffering is seen to lie not just in attitudes (patience, faith, and so forth) but also in our capacity to change those attitudes in light of such experiences. Our freedom now plays an integral part.[71]

Stump's interpretation of Job differs from Brown's in many respects, and perhaps the best way in is by noting their contrasting appeals to the instigating conversations between God and *ha-satan*, 'The Accuser', in chapters 1—2. Brown does not dwell on this exchange at length, but simply notes that 'Job's complaints would lack the power of specificity without the opening prose section; so we can be sure that, even if from a different author, the poetry was intended to expand upon the basic prose plot'.[72] For Stump, by contrast, what she calls the 'framing story' – both the prologue and the conclusion – is essential to understanding the book, which on her reading is as much about 'Satan' as Job himself.[73] In addition to the prologue and conclusion she focuses on the 'dramatic episode when God intervenes to talk to Job, which is the culmination of the dialogues among Job and his comforters', rather than on those dialogues themselves, although she acknowledges that they contain much material of interest.[74]

As with Abraham, Stump reads the story of Job as about losing and regaining the desires of his heart, but her distinctive take on this story is also to probe the inner life of 'Satan' as revealed by his conversations with God about Job. In a tour de force of psychological subtlety, Stump draws a detailed character analysis out of 'Satan's' incongruous arrival among the 'sons of God', God's greeting to him and their subsequent exchanges leading on to Job's trials. On Stump's reading, God is motivated by care and love for 'Satan' and yet 'Satan' is an internally divided self not integrated around the good and thus cynically out of fellowship with God and everything else.[75] As Stump reads the book of Job, the framing story 'is a complicated second-person account within which the nested second-person accounts comprising the story of Job's relations with God are embedded'.[76]

Again, as with Brown's chapter I cannot here do justice to the remaining 25 pages of detailed analysis in which, as Stump sees it, God tests Job in order to provide 'Satan' an exemplar of a self truly integrated around the good, but also to make Job into a greater person than he had been before his trials began:

> Because of Satan's second attack and Job's endurance under it, in the story Job becomes the sort of person whose life captures the imagination of anyone who learns of it. Job stood up to the ruler of the universe, and in response God came to talk to him in one of the longest conversations between God and human beings in any of the biblical stories.[77]

In resisting the arguments of his friends, Job 'takes his stand with the goodness of God, rather than with the office of God as ruler of the universe', and in so doing Job chooses 'to be on the side of goodness rather than on the side of power, even if the side of power should be God's side'.[78]

Perhaps most distinctively, Stump sees the book of Job as a 'fractal' vision of divine–human reality in which

> tucked within the overarching story of Satan's relations with God is the story that is focused on Job. In regard to *that* story, considered not as a detail in Satan's story (which it is) but as its own whole story – namely the story of Job's life (which it also is) – *Job* is the primary beneficiary of the events involving his suffering.[79]

Thus in Stump's reading, Job is not

> a pawn heartlessly used in a wager between God and Satan. On the contrary, the nested stories of Satan and Job show us God's providence operating in a fractal way, to deal with each of God's creatures as an end in himself, even while interweaving all the individual stories into one larger narrative.[80]

Mary Magdalene/Mary of Bethany

This final comparison must be extremely compressed, but in the service of completeness it is essential to include, both because it takes us into the New Testament and because Brown's and Stump's respective interpretation of this figure is among their most interesting and provocative. Fortunately, in both cases their conclusions can be summarized briefly, if regrettably shorn of nuance.

Acknowledging that it is almost certainly a historical and exegetical error, Brown nevertheless endorses the literary, theological and moral value of Gregory the Great's influential conflation of Mary Magdalene, Mary of Bethany and the unnamed penitent sinner who washes Jesus' feet with her tears.[81] Here we see Brown's penchant for splitting the difference between modernism and postmodernism. He argues that

> though what emerged was less than loyal to history, it embodied the more important truth, one which has very effectively engaged the imagination of believers over the centuries in establishing and deepening their relation with Christ and one which we will now lose at our peril: what is involved in the dialectics of discipleship, in the growth of the disciple from sin and misunderstanding through forgiveness to intimacy and empowerment.[82]

Against both historical-critical and feminist 'rehabilitations', Brown thus defends the traditional figure of Mary Magdalene/Mary of Bethany as the reformed prostitute who becomes the Apostle to the Apostles, contemplative exemplar and missionary preacher. As with Abraham and Job, Brown supports his case with artistic examples, drawing from painting, poetry, sculpture and film. Although this composite figure is almost completely imaginary, in the Christian tradition she has become 'the primary symbol for understanding what our own discipleship and commitment entail'.[83]

By contrast, although Stump is well aware of the patristic and medieval tradition of conflating Mary Magdalene, Mary of Bethany and the penitent sinner, and is even personally inclined to accept it, she deliberately avoids arguing for such conflation in *Wandering in Darkness*.[84] She rather proposes that the motivation of Mary of Bethany's anointing of Jesus in John 12 may be found not in a life of notorious sin imported from Luke 7 but from the previous chapter of John's Gospel. When Martha and Mary informed Jesus that his friend and their brother Lazarus was ill, Jesus deliberately waited until Lazarus was dead before making his way to Bethany (John 11). Although he knew he would restore their brother to them alive in a glorious miracle, in different ways the sisters responded in anger when Jesus finally arrived, and Stump contends that he made a human – but not divine – error of judgement in not informing them of his plan. Martha confronts Jesus directly whereas Mary withdraws and only comes when told by Martha – truthfully or not – that Jesus was asking for her. Stump reads Mary's subsequent anointing of

Jesus (John 12) as an act of gratitude for the restoration of her brother, but also as an act of repentance and reconciliation. According to Stump, Mary thought that Jesus had betrayed her trust in him, but belatedly came to see that, if there was a betrayal of trust here, through her anger and grief she had betrayed his trust in her rather than the other way around. But whatever the motivation, this image of Mary of Bethany has come down to us as the paradigm of Christian devotion and discipleship: 'Even images of that fervent disciple Peter at his most generous are no match for this picture of Mary, with her hair down, heedless, anointing [Jesus'] feet in an outpouring of love.'[85]

Conclusion: Left-Brain/Right-Brain

As with their interpretative methodologies, comparing Brown and Stump on these biblical narratives reveals many interesting similarities and differences that cry out for further analysis, commentary and critique. Note, for example, that despite highly divergent interpretations, their evaluations of Mary Magdalene and Mary of Bethany arrive at precisely the same point. Collectively weighing in at 1,500 pages, I have barely scratched the surface of *Tradition and Imagination*, *Discipleship and Imagination* and *Wandering in Darkness* and their implications for biblical studies, philosophy and theology, nor begun to do justice to the subtleties of their respective arguments. For this chapter my concern is more expository than critical, but having summarized their methodological positions and exegetical offerings I must now offer some brief interim conclusions.

To begin with, even when Brown and Stump engage in biblical interpretation they clearly do so with an eye for the theological and philosophical significance of these texts, although I have resisted engaging with them on these normative matters, either pro or con. For example, they disagree regarding the nature of an adequate defence for the theistic problem of human suffering, and I contend that their disagreement turns first on their views of particular providence and only secondarily on their readings of Job.[86] While I cannot adjudicate this debate here, it is indeed fascinating that Stump offers a mathematical example to explain the narrative of Job while Brown points to aesthetic considerations. Hence Stump's 'fractal' reading, where God interweaves all the individual stories into one larger narrative in which each story has its place in the whole while maintaining the integrity of each character as an end in herself; and hence Brown's preference for Blake's illustrations of a world in which the minute details of our experience are enabled but not engineered by God. This generic difference – math versus art – correlates with Stump's methodological appeal to neuroscience and mirror neurons against Brown's preference for hermeneutics and a fluid reception exegesis of moving texts. When it comes to method, Stump's approach to the biblical texts is thus still more 'left-brain' than she may have desired or intended, and is more likely to appeal to philosophers and scientists, whereas Brown's more 'right-brain' approach is more likely to appeal to readers in the arts and humanities.

When it comes to their interpretations of the compared biblical narratives, Brown typically lifts up a neglected stage of a traditional reading discerned through the written and artistic record, explains why it was abandoned as a result of various critiques, and then argues for its continuing value for contemporary audiences. Stump, by contrast, while familiar with those traditional readings and historical-critical demolitions of them, typically offers an original and highly creative reading unprecedented in the history of interpretation. Stump is thus more 'right-brain' in practice than in method, and has indeed been accused by historical-critical scholars of 'rewriting' the biblical narratives to suit her purposes.[87] Ironically, whether this is a fair characterization of her interpretations or not, this is precisely what Brown claims that other interpreters have done as well, including canonical authors and editors, namely rewritten the biblical narratives in order to address specific social and religious concerns.[88] Also ironically, Brown now seems more 'left-brain' in practice than in method, at least in comparison with Stump, as he has identified the creative process at work in interpretation but draws his own understanding of the narratives from the various stages of rewriting through commentary, art and literature rather than – à la Stump – contributing a 'moving text' of his own. Unless, that is, one reads *Tradition and Imagination* and *Discipleship and Imagination* as intentional palimpsests of such 'moving texts' and thus as intellectually imaginative acts in their own right.[89]

Notes

1 Eleonore Stump, review of *The Divine Trinity* by David Brown, *Faith and Philosophy* 3.4 (1986), 463–8. *The Divine Trinity* was published in 1985 by Duckworth in the UK and Open Court in the USA.
2 Ibid., 463.
3 Ibid.
4 Ibid., 464. Some of this review is also included in Eleonore Stump, 'Modern Biblical Scholarship, Philosophy of Religion, and Traditional Christianity', *Aletheia* 1 (1985), 75–80.
5 Eleonore Stump, 'Visits to the Sepulcher and Biblical Exegesis', *Faith and Philosophy* 6.4 (1989), 353–77; 'Biblical Commentary and Philosophy', in *The Cambridge*

Companion to Aquinas, ed. Norman Kretzmann and Eleonore Stump (Cambridge: Cambridge University Press, 1993), 252–68; 'Aquinas on the Sufferings of Job', in *Reasoned Faith: Essays in Philosophical Theology in Honor of Norman Kretzmann*, ed. Eleonore Stump (Ithaca, NY: Cornell University Press, 1993), 328–57; 'Revelation and Biblical Exegesis: Augustine, Aquinas, and Swinburne', in *Reason and the Christian Religion: Essays in Honour of Richard Swinburne*, ed. Alan G. Padgett (Oxford: Clarendon Press, 1994), 161–97. Brown also contributed a chapter – 'Did Revelation Cease?' (121–41) – to the Swinburne Festschrift.

6 See *Hermes and Athena: Biblical Exegesis and Philosophical Theology*, ed. Eleonore Stump and Thomas P. Flint (Notre Dame, IN: University of Notre Dame Press, 1993). Meeks's chapter is '"To Walk Worthily of the Lord": Moral Formation in the Pauline School Exemplified by the Letter to Colossians' (37–58), and Stump's reply is, 'Moral Authority and Pseudonymity: Comments on the Paper of Wayne A. Meeks' (59–70). Meeks followed up with a 'Response to Stump' (71–4).

7 See *Divine Evil? The Moral Character of the God of Abraham*, ed. Michael Bergmann, Michael J. Murray and Michael C. Rea (Oxford: Oxford University Press, 2011). Stump's contributions are 'Comments on "Does God Love Us?"' (47–53) – a response to Louise Antony's 'Does God Love Us?' (29–46), and see also Antony's 'Reply to Stump' (54–7) – and 'The Problem of Evil and the History of Peoples: Think Amalek' (179–97); and see also Paul Draper's 'Comments on "The Problem of Evil and the History of Peoples"' (198–203) and Stump's 'Reply to Draper' (204–7).

8 Eleonore Stump, *Wandering in Darkness: Narrative and the Problem of Suffering* (Oxford: Oxford University Press, 2010). Brown reviewed *Wandering in Darkness* in *The Church Times* (8 November 2011) – available online at www.churchtimes.co.uk/articles/2011/11-november/reviews/book-reviews/the-trials-that-beset-you; accessed 18 May 2018 – and engages with both Swinburne and Stump in 'Present Revelation and Past "Problematic" Texts', in David Brown, *God in a Single Vision: Integrating Philosophy and Theology*, ed. Christopher R. Brewer and Robert MacSwain (London and New York: Routledge, 2016), 73–85, on 78–81. For my joint review of *Wandering in Darkness* and *Divine Evil?*, see *Sewanee Theological Review* 57 (2014): 582–6.

9 Both Oxford University Press, 1999 and 2000 respectively.

10 All three Oxford University Press, 2004, 2007 and 2008 respectively.

11 Robert MacSwain, 'Introduction: Theology, Aesthetics, and Culture', in *Theology, Aesthetics, and Culture: Responses to the Work of David Brown*, ed. Robert MacSwain and Taylor Worley (Oxford: Oxford University Press, 2012), 1–10, citation from 5. See also my review of these five volumes in *Faith and Philosophy* 29.3 (2012): 362–6.

12 Brown expresses his interest in the newer project of 'reception exegesis', rather than the older approach of 'reception history', because of the former's concern with 'possible meanings for today': see 'From Past Meaning to Present Revelation: Evaluating Three Approaches', in *God in a Single Vision*, ed. Brewer and MacSwain, 73–85, esp. on 81–3, where he lifts up the work of Paul M. Joyce, Diana Lipton, Judith Kovacs and Christopher Rowland as examples of the sort of biblical scholarship he has in mind. I am grateful to David Brown and Chris Brewer for clarifying comments on this point.

13 See David Brown, *Continental Philosophy and Modern Theology: An Engagement* (Oxford: Blackwell, 1987).

14 See David Brown, *Tradition and Imagination: Revelation and Change* (Oxford: Oxford University Press, 1999), ch. 1, 'Narrative and Enlightenment: The Challenge of Postmodernism', 9–59.

15 David Brown, *Discipleship and Imagination: Christian Tradition and Truth* (Oxford: Oxford University Press, 2000), 390.

16 Brown, *Tradition and Imagination*, 11.

17 Ibid., 22.

18 Ibid., 32. For further discussion of appeals to probability as a distinctively 'Angli-

can epistemology', see William J. Abraham, *Canon and Criterion in Christian Theology: From the Fathers to Feminism* (Oxford: Oxford University Press, 1998), 188–214, esp. 212, n. 50, and Robert MacSwain, *Solved by Sacrifice: Austin Farrer, Fideism, and the Evidence of Faith* (Leuven: Peeters, 2013), 65–9.

19 See, for example, his discussion of historical and empirical criteria in *Discipleship and Imagination*, 390–5.

20 See Brown, *Tradition and Imagination*, 6, 9–10, 32, and then 32–44 for a more detailed engagement.

21 Ibid., 44–54.

22 Ibid., 51, citing Hans-Georg Gadamer, *Truth and Method* (London: Sheed & Ward, 1979), 245.

23 Brown, *Tradition and Imagination*, 51.

24 Ibid., 50.

25 Ibid., 41–43, 55, and Brown, *Discipleship and Imagination*, 26, where he says it is highly improbable that Paul held to the equal status of men and women in either church or society, as this verse is often now interpreted to mean.

26 Brown, *Tradition and Imagination*, 56.

27 Ibid., 1.

28 Ibid., 6.

29 Ibid., 2.

30 Ibid., 366. For engagements with Brown that expand on these various themes, see William J. Abraham, 'Scripture, Tradition, and Revelation: An Appreciative Critique of David Brown', in *Theology, Aesthetics, and Culture*, ed. MacSwain and Worley, 13–28; Douglas Hedley, 'Revelation Imagined: Fiction, Truth, and Transformation', in ibid., 79–90; and Nicholas Wolterstorff, Review of *Theology, Aesthetics, and Culture*, ed. by MacSwain and Worley, *International Journal of Systematic Theology* 17.4 (2015), 473–5.

31 Stump, *Wandering in Darkness*, 23.

32 Ibid., 24.

33 Ibid., 25.

34 Ibid., 26.

35 Ibid., 27.

36 Ibid., 29.

37 Ibid., 30. See 29–35 for the full discussion.

38 Ibid., 37.

39 See, for example, her substantial chapter, 'Revelation and Biblical Exegesis: Augustine, Aquinas, and Swinburne', in *Reason and the Christian Religion*, ed. Padgett, 161–97.

40 Stump, *Wandering in Darkness*, 65.

41 Ibid., 68 (original emphasis). See 67–75 for the full discussion.

42 Ibid., 78.

43 Ibid., 79. See 75–80 for the full discussion. In comments on an earlier version of this chapter, Chris Bryan pointed out that such second-person experience is also mediated through theatre, and one could add film as well.

44 Although I focused above on Stump's *avoidance* of historical-critical method in *Wandering in Darkness*, in the context of her other work in this area it is clear that she is also highly *critical* of it, and that criticism emerges here as well. For a response from a biblical scholar, addressing both Stump and Alvin Plantinga, see C. L. Brinks, 'On Nail Scissors and Toothbrushes: Responding to the Philosophers' Critiques of Historical Biblical Criticism', *Religious Studies* 49.3 (2013), 357–76.

45 As indicated above, Stump also engages with the story of Samson, but as Brown does not I will omit it here. See Stump, *Wandering in Darkness*, 227–57. Stump also treats the shared stories in the order of Job, Abraham and Mary of Bethany, but I will

follow their canonical sequence and start with Abraham. Brown deals with Abraham in *Tradition and Imagination*, and with Job and Mary Magdalene/Mary of Bethany (I explain the conflation below) in *Discipleship and Imagination*.

46 Brown, *Tradition and Imagination*, 208-9.
47 Ibid., 239, citing Philo's *De Abr.*, 32.
48 Brown, *Tradition and Imagination*, 242.
49 Ibid., 247.
50 Ibid., 249.
51 Ibid., 251. See 247-54 for details.
52 Ibid., 257. See 254-7 for details.
53 Ibid., 256-60, discussing the work of G. D. Tiepolo, Ghiberti and Rembrandt, among others. Caravaggio, for example, shows what is 'so profoundly wrong with the biblical version: Abraham is shown pinning down his victim, a squirming and screaming son' (ibid., 258). Of course, such graphic details are not in the biblical text itself, but Brown's point is that they are imaginatively implied by it if Isaac is a mere child without any self-determination.
54 Stump, *Wandering in Darkness*, 259. For her discussion of Kierkegaard, see 260-3, 302-4.
55 Ibid., 263-93.
56 Ibid., 293.
57 Ibid., 295.
58 Ibid., 300 (original emphasis).
59 See ibid., 593, n. 133. In 592, n. 121, Stump acknowledges the midrash discussed by Brown that derives Isaac's age of 37 from Sarah's age at her death, but says that 'there is no tangible evidence for it, and in my view it assigns an age to Isaac at the time of the binding that is improbable as the narrative portrays him in that episode'.
60 Ibid., 302.
61 Brown, *Discipleship and Imagination*, 177. For a more formal philosophical and theological approach, see his 'The Problem of Pain', originally published in 1989 and now reprinted in Brown, *God in a Single Vision*, ed. Brewer and MacSwain, 28-40.
62 All subsequent citations in this paragraph from Brown, *Discipleship and Imagination*, 177.
63 Ibid., 183.
64 Ibid.
65 Ibid., 182-94.
66 Ibid., 187.
67 Ibid., 194-225.
68 Ibid., 198.
69 In Brown's discussion of Aquinas he cites Stump's chapter on Aquinas's biblical commentaries but not 'Aquinas on the Sufferings of Job', both cited in note 5 above.
70 Brown, *Discipleship and Imagination*, 220.
71 Ibid., 223.
72 Ibid., 183.
73 Stump, *Wandering in Darkness*, 179. I place Satan's name in scare quotes to indicate Stump's decision to read *ha-satan* as a proper noun and thus as the Devil of Christian tradition rather than as 'the adversary' or 'the accuser' among the 'sons of God' more naturally suggested by the Hebrew text: on this point, see Brinks, 'On Nail Scissors and Toothbrushes', 372.
74 Ibid. For rather different earlier interpretations of Job see Stump's 'Aquinas on the Sufferings of Job' and 'Revelation and Biblical Exegesis: Augustine, Aquinas, and Swinburne', cited in note 5 above.
75 Ibid., 197-203.
76 Ibid., 197.

77 Ibid., 217.

78 Ibid. Although Stump does not mention him, Huck Finn comes inevitably to mind.

79 Ibid., 219 (original emphasis). 'In my view, the book of Job is to second-person accounts what a fractal is to mathematics. A fractal is a set of points with this peculiar feature: when it is graphed, the shape of each part of the whole resembles the shape of the whole; and the shape of each of the parts of any one part also resembles that of the whole, indefinitely ... A graphed fractal is thus a picture within a picture within a picture, and so on, each picture of which is similar to the picture of the whole, only reduced in scale' (ibid., 220).

80 Ibid., 225.

81 Brown, *Discipleship and Imagination*, 32–3.

82 Ibid., 32.

83 Ibid., 54. For details see the whole chapter, 'Prostituting and Valuing Women: Equality and Mary Magdalene', 31–61.

84 Stump, *Wandering in Darkness*, 605–6, n. 121.

85 Ibid., 353. For details see the whole chapter, 'The Story of Mary of Bethany: Heartbrokenness and Shame' (308–68). Although she does not explore further the conflation between Mary Magdalene and Mary of Bethany, later in the chapter Stump does consider the possibility that Mary of Bethany is the woman in Luke 7, but the main aspect of her argument does not depend on that potential identification. The above paragraph in the main text is adapted from my 'Sermon for 13th March: 5th Sunday in Lent', *The Expository Times* 127.5 (2016): 235–6.

86 For details, see 'The Problem of Pain: Why Philosophers and Theologians Need Each Other', in Brown, *God in a Single Vision*, ed. Brewer and MacSwain, 28–40 (esp. 34), and the theodicy section of Stump, *Wandering in Darkness*, 371–481.

87 See, for example, Brinks, 'On Nail Scissors and Toothbrushes', 373.

88 Brown, *Discipleship and Imagination*, 177.

89 Although I came up with this literary analogy to describe creative scholarship such as Brown's on my own, I eventually realized that others had done so as well and that it has indeed become a significant concept in a number of fields: see, for example, Sarah Dillon, 'Reinscribing De Quincey's Palimpsest: The Significance of the Palimpsest in Contemporary Literary and Cultural Studies', *Textual Practice* 19.3 (2005), 243–63. Dillon's discussion of Foucault on 253–4 suggests that while historical-critical biblical scholars are archaeological 'palimpsest readers', only interested in recovering the original text, Brown's reading is genealogically 'palimpsestuous', interested in the layered rewritings and their interactions.

PART 2

The Visual Imagination

5

Paradise Reclaimed: Kerry James Marshall and Chris Ofili in the Garden of Eden

TAYLOR WORLEY

'Who told thee that thou wast naked?' (God, Genesis 3.11)
Kerry James Marshall[1]

Kerry James Marshall's quotation from Genesis 3 may well seem a startling, out-of-place insertion within his art critical writing. After all, he employs it as an epigraph for an essay on the pioneering black artists Bill Traylor (1853–1949) and William Edmondson (1874–1951). As with Marshall's paintings, however, nothing is random. There are no meaningless details. He perceptively acknowledges the fact that even in twenty-first-century America the question of artistic prowess for African-American artists is still tied to the question of basic human dignity. Race, ethnicity and culture are not incidental to criticism, not even in the elitist world of art theory and criticism. Ideological narratives dominate here as well. But Marshall charges the question of merit with something even more volatile than politics, economics or culture by taking it back to the Bible. Admittedly, it is a fraught question. How do we read the biblical account of human origins *today*? After the dominance of racist myths like 'the mark of Cain' and 'the curse of Ham', there is no pristine, uncomplicated reading of Adam and Eve. In the land of Uncle Tom and Jim Crow, where the founding document of the land claims that 'all men were created equal' but was, in fact, signed by many slaveholders, there is no community where racialization or privilege do not dramatically affect interpretation. Indeed, how can we access the meaning of Genesis and its portrayal of the beginning of the human story in the context of this racist past and the enduring effects of its trauma?

In his *Tradition and Imagination*, David Brown helpfully acknowledges that the Bible is much more than a compendium of historical facts and that the living traditions embracing it access new insights and meanings from it. He holds out the notion of a 'moving text', for which 'changing social circumstances help generate fresh insights'.[2] In the case of the pre-history found in Genesis 1—11, Brown is right to note that 'the stories within Scripture itself have not stood still'.[3] According to Brown, 'almost all biblical narratives have been subject to huge transformations over the course of the Church's history'.[4] However, such transformations are, as Brown admits, not always positive. In fact he reminds us that we cannot deny 'the existence of many negative creations'.[5] As an exceptionally negative example, both 'the mark of Cain' and 'the curse of Ham' have been used by white supremacists as explanations for the dark skin of African peoples and hence justification for their subjugation and prejudicial treatment by Whites.[6] Surely these racialized interpretations represent some of the worst extensions of the Christian tradition. With his characteristic optimism for God's ongoing revelation in tradition, then, Brown would not be surprised to see two contemporary artists offering their own creative, corrective retellings of that biblical pre-history. Moreover, in Brown's conception of tradition as revelation, these new interpretations should be expected and welcomed. As Kerry James Marshall and Chris Ofili return to the Garden of Eden in their paintings and offer through their evocative use of 'black aesthetics' a rewriting of the tale of the primordial couple, we find not only a corrective to the racist myths that have blighted the Church's reading of Genesis but also a generative vision of recovering paradise.

In their own ways, both Marshall and Ofili eschew the efforts of critics and theorists to appropriate their respective body of paintings into a simple narrative of art history that can be finally credited as truly 'multicultural'. Neither artist aspires merely for inclusion, but are instead developing their own painterly trajectories.[7] Perhaps surprisingly, both Marshall and Ofili return to the biblical image of the primordial couple – the first inhabitants of paradise. These portraits are, however, not easily compared with the famous examples of Dürer or Rubens.[8] Nor do they fit alongside the African-American artist Jacob Lawrence's (1917–2000) *Genesis Creation Sermon VII: And God Created Man and Woman* (1989), for while the scene complements the elegant congregation of Harlem's historic Abyssinian Baptist Church its Adam and Eve still appear ghostly white in contrast to the parishioners.[9] There is a distinct break from such aesthetic traditions with Marshall and Ofili. Their aesthetic emerges much more akin to what critics and theorists have described recently as 'Afrofuturism'. This fantastical, loosely defined genre can be seen in contemporary science fiction, art, popular music, film, comic books and more, but the fundamental character of Afrofuturism as it emerges in art and culture is its peculiarly hopeful vision of what lies ahead for the African diaspora. According to Mark Dery (an early proponent the term), Afrofuturism embodies 'a troubling antinomy: can a community whose past has been deliberately rubbed out, and whose energies have subsequently been consumed by the search for legible traces of its history, imagine possible futures?'[10] Projection of possible futures, however, does not alone characterize Afrofuturism. The past remains an integral piece of its aesthetic, and De Witt Douglas Kilgore thus highlights the fact that Afrofuturism is seen as 'responsible storytelling, a challenge to remember a past that instructs the present and can build a future'.[11] Or, in the words of Kodwo Eshun:

> Afrofuturism may be characterized as a program for recovering the histories of counter-futures created in a century hostile to Afro-diasporic projection and as a space within which the critical work of manufacturing tools capable of intervention within the current political dispensation may be undertaken.[12]

Since both Marshall and Ofili have dabbled quite blatantly with Afrofuturism in their painting, it seems entirely reasonable to read them as bridging past, present and future with their unique depictions of Eden.[13] Thus, seen in the context of a painterly hermeneutic of 'recovering the histories of counter-futures', Marshall's *They Know That I Know* (1992) and Ofili's *Afronirvana* (2002) offer a glimpse of paradise reclaimed and, as such, provide a more imaginative encounter with the biblical text than has previously been possible.[14] Marshall and Ofili's works alert us in new ways to the racialized patterns of interpretation for Genesis and at the same time refuse to allow the traumas of history to be buried beneath the surface when picturing Eden. The result is a fresh and corrective engagement with the meaning of paradise in dialogue with Scripture that has a distinctly redemptive eschatological vision.

Kerry James Marshall's *They Know That I Know* (1992)

> 'All great art was in essence religious art.'
> *Kerry James Marshall*[15]

In framing his artistic project, Marshall begins with the problem of visibility for black folks in art spaces and institutions. Reflecting on the scarcity of black faces in works of Western art history, he concludes: 'It would not be a stretch to suggest that low "African American" attendance correlates with their low visibility in the art.'[16] This phenomenon, however, constitutes more than an issue of mere representation.[17] Catherine Womack notes that in Marshall's work the commonplace issue of invisibility is taken up and treated as the problem of 'un-visibility'.[18] Drawn from Ralph Ellison's novel *The Invisible Man*, 'un-visibility' names the shift from ignorance to avoidance, passive neglect to active suppression. Over time, withholding approval and acceptance becomes a form of oppression. When the fact of black invisibility in art history persists, it becomes clear that the system does not wish to see what is not there, and hence black folks are un-visible in art history. Marshall's work operates in acknowledgement and defiance of these unjust social conditions. Rather than accept this state of affairs, he takes up the challenge to overcome and undo it.[19] Marshall responds to the un-visibility of black folks in art history by positioning his practice squarely in contradistinction to the 'mainstream'. Again, Marshall: 'It is this difference from the mainstream, not the performance of any particular work, which must concern me as a black painter in ways "mainstream" artists are indifferent to.'[20] But his posture is not mere protest, as he explains: 'My interest in being a part of it [the art-historical canon] is being an expansion of it, not a critique of it.'[21] His social and historical awareness is evident from the very beginning of his mature art practice and can be traced to his earliest return to painting after art school, *Portrait of the Artist as a Shadow of His Former Self* (1980).[22] Produced in response to his reading of Ellison's *The Invisible Man*, this self-portrait – described by the art critic Jerry Saltz as a 'tiny egg-tempura icon' and 'an avenging angel of art history'[23] – bears within it the aesthetic seed of Marshall's sprawling oeuvre. With his signature deployment of a few shades of black paint, Marshall renders all of the figures in his paintings as purposively opaque and unmistakably black people. Catherine Womack eloquently describes this most critical and conspicuous aspect of his work, noting:

> Kerry James Marshall is a black artist who paints black people. The men and women in Marshall's paintings are not people of a range of colors. They are not painted in differing shades of brown. They are painted in the darkest, inkiest black, consistently, exclusively, insistently and masterfully.[24]

In this way Marshall defies the despair of invisibility and disarms the militancy of un-visibility by continually transforming himself as a black artist for today.

In the process of confronting art history, Marshall has put forward his own characterization of the distinctly 'black aesthetic' that is informed as much by historic thinkers as that of Afrofuturism. In his own words:

> 'Black aesthetics' is an atmosphere, a tone, a 'vibe'. 'Black aesthetics' embody the 'twoness' [W. E. B.] Dubois wrote about in *The Souls of Black Folk*: it is glamorous and impoverished, structured and improvisational, naïve and sophisticated, brash and abject. Its first principle is a desire for self-representation.[25]

Marshall participates in this conversation on 'black aesthetics' with voices from the past as well as current artists like Ofili. In 2012's *School of Beauty, School of Culture*, Marshall paints an official poster for Ofili's major exhibition at Tate Britain in 2010 into the scene.[26] In his essay 'Just Because', written for the catalogue to Ofili's *Afrotranslinear* exhibition at the Arts Club of Chicago in 2010, Marshall playfully frames the conversation around the phrase 'Because but not just because'. He concludes:

> Do I say this [i.e. Ofili epitomizes black aesthetics] because Chris himself is 'black', because his parents are Nigerian? Yes. But not just because … I say it because I think this is what he really wants. The work, quite frankly, cries out to be understood in this context, and yet it is not 'identity' work in the soporific mode lovers of 'real' art find so tedious.[27]

In other words, he commends the work because Ofili is a black artist self-consciously making paintings with his own 'black aesthetic', but also not just because Ofili is black – 'Because but not just because'. Inherent to Marshall's 'black aesthetic', then, is the expectation that certain intramural conversations will be happening among black artists, what he describes as 'responding to and riffing on the work of "other" black artists, and on "black" vernacular traditions'.[28] Neither artist is willing to surrender to the opposition of un-visibility, and we see that quite clearly in their independent but remarkably related choices to revisit the Bible's Garden of Eden.

Similarly, as a painter of the black experience Marshall embraces the whole of it, and this certainly includes the legacy of the Black Church in America. It is thus no surprise to see consistent and conflicted inclusion of explicitly Christian religious imagery and symbols in his work. It would, however, be a mistake to overestimate the significance of their inclusion, as Marshall also invokes freely the imagery of Haitian vodou as well as symbols and references to indigenous religions of various African peoples. We must be careful to avoid what Marshall himself calls 'strip-mining for symbolism'.[29] That said, many of his early works – such as *The Ecstasy of Communion* (1990),[30] *The Face of Nat Turner Appeared in a Water Stain (Image Enhanced)* (1990),[31] *So This Is What You Want?* (1992)[32] and *Stigma Stigmata* (1992)[33] – clearly draw on hagiographic forms of portraiture. In his mature work such saintly depictions settle beneath the surface of the work, operating as a central set of images within his overall visual vocabulary. One of these key tropes is the image of the couple. As one of the most consistent subjects within his practice, Marshall returns again and again to pictures of the black man and woman at rest and at play, in domestic and public settings, troubled and at ease. The range of his depictions of the simple black couple spans every period of his painting's development and can be easily seen in works such as *Slow Dance* (1992–3),[34] *Better Homes, Better Gardens* (1994),[35] *Vignette* (2003)[36] and *Club Couple* (2012).[37] For almost any other community, straightforward depictions of a solitary couple would be just that: straightforward and simple. In the case of the black community, however, political discourse and media attention over the last few decades have made the nuclear family in black communities a matter of public concern. Politicians and pundits alike bemoan the disintegration of the family in the black community as an isolated talking point to the degree that it has become a cliché of American political discourse. Amid the din, Marshall's canvases – and the couples they depict – offer a serene sanctuary enabling viewers to return to reality. Marshall believes that despite its trials and failures the black family remains strong. In this way his couples protest the lack of faith that America has in the black community, and in a few instances their political power is mixed with religious poignancy too. The best example of this potent mixture is his *They Know That I Know* (1992).[38]

Once more, in this early painting we see Marshall's iconic black couple. They do not invest themselves here in any activity or event but rather enjoy a moment's rest. What is most notable about this couple is their simple and subtle repose. They do not dominate or fill the composition but simply settle into the safe space beneath the branches of the trees. And what resides within this primitive garden? The biblical trees – the tree of life and the tree of the knowledge of good and evil (Gen. 2.9) – have been removed, and in their place we find a new cultivation of man: family trees. The genealogical lumber of racial history is planted here. Left to right, we notice first a green trunk that reads 'Mongoloid' with branches that read 'Huns Tungus' and 'Turks'. In the centre of the canvas stands a trunk of pale pink covering over the dull green, with offshoots that read 'Laps' and 'Proto-Indos' and branches that read 'Slavs', 'Finns, Bulgars', 'Nordics', 'Modern Mediterraneans', 'Alpines', 'Greeks, Romans, Celts' and 'Armenians'. Finally we see a tree of inky black opacity that reads along the trunk 'Negroid' and short broken branches, of which two are labelled alternately 'Pygmies' and 'Bush'. Racial ideology, Marshall seems to suggest, is the most primitive of all social constructs, and in our world, these genealogical trees become false trees of life and knowledge.

Like other paintings from this period, Marshall builds up the surface of his canvas with many layers of found material. Images of mainstream beauty fade into the pale background of this scene. These resemble advertising images from the 1950s and 1960s of beauty products for white women, but in fact they are in several instances covers of cheap romance novels from the period. Curiously, the one floating closest to the base of the black tree reads 'Yesterday, Today, and Tomorrow'. Each cover is mostly obscured by layers of paint applied quickly to highlight the portraits of the white women on each surface. Almost exclusively rendered with a thin wash of yellow paint, they float in the visual field as if they are the fruit of these incomplete trees, tempting us like apparitions of plastic, Barbie-doll beauty. We also find three curious creatures near the reclining couple. A lone, minuscule field mouse populates the lower left-hand corner of the canvas. Perched atop one of the offshoots of the central tree, there rests a chameleon with a curled tail. He is not easily spotted in the composition because his skin matches the same dull green of the trees. Most present in the composition, however, is an opaque and coiled black serpent. In the case of the snake, Marshall has chosen a more symbolic figuration than the naturalistic rendering of the chameleon and the field mouse. In this way, we cannot easily identify the coiled serpent as merely another participant in the scene or an instance of Marshall's layering and crowding the composition with thematic references all his own. In the same way, we might inquire as to the presence of the golden book laid open and floating just above the heads of the reclining couples. Is this a visual invitation to return afresh to the scriptural canon? Is Marshall, as this open book floats opposite the novel entitled 'Yesterday, Today, and Tomorrow', perhaps suggesting that the whole story has not been told?

Among the green trees and the lone black tree congregate a beautiful host of small, wild birds, each a different species arrayed in feathers of various colours with their distinctive markings. These seven birds bring life and vitality to the garden. In contrast to the bare branches and hurriedly rendered trunks of the trees, each bird is painted with the utmost care and detail. They populate the branches of all the trees, resting here and there and taking flight to move about within the scene. Not unlike Charlie Parker's sumptuous be-bop suite 'Ornithology', these birds are the music of the picture. They signal renewed life and vitality the way that Revelation 22.2 describes the tree's fruit as a source of healing for the nations. They suggest to us that variety and diversity are as much a part of the beginning of our story as they are in our desired future.

Symbols cannot always be trusted, and interpretations vary from one community to the next. This unfinished canvas by Kerry James Marshall is not merely an attempt at correcting the false narratives of a white supremacist history but also his vision of defiant faith in a paradise to come. As an artist who trades regularly in mixed messages, Marshall here evokes both the current anthropological discourse on human origins and the cultural narrative within the black community of Egypt's 'original man'. He explains:

> The Black Muslims taught that the 'black' man was the original man. They said, 'Egyptian civilization,' which European historians managed to de-link from the 'Mother Continent,' was a black African civilization. For people desperate to recover a sense of dignity, this is pretty great stuff.[39]

The subtle, almost attached, repose of the figures here belies a more significant theme. The couple included here is more than the embodiment of black sexuality or familial tranquillity or leisure and frivolity, but instead mere presence – collapsing together a primordial rootedness and its future restoration in a single space. Whereas the influence of Afrofuturism invites the artist to play loose and free with past, present and future, Marshall acknowledges that some audiences will not pick up on that freedom. He notes how easy it is for viewers to misread his works, in particular the expressions of his figures. Whereas the white gaze perceives desperation or hopelessness, Marshall portrays something else. Describing a figure from another work, he explains: 'When I look at his demeanor, I see contentment. That's what I see. The gaze out at the spectator, there's a certain uncertainty about the way he sees himself being perceived by the spectator.'[40] With our Edenic example, we see a consistent 'certain uncertainty' in the way Marshall's Adam and Eve view their spectators. Their sense of belonging in the Garden is not contingent on the acceptance of all viewers of the work. Hence we have the work's curious title: *They Know That I Know*. Here Marshall envisages the free and final emplacement of his black figures, reclaiming paradise not through violence or the forced removal of their oppressors but instead through their persistent and defiant presence: personal, familial and cultural endurance despite all attempts to denigrate and destroy black folks. Again, Marshall:

> What you're trying to create is a certain kind of indispensable presence ... Where your position in the narrative is not contingent on whether somebody likes you, or somebody knows you, or somebody's a friend, or somebody's being generous to you. But you want a presence in the narrative that's not negotiable, that's undeniable.[41]

And marked by the joy of the birds in paradise, it is as if the land has been groaning under its bondage and the return of this couple signals its relief as well. Paradise reclaimed, through hopeful and defiant witness, is paradise regained.

Chris Ofili's *Afronirvana* (2002)

> 'The original paradise, let's say the Garden of Eden, was always a complicated space.'
> *Chris Ofili*[42]

As with Marshall, there is a powerful duality at work in the paintings of Chris Ofili (b. 1968). While Marshall explores the political and ethical tensions inherent in a contemporary black aesthetic, Ofili probes similar themes but along provocative and more playful lines. Instead of seeking mastery, Ofili invites open mockery. Whereas Marshall joins conspicuously black figures with the overwhelmingly lily white conventions of Western art history, Ofili generates his odd pairs in much less straightforwardly aesthetic terms, involving a 'formal and conceptual dualism'.[43] Besides the fantastic allure of the sparkling, bedazzling surfaces of his elaborate canvases, Ofili's project targets the facile attitudes of cultured liberals towards issues like political identity and multiculturalism. Not unlike the dialogical nature of Marshall's black aesthetic, his practice derives its overarching strategy from the culture of hip-hop and its chief music innovation: 'sampling' – the recording process whereby one artist lifts the work of another and creates a musical collage of familiar and original material. The novelty of his work, however, results from sampling the conceptual genius of artists like David Hammons and Jean-Michel Basquiat with the visual allure of African craftsmanship, the fantastic imagination of Afrofuturism and hip-hop commodity culture.[44] While scholars have debated the authenticity of his 'African-ness' and the problems with labelling his work 'African art', the issue of identity as a primary concern motivating the work remains incidental to the larger project at stake.[45] In her essay 'Confounding the Stereotype', Lisa Corrin further elucidates what exactly is at stake in Ofili's project:

> Ofili is merely trying to get from under what he believes is an excess of talk about 'issues' over the past decades. His 'issue' is his paintings and his context is one in which the presentation of a stable, unitary identity realised in a work of art has given way to its fluid, sliding, global annunciation. He has adapted 'aesthetic strategies that reveal happy accidents in the traffic of visual interculturation.' An understanding of collective and personal identity in a global and electronic context offers artists the possibility of absorbing its benefits without feeling pressed to make it the focal point of their subject matter.[46]

Corrin also points out that appearances can be quite deceiving in making sense of Ofili's practice as the 'African' craftwork is no more exotic than the King's Cross studio the artist utilized for the early part of his career (e.g. the elephant dung comes from London Zoo and the multicoloured beads are manufactured in Taiwan). In this light, issues of identity serve essentially as an ironic subtext to his primarily aesthetic enterprise: making gorgeous paintings. His is a story, however, that could enlist both sentiment and sympathy; hence Stuart Morgan's initial perception of Ofili. In a 1994 interview Morgan introduces the artist in this way:

> Born in Britain, Ofili had always felt African. But despite his black skin and the fact that his parents' first language was Yoruba, how African could he be, living first in Manchester, then in London? For him the question was crucial.[47]

The artist himself explains: 'My project is not a p.c. project, that's my direct link to blaxploitation. I'm trying to make things you can laugh at. It allows you to laugh about issues that are potentially serious.'[48] Whereas much of contemporary art employs a corrosive and cynical irony, Ofili strives for a poignant, almost redemptive levity in his work. Even in his most shocking displays of humour, irony and absurdity, the artist remains present to the weight of his provocations and their quest to see the sacred and profane collide.[49] Celebrating, for instance, the delicate figure of the hip-hop muse, he populates his collection of polymorphous cultural icons from blending disparate sources such as 1970s psychedelic funk and blaxploitation films with the tradition of Roman Catholic hagiography. Throughout his visual landscape of black culture, his interpretation of Afrofuturism remains playful, hopeful and dripping with colourfully sexy, ethereal splendour. In this way Godfrey Worsdale offers some helpful advice on assessing the work when he claims: 'Ultimately, to engage fully with the work it must be experienced as a group of complex, conflicting and sometimes deceptive possibilities rather than a statement of uncompromising intent.'[50] Or as Klaus Kertess relates concerning the 'Devil's Pie' show, the artist 'renders holy sexy and vice versa. Ofili provides aesthetic pleasure in generous portions but intends that pleasure to draw the viewer in to question and/or reconsider conventional beliefs.'[51] The proportions, however, represented in his choice of cultural references appear to doubly favour what Kodwo Eshun calls the '90s communication landscape', and this fact only further obscures the reasons behind Ofili's treatment of religious subjects. While his body of work envelopes all manner of readily available cultural touchstones, and privileges none, the emergence of Ofili's religious renderings – such as *The Holy Virgin Mary* (1996),[52] *The Upper Room* (1999–2002),[53] *Annunciation* (2006)[54] and *Saint Sebastian* (2007)[55] – remains quite irreconcilable, that is unless what the commentators repeat is true: Ofili remains a practising Catholic.[56]

Again, like Marshall, Ofili seems to be fascinated with the image of the lone couple, what Katherine Brinson calls his 'rapt Edenic couplings'.[57] The romantic union of man and woman appears and reappears throughout his more mature work, but his vision of the primordial couple begins with *Afronirvana* and other works from the same time.[58] Here the first man and woman rest comfortably amid the lush interiors of a tropical forest. As the title suggests, they are identified chiefly by their grand afros and their long, luxuriating nude forms. Reclining on trees opposite each other, their legs and bodies mingle together in the composition's centre such that we cannot make out the lines of their forms any longer. They are perfectly at ease; as natural, contented and easy as the plants and flowers that hang about them. Or as the art critic Okwui Enwezor relates, we have here a 'love story, set in a fecund African Eden, a lost paradise of tangled luxuriant foliage emitting the glow of sexual heat'.[59] Beaming like a black sun, a ball of elephant dung hangs overhead and orientates the grand, geometric overlay of the canvas to its centre. Masterfully, this rich scene is rendered completely in but a few shades of green, red and black. Ofili limits himself to this austere palette of green, a single red and black drawn from Marcus Garvey's pan-African flag, and in this way his paradise portrait remains decidedly and unmistakably African.

Afronirvana – along with *Afro Apparition* (2002–3),[60] *Afro Jezebel* (2002–3)[61] and *Afro Green* (2005–8)[62] – operate as a dramatic pivot point in Ofili's painterly journey. These works preserve certain stylistic staples of the early, large-scale canvases and at the same time introduce powerful new elements that will feature prominently in the major projects that follow. They carry on with Ofili's characteristically complex surfaces: flat backgrounds of vibrant colour, intricate constellations of small dots comprising the lines and mass of his figuration, miniature images from magazines collaged into the delicate paint work and balls of elephant dung affixed to the canvas and supporting the weight of it on the floor. This set of works diverges, however, from several new developments in Ofili's visual vocabulary: darkness, instinct and romanticism. The tone of his work changes here with a marked descent into darker canvases. These darker, denser settings pave the way for later experiments in the fully darkened, almost completely opaque canvases of works in 'The Blue Rider' or 'Devil's Pie' shows, such as *Blue Riders* (2006)[63] or *Iscariot Blues* (2006)[64]. Along with these heavier surfaces, Ofili also relies more consistently on instinct and introduces a more gestural, intuitive brand of figuration. Instead of working from found images and recreating them in his own fashion, the figures of *Afronirvana* or *Afro Apparition* relate a sense of the artist's free and instinctual hand, and in this way more closely resemble his drawings. While Ofili still harvests images for inspiration from various places, his rendering of the figures in works since this period continues to demonstrate a stylistic family of iconic figures from his own imagination. Lastly, he seems to be trading in his sly, irreverent jabs at multiculturalism for a much more earnest romanticism of his own. The emotional maturity of the later works begins here with his choice to explore the question of paradise. Though complicated in all sorts of ways, paradise is not a punchline. The shifts in his work from the time of *The Holy Virgin Mary* are dramatically evident to all, but the first, tentative steps towards something more subtle – more honest, sober and grave – can be seen in *Afronirvana*.

Perhaps the most abrupt of all his shifting turns, *Afronirvana* presents plenty of problems for Ofili's critics. Katherine Brinson notes the inherent tensions of the work from this period when she describes them as conjuring 'a fragile moment of prelapsarian fulfilment that is temporary and therefore tragic'.[65] Ofili himself confesses that Eden 'always was a complicated space'.[66] In response to Christy Lange's question about the seemingly less complicated presence of religious imagery in *Afronirvana*, the artist responds: 'I wonder if the biblical was, for me, always a way to get to the spiritual.'[67] And in conversation with Jonathan Jones, Ofili reflects more seriously on the shift in his new work and the trajectory represented by his explorations of paradise. Jones relates:

> He worries that, with his new works, he might be seen as a preacher, a stern moralist calling for a return to traditional values. 'I suppose in these paintings I'm sort of trying to say that maybe Paradise is achievable right now. But that's with the risk of sounding like a preacher – you know, change your ways.' The reward Ofili offers is utopia, the good life – not just for a couple of weeks' holiday. 'It's dreaming of a place where at least two people are happy. Starting from that premise, where two people are happy being in the same place with each other, and hoping that that's infectious.'[68]

Curiously, Ofili includes some details of his figures and abandons others. For instance, the woman's neck is adorned with a string of beads in *Afronirvana*. Could this cultural artefact suggest something profound? Something profoundly self-aware? Just like the Africa pendant necklace worn by the man in Marshall's *Vignette* (2003), paradise is not a simple fiction of a deprived or evacuated pre-history. No, a reductionist origin story will not do. Paradise must be pictured with the stuff of history – the traumas and triumphs of the human story in the lives of black folks.

Conclusion: Tradition *with* Imagination

Perhaps the significance of these two works could be felt to a greater degree when placed in their proper context. Both emerge, or re-emerge, at highly significant moments. *Afronirvana* was exhibited as part of *Within Reach*, a suite of paintings and other works for the British pavilion at the 50th Venice Biennale in 2003. Chris Ofili was chosen to represent the United Kingdom in Venice that year. Given this fact, those works – *Afronirvana* in particular – take on a social and political resonance of grand proportions. Tracing these developments, Enwezor writes:

> Ofili's career as an artist, and the narrative that unfolds in *Within Reach*, can only be fully understood in light of his early attempt to confront the entire tradition of Western painting that either eschewed, objectified or caricatured the black figure.[69]

He further describes the import of Ofili's show as 'shattering the mirror of tradition' in Western art history and troubling the epistemological foundations of modernism.[70] While Marshall's *They Know That I Know* is one of his earliest paintings, the work garners new significance and meaning as a part of the late career retrospective *Mastry*, which began in Chicago and travelled next to New York City and then Los Angeles. This hugely important and timely survey of Marshall's career comes at a moment when the victimization of black folks is once again unavoidably obvious in the mainstream American consciousness, due to the shocking murders of young black men like Michael Brown and Laquan McDonald.[71] Whereas Ofili sought direct confrontation with the values of representation in his home country, Marshall's consistent practice of addressing such issues through his work means that when national attention returns to such crimes, his art addresses us most. In both cases, one active and the other passive, these artists have allowed their paintings to address uneasy social, political and religious assumptions about the black community in society today. Such works prove so timely for these fraught days that we could almost assume divine providence in regards to their appearance. But do these works matter to art history, to theologians, to the majority culture? David Brown offers a reply:

> To locate divine activity only within the tradition would be to ignore what is sometimes an indispensable contribution from the wider cultural context. Equally, though, to leave the final say with the present would also seem a mistake, since tradition gains its power not only through its capacity for change but also sometimes from its past returning to haunt it, requiring a return to earlier views. In other words, God defies our

desire for tidy categories, and so in trying to tell the revelatory story we need to recognize a God at work everywhere in his world in helping to shape our comprehension of his purposes. That of course does not mean that he is at work equally everywhere, but it should mean our readiness to listen even where he seems most distant.[72]

If the 'mark of Cain' and the 'curse of Ham' – as thoroughly tragic examples of reading Genesis – substitute ideology for imagination when engaging with the text, Marshall and Ofili do not, for their part, respond in kind. Rather than rewriting the story of Cain or Ham, they go further back *and* further forward by asking what it would feel like to see an African Adam and Eve. Their hermeneutic – informed as it is by Afrofuturism – lends to us something entirely new and unforeseen. We must allow these artistic developments to inform our contemporary reading of Genesis' account of human origins. We should follow where these artists lead and ask: What does the lack of ethno-cultural specificity in Genesis 1—2 permit? Does this origin story belong to the whole human family? Indeed it does. The most faithful reading of Eden then should be, as Ofili and Marshall intimate, one of access, inclusion and justice: 'paradise reclaimed'.

It does not take long – when one stands before these paintings – to recognize that they were not constructed for the white male gaze. That experience can prove shocking and unsettling to most. Sometimes even controversy ensues. But I would argue, for theological reasons, that such displacement of the white male gaze ultimately serves everyone. With their hermeneutic for 'recovering the histories of counter-futures', Marshall and Ofili provide a compelling vision of justice – what should be and what could be in the end. In contrast with the unaccountably shallow consolation of 'colour blindness' from the majority culture, Ofili and Marshall force all viewers to see the beautiful otherness of blackness, not as mere code or symbol to be dismissed but as a presence to be acknowledged with all due respect. As emblems of Afrofuturism, their paintings are much more but also never less than a defiant assertion about the basic human dignity of their subjects. Recall Marshall's words:

> What you're trying to create is a certain kind of indispensable presence … Where your position in the narrative is not contingent on whether somebody likes you, or somebody knows you, or somebody's a friend, or somebody's being generous to you. But you want a presence in the narrative that's not negotiable, that's undeniable.[73]

Such demands from the 'moving text' – when brought together with the scriptural canon – constitute much more than political protest or social activism. In the words of Marshall, 'there's a certain uncertainty' at play in the work, and that aporia bears witness to the mystery and meaning of the text upon which they draw, even as the text reveals its own 'indispensable presence' in the imagination of its readers.[74] Such aporias are urgently needed if we are to hear with fresh attention the divine call in the words of Christian Scripture concerning God's promise to bless all people through Christ.

Notes

1 Kerry James Marshall, 'Sticks and Stones ..., but Names ...', in *Kerry James Marshall: Mastry*, ed. Helen Molesworth (New York: Skira Rizzoli, 2016), 231.
2 David Brown, *Tradition and Imagination: Revelation and Change* (Oxford: Oxford University Press, 1999), 170.
3 Ibid., 55.
4 Ibid., 58.
5 Ibid., 75.
6 For additional discussion, see David M. Goldenberg, *The Curse of Ham: Race and Slavery in Early Judaism, Christianity, and Islam* (Princeton, NJ: Princeton University Press, 2005); Stephen R. Haynes, *Noah's Curse: The Biblical Justification of American Slavery* (Oxford: Oxford University Press, 2007); and David M. Whitford, *The Curse of Ham in the Early Modern Era: The Bible and the Justifications for Slavery* (Abingdon: Ashgate, 2009; London and New York: Routledge, 2016).
7 For Brown's discussion of Ofili's works, see David Brown, *Divine Generosity and Human Creativity: Theology through Symbol, Painting and Architecture*, ed. Christopher R. Brewer and Robert MacSwain (London and New York: Routledge, 2017), 20 (n. 30), 46, 48 (n. 38); David Brown, 'Context and Experiencing the Sacred', *Royal Institute of Philosophy Supplement* 79 (2016), 125–6.
8 For illustration of Albrecht Dürer, *Adam and Eve* (1504), see online: www.metmuseum.org/toah/works-of-art/19.73.1; accessed 27 August 2017. For illustration of Peter Paul Rubens, *Adam and Eve* (1628–9), see online: www.museodelprado.es/en/the-collection/art-work/adam-and-eve/de0047db-6f8b-4761-a55b-ad41e959cca2; accessed 27 August 2017.
9 For illustration of Jacob Lawrence, *Genesis Creation Sermon VII: And God Created Man and Woman*, see online: www.scadmoa.org/art/collections/genesis-creation-sermon%20vii-and-god-created-man-and-woman; accessed 3 September 2017.
10 Mark Dery, 'Black to the Future: Interviews with Samuel R. Delaney, Greg Tate, and Tricia Rose', in *Flame Wars: The Discourse of Cyberculture*, ed. Mark Dery (Durham, NC: Duke University Press, 1994), 180.
11 De Witt Douglas Kilgore, 'Afrofuturism', in *The Oxford Handbook of Science Fiction*, ed. Rob Latham (Oxford: Oxford University Press, 2014), 563.
12 Kodwo Eshun, 'Further Considerations on Afrofuturism', *CR: The New Centennial Review*, 3.2 (2003), 301.
13 For example, consider Marshall's *Keeping the Culture* (2010) and Ofili's *Spaceshit* (1995). For illustration of Marshall's *Keeping the Culture*, see online: www.artnet.com/artists/kerry-james-marshall/keeping-the-culture-d2b-l9BmC9NRjFz1rqk9Xg2; accessed 27 August 2017. For illustration of Ofili's *Spaceshit*, see online: www.saatchigallery.com/artists/artpages/chris_ofili_7.htm; accessed 27 August 2017.

14 In addition to the two primary artworks under review here, all subsequent works by Marshall and Ofili can be found in either of these two volumes: *Kerry James Marshall*, ed. Molesworth, and *Chris Ofili* (New York: Rizzoli, 2009).

15 Quoted in 'Plates with catalogue entries by Anna Katz, Karsten Lund, and Abigail Winograd', in *Kerry James Marshall*, ed. Molesworth, 94.

16 Kerry James Marshall, 'Just Because', in *Kerry James Marshall*, ed. Molesworth, 242.

17 For illustration of works from Marshall's recent retrospective *Mastry*, see online: www.metmuseum.org/exhibitions/objects?exhibitionId=175f55d3-dbd8-4be6-b248-9dc2025021f0; accessed 22 July 2017.

18 Catherine Womack, 'Kerry James Marshall Brings Blackness to the White Walls of a White Space', *LA Weekly* 21 March 2017. Online: www.laweekly.com/arts/kerry-james-marshalls-moca-retrospective-mastry-brings-blackness-to-a-traditionally-white-space-8045004; accessed 1 June 2017.

19 He writes: 'This dependence on white acknowledgement and stewardship (engineered over the centuries) remains a major hurdle facing even the academy-trained visual artists.' Marshall, 'Sticks and Stones ..., but Names ...', 233.

20 Kerry James Marshall, 'Horace Pippin: The Way I See Him', in *Kerry James Marshall*, ed. Molesworth, 252.

21 Wyatt Mason, 'Kerry James Marshall is Shifting the Color of Art History', *The New York Times Style Magazine*, 17 October 2016. Online: www.nytimes.com/2016/10/17/t-magazine/kerry-james-marshall-artist.html?_r=1; accessed 31 March 2017.

22 For illustration, see online: http://metmuseum.org/exhibitions/view?exhibitionId=%7B175f55d3-dbd8-4be6-b248-9dc2025021f0%7D&oid=668284; accessed 22 July 2017.

23 Jerry Saltz, 'The Painting that Jerry Saltz Can't Stop Thinking About', *Vulture* 3 November 2016. Online: www.vulture.com/2016/11/kerry-james-marshall-mastry.html; accessed 7 July 2017.

24 Womack, 'Kerry James Marshall Brings Blackness to the White Walls of a White Space'.

25 Kerry James Marshall, 'Mickalene's Harem', in *Kerry James Marshall*, ed. Molesworth, 241.

26 For illustration, see online: http://metmuseum.com/exhibitions/view?exhibitionId=%7B175f55d3-dbd8-4be6-b248-9dc2025021f0%7D&oid=668407; accessed 19 August 2017.

27 Marshall, 'Just Because', in *Kerry James Marshall*, ed. Molesworth, 246.

28 Ibid.

29 Marshall, 'Mickalene's Harem', 241.

30 For illustration, see online: www.metmuseum.org/exhibitions/view?exhibitionId=%7B175f55d3-dbd8-4be6-b248-9dc2025021f0%7D&oid=668297; accessed 27 August 2017.

31 For illustration, see online: www.metmuseum.org/exhibitions/view?exhibitionId=%7B175f55d3-dbd8-4be6-b248-9dc2025021f0%7D&oid=668300&pkgids=368&pg=0&rpp=20&pos=8&ft=*&offset=20; accessed 27 August 2017.

32 For illustration, see online: www.metmuseum.org/exhibitions/view?exhibitionId=%7B175f55d3-dbd8-4be6-b248-9dc2025021f0%7D&oid=668310; accessed 27 August 2017.

33 For illustration, see online: www.muhka.be/collections/artworks/s/item/4748-stigma-stigmata; accessed 27 August 2017.

34 For illustration, see online: www.contemporaryartdaily.com/2014/05/kerry-james-marshall-at-kunsthal-charlottenborg/kerry-james-marshall-slow-dance-1992-1993-05092014; accessed 27 August 2017.

35 For illustration, see online: http://denverartmuseum.org/sites/default/files/marshall_final-image_1995771.jpg; accessed 27 August 2017.

36 For illustration, see online: www.christies.com/lotfinderimages/D58450/kerry_james_marshall_vignette_d5845010g.jpg; accessed 27 August 2017.

37 For illustration, see online: http://media.npr.org/assets/img/2017/03/27/kjm_dz_club_couple_custom-bea7d3692cacddecd45bd3c5523020f42b9aa762-s900-c85.jpg; accessed 27 August 2017.

38 For illustration of this work, see online: https://goo.gl/images/JCxkPL; accessed 19 August 2017.

39 Marshall, 'The Legend of Sun Man Continues', in *Kerry James Marshall*, ed. Molesworth, 250. Revealingly, he writes: 'Reading history taught me that current attitudes, ideas, and behaviors are linked in a continuum that stretches back for millennia.' Ibid., 248.

40 Susan Stamberg, 'Kerry James Marshall: A Black Presence in the Art World is "Not Negotiable"', *NPR: Morning Edition*, 28 March 2017. Online: www.npr.org/2017/03/28/521683667/kerry-james-marshall-a-black-presence-in-the-art-world-is-not-negotiable; accessed 10 August 2017.

41 Ibid.

42 Christy Lange, 'In Search of the Real Me: Interview with Chris Ofili', *TATE ETC.* 18 (Spring 2010), 95.

43 Katherine Brinson, 'After the Fall', in *Chris Ofili: 2000 Words*, ed. Karen Marta (New York: Artbook/D.A.P., 2015), 7.

44 Whereas Ofili admits directly sampling David Hammons's *Bliz-aard Ball Sale*, much of the attitude towards contemporary issues of identity in his work draws inspiration from Hammons's prolific career. Cf. Terry R. Myers, 'Chris Ofili: Power Man', *Art/Text* 58 (August–October 1997), 38.

45 For one such debate, see Donald J. Cosentino, 'Hip-Hop Assemblage: The Chris Ofili Affair', *African Arts* 33.1 (2000), 40–51, 95–6; Sidney Kasfir, 'Assigning Identity: Cosentino's "Hip-Hop Assemblage: The Chris Ofili Affair"', *African Arts* 34.1 (2001), 9; Nancy Hynes, 'Africanizing Chris Ofili?', *African Arts* 34.1 (2001), 9–10; Donald J. Cosentino, 'Cosentino Replies', *African Arts* 34.1 (2001), 10.

46 Lisa G. Corrin, 'Confounding the Stereotype', in *Chris Ofili* (London: Serpentine Gallery, 1998), 15.

47 Stuart Morgan, 'The Elephant Man', *Frieze* 15 (1994), 40.

48 Kodwo Eshun, 'Plug Into Ofili', in *Chris Ofili* (London: Serpentine Gallery, 1998), n.p.

49 For additional discussion, see the short documentary, 'Chris Ofili: Exploding the Crystal', available online: www.tate.org.uk/whats-on/tate-britain/exhibition/chris-ofili; accessed 10 August 2017.

50 Godfrey Worsdale, 'The Stereo Type', in *Chris Ofili* (London: Serpentine Gallery, 1998), 10.

51 Klaus Kertess, 'Just Desserts', in *Chris Ofili: Devil's Pie* (New York: Steidl/David Zwirner Gallery, 2008).

52 For illustration, see online: www.khanacademy.org/humanities/global-culture/identity-body/identity-body-europe/a/chris-ofili-the-holy-virgin-mary; accessed 27 August 2017.

53 For illustration, see online: www.tate.org.uk/whats-on/tate-britain/exhibition/chris-ofili-upper-room; accessed 27 August 2017.

54 For illustration, see online: www.artnet.com/magazineus/features/saltz/saltz10-22-07_detail.asp?picnum=10; accessed 27 August 2017.

55 For illustration, see online: http://newmuseum.tumblr.com/post/105009157857/chris-ofili-night-and-day-is-on-view-through ; accessed 27 August 2017.

56 See, for example, Eleanor Heartney, *Postmodern Heretics: Catholic Imagination in Contemporary Art* (New York: Midmarch Arts, 2004), 143.
57 Brinson, 'After the Fall', 7.
58 For illustration of this work, see online: www.victoria-miro.com/artists/6-chris-ofili/works/artworks2929; accessed 19 August 2017.
59 Okwui Enwezor, 'Shattering the Mirror of Tradition: Chris Ofili's Triumph of Painting at the 50th Venice Biennale', in *Chris Ofili* (New York: Rizzoli, 2009), 156.
60 For illustration, see online: https://flavorwire.files.wordpress.com/2009/10/ofili_afro.jpg?w=1920; accessed 27 August 2017.
61 For illustration, see online: www.tate.org.uk/sites/default/files/styles/grid-normal-12-cols/public/images/chris_ofili_afro_jezebel_2002_2003.jpg?itok=u-j6MoHg; accessed 27 August 2017.
62 For illustration, see online: https://d2u3kfwd92fzu7.cloudfront.net/catalog/artwork/gallery/1103/photo/2005-2008_OFICH0293Z_REPRO_edited-1.jpg; accessed 27 August 2017.
63 For illustration, see online: www.tate.org.uk/whats-on/tate-britain/exhibition/chris-ofili/exhibition-guide/room-6; accessed 27 August 2017.
64 For illustration, see online: www.artnet.com/magazineus/features/saltz/saltz10-22-07_detail.asp?picnum=7; accessed 27 August 2017.
65 Brinson, 'After the Fall', 11.
66 Lange, 'In Search of the Real Me: Interview with Chris Ofili', 95.
67 Ibid.
68 Jonathan Jones, 'Paradise Reclaimed', *The Guardian Weekend* (June 15 2002), online: www.theguardian.com/artanddesign/2002/jun/15/artsfeatures; accessed 5 July 2017. The choice of title for this chapter and the above article in *The Guardian* compose a happy, if unexpected coincidence.
69 Enwezor, 'Shattering the Mirror of Tradition', 152. He continues: 'If this is the philosophical pivot on which the reception and analysis of Ofili's work can proceed, it seems then that the problem posed by modernism in relation to the figure of the black subject in painting, and the question of modernity in relation to its denial of the black citizen as a member of the nation in various instances are both central to his work. Modernism and modernity have made the presence of black subjectivity anathema to modern conceptions of identity. Both, whether in situations of colonization or in the repressed images of the black figure in canonical representation, deny the counter-history of African identity in the making of the narrative of the modern Western nation.' Ibid.
70 Ibid.
71 For context, consider Ben Austen, 'Chicago After Laquan McDonald', *New York Times Magazine* (20 April 2016), online: www.nytimes.com/2016/04/24/magazine/chicago-after-laquan-mcdonald.html?mcubz=1; accessed 27 August 2017.
72 Brown, *Tradition and Imagination*, 374.
73 Ibid.
74 Stamberg, 'Kerry James Marshall: A Black Presence in the Art World is "Not Negotiable."'

6

Re-visions of Sacrifice: Abraham in Art and Interfaith Dialogue

AARON ROSEN

David Brown has tremendous faith in art. While an increasing number of contemporary Christian thinkers, including John Drury, Richard Harries, George Pattison and Ben Quash,[1] have recognized visual art as a powerful resource for thinking about Christian theology and identity, Brown has made especially bold claims for its revelatory capacity. He lays out the foundations for this claim in two volumes from the turn of the twenty-first century: *Tradition and Imagination* (1999) and *Discipleship and Imagination* (2000). God's self-disclosure within human history, he argues, is just as discernible in the past two millennia of Christian experience as it was during biblical times. Because God made himself subject to the constraints of history and materiality in the Incarnation, Brown argues, it is reasonable to speak of God's revealing activity continuing through history, especially within Christian tradition. Scripture and tradition are thus interwoven in a 'single, ongoing process of revelation'.[2] While tradition might carry staid, conservative connotations for some, for Brown it entails a dynamic process by which the original text is rewritten and recharged with meaning. In fact, submits Brown, creative reworkings might even critique or correct the original narratives, providing the more profound theological truth.[3] This claim would be controversial enough were it only to apply to literary or liturgical innovations, but Brown makes clear that visual art has an important – at times even primary – role to play in this process. It not only illuminates Scripture, it reimagines it.

While Brown's wide-ranging interests prevent him from dwelling too extensively on specific examples from art history, he has provided some very tantalizing case studies. In *Tradition and Imagination*, for instance, he presents a cogent analysis of theological insights to be gleaned from Romanesque and Gothic art. A later essay on 'Sinai in Art and Architecture' notes productive parallels and cross-pollinations between Jewish and Christian artists,[4] and indeed helpfully telegraphs some of the kinds of interreligious conversations that art can enable, which is a dialogue I will pick up on later in this chapter. Not surprisingly, given the incarnational emphasis in his theology, Brown writes illuminatingly on images of the Incarnation,[5] simultaneously demonstrating his willingness to engage with works of modern art. And a volume of collected essays, *Divine Generosity and Human Creativity: Theology through Symbol, Painting and Architecture*, promises further insights into art as a source of revelation and a focus for worship.[6] With some noted exceptions above, Brown tends to take a synoptic approach to art, surveying works from various periods on given themes rather than focusing on particular periods. This makes complete sense, of course, given Brown's abiding concern to emphasize the progressive and purposive unfolding of tradition. But it does pose some critical questions. To what extent do modern – and especially contemporary artists, mentioned only sporadically by Brown – follow and extend the flow of tradition, as Brown conceives it? How does he take account of the many works that seem to disrupt previous tradition or turn it on its head? Can these still serve as vehicles for revelation? He comments encouragingly in *Discipleship and Imagination* that 'the recognition of disorder can surely also be a form of truth',[7] but does not take the opportunity to extend this promising insight to contemporary art. While contemporary art might seem a somewhat ancillary concern at first, the issues it raises reach to the core of Brown's theological project. If the claims he makes for art falter at the gates of the twenty-first century, his model of continuous revelation risks being compromised where it is needed most: the present.

I think Brown can meet these challenges, but perhaps not in precisely the way he envisages. In earlier eras, church patronage led to art that had to be, to a greater or lesser extent, in step with the theology of the day and in touch with its developing traditions. That changed, of course, in the modern period, with artists following a host of competing imperatives, largely without the shaping influence of religious institutions directing them towards particular texts or traditions. This certainly should not be taken to mean that modern artists have abandoned theology or have less to say about spiritual matters, and Brown wisely avoids the trope of the modern artist as intemperate iconoclast.[8] Artists today can be a profound source of religious reflection. What is much harder to establish is how contemporary artists, an incredibly varied group, propelled by an equally diverse array of concerns, fit within the metanarrative of tradition and revelation adumbrated by Brown. While there are certainly artists who do seek to engage with this theological heritage directly, mining the kinds of seams mapped out by Brown, they remain in the minority. For many modern and contemporary artists, religious insights are just as likely to come from rejecting, ignoring or even randomly appropriating religious subject matter as they are from careful or prayerful consideration of religious tradition. The question becomes: Just how elastic is Brown's concept of tradition? Is it capable of stretching to include art that, so to speak, *misbehaves*?

To get our answer we need to put Brown to the test, like a patriarch of old. Appropriately enough, I intend to do so by exploring how modern artists have rendered Abraham's 'test' on Mount Moriah, and how this problematizes – but I think ultimately enriches – Brown's argument for tradition. To my mind, one of the great strengths of Brown's project is his willingness to listen for revelation beyond the borders of Christianity, even allowing for the possibility 'that sometimes at least God might have spoken more effectively through the history of faiths other than one's own'.[9] Abraham's near sacrifice of his son provides an optimal, if uncomfortable opportunity to listen for this voice. This traumatic event, known to Jews as the *Akedah*, to Christians as the Sacrifice of Isaac and to Muslims as the *Dhabih*, is a major theme in the Scriptures, interpretative traditions and practices of all three faiths. According to Brown, both Jewish and Christian tradition have progressively pivoted away from the biblical Abraham's apparent willingness to slaughter his son, developing instead a tradition in which 'Isaac's self-sacrificial offering [constitutes] the "real" text'.[10] In the section that follows, I will review some examples of this tendency, alongside evidence from Islam. Broadly speaking there is good textual support for Brown's argument, and an even better moral rationale for imagining a son who *voluntarily* submits to his father's blade.

But even Brown admits that a challenge presents itself when we come to modernity. 'It would be a tragedy', he warns ominously, 'if our modern retreat from tradition also meant a return to what is in the end not only the more troubling but also the less evocative image.'[11] Judging by visual art, the situation is worse than Brown suspects: modern artists have shown a marked preference for the 'more troubling' image of the scriptural Abraham, ready and willing to draw innocent blood. Brown makes a misstep, I think, by writing this off as a 'retreat from tradition'. This is indeed a paradigmatic example of modern artists' prevailing preference for the raw immediacy of the Bible over exegetical accretions. But it is possible, at a more fundamental level, to see this turn as an extension of tradition rather than its repudiation. After all, as Brown himself frequently reminds us, one of tradition's most important upshots is the potential to cast Scripture in a more revealing light, that it might better address us in the present. Earlier interpreters felt compelled to exculpate Abraham by inventing a more mature Isaac who takes up God's command with sober obedience. Rather than seeking to excuse Abraham by inventing mitigating factors, modern artists have preferred to indict him directly for his meek compliance. While this might look like an inversion of tradition, it responds to the same thorny problem that earlier traditions diagnosed so adroitly within the norms and conventions of their own eras. The answer differs, but the question remains the same: How could a parent consent to slaughter a child? Modern art takes tradition in a more radical but no less revealing direction. It gives us the unvarnished Abraham we need if we are to confront ourselves – and our interconnected, 'Abrahamic' faiths – more honestly.

Textual Traditions

Before we turn to imaginings from modern art, we need to review how the story of Abraham and his beloved son surfaces in the Scriptures and interpretative traditions of Judaism, Christianity and Islam.[12] Not only will this set the stage for the artistic references to follow, it will offer an opportunity to consider Brown's contention that ancient and medieval interpreters progressively massaged the narrative into a tale of willing self-sacrifice. I begin with Judaism. Traditionally, Jews read Genesis 21 on the first day of Rosh Hashanah, the Jewish New Year, while Genesis 22 is read on the second day of the holiday.[13] The pairing provides a critical insight. Before he trudges to the altar with Isaac, Abraham demonstrates his willingness to sacrifice his offspring by casting out Ishmael, his firstborn son (Gen. 21.14). While Ishmael's survival signals the potential for Isaac's own deliverance, it raises genuine concerns about Abraham's paternal commitment. Genesis 22 opens:

> After these things God tested Abraham. He said to him, 'Abraham!' And he said, 'Here I am.' He said, 'Take your son, your only son Isaac, whom you love, and go to the land of Moriah, and offer him there as a burnt-offering on one of the mountains that I shall show you.'[14]

Abraham's reply, *hinneni*, indicates absolute attention. God calls; Abraham responds.[15] This alacrity, confirmed when Abraham rises 'early in the morning' (Gen. 22.3), sets the tone for the story.[16] Rather than extraordinary faith – as Christian interpreters would later argue – the text seems to emphasize Abraham's 'radical obedience',[17] a distinction also noted by Brown, who finds the Jewish emphasis more 'natural'.[18] Disclosing his plan to no one, not even his wife (a fact that has particularly disturbed modern critics), Abraham sets off with his son and servants on a three-day journey. When they reach the foot of Mount Moriah, father and son tread the final leg of the journey alone. Isaac calls to him, perhaps naively, or maybe because a sense of foreboding has begun to stir. 'He said, "The fire and the wood are here, but where is the lamb for a burnt-offering?" Abraham said, "God himself will provide the lamb for a burnt-offering, my son."' (Gen. 22.7–8); a careful reply that has been interpreted as everything from prophetic to evasive, resigned or ironic.[19] When they finally reach the appointed place, Abraham binds his son on the altar and raises his knife to slay him. At the last instant, an angel of the Lord calls to him, 'Do not lay your hand on the boy or do anything to him; for now I know that you fear God, since you have not withheld your son, your only son, from me' (Gen. 22.12). Glancing up, Abraham spies a ram caught in a thicket, which he slaughters instead. After a second encomium booms down from heaven, the story concludes on a seemingly prosaic note. 'Abraham returned to his young men' – curiously Isaac is not mentioned – and journeys back to Beersheba (Gen. 22.19).

Surprisingly, the *Akedah* barely features in the remainder of the Hebrew Bible. That, together with the episode's sparse and cryptic narration, means the narrative positively clamours for interpretation. The rabbis were happy to oblige, requiring only the smallest foothold in the text. Even the opening words, 'After these things', could suggest a whole scene in which Satan baits God into testing Abraham, just as he does in Job (1.6–12).[20] In another tradition – of central importance in Islam – a devil appears to Abraham, Isaac and Sarah, arguing that such a monstrous demand transgresses God's own moral law.[21] While Brown finds the insinuation of Satan to be merely 'a dramatic way of labelling the problem',[22] it may be this embellishment more than any other that intuits modern reactions to the story. Other *midrashim* fly directly in the face of the text's plain sense, claiming that Abraham had wounded or even slaughtered his son. In one version Isaac is whisked away to the Garden of Eden for three years to rehabilitate.[23] According to another, 'When Father Isaac was bound on the altar and *reduced to ashes and his sacrificial dust was cast* on to Mount Moriah, the Holy One, blessed be He, immediately brought upon him dew and revived him.'[24] The site of Isaac's sacrifice became identified with the Temple in Jerusalem and – as Brown notes[25] – Isaac himself came to be construed as a willing adult[26] and thus an exemplar for martyrs (e.g. 4 Macc. 13.12). As Jews looked to the merit of their ancestors to find strength in the face of oppression, especially during the Crusades, Isaac's noble sacrifice even came to be viewed as an act that could grant atonement to his descendants. In the ensuing centuries, according to Brown, 'Within Judaism, Isaac was to become the norm for life understood as self-sacrificial dedication to God.'[27] While this remains broadly true, it requires revision for the modern period, when progressive Jews began to turn their attention back towards the original text. And in the aftermath of the Holocaust, the reception of Isaac focused even more squarely on his status as an innocent victim in a drama beyond his control.

In Christianity, atonement comes to the forefront. Early followers of Jesus recognized a powerful affinity between Abraham's offering of Isaac and God's sacrifice of his own beloved son. When Paul asserted in his Letter to the Romans that God 'did not withhold his own Son, but gave him up for all of us' (8.32), he echoed the language of the Hebrew Bible, which praises Abraham for not withholding his cherished son (Gen. 22.12, 16).[28] The Letter to the Hebrews develops another influential line of thought:

> By faith Abraham, when put to the test, offered up Isaac. He who had received the promises was ready to offer up his only son, of whom he had been told, 'It is through Isaac that descendants shall be named after you.' He considered the fact that God is able even to raise someone from the dead – and figuratively speaking, he did receive him back. (11.17–19)

The author boldly interpolates the patriarch's reasoning. Abraham's deed becomes – first and foremost – a measure of faith; a touchstone in Christian interpretations from Paul to Søren Kierkegaard (the latter roundly critiqued by Brown).[29] While Hebrews does not explicitly link the sacrifice of Isaac to Christ's resurrection,[30] later interpreters would soon cement this connection. The Letter of James, meanwhile, concentrates on another aspect: 'Was not our ancestor Abraham justified by works when he offered his son Isaac on the altar? You see that faith was active along with his works, and faith was brought to completion by the works' (James 2.21–22). This reading is strikingly Jewish, and rubs against a Pauline emphasis on faith over works. As Brown wisely notes, 'we should guard against too easy a reconciliation between Paul and James', looking instead to the productive tension these readings generate.[31] Over the next several centuries, many of the Church Fathers wrote extensively on Genesis 22, frequently reading it as a prototype for the perfected sacrifice of Christ. Thus, for Saint Augustine, Isaac carrying the wood for the burnt offering anticipated Jesus shouldering the cross on his way to Golgotha.[32] And the ram caught in thicket also became a symbol for the Saviour, 'crowned with Jewish thorns before he was offered in sacrifice'.[33] Taking their cue from such typologies, many churches today read Genesis 22 during the Easter Holy Week, when Christians remember Jesus' sacrifice as the Paschal Lamb.[34] The willing Isaac thus carries the day through most of Christian history, as Brown contends. Even so, it is worth noting how an *un*willing Isaac, forced on the altar, may offer an increasingly impactful image for some Christians, especially in the wake of abuse.

If, as Erich Auerbach put it, '[e]verything remains unexpressed' in Genesis 22,[35] the Qur'anic story is startlingly clear about the intentions of the protagonists. Here is the account in its entirety:

> And when (his son) was old enough to walk with him (Abraham) said: O my dear son, I have seen in a dream that I must sacrifice thee. So look, what thinkest thou? He said: O my father! Do that which thou art commanded. Allah willing, thou shalt find me steadfast. Then, when they had both surrendered (to Allah), and he had flung him down upon his face, we called unto him: O Abraham! Thou hast already fulfilled the vision. Lo! Thus do we reward the good. Lo! that verily was a clear test. Then we ransomed him with a tremendous victim. (37.102–7)[36]

Certain elements are familiar, of course, but the differences are crucial. Abraham receives God's call in a dream, and rather than deliberately keeping his son in the dark, he immediately asks his opinion. For his part, the son is less like the naïve Isaac of Genesis and more like the steadfast martyr of *midrash*. Significantly, it is not clear which son is the protagonist. Early Islamic interpreters leaned towards Isaac and imagined the events transpiring in Syria, while later interpreters favoured Ishmael, and the Muslim holy city of Mecca as the setting.[37] Although overall Ishmael features as the hero in only slightly more authoritative Islamic texts than Isaac,[38] he is the overwhelming consensus among Muslims today. Picking up elements from both Jewish exegesis and pre-Islamic traditions, numerous sources describe Abraham and either Isaac or Ishmael stoning Satan as he attempts to dissuade them from their sacrifice.[39] This is the basis for the ritual during the Hajj in which pilgrims hurl pebbles at stone pillars representing the devil. The pilgrimage culminates with the *Eid al-Adha*, the Feast of the Sacrifice, in which an animal is slaughtered in memory of Abraham and his son's great trial. While Brown touches only briefly upon Islamic renditions of this story, it is here that his argument finds its strongest anchor: a father who asks permission, and a son who gives it freely. And yet, as we shall see, also within Islam we can locate an emerging interest in an Ishmael or Isaac who is as much reluctant sacrifice as ready martyr. With that in mind, we turn now to see what revelations art might provide.

Picturing the Patriarchs

The self-sacrificing Isaac that Brown prefers makes regular appearances in the history of art, beginning in antiquity. From Christian tradition, Brown might look to the sixth-century mosaic at San Vitale in Ravenna, in which Isaac kneels in dutiful submission, his form mirroring the meat Abraham serves to the visiting angels on the opposite side of the image. Medieval Islamic manuscripts typically display Abraham and his son as equally stalwart, with an angel rushing down from heaven to deliver a ram. Meyer Schapiro notes that a handful of medieval Christian manuscripts actually share this iconography.[40] He speculates that this motif may even have spread via Jewish exegetes, bringing all three faiths into visual dialogue.[41] An interesting Jewish example, which serves Brown's argument well, comes from the *Venice Haggadah* (1609), in which a grown Isaac kneels contemplatively on the altar, his loosely bound hands crossed in a prayerful pose. While the image of the self-sacrificing son never disappears entirely, it begins to taper from the Renaissance onwards. Unfortunately – and quite unusually in his work – Brown is reticent to follow the evidence where it leads. He notes approvingly that in the famous competition to design the north doors for Florence's Baptistery in the early fifteenth century, Ghiberti's image of a confident Isaac, gazing towards the angel, was selected over Brunelleschi's more gruesome design, in which Abraham wrenches his son's neck into position.[42] 'That, then, is overwhelmingly how the tradition came to read the narrative', concludes Brown.[43] In actuality, that is only half the story. When Ghiberti was commissioned two decades later to create a new series for the Baptistery – his resplendent *Gates of Paradise* (1425–52) for the eastern portal – he carved out a different Isaac: his face downcast, his body slumped and dejected. Brown continues his search for a willing Isaac in later works, finding 'gentleness and acceptance', for example, in Rembrandt's etching of the subject.[44] Even if we follow this tendentious reading, we are still left with the Rembrandt's masterpiece in the Hermitage (1635), in which Abraham's massive hand is clamped over Isaac's face like an octopus, while his phallic blade slices through the air towards Isaac's midsection. When Brown comes to Caravaggio's *The Sacrifice of Isaac* (c.1603), he knows he has met his match, wisely avoiding any attempt to mitigate its brutal vision of a screaming adolescent, writhing beneath his father's knife. To Brown, this 'shows us what is so profoundly wrong with the biblical version'.[45] I agree, but I prefer to extract a different lesson. For Brown, Caravaggio represents a dead end, a betrayal of tradition. To me he constitutes its logical extension. And with this unabashed, prophetic critique of the original text, Caravaggio passes the torch – or rather the knife – to modern artists.

Perhaps no modern artist has treated the subject of Abraham and Isaac more frequently than Marc Chagall, beginning with a series of biblical etchings in the 1930s. Chagall's authoritative statement of the theme came some 30 years later with *The Sacrifice of Isaac* (1960–6), a large, ambitious canvas in the manner of Rembrandt and Caravaggio's masterpieces of the same title. The composition unfolds along a bold diagonal, with two angels leading the way. The first raises an arm in warning. The second – most likely the same angel shown a second later – swoops to earth with both arms urgently extended. The image echoes midrashic accounts in which the angel calls out a second time because Abraham has not heard the first. However, even this second effort may have come too late. In Chagall's imagination, Isaac's limp body glows a fiery yellow as flickering strokes of orange and red engulf both father and son. Are these the 'ashes of Isaac' of rabbinic tradition?[46] Has the anguished patriarch leapt on to the pyre himself? Perhaps the azure angel has not come to prevent the sacrifice but to supply the 'resurrecting dew' that will revive the patriarchs.[47] According to several Jewish legends, Sarah died from shock on hearing what transpired on Mount Moriah.[48] Here she emerges from behind a tree in the background, wailing at what she perceives in the foreground. The tiny ram poking out behind the tree-trunk seems to have arrived too late, or proved an inadequate substitute. At the top of the picture, suspended in the smoky space above the sacrifice, float various figures, seemingly unaware of one another. A wandering Jew, a familiar character in Chagall's paintings, slouches along, book in hand. To his left stumbles Jesus, hauling the crucifix on his back. To his right a woman nervously cradles her child. Based on a Chagall pen and ink drawing from 1956, we can identify the figures as Hagar and Ishmael. Thus for all the work's Jewish resonances, Chagall makes a point of acknowledging the centrality of the sacrifice for both Christianity and Islam. Each of the three faiths, he seems to suggest, has a stake in this story. And yet the story itself, he intimates, may not be a tale of deliverance so much as a test gone horribly awry, ending in flames.

The image of a slaughtered Isaac has been a dominant motif in Zionist thought and Israeli culture. From the 1940s onward it began to be utilized paradoxically to express 'both the slaughter of the Holocaust and the national warrior's death in the old-new homeland'.[49] In the 1980s the Lebanon War (1982) – regarded as a conflict of choice by many Israelis – served as the catalyst for another transformation, as Isaac was increasingly read as the victim of unnecessary sacrifice demanded by the state.[50] Writers including A. B. Yehoshua, Yitzhak Laor and Yehuda Amichai, and painters such as Avraham Ofek and Moshe Gershuni, cast Abraham as villain or patsy rather than hero.[51] For Amichai, 'the real hero of the Binding of Isaac was the ram', who remained on the altar long after Isaac, Abraham and even God had departed.[52] The ram also caught the attention of Menashe Kadishman, an artist who in his youth had worked as a shepherd and famously corralled a herd of painted sheep for the 1978 Venice Biennale. For Kadishman, however, the ram is anything but innocent. In his massive Corten steel sculpture, *Sacrifice of Isaac* (1982–5),

Kadishman gives the animal a demonic glare as he exalts over the slain Isaac. Abraham is nowhere to be seen, although two women – Sarah and Hagar? – fearfully huddle together in a single, mountainous heap. In a subsequent version, *Sacrifice of Isaac II* (1986–7), installed on the steps of Saint John the Divine Cathedral in New York City, Kadishman joined the ram and Isaac into a single looming figure. The location is crucial to Kadishman's point. By continually reinventing and reconfiguring the *Akedah* he sets out to disrupt the symbolic economy of sacrifice wherever it exists, whether in Israeli political culture or Christian worship. In the end, there is neither Abraham nor God in Kadishman's *Akedah*, just boy and beast, welded together in purposeless death.

Palestinian artists and writers – sometimes in dialogue with their Israeli counterparts – have also recognized the symbolic potential of the sacrifice story as a vehicle for social and political protest, often emphasizing Ishmael as an unwilling victim. Since the late 1990s the Palestinian painter and sculptor Sliman Mansour has created more than a dozen works in a series entitled *I, Ishmael*. Each piece consists of a single, life-sized body shaped from mud smeared across a wooden door. At times, Mansour displays these desiccated figures in groups along a gallery wall, while at others he lays them to rest outdoors, directly on the ground. Despite their dearth of narrative detail, the panels tap into several intersecting stories. By calling himself Ishmael, the artist deliberately evokes the Islamic tradition of Abraham's eldest son as the forefather of the Arab people and the ancestor of the Prophet Muhammad. While Mansour – the grandson of a Greek Orthodox priest[53] – comes from a Christian background, he turns to a key marker of Islamic heritage, the faith of the majority of Palestinians, in order to forge an icon of national longing and resistance. Mansour's Ishmael becomes a literal 'father-land', the fate of the Palestinian homeland etched into his arid, cracking flesh. And yet while Mansour calls on Islamic associations to emphasize Palestinian *sumud*, or rootedness to the land, his quarrel is not with Jews or Judaism. Indeed, he addresses Israelis in a language that also reverberates with biblical associations. To borrow the words of an Israeli poet, Mansour's sculptures seem to call out: 'Isaac, Isaac, remember what your father did to your brother Ishmael.'[54] The same father that binds Isaac on the sacrificial altar began by sending Ishmael out into the desert. Mansour reminds us that the sons of Abraham – and their descendants – each suffer the excesses of uncompromising power.

But what if these children were not sons? Would it make a difference if they were daughters? 'Would the logic of sacrificial responsibility', Jacques Derrida asks, 'be altered, inflected, attenuated, or displaced, if a woman were to intervene in some consequential manner?'[55] While Chagall and Kadishman both introduce women as witnesses, the Turkish photographer Nazif Topçuoğlu imagines the same events enacted exclusively by women. Topçuoğlu explicitly bases the composition of his *Sacrifice: The Story of Isaac* (2008) on Rembrandt's *Sacrifice* in St Petersburg. These parallels underscore the significance of Topçuoğlu's deliberate variations. In a space that could be either a library or a courtroom – both equally appropriate for staging this biblical trial – Topçuoğlu poses the victim with her hands tucked (bound?) behind her back, arched over a bolster. Compared to Rembrandt's Abraham, the executioner's hand rests almost gingerly across her victim's throat. Where Isaac's voice, breath and even sight are smothered, leaving him utterly bereft of agency,[56] Topçuoğlu's heroine is free to cry out or confront her executioner, although she seemingly opts for the path of 'infinite resignation', to use Kierkegaard's terminology.[57] The young women in this tableau may be acting out the patriarchal roles assigned to them, but they do so dispassionately, rather than fired by religious fervour, like Rembrandt's Abraham. And instead of the knife that plummets towards Isaac in Rembrandt, in Topçuoğlu the executioner brandishes the sharp edge of a book. But is the book ultimately any less dangerous? Is it any less of a weapon? The real risk of violence, Topçuoğlu suggests, is hermeneutic: the way we interpret the Holy Book. As disturbing as Abraham's readiness to sacrifice his child may be, his most dubious and enduring legacy may be his literalism, which he passes on to male and female descendants alike.

From the metaphorical papercuts inflected by Topçuoğlu, we turn finally to the works of Adel Abdessemed, whose Abraham threatens to draw real blood from its viewers. In a charcoal sketch from 2014, Abdessemed began to meditate on and re-envisage Caravaggio's *Sacrifice of Isaac* from the Uffizi Gallery. As Philippe-Alain Michaud notes, 'Abdessemed uses the flat edge of the chalk, as though sharpening a knife. Lines are thus applied like thrusts of a blade.'[58] But Abdessemed goes a step further. By pasting a surgical blade on to his drawing, the artist implies that the story of Abraham's sacrifice slices into itself, paring away at its own pieties. Abdessemed extends this insight in a life-size sculpture, *Untitled* (2014), in which his own father – studiously positioned like Caravaggio's Abraham – brandishes a knife while the adult artist kneels below him in submission. The intoxicating God-sickness of Abraham, Abdessemed suggests, is a disease that travels the generations, infecting every father and jeopardizing every son.[59] Encased in a skin of scalpel blades, there can be no embrace between this father and son; no caress to heal the wound inflicted by a zealous parent. Every touch simply whets the blade and sharpens the taste for sacrifice. For all the horror of Caravaggio's canvas, the angel still manages to grasp Abraham's wrist in time, pointing towards a benevolent, watery-eyed ram who has just entered the picture. No such angelic hope waits in the wings in Abdessemed's sculpture. And no substitute victim emerges from the thicket to spare this Isaac-Ishmael-Adel. He is the victim not just of one faith, but three. The artist conceives of this role as a sort of birthright from his native Algeria, where the Abrahamic faiths intersected in daily life. 'I was born in Constantine to a Muslim mother in a Jewish house and with Christian nuns as midwives', he recalls. 'On that day, I think I brought the gods of monotheism together.'[60] What might seem like a blessing, however, may also be a curse. In *Untitled*, this favourite son of monotheism suffers the menace of all three faiths, their sacrificial demands projected on to his bowed and terrified body.[61]

Trajectories for Dialogue

At the end of his survey of Genesis 22 and its subsequent imaginings, Brown notes 'the opportunities thereby created for fruitful dialogue, and indeed the possibility of mutual enrichment'.[62] While he concludes that it is 'not the place to begin such dialogue', he pauses to emphasize 'how much is lost if either or both religions seek to recover a primary place for the passage in something like its original significance'.[63] In this chapter I have sought to pick up and develop the dialogue so helpfully framed by Brown, drawing in Islamic art and tradition alongside that of Judaism and Christianity. In doing so, however, I have called on resources largely neglected in Brown's account of this tradition, namely modern and contemporary visual art. The result, I hope, has been to demonstrate that Brown's own notion of tradition is more capacious than he gives it credit for in this instance. While later art might appear to reject earlier traditions, in many cases it actually sharpens the critique that lies at their core. The artists we studied above do not attempt to 'recover' Abraham's act in anything 'like its original significance'. But nor are they content to imagine their way out of the horrors their respective texts introduce. They return to the scene of the crime in order that we might study it with fresh eyes, investigating the origins of our traditions – and our religious selves – with unflinching honesty.

However stark the results, this is not the end of a dialogue but rather a new, more self-critical beginning. Abraham's attempted sacrifice may constitute an ambivalent heritage for Jews, Christians and Muslims, but it is a *shared* inheritance nonetheless. As such, it may represent – even in its contestation – a critical stimulus for interreligious dialogue.[64] This task is especially critical at a time when 'the Abrahamic' has become ubiquitous in the practice, organization and promotion of interfaith dialogue. Various national and international organizations have taken

Abraham as a figurehead, including the Abraham Fund in Israel, Children of Abraham in the United Kingdom and Abraham's Vision and the Abrahamic Alliance International headquartered in the United States.[65] Universities have followed suit, with Oxford and Cambridge respectively establishing professorships in 'The Study of the Abrahamic Religions' and 'Abrahamic Faiths and Shared Values'. The proliferation of such institutions and positions is certainly a boon to interfaith dialogue and academic study. The more traction the idea of the Abrahamic has attained, however, and the more it has solidified its place within our vocabulary, the less attentive we have become to what this label might obscure or ignore. If we are really aiming at an informed practice of interfaith dialogue, one of our first steps must be to reflect rigorously on the language we employ. If we are going to call for interfaith dialogue under the banner of 'the Abrahamic', we need to wrestle honestly, first of all, with the legacy of Abraham himself. It is time to stop trying to paint a benevolent portrait of the patriarch to hang above our mantle, expecting him to gaze down approvingly on our interfaith salons and seminars. The future of interfaith dialogue depends on our ability to perforate our pieties as much as reinforce them.

Notes

1 It is interesting to note the high proportion of British theologians in the field, which Ben Quash attributes to a number of factors, not least a strong and abiding historical sensibility within Anglicanism. His own recent volume is a particularly fruitful contribution to this area. See Ben Quash, *Found Theology: History, Imagination and the Holy Spirit* (London: Bloomsbury T&T Clark, 2013), 1–2.

2 David Brown, *Tradition and Imagination: Revelation and Change* (Oxford: Oxford University Press, 1999), 111.

3 Ibid., 60, 376.

4 David Brown, 'Sinai in Art and Architecture', *The Significance of Sinai: Traditions about Sinai and Divine Revelation in Judaism and Christianity*, ed. George J. Brooke, Hindy Najman and Loren Stuckenbruck (Leiden: Brill, 2008), 313–31. See also David Brown, 'Interfaith Dialogue through Architecture', in *Divine Generosity and Human Creativity: Theology through Symbol, Painting and Architecture*, ed. Christopher R. Brewer and Robert MacSwain (London and New York: Routledge, 2017), 167–77.

5 David Brown, 'The Incarnation in Twentieth-Century Art', in *The Incarnation: An Interdisciplinary Symposium on the Incarnation of the Son of God*, ed. Stephen T. Davis, Daniel Kendall and Gerald O'Collins (New York: Oxford University Press, 2002), 332–72. He also engages with modern works in, for example, 'The Glory of God Revealed in Art and Music: Learning from Pagans', in *Celebrating Creation: Affirming Catholicism and the Revelation of God's Glory*, ed. Mark Chapman (London: Darton, Longman & Todd, 2004), 43–56, republished in Brown, *Divine Generosity and Human Creativity*, ed. Brewer and MacSwain, 37–48.

6 Other relevant works in which Brown engages with visual art include: David Brown, 'The Trinity in Art', in *The Trinity: An Interdisciplinary Symposium on the*

Trinity, ed. Stephen T. Davis, Daniel Kendall and Gerald O'Collins (New York: Oxford University Press, 1999), 329–56, republished as 'Artists on the Trinity', in David Brown, *Divine Generosity and Human Creativity: Theology through Symbol, Painting and Architecture*, ed. Christopher R. Brewer and Robert MacSwain (London and New York: Routledge, 2017), 130–49; David Brown, 'Images of Redemption in Art and Music', in *The Redemption: An Interdisciplinary Symposium on Christ as Redeemer*, ed. Stephen T. David, Daniel Kendall and Gerald O'Collins (New York: Oxford University Press, 2004), 295–319 (plus plates); David Brown, 'Science and Religion in Nineteenth- and Twentieth-Century Landscape Art', in *Reading Genesis After Darwin*, ed. Stephen Barton and David Wilkinson (New York: Oxford University Press, 2009), 111–24.

7 David Brown, *Discipleship and Imagination: Christian Tradition and Truth* (Oxford: Oxford University Press, 2000), 378.

8 For further discussion of stereotypes of contemporary artists, see: Aaron Rosen, *Art and Religion in the 21st Century* (London: Thames & Hudson, 2015), 10.

9 Brown, *Tradition and Imagination*, 112.

10 Ibid., 257.

11 Ibid., 259.

12 An early, abbreviated version of this section and the next appeared in 'Re-visions of Sacrifice: Abraham in Art and Interfaith Dialogue', *Jewish Quarterly* 61.2 (2014), 10–5, and I thank the publisher for their permission to reprint this material in expanded form here.

13 Reform Jews, who tend to celebrate one day of Rosh Hashanah, usually recite only Genesis 22.

14 Genesis 22.1–2. All biblical citations are from the NRSV, Anglicized Edition unless otherwise noted.

15 Emily Dickinson captures the tone well: 'Not a hesitation- / Abraham complied / Flattered by obeisance / Tyranny demurred'. Emily Dickinson, '1317' (First Line: 'Abraham to Kill Him'), *The Complete Poems of Emily Dickinson*, ed. Thomas Johnson (Boston, MA: Back Bay Books, 1960), 571.

16 Franz Kafka imagines an Abraham 'who was prepared to satisfy the demand for a sacrifice immediately, with the promptness of a waiter, but was unable to bring it off because he could not get away, being indispensable'. Franz Kafka, *Parables and Paradoxes* (New York: Schocken, 1974), 41.

17 Jon D. Levenson, *Inheriting Abraham: The Legacy of the Patriarch in Judaism, Christianity, and Islam* (Princeton, NJ: Princeton University Press, 2012), 78.

18 Brown, *Tradition and Imagination*, 219.

19 According to Jacques Derrida, 'We share with Abraham what cannot be shared, a secret we know nothing about, neither him nor us … What is a secret', he asks cryptically, 'that is a secret about nothing and a sharing that doesn't share anything?' Jacques Derrida, *The Gift of Death*, trans. David Wills (Chicago, IL: University of Chicago Press, 1995), 80.

20 B. Sanhedrin 89b; cf. Jubilees 17.15–18.

21 Shalom Spiegel, *The Last Trial: On the Legends and Lore of the Command to Abraham to Offer Isaac as a Sacrifice*, trans. Judah Goldin (Woodstock, VT: Jewish Lights Publishing, 2007), 104–5.

22 Brown, *Tradition and Imagination*, 246.

23 Spiegel, *The Last Trial*, 5–6.

24 Ibid., 33; emphasis original. According to a poem by Rabbi Ephraim of Bonn, written in the Middle Ages, Isaac was even slain twice! 'Down upon him fell the resurrecting dew, and he revived. / (The father) seized him (then) to slaughter him once more. / Scripture, bear witness! Well-grounded is the fact: / And the Lord called

Abraham, even a second time from heaven. / The ministering angels cried out, terrified: / Even animal victims, were they ever slaughtered twice?' Spiegel, *The Last Trial*, 148-9.

25 Brown, *Tradition and Imagination*, 240.

26 The rabbis concluded he was either 26 or 37, while Flavius Josephus calculated his age at 25. Levenson, *Inheriting Abraham*, 96.

27 Brown, *Tradition and Imagination*, 251.

28 In fact, Paul uses the same Greek verb that the Septuagint uses for 'withhold' in Genesis 22. Jon D. Levenson, *The Death and Resurrection of the Beloved Son: The Transformation of Child Sacrifice in Judaism and Christianity* (New Haven, CT: Yale University Press, 1993), 222. In a sense, God might be said to be following in the footsteps of his faithful servant Abraham. Levenson, *Death and Resurrection*, 222.

29 Brown, *Tradition and Imagination*, 243.

30 Jeffrey Siker, *Disinheriting the Jews: Abraham in Early Christian Controversy* (Louisville, KY: Westminster/John Knox Press, 1991), 95.

31 Brown, *Tradition and Imagination*, 234.

32 Saint Augustine, *Concerning the City of God against the Pagans*, trans. Henry Bettenson (London: Penguin, 2003), 694 (Part II, Book XVI, Chapter 32).

33 Augustine, 695 (Part II, Book XVI, Chapter 32).

34 Ironically, Christianity thus revives an ancient Jewish connection between the *Akedah* and Passover, which today has all but faded. Levenson, *Death and Resurrection*, 198; cf. Levenson, *Inheriting Abraham*, 91-3.

35 Erich Auerbach, *Mimesis: The Representation of Reality in Western Literature*, trans. Willard Trask (Princeton, NJ: Princeton University Press, 2003), 11.

36 *The Glorious Koran*, trans. Marmaduke Pickthall (London: Everyman's Library, 1992).

37 Reuven Firestone, *Journeys in Holy Lands: The Evolution of the Abraham-Ishmael Legends in Islamic Exegesis* (Albany, NY: State University of New York Press, 1990), 144-51.

38 Ibid., 135.

39 Ibid., 111-15.

40 Meyer Schapiro, *Late Antique, Early Christian and Mediaeval Art: Selected Papers* (New York: George Braziller, 1979), 289-95.

41 Ibid., 305-7.

42 Brown, *Tradition and Imagination*, 256-7.

43 Ibid.

44 Ibid., 258.

45 Ibid.

46 The traditional supplication for the person sounding the shofar is: 'O, do Thou regard the ashes of Father Isaac heaped up on top of the altar, and deal with Thy children in accordance with the Mercy Attribute.' Spiegel, *The Last Trial*, 38.

47 Spiegel, *The Last Trial*, 148.

48 Her shrieks have also been likened to the blowing of the shofar. Lev. R. 20.2 cited in Spiegel, *The Last Trial*, 75.

49 Yael Feldman, *Glory and Agony: Isaac's Sacrifice and National Narrative* (Stanford, CA: Stanford University Press, 2010), 20.

50 This trend itself built on a protest tradition dating back at least to the First World War. See: Wilfred Owen, 'The Parable of the Old Man and the Young', *The Collected Poems of Wilfred Owen* (New York: New Directions, 1965), 42.

51 For an examination of the *Akedah* in Israeli cinema, see Anat Zanger, 'Hole in the Moon or Zionism and the Binding (Ha-Ak'eda) Myth in Israeli Cinema', *Shofar: An Interdisciplinary Journal of Jewish Studies* 22.1 (2003), 95-109.

52 Yehuda Amichai, 'The Real Hero', *The Selected Poetry of Yehuda Amichai*, trans.

Chana Bloch and Stephen Mitchell (Berkeley, CA: University of California Press, 2013), 156.

53 Gannit Ankori, *Palestinian Art* (London: Reaktion Books, 2006), 60–1.

54 Yitzhak Laor, 'This Idiot, Isaac'; quoted in Feldman, *Glory and Agony*, 278.

55 Derrida, *The Gift of Death*, 76.

56 Alice Miller, *The Untouched Key: Tracing Childhood Trauma in Creativity and Destructiveness*, trans. Hildegarde Hunter Hannum (New York: Doubleday, 1991), 137.

57 Søren Kierkegaard, *Fear and Trembling*, trans. Sylvia Walsh (Cambridge: Cambridge University Press, 2008), 39.

58 Philippe-Alain Michaud, 'Funambule', *Adel Abdessemed*, trans. Deke Dusinberre (Paris: Manuella Editions, 2016), n.p.

59 Abdessemed and Hélène Cixous return several times in their correspondence to the imagery of Abraham's sacrifice, which becomes a metaphor for multiple instantiations of internecine struggle. In a letter from 30 April 2013, Abdessemed intertwines a story of family squabbles in Algeria with the story of Abraham and Isaac, grafting together religious and genetic origin stories. 'I was born twins with a grapevine', he writes. 'I saw my father and his half brother fight about sharing space between them … They decided to build a separation wall … and it was the vine that suffered … ripped out … truncated … cut … unearthed … uprooted … dismembered … killed … In reality and in the imagination it was her or me … only one of us would survive the argument … a sort of sacrifice of Isaac. I see the disappearance of that vine as an essential link … It is a dark image … that has remained imprinted.' Hélène Cixous, *Insurrection de la poussiere: Adel Abdessemed*, trans. Eric Prenowitz (Paris: Galilée, 2014), n.p.

60 *Adel Abdessemed Conversation with Pier Luigi Tazzi* (Arles: Actes Sud, 2012), 9.

61 A version of this paragraph appears in Aaron Rosen, 'The Sacrifices of Adel Abdessemed', *Adel Abdessemed: Bristow*, ed. Hans Ulrich Obrist, Hannah Barry and Donatien Grau (London: Bold Tendencies, 2017), 142. There I set the work alongside Abdessemed's *Décor* (2011–12), an homage to Matthias Grünewald's *Isenheim Altarpiece* (c.1515) fashioned out of razor wire.

62 Brown, *Tradition and Imagination*, 257.

63 Ibid., 258.

64 Levenson makes a related point. 'Radically transformed but never uprooted', he writes, 'the sacrifice of the first-born son constitutes a strange and usually overlooked bond between Judaism and Christianity and thus a major but unexplored focus for Jewish-Christian dialogue.' Levenson, *Death and Resurrection*, x.

65 There are also numerous local initiatives around the world named after Abraham. Just in the United States, for instance, there is the Daughters of Abraham reading group in Massachusetts, the Abraham House Interfaith Build in Texas, which works with Habitat for Humanity, and Abraham's Tent in Illinois, which brings groups together for interfaith dinner parties. In New Haven, Connecticut, where I first began thinking about the figure of Abraham in art, I met volunteers who worked on their own initiative named Abraham's Tent, in which local congregations collaborate to provide food and shelter to the homeless for a week.

7

'Surely the Lord is in this Place': Jacob's Ladder in Painting, Contemporary Sculpture and Installation Art

CHRISTOPHER R. BREWER

In the final chapter of *Tradition and Imagination* ('Art as Revelation'), David Brown argues that for the bulk of Christian history, the primary experience of faith has been visual, and that

> artists, like expositors of the word, operated within a tradition of interpretation ... one that was no less 'a moving text': a gradually changing content, whose images had the latent power radically to reshape the nature of the faith they were expounding.[1]

Innovative and potentially revelatory, art has, according to Brown, 'the capacity to transmit the biblical story in ways which at times could speak more powerfully to contemporaries than the original deposit'.[2] Genesis 28.10–17, and more specifically the *sullam* (aka 'ladder', 'stairway') of verse 12, is, I suggest, a case in point.[3]

Jacob's dream (Gen. 28.12–13) has been variously depicted, the earliest known example being a third-century wall painting on the north wall of the synagogue at Dura-Europos in present-day Syria.[4] A second example comes from the fourth century and is located in the Via Latina Catacomb near Rome.[5] Both frescoes opt for a ladder, and while many commentators are keen to point this out as a mistake, doing so obscures the fact that the Hebrew word *sullam* is a *hapax legomenon* with multiple possible meanings.[6] Standard glosses include 'ladder' (BDB, BDAG for LXX) or 'flight of stairs' (BDAG for LXX), but Yitzhak (Itzik) Peleg suggests a wider range of meanings, including 'a ramp, a ziggurat, a mountain, a rope or roots of a cosmic tree, or even a ray of the sun (Egypt)'.[7] This may well explain why artistic examples are so varied, with examples covering a broad semantic range. In addition to this semantic concern (i.e. 'past text'), there is however, according to Brown, the question of meaning and significance for contemporary believers (i.e. 'current reality').[8] This question, I will argue, has as much to do with metaphysics as it does with semantics.

Wishing to affirm Brown's emphasis on the power of art to in some cases transmit the biblical story more effectively than the original deposit, I will argue that we must go further still, and by this I mean not only that we must turn our attention to art but that we should, as Terry Smith suggests, 'profess *contemporary* art', 'questioning it for its questions'.[9] That said, as the Brooklyn-based artist Alfonse Borysewicz has suggested:

> [T]here is an unfortunate fog in religious circles concerning contemporary art. Though the art world has no doubt contributed to the problem, in much of the church there is what Louis Bouyer in his classic book *Liturgical Piety* calls 'archeologism.' This attitude rejects contemporary art – and ultimately, contemporary experience – in favour of the artificial restoration of the religious imagery of the past. Archeologism says, if it's not an icon, if it hasn't acquired the patina of age, it's not art and doesn't belong in our sacred space. 'Nothing could be more of an abortion,' writes Bouyer, 'dead at the very moment of its birth, than this soulless and uninspired false Byzantinism.'[10]

In response, Borysewicz concludes: 'Indeed, we as the church must have minds and hearts open to the work of living artists around us. This is necessary for the sake of the young, who are desperately searching for fresh images.'[11]

I will argue, with reference to Jacob's ladder, that contemporary sculpture and installation art are among the most effective – and yet most often neglected[12] – media for getting at contemporary meaning and significance. Add to this that the most successful examples are by those individuals to whom Brown refers in one essay as 'pagans', for these artists are not concerned with – nor burdened by – the need to depict the text. As Brown has noted:

> The twentieth century is often described as a time of loss of faith and in many ways that is true, but a surprising number of artists continued to engage actively with the Christian faith in their art. The natural tendency of Christians has been to focus on those who are explicit believers ... but to do so exclusively would be merely to repeat the mistake against which I have been protesting. God does not just speak through the like-minded.[13]

Put simply: I mean to focus on *contemporary* art, and more specifically, contemporary sculpture and installation art, by artists beyond the confines of the Christian Church. In order to do so, however, I must begin with traditional, literal depictions, and this to establish what I refer to as the ladder-to-heaven motif. With this motif in place, examples standing at a remove from the original deposit can then be recognized as drawing on more literal, traditional depictions and contributing to 'the moving text'. In keeping with Brown's concerns, however, I seek to 'wrestle with possible meanings for today'.[14] Central to this discussion is Brown's call for 'a different criterion of truth ... one more directly related to the operation of the imagination: the truth of imaginative "fit" rather than literal fact'.[15] I argue that depictions of Jacob's ladder as well as the ladder-to-heaven motif not only explore semantic possibilities more effectively but more fundamentally raise the metaphysical question – that is, ultimate transcendence, aka God – in ways more engaging than Scripture itself. Put simply, these depictions say with Jacob, 'Surely the Lord is in this place' (Gen. 28.16).

Jacob's Ladder in Painting, Contemporary Sculpture and Installation Art

Genesis 28.12–13 describes a dream with three elements: 1) a ladder or stairway reaching from earth to heaven; 2) the angels of God ascending and descending; and 3) the Lord above it. Depictions of this scene may or may not include all, or in some cases any of these three elements.[16] Some examples are more or less literal, others have little to nothing to do with the narrative but nevertheless adopt its imagery to make various related points. Still others adopt the imagery to make points that are, to some degree, 'secular'. These examples sometimes also adopt the title, imagery or in some cases both, all the while distancing themselves from the narrative. Others make no explicit reference to the narrative but clearly draw on the imagery. Some examples adopt the title but not the imagery.

All of this makes things difficult for the biblical scholar or theologian seeking to follow 'the moving text' (i.e. the interpretative canon). In fact the scholar's default preference for the illustrative may well be the result of difficulty identifying examples of the more general motif rather than some underlying theological or philosophical commitment. If so (and perhaps even if not), this non-comprehensive taxonomy will be useful. I have organized artistic examples of Jacob's ladder into four types: 1) Literal; 2) Metaphorical; 3) Allegorical; and 4) Secular.[17] The first type will for the most part include examples that depict the past text, with scholarly discussion focusing on how many of the three textual elements are present, what form they take (e.g. ladder or staircase) as well as the degree of artistic innovation. Discussion of the second type will focus almost entirely on current reality with, for example, Saint Romuald standing in for Jacob and monks for the angels. While these examples may seem less relevant with reference to 'past text' and/or our 'current reality',[18] treating the text as representative emphasizes 'imaginative rewriting' that may well expose and highlight what Brown refers to as 'open trajectories ... pressure points that almost demand further development'.[19] The same could be said for depictions of the third type, though the emphasis in these cases rests on the moral (rather than the post-textual historical, e.g. the dream of Saint Romuald). Images of this sort seem further from the 'past text' insofar as they move beyond one-to-one correspondence. Finally, there are a number of artworks that allude to or reference the narrative but from what might be called a 'secular' perspective. No less important, and perhaps even more so in terms of 'current reality', these examples are consistent with Brown's emphasis on looking to the margins and learning from pagans. While these artworks could be judged along the same lines as Type 1 examples, Type 4 examples are not driven by a desire to depict but instead to engage viewers, and so explore contemporary and often metaphysical concerns more explicitly.[20] I begin with literal ladders.

Type 1: Literal

In addition to the third- and fourth-century frescoes referenced above, Raphael's sixteenth-century frescoes (Palazzi Vaticani, Rome) are prime examples of this type. The first is on the ceiling of the *Stanza di Eliodoro* (*c.*1508–9), and the second is in the sixth arcade of the loggia (1518).[21] Focusing upon the latter, *sullam*, angels and Lord are present, and the *sullam* takes the form of a single stairway. While a recent commentator has suggested that 'no doubt accidentally, Raphael manages to capture something of the *original* intent (a stairway)',[22] I see no reason to think Raphael's choice accidental. As Brown points out, while 'there is perhaps a natural temptation to suppose that artists are mere amateurs in theology compared to preachers and professional theologians', several factors 'pull in the other direction', namely input from their – often clerical – patrons, traditions of representation as well as the artist's own reflective capacities.[23] Worth noting is that Raphael connects rock and cloud, reinforcing the connection between heaven and earth established by the stairway. The scene suggests a mountain on which God rests, and so even in choosing a staircase, Raphael acknowledges the closely related symbol of the mountain and so suggests more.

Influenced by Raphael, Giorgio Vasari painted *Jacob's Dream* (1558).[24] Again, all three elements are present, and though Jacob's position and posture are similar to those in Raphael's loggia fresco, the simple staircase has now become an elaborate Renaissance-style double staircase. The angels are more numerous and the Lord hovers above Jacob rather than the top of the staircase. Perhaps Vasari was aware that the preposition *al* in verse 13, traditionally translated 'above it', might also be rendered 'upon it',[25] not to mention 'beside him' (NRSV) or even 'poised over him'.[26] This depiction suggests that semantic concerns in visual art reach beyond the word *sullam*, inching closer to metaphysical concerns while remaining firmly rooted in the semantic. The Lord may well be in this place, but where, more precisely?

Other notable examples of this type include paintings by Ludovico Carracci (sixteenth century), Tintoretto (1577–78),[27] Ludovico Cigoli (1593),[28] Domenico Feti (1616),[29] José de Ribera (1639),[30] Ferdinand Bol (1642),[31] Salvator Rosa (1665),[32] Murillo (c.1670),[33] Joseph Goupy (after Rosa, c.1720),[34] William Blake (1799–1806),[35] Washington Allston (1817),[36] Evelyn Dunbar (1960)[37] and Marc Chagall (1966).[38] In addition to paintings, there are a number of Type 1 illuminations, woodcut prints and etchings, including those found in the Lambeth Bible,[39] the Egerton Genesis (fourteenth century),[40] the Nuremberg Chronicle and the Luther Bible, not to mention Rembrandt.[41] Particularly interesting are two seventeenth-century etchings, the first by Matthäus Merian, the second by his apprentice Wenceslaus Hollar. In both etchings the textual 'YHWH' stands in place of a visual depiction of the Lord.[42] The image is, in this regard, similar to Hollar's etching of Abraham's dream (Gen. 15.5), as well as a much later etching by Chagall.[43] Also worth noting is that Jacob here sleeps under a tree and, like Raphael, who blurred the line between stairway and mountain, both Merian and Hollar blur the line between ladder and tree.

The earliest example of Jacob's ladder in sculpture of which I am aware is located on the west front of Bath Abbey. Seemingly flat against a plumb stone surface, these architectural reliefs (c.1520) are frozen in gothic time and do little, from my perspective, to invite imagined ascent. That said, all three elements are present and, as part of the gothic abbey, draw the viewer upward. A more interesting example is *Staircase* (1980) by Ezra Orion (b. 1934), an Israeli artist best known for his earthworks.[44] Made of reinforced concrete, the work is 18 metres tall, includes no angels or Lord and stands at the entrance to Givat Mordechai, a neighbourhood in southwest-central Jerusalem.[45] An earlier work – *Endless Ladder* (1979) – also draws on the motif but is, to my mind, less compelling.[46]

To summarize: Type 1 depictions wrestle with various semantic concerns, including how best to visualize *sullam* and also where to place the Lord (if he appears at all). Priority is, in some works, given to Jacob, but in others to the angels or their Lord. Even literal depictions of Jacob's ladder vary.

Type 2: Metaphorical

While rooted in the literal, depictions of this type focus on analogical or symbolic relationships. A prime example of this type is *The Dream of Saint Romuald*. Romuald (*c*.950–1027), who was the founder of the Camaldolese order, built a new hermitage and monastery at Camaldoli (*c*.1012) as the result of a vision of Jacob's ladder.[47] In a mid-fifteenth-century example attributed to Belbello da Pavia,[48] Romuald takes the place of Jacob at the ladder's base, and is sleeping surrounded by monks. Directly above Romuald a ladder extends to the heavens. The Lord sits on the ladder, and beneath him three angels ascend/descend. Contrast this first example with Attavante's illumination (1452–*c*.1525), in which the ladder is replaced by a staircase and, more importantly, there are no angels but instead monks ascending.[49] Attavante's illumination differs from the lower-right panel of Nardo di Cione's fourteenth-century *Trinity, with SS Romuald and John the Evangelist*, in which the monks ascend a ladder rather than a staircase, but in both examples humans rather than angels ascend. Depictions of this sort visually break the metaphysical barrier, with humans rather than angels ascending to heaven.

A second example of this type is the inviolate mountain icon in which Mary is – in the words of the *Akathist* hymn – 'the heavenly Ladder whereby God came down'.[50] The Virgin – who is also the inviolate mountain and whose throne, in some examples, has sprouted shoots – is depicted holding the Son in her left arm, and in her right hand a small version of Jacob's ladder that points to Christ, drawing on John 1.51. While some might think examples of this type insignificant with reference to Genesis 28.12–13, they demonstrate a willingness to reimagine the text in ways that clearly depart from its assumed historical context but nevertheless emphasize presence and *access*. This is indeed significant. While semantic decisions are still evident, the metaphysical has come to the fore, with Mary, monks and, by extension, perhaps also the viewer climbing the ladder or staircase to heaven. For a more recent example of this type in sculpture (with reference to the Holocaust), see Ales Vesely, *Gate of Infinity* (2015, Praha Bubny Railway Station, Prague, Czech Republic). In some ways similar to the metaphorical is the allegorical, and it is to this type that I now turn.

Type 3: Allegorical

Leaving the literal behind, the allegorical adopts and adapts the imagery – ladder, angels and Lord – for a different purpose. Highlighting morality, the emphasis here shifts from divine presence to spiritual progress. A representative example of this type is the ladder icon, which has its roots in the seventh century; more specifically, *The Ladder of Divine Ascent* (St Catherine's Monastery, Sinai), a visual work inextricably tied to *The Ladder of Divine Ascent* by Saint John Climacus.[51] There are numerous examples of the ladder icon. In addition to *The Ladder of Divine Ascent* we might consider three ladder icons from the collection of the Museum of Russian Icons in Clinton, Massachusetts. Regarding these icons, Raoul N. Smith notes:

> The Museum's three icons follow traditional iconography for Ladder icons – the ladder (with a variety of number of rungs), Saint John holding a scroll, Christ welcoming successful climbers into Paradise, personages climbing the ladder, some falling or being pulled down, and the jaws of hell open to receive falling climbers.[52]

These icons are, then, clearly related to Genesis 28.12–13, including a ladder, and also the Lord above. The chief difference is that human beings rather than angels ascend the ladder. There has, again, been a shift from presence to progress, and in the case of the latter, it seems imaginatively fitting that human beings ascend the ladder.

Type 4: Secular

Acknowledging that 'secular' is a difficult word,[53] I am using it to mean something like what Jane Dillenberger meant when she spoke of 'Secular Art with Sacred Themes'.[54] The point is that the artist need not be a Christian, nor the work explicitly or even intentionally religious, to be considered as part and parcel of 'the moving text'. As Brown notes: 'All creation, however odd, is his, as is all human creativity, whether explicitly Christian or not.'[55] Brown thus advocates a 'readiness to listen even where [God] seems most distant',[56] and elsewhere suggests that

> art can of course illustrate faith but to insist that this is its only appropriate role is to belittle its achievements. Whether there are specific allusions to Christianity or not, it can offer a religious vision that we need to take seriously and engage with.[57]

I will here focus on three examples from contemporary sculpture and installation art: Martin Puryear's *Ladder for Booker T. Washington* (1996, hereafter *LBTW*),[58] Jonathan Borofsky's *Walking to the Sky* (2005, 2006 and 2008, hereafter *WS*) and Kader Attia's *Continuum of Repair: The Light of Jacob's Ladder* (2013–14).

Martin Puryear (b. 1941) is an American artist who works primarily in wood, and *LBTW* is consistent with this sensibility. The ladder's vertical rails are made from a sapling that came from the property behind his studio. The choice here to use not only wood but a sapling reinforces the connection between ladder and tree as symbol.[59] The work is approximately 11 metres tall, 57.785 centimetres wide at the base, narrowing to 3.175 centimetres wide at the top. Initially one might think of 'ambition, ascension, and ultimately transcendence, a ladder can symbolize our desire to separate ourselves from the physical world'.[60] But as Margo A. Crutchfield notes: 'The ladder can – perhaps with difficulty – be climbed, but ultimately access to the top is denied. There is, however, no simple reading of this object, and any number of differing interpretations are possible.'[61] Like Georgia O'Keeffe's painting, *Ladder to the Moon* (1958),[62] *LBTW* floats in mid-air, and yet unlike O'Keeffe's *Ladder*, *LBTW*'s rungs are within reach, and so suggest if not the possibility of ascent, then at the very least – via the gap – otherness and excess.[63]

In any case, Puryear's *Ladder* makes no explicit reference to Genesis 28.12–13, and yet as Crutchfield notes: 'The ladder is rich with associations. It often refers to ambition, and in many cultures it is a symbol of ascension, or in more spiritual terms, transcendence, from the mortal to the celestial realms.'[64] From this I conclude that a piece need not make explicit reference to the narrative but can, instead, rely on the power of the symbol in which both narrative and artwork have their genesis. Related to this is that the artwork need not include all three elements (i.e. ladder/stairway, angels ascending/descending, and the Lord above), but can, via this central symbol (i.e. the ladder), evoke the narrative as part of the ongoing pattern of development.

Going further, some examples omit ladder/stairway, angels ascending/descending and Lord above. And yet they still effectively, even if unwittingly, evoke the narrative. Here I am thinking of Borofsky's *Walking to the Sky*, a 30.5 metre tall pole set on a 75 degree angle with ten life-size human figures.[65] It has been noted with reference to this series that 'Borofsky was fascinated by the philosophical title of a Paul Gauguin painting, "Where Do We Come From? What Are We? Where Are We Going?"'[66] In fact Borofsky has suggested: 'Maybe the sculpture represents every one of us being involved in the same question, in the deepest sense.'[67] And yet as Samantha Baskind observes:

> Borofsky's engagement in projects that relate to his Jewish background do not emerge from a religious perspective. As the artist explains: 'I'm not a fan of any organized religion that separates itself out from other religions or peoples ...' In answer to the question 'What, if anything, do you consider Jewish about your art?' Borofsky again provides a universalist response: 'Nothing, and everything' ([Email correspondence]).[68]

Borofsky's response might be taken as the motto for this type. What does this artwork have to do with the text? Nothing, and everything. Less concerned with the details of a text, this work transposes the central metaphysical concern – presence, and related to this, access; that is, transcendence in immanence – into a contemporary context. Recall Brown's suggestion that art may, in some cases, transmit the biblical story more effectively than the original deposit. Borofsky's *WS* is, I suggest, a choice example of this phenomenon, one that raises not only semantic but also metaphysical questions, and both of these with an eye on significance.

Unlike these first two examples, my third example makes explicit reference to Jacob's ladder, but its use of the narrative in relation to the concept of 'repair' is thoroughly secular.[69] Even so, I think this artwork is the most successful of the lot. Kader Attia (b. 1970) is a French Algerian artist whose work I saw at Whitechapel Gallery in September 2014. *Continuum of Repair: The Light of Jacob's Ladder* (2013-14)

> gives us a glimpse of infinity. He revisits the story of Jacob's Ladder describing the prophet's vision of angels ascending from earth to heaven. A towering floor to ceiling structure fills the lofty spaces of the Gallery as a cabinet of curiosities, artefacts and books ... The installation is the latest chapter in Kader Attia's research into the concept of repair, which he sees as an underlying principle of development and evolution in both culture and nature.[70]

Walking into Gallery 2, I saw metal bookcases piled high with books, and through the spaces between the shelves an inner sanctum of sorts in which a large cabinet sat. Walking around the bookcases to the rear of the Gallery where there was an opening between two bookcases through which one can gain access to the inner sanctum, I noticed all manner of books. Upon entering the inner space I began looking at the various artefacts in the cabinet, and then after several minutes walked around to the steps. I had read that 'you eventually come across a real ladder that takes you up above the ground. And there you will see a very simple and beautiful vision of infinity.'[71] I climbed the stairs, still sceptical, and reaching the top, saw a mirror laid flat on top of the cabinet and, on the mirror, a fluorescent tube. At that moment I thought my trip had been for naught, and then I saw it. Above the mirror on top of the cabinet was an identical, opposing mirror suspended from the ceiling, and the mirrors, working in tandem, reflected the image of the fluorescent tube into infinity. Brown speaks – with reference to narrative painting – of 'the scene being placed at such an angle to compel some sense of personal presence, and so, when narrative is involved, the effect is to make the viewer one of the participants in the story'.[72] The same could be said of Attia's installation, and this is significant, for as Brown notes, 'the external and internal presentation of the painting [or, in this case, installation] can themselves invite the participation of the viewer and so compel a more contemporary version of what may have happened and its significance'.[73] Brown provides additional clarification in a footnote:

> 'External' in the sense of where and how the painting is hung; 'internal', in the sense of the angle of vision set by the painter by which he tries to draw us within the frame, or the gaze of some of the participants designed to effect the same purpose.[74]

It is in this sense that I think sculpture and installation art potentially more effective than 2D media in conveying contemporary meaning and significance for they, quite literally, invite participation by placing the viewer within the scene. In that moment beneath the infinitely reflected fluorescent tube, I was Jacob, it was my vision, and God was surely in that place. Past text had become current reality.[75]

'It is not possible', says Claus Westermann, 'to form a precise image of what Jacob saw in his dream.'[76] That may well be so, but if Brown is right, then the *sullam* is perhaps less important than its *significance*, and this has been imaginatively mediated through a succession of new images. And what is this significance? First, that Beth-el (Gen. 28.19) was, and these various artworks can be, a point of contact, what the sociologist Peter Berger called a 'signal of transcendence'. We can be drawn through the material beyond our reality (transcendence), and the divine also invades the material order (immanence).[77] With Jacob, we say: 'Surely the LORD is in this place, and I was not aware of it' (Gen. 28.16b NIV). Going further, Brown argues that we are not only drawn or 'pulled into the unknown beyond', but also strain, and that 'we should welcome those human strainings, for, if nothing else, they at least represent the realization that there might be more to this world than what first meets the eye'.[78] Self-transcendence precedes ultimate transcendence. There are, in other words, varieties of transcendence.[79] In any case, as Thomas L. Broadie concludes, Genesis 28.12-13 'suggests some form of breakthrough'.[80] For Brown, though, the 'scene' extends beyond Scripture, the dialogue continues and this is because 'heaven and earth are linked, made sacramentally one by realization of the divine presence here on earth'.[81]

Notes

1 David Brown, *Tradition and Imagination: Revelation and Change* (Oxford: Oxford University Press, 1999), 323. See also David Brown, 'Revelation through Art', in *Where Shall We Find God? Lincoln Lectures in Theology 1997* (Lincoln Cathedral: Lincoln Cathedral Publications, 1998), 41–51.

2 Brown, *Tradition and Imagination*, 324. William Desmond explains development along these lines in terms of what he calls '"open" wholeness', writing: 'The art work exhibits a certain wholeness, but if we attend to this we find there is a kind of compacted fullness which seems to be inexhaustible in terms of finite analysis. For this compacted fullness of the art work is not just a recollective gathering up of the past. It is also a kind of implicit spanning of the future. The art work is always a promise of repeated reinterpretations, repeated resurrections.' William Desmond, *Art and the Absolute: A Study of Hegel's Aesthetics*, SUNY Series in Hegelian Studies (Albany, NY: State University of New York Press, 1986), 70–1; cf. Brown, *Tradition and Imagination*, 54.

3 See also 'Ladder of Jacob', in James H. Charlesworth (ed.), *The Old Testament Pseudepigrapha: Expansions of the 'Old Testament' and Legends, Wisdom and Philosophical Literature, Prayers, Psalms and Odes, Fragments of Lost Judeo-Hellenistic Works*, vol. 2 (New Haven, CT: Yale University Press, 1983), 401–11. For a survey of approaches to the narrative, including some discussion of the aforementioned pseudepigraphical text, see James L. Kugel, *The Ladder of Jacob: Ancient Interpretations of the Biblical Story of Jacob and His Children* (Princeton, NJ: Princeton University Press, 2006), 9–35.

4 For illustration and discussion, see Kurt Weitzmann and Herbert L. Kessler, *The Frescoes of the Dura Synagogue and Christian Art* (Washington, DC: Dumbarton Oaks Research Library and Collection, 1990), Fig. 10 (illustration), 17–21 (discussion). For a more recent, general discussion, see Michael Peppard, *The World's Oldest Church: Bible, Art, and Ritual at Dura-Europos, Syria* (New Haven, CT and London: Yale University Press, 2016).

5 For illustration, see William Tronzo, *The Via Latina Catacomb: Imitation and Discontinuity in Fourth-Century Roman Painting* (University Park, PA and London: Pennsylvania State University Press, 1986), Fig. 37.

6 For the classic discussion, see C. Houtman, 'What Did Jacob See in his Dream at Bethel?', *Vetus Testamentum* 27.3 (1977), 337–51.

7 Yitzhak (Itzik) Peleg, 'What Do Jacob's Ladder, the Tower of Babel, and the Babylonian Ziggurat Have in Common?', in *Bethsaida in Archaeology, History and Ancient Culture: A Festschrift in Honor of John T. Greene*, ed. J. Harold Ellens (Newcastle upon Tyne: Cambridge Scholars, 2014), 342. See also Yitzhak (Itzik) Peleg, *Going Up and Going Down: A Key to Interpreting Jacob's Dream (Genesis 28:10–22)*, trans. Betty Rozen (London and New York: Bloomsbury, 2015), 88–100.

8 David Brown, *God in a Single Vision: Integrating Philosophy and Theology*, ed. Christopher R. Brewer and Robert MacSwain (London and New York: Routledge, 2016), 77.

9 Terry Smith, *What is Contemporary Art?* (Chicago, IL: University of Chicago Press, 2009), xi; emphasis added.

10 Alfonse Borysewicz, 'Naked Grace', *Image* 32 (2001), 28. Borysewicz is quoting from Louis Bouyer, *Liturgical Piety*, Liturgical Studies (Notre Dame, IN: University of Notre Dame Press, 1954), 20.

11 Borysewicz, 'Naked Grace', 28.

12 For a notable exception in religion/arts more generally, see Jeffery L. Kosky, *Arts of Wonder: Enchanting Secularity – Walter DeMaria, Diller + Scofidio, James Turrell, Andy Goldsworthy* (Chicago, IL: University of Chicago Press, 2013).

13 David Brown, 'The Glory of God Revealed in Art and Music: Learning from Pagans', in *Celebrating Creation: Affirming Catholicism and the Revelation of God's*

Glory, ed. Mark Chapman (London: Darton, Longman & Todd, 2004), 47–8; republished as 'Learning from Pagans', in David Brown, *Divine Generosity and Human Creativity: Theology through Symbol, Painting and Architecture*, ed. Christopher R. Brewer and Robert MacSwain (London and New York: Routledge, 2017), 40–1.

14 Brown, *God in a Single Vision*, ed. Brewer and MacSwain, 82. Following Paul M. Joyce and Diana Lipton, Brown prefers the nomenclature 'reception exegesis' to 'reception history'. Ibid., 81–3.

15 Brown, *Tradition and Imagination*, 7. See also David Brown, *Discipleship and Imagination: Christian Tradition and Truth* (Oxford: Oxford University Press, 2000), 343–406; esp. 373–84.

16 See Peter and Linda Murray and Tom Devonshire Jones (eds), *The Oxford Dictionary of Christian Art and Architecture*, 2nd edn (Oxford: Oxford University Press, 2013), s.v. 'Ladder'; Leslie Ross, in *Medieval Art: A Topical Dictionary* (Westport, CT and London: Greenwood, 1996), s.v. 'Jacob's Ladder'; and in Paul Corby Finney (ed.), *The Eerdmans Encyclopedia of Early Christian Art and Archaeology*, vol. 1 (Grand Rapids, MI: Eerdmans, 2017), s.v. 'Jacob'.

17 Additional taxonomies from Paul Tillich to James Elkins can be referenced. For discussion of Tillich's taxonomies, see John Dillenberger, 'Introduction', in Paul Tillich, *On Art and Architecture*, ed. John Dillenberger and Jane Dillenberger (New York: Crossroad, 1987), xxii–xxv. For Elkins's: James Elkins, *On the Strange Place of Religion in Contemporary Art* (London and New York: Routledge, 2004), esp. 47.

18 Brown, *God in a Single Vision*, ed. Brewer and MacSwain, 77.

19 Brown, *Tradition and Imagination*, 5, 54.

20 For additional discussion, see Brown, *Divine Generosity and Human Creativity*, ed. Brewer and MacSwain, 16–17.

21 For illustration of the first, see Konrad Oberhuber, *Raphael: The Paintings* (Munich, London and New York: Prestel Verlag, 1999), 122; and for the second, Nicole Dacos, *The Loggia of Raphael: A Vatican Art Treasure*, trans. Josephine Bacon (New York and London: Abbeville, 2008), 160.

22 Iain Provan, *Discovering Genesis: Content, Interpretation, Reception* (Grand Rapids, MI: Eerdmans, 2016), 162.

23 Brown, *Divine Generosity and Human Creativity*, ed. Brewer and MacSwain, 101; cf. Brown, *Tradition and Imagination*, 324–5.

24 For illustration, see online: http://art.thewalters.org/detail/17863/jacobs-dream; accessed 26 December 2016. Vasari mentions Raphael's painting in *The Lives of Artists*, trans. Julia Conaway Bondanella (Oxford: Oxford University Press, 1991), 322.

25 For discussion, see Bruce K. Waltke, *Genesis: A Commentary* (Grand Rapids, MI: Zondervan, 2001), 390.

26 Robert Alter, *The Five Books of Moses: A Translation with Commentary* (New York and London: W. W. Norton, 2004), 149. For additional discussion, ibid., 149, n. 13.

27 For illustration, see online: www.wikiart.org/en/tintoretto/jacob-s-ladder-1578; accessed 26 December 2016.

28 For illustration and discussion (in relation to various studies), see Ann H. Sievers et al., *Master Drawings from the Smith College Museum of Art* (New York: Hudson Hills, 2000), 52–6.

29 For illustration, see *The Bible in Art: Miniatures, Paintings, Drawings and Sculptures Inspired by the Old Testament* (London: Phaidon, 1956), Plate 57 (black and white).

30 For illustration, see ibid., Plate 59 (black and white); for full-colour, online: www.museodelprado.es/en/the-collection/art-work/jacobs-dream/c84dbc72-af49-4a7c-88df-a66046bc88cd; accessed 14 January 2017.

31 For illustration, see online: https://commons.wikimedia.org/wiki/File:Ferdinand_Bol_-_Jacob's_Dream_-_WGA02362.jpg; accessed 14 January 2017.

32 For illustration, see online: https://commons.wikimedia.org/wiki/File:Salvator_Rosa,_Jacob's_Dream,_c._1665,_oil_on_canvas.jpg; accessed 14 January 2017.

33 For illustration, see *The Bible in Art*, Plate 60 (black and white).

34 For illustration, see online: www.clevelandart.org/art/1970.362; accessed 14 January 2017.

35 For illustration, see online: www.bmimages.com/preview.asp?image=00133517001&imagex=2&searchnum=0002; accessed 26 December 2016.

36 For illustration, see William H. Gerdts and Theodore E. Stebbins, Jr, '*A Man of Genius': The Art of Washington Allston (1779–1843)* (Boston, MA: Museum of Fine Arts Boston, 1979), 190 (black and white); for full-colour, see online: www.artuk.org/discover/artworks/jacobs-dream-219777; accessed 5 January 2017.

37 For illustration, see Sacha Llewellyn and Paul Liss (eds), *Evelyn Dunbar (1906–1960): The Lost Works* (Chichester: Pallant House Gallery, 2015), 165. Published in conjunction with the exhibition of the same name, shown at Pallant House Gallery, Chichester.

38 For illustration, see Marc Chagall, *The Biblical Message of Marc Chagall* (New York: Tudor, 1973), 44–5. For discussion, see Aaron Rosen, *Imagining Jewish Art: Encounters with the Masters in Chagall, Guston, and Kitaj*, Studies in Comparative Literature 16 (Oxford: Legenda, 2009), 21, 44–45, n. 52.

39 For illustration and discussion, see C. R. Dodwell, *The Great Lambeth Bible* (London: Faber & Faber, 1959), 20–1.

40 For illustration and discussion, see Mary Coker Joslin and Carolyn Coker Joslin Watson, *The Egerton Genesis* (Toronto and Buffalo, NY: The British Library and University of Toronto Press, 2001), Plate 105 (illustration), 109 (discussion).

41 For illustration, see Oswald Goetz, *The Rembrandt Bible: A Selection from the Master's Graphic Work* (New York: Greystone, 1941), illustration 9.

42 For illustration of the first, see Matthäus Merian, *Iconum Biblicarum* (Wenatchee, WA: AVB, 1981), 69; for the second, see online: https://commons.wikimedia.org/wiki/File:Wenceslas_Hollar_-_Jacob's_ladder_(State_2).jpg; accessed 26 December 2016.

43 For illustration, see online: https://commons.wikimedia.org/wiki/File:Wenceslas_Hollar_-_Abraham's_dream_(State_2).jpg; accessed 31 December 2016. This work is listed in Richard Pennington, *A Descriptive Catalogue of the Etched Work of Wenceslaus Hollar 1607–1677* (Cambridge: Cambridge University Press, 1982), 5.

44 For illustration, see online: http://ezraorion.org/maalot/; accessed 14 April 2018. Cf. Rachel Whiteread, *Untitled (Stairs)* (2001), *Untitled (Domestic)* (2003) and *Stairs* (2003). For illustration, see Ann Gallagher and Molly Donovan (eds), *Rachel Whiteread* (London: Tate, 2017), 128–9, 138. Whiteread has apparently 'long wanted to work with stairwells, since the time of making *House* [1993]' (ibid., 18), and this is evidenced by a number of drawings from 1995. For illustration, see ibid., 90–3. The stairs were cast from a building in Bethnal Green in London's East End, 'an old synagogue, which had been used ... as a textile warehouse' (ibid., 18) and is now Whiteread's home and studio.

45 Cf. David McCracken, *Walking to the Mainland* (2005), *Diminish and Ascend* (2013). For illustration, see online: www.gowlangsfordgallery.co.nz/artists/david-mccracken/works; accessed 16 January 2017.

46 Cf. Daniel Kafri, *Gate of Faith* (1977, Abrasha Park, Jaffa), left column. Online: http://israelpublicart.com/public_art/?art=gate_of_faith; accessed 22 January 2017.

47 For additional context, see *The Oxford Dictionary of Christian Art and Architecture*, 2nd edn, s.v. 'Romuald, Saint'; Rosa Giorgi, *Saints in Art*, ed. Stefano Zuffi, trans. Thomas Michael Hartmann (Los Angeles, CA: Getty, 2003), 321–2.

48 For illustration and discussion, see online: www.mfa.org/collections/object/the-dream-of-saint-romuald-cutting-from-an-antiphonary-or-a-gradual-49048; accessed 24 January 2017.

49 Armelle Le Gendre, in Bernard Wooding (ed.), *Illuminations from the Wildenstein Collection*, trans. David Wharry (Paris: Musée Marmottan Monet, 2010), 31.

50 Quoted in Alfredo Tradigo, *Icons and Saints of the Eastern Orthodox Church*, trans. Stephen Sartorelli (Los Angeles, CA: Getty, 2006), 202. For examples, see ibid., 202–4. An early sixteenth-century example of *The Virgin: Inviolate Mountain* from the collection of the Musée des Beaux-Arts de la Ville de Paris can be seen online, as can *Our Lady of Mount Nerukosechnaya* from the collection of the Kolomenskoe Museum, Moscow.

51 See Saint John Climacus, *The Ladder of Divine Ascent*; 'Ladder', in *The Oxford Dictionary of Christian Art and Architecture*, ed. Murray, Murray, and Jones, 123. For a contemporary example along these lines, but in fictional literature rather that iconography, see Flannery O'Connor, 'Revelation', in *The Complete Stories* (New York: Farrar, Straus & Giroux, 1971), 508–9.

52 Raoul N. Smith, 'The Ladder of Divine Ascent – A Codex and an Icon', 15. Online: www.museumofrussianicons.org/wp-content/uploads/2016/09/LadderOfDivine AscentFINAL2013Opt.pdf; accessed 28 June 2017.

53 For discussion, see Charles Taylor, *A Secular Age* (Cambridge, MA and London: Belknap, 2007), 1–4.

54 Jane Dillenberger, 'Secular Art with Sacred Themes', in *Secular Art with Sacred Themes* (Nashville, TN: Abingdon, 1969), 117–129; esp. 127.

55 Brown, *Tradition and Imagination*, 342.

56 Ibid., 374.

57 Brown, 'The Glory of God Revealed in Art and Music', in *Celebrating Creation*, ed. Chapman, 53; and in Brown, 'Learning from Pagans', in *Divine Generosity and Human Creativity*, ed. Brewer and MacSwain, 45.

58 For illustration, see Margo A. Crutchfield, *Martin Puryear* (Richmond, VA: Virginia Museum of Fine Arts, 2001), 32, 35 (on the floor of the artist's studio); or John Elderfield (ed.), *Martin Puryear* (New York: Museum of Modern Art, 2007), 69.

59 Cf. David Nash, *Willow Ladder* (1978), *Willow Ladder II* (1979), *Big Ladder* (1984), *Through the Trunk, Up the Branch* (1985), *Apple Jacob* (1986), *Sylvan Steps* (1987), *Ladder* (1989) and *Small Napa Ladders (Part 1)* (1990). For illustration and discussion of some of these examples, see Julian Andrews, *The Sculpture of David Nash* (London: Lund Humphries; Berkeley, CA and Los Angeles, CA: University of California Press, 1996), 132–5. See also Aristotle Georgiades, *Newoldgrowth* (2012). Online: www.carlhammergallery.com/artists/aristotle-georgiades/featured-works?view=slider#4; accessed 21 April 2017.

60 Elderfield (ed.), *Martin Puryear*, 68.

61 Crutchfield, *Martin Puryear*, 34.

62 For illustration and discussion, see Barbara Buhler Lynes, *Georgia O'Keeffe: Catalogue Raisonné*, vol. 2 (New Haven, CT and London: Yale University Press, 1999), 838; cf. Tom Van Sant, *Jacob's Ladder* (1976), a quarter-mile long kite; and Ken Goldman, *Jacob's Ladder* (2011), a performance piece featuring a white ladder tied to a cluster of white helium-filled balloons that drift across the sky. For illustration, see online: www.drachen.org/collections/tom-van-sant-jacobs-ladder; www.kengoldman art.com/jacobs-ladder.html; accessed 16 January 2017.

63 Cf. Zatorski + Zatorski, *The Practical Impossibility of Faith* (2006). For illustration, see online: www.zatorskiandzatorski.com/the-practical-impossibility-of-faith; accessed 27 December 2016.

64 Crutchfield, *Martin Puryear*, 34. While some might think this insufficient to make the connection, Crutchfield clearly had no difficulty, as is evidenced by reference to Jacob's ladder and Genesis 28.12. See ibid., 57, n. 42. See also David Brown, *Discipleship and Imagination*, 380–1.

65 For illustration, see online: www.borofsky.com/index.php?album=walkingdallas;

accessed 15 February 2017. This work is also featured on the front cover of Brown, *Divine Generosity and Human Creativity*, ed. Brewer and MacSwain. The other two sculptures from this series are located at Carnegie-Mellon University, Pittsburgh, PA, and in Seoul, South Korea. Cf. Borofsky's earlier, related works, *Man Walking to the Sky* (1992) and *Woman Walking to the Sky* (1994), as well as Cedric Wentworth, *Jacob's Ladder* (2005). For illustration of the latter, see online: www.campbellgallerysf.com/cw/2.htm; accessed 16 January 2017.

66 Cathy Rose A. Garcia, 'Walk to the Sky With Jonathan Borofsky', *The Korea Times*, 31 October 2008. Online: www.koreatimes.co.kr/www/news/art/2009/07/148_33617.html; accessed 2 March 2017. For illustration and additional discussion, see George T. M. Shackelford, *Paul Gauguin: Where Do We Come From? What Are We? Where Are We Going?* (Boston, MA: MFA Publications, 2013), esp. 27.

67 Garcia, 'Walk to the Sky With Jonathan Borofsky'.

68 Samantha Baskind, *Encyclopedia of Jewish American Artists* (Westport, CT: Greenwood, 2007), s.v. 'Jonathan Borofsky'.

69 As Kim West notes, 'the biblical image is employed here for its metaphorical value – as an event of miraculous rupture with continuity and the logic of ordinary existence – as much as for its properly doctrinal significance.' Kim West, 'Repair as Redemption or Montage: Speculations on Kader Attia's Ladder of Light', in Kader Attia, *Continuum of Repair: The Light of Jacob's Ladder* (London: Whitechapel Gallery, 2013), 57. See also Kader Attia, *The Repair: From Occident to Extra-Occidental Cultures* (Berlin: The Green Box, 2024), esp. 163–6.

70 Whitechapel Gallery, Winter 2014 (gallery brochure).

71 Laura Cumming, 'Kader Attia: Continuum of Repair: The Light of Jacob's Ladder' – review, *The Guardian*, 15 December 2013. Online: www.theguardian.com/artanddesign/2013/dec/15/kader-attia-jacobs-ladder-review-whitechapel; accessed 2 March 2017.

72 Brown, *Discipleship and Imagination*, 383.

73 Ibid., 384.

74 Ibid., 384, n. 129.

75 Additional examples of this type include Helen Frankenthaler (1957), Pavel Baňka (1986), Jasper Johns (1999), Damien Hirst, *The Soul on Jacob's Ladder* (2005), *The Souls on Jacob's Ladder Take Their Flight* (2007, a series of six etchings) and *Jacob's Ladder* (2008). For illustration of these works, see Barbara Rose, *Frankenthaler* (New York: Harry N. Abrams, 1970), Plate 63; for Baňka, Lynn Gamwell (ed.), *Dreams 1900–2000: Science, Art, and the Unconscious Mind* (Ithaca, NY: Cornell University Press, 2000), 216; for Johns, online: http://archive.artsmia.org/until-now/artworks/johns_catenary.html; accessed 26 December 2016; for Hirst, online: http://paragonpress.co.uk/works/the-souls-on-jacobs-ladder-take-their-flight; accessed 10 January 2018. For additional examples in sculpture, see Wolfgang Laib's *Untitled (Stairs)* (2002), *Without Beginning and Without End* (2005), or any one of Gao Weigang's ladders or staircases, e.g. *Superstructure* (2010).

76 Claus Westermann, *Genesis 12–36: A Commentary*, trans. John J. Scullion, SJ (London: SPCK; Minneapolis, MN: Augsburg, 1985), 454 in the Augsburg edition.

77 Brown, *God and Enchantment of Place*, 37.

78 Brown, *God and Grace of Body*, 6.

79 William Desmond identifies three senses of transcendence in *God and the Between*, Illuminations: Theory and Religion (Oxford: Blackwell, 2008), 22–3.

80 Thomas L. Broadie, *Genesis as Dialogue: A Literary, Historical, and Theological Commentary* (New York: Oxford University Press, 2001), 312. Desmond refers to this as 'a hyperbolic sense of transcendence, bringing to mind the question of God beyond the immanence of transcendence in nature and human being'. Desmond, *God and the Between*, 22.

81 Brown, *God and Enchantment of Place*, 248.

8

Understanding John's Visions: Unlocking the Insights of Revelation's Visual History

NATASHA O'HEAR

Engaging with David Brown's work in both *Tradition and Imagination* and *Discipleship and Imagination* has been enlightening. In the introduction to this volume, Christopher R. Brewer rightly bemoans the fact that Brown's work has not been engaged with in a meaningful way by biblical scholars. I would go further than this and argue that these books should be compulsory reading for all those working in the field of biblical reception history in particular. In these two works, Brown provides a wealth of arguments in favour of treating the 'tradition' inspired by Scripture – the 'story in-between the [biblical] text' and the present – with much more respect and curiosity than is often the case.[1] In doing so, Brown gradually provides a clear rationale for the vital importance of the work of the biblical reception historian, a rationale that goes beyond an assertion that this tradition should be studied because it is interesting to understand the diverse ways the same text has been interpreted. Rather, Brown confidently asserts that engaging with the imaginative responses inspired by biblical texts helps us better understand the original or 'source-text' and in some cases assists in forming an informed critique of that source-text. Brown calls on us to reject the 'deposit' view of revelation that has developed – the idea that the Bible is an isolated 'deposit' that cannot be meaningfully developed or extended – and also to free ourselves from the idea of the 'tyrannical' text, or one that forbids its readers from going beyond it.[2]

In many ways, *Tradition and Imagination* and *Discipleship and Imagination* need to be read alongside one another, particularly if one engages in visual reception. My particular focus is the visual history of the book of Revelation, a subject Brown touches on in the first volume and returns to at greater length in the second. Thus Brown's initial comments on Revelation, which he finds narrow-minded and unimaginative, and its 'overly literal' visual history are helpfully developed in chapter 3 of *Discipleship and Imagination*. Here he explores more imaginative and ambiguous visualizations of Revelation.³ Two extensions of Brown's work on the visual history of Revelation will be offered here. The first explores how artistic interpretations of Revelation have offered a much deeper understanding of the visionary experience that purports to be the source of the text, than the text itself. We will engage a range of images, including those from the thirteenth-century *Lambeth Apocalypse Tapestry*, Memling's *Apocalypse Panel* of 1474–9 and two images from Dürer's *Apocalypse Series* of 1498. To use Brown's own words, such images add the 'body and colour' to the outline of what it means to have a visionary experience like the one in Revelation.⁴ As Brown argues, visions were an important part of Jesus' own earthly experience, and the images considered below help to flesh out what form these experiences might have taken. This analysis is not only relevant to the study of Revelation but to our understanding of revelation.⁵

The second extension to Brown's work explores some images of Revelation's Beasts. First we look more closely at some images that provide a fixed and/or polemical interpretation of the Beasts, namely *The Master Bertram Apocalypse Altarpiece* of c.1400 and Cranach the Elder's image of the Beast from the Abyss of Revelation 11 from his Apocalypse series of 1522. These provide a useful point of comparison with two images of Revelation's Beasts (William Blake's *The Great Red Dragon and the Woman Clothed with the Sun: The Devil is Come Down*, c.1805–9 and Yolanda Lopez's *Virgin of Guadalupe* Triptych of 1978), which embody the element of self-critique and ambiguity Brown praises in other visualizations of Revelation.⁶

These two extensions to Brown's work will provide further exemplification of the way carefully selected artistic interpretations of a biblical text can deepen our understanding of it, providing illumination of hitherto neglected aspects. Other visualizations, in their complexity and ambiguity, serve to open up or endorse alternative interpretative avenues and introduce new and often welcome layers of complexity to the task of exegesis.

Brown on Revelation and its visual history

Brown's arguments in the two volumes are impressively wide-ranging, both in terms of their chronological scope, their breadth across many disciplines and even in terms of the wide range of artistic examples he examines. However, in the interests of brevity and precision (and safe in the knowledge that others in this volume have engaged with Brown more holistically), I will engage in detail only with his comments on Revelation and the art it has inspired. Brown's observations in *Tradition and*

Imagination are fairly negative. He argues that Revelation fails to work imaginatively for most Christians and is mostly left unread.[7] In addition he argues that the text has been very difficult to visualize. Even such widely accepted masterpieces as *The Angers Apocalypse Tapestry* and Dürer's *Apocalypse Series* of 1498 are condemned by Brown as lacking conviction and impact due to the imaginative failings of the source-text.

However, in *Discipleship and Imagination* his position on the art inspired by Revelation – if not the text itself – is extended and softened. Brown's comments here have to be seen against his wider argument regarding the development of ideas about hell and judgement.[8] Unsurprisingly, given the preponderance of hellish figures and imagery in Revelation, many details of the 'Christian hell' are drawn from this text. Brown sees in the developing artistic tradition of Revelation's Beasts a gradual freeing from the condemnation of others and a summons to penitence and self-critique. In some visual examples he sees a clear critique of Revelation's close-mindedness.[9] While Revelation's author seems willing to engage in a critique of members of his own church in Revelation 2—3, the subsequent visions lack any element of self-critique, willingness to compromise or awareness that, as Brown eloquently puts it, the double-edged sword might fall on him.[10] It is for these reasons that Brown 'would not hesitate to describe some later adaptations ... as both artistically and morally superior to revelation itself'.[11] These include Signorelli's fifteenth-century Antichrist frescoes, Botticelli's early sixteenth-century *Mystic Crucifixion* and *Mystic Nativity*, Lorenzo Lotto's sixteenth-century *Michael Defeating the Dragon* and John Martin's *Belshazzar's Feast* (1821).[12] In the Signorelli frescoes, for example, Brown perceives not only an ecclesial critique but also an implied critique of the viewer who, due to the positioning of the frescoes, finds themselves a part of the crowd that has to decide whether to succumb to Antichrist or not.[13] He argues that Signorelli and Botticelli's images provide a welcome reinterpretation of Revelation's rigidly deterministic and pessimistic outlook. Instead, they suggest that repentance *could* produce a different kind of world, and 'one in which no necessity attached to the work of Antichrist or other demons'.[14]

There is much one could engage with here, not least the polemic against Revelation, a text in which many have found solace and inspiration and which for many is much more than a 'dry, literary' text. Indeed, many have written persuasively on the power and importance of the political critique of Rome set out in Revelation (especially chs 12, 13 and 17). The metaphorical and multivalent nature of the language of the work has meant that this critique has been applied again and again to other superficially attractive yet deeply pernicious regimes and religions.[15] Brown's comments about the interpretative limitations of Dürer's Apocalypse Series also seem to miss the artistic context of this great work, an issue to which we return below.

However, for a reception historian working with images of Revelation, this section is exciting in its persuasive legitimation of the reinterpretative power of art in a way that I have rarely encountered. In Brown's view, the 'best' visualizations of Revelation provide an 'imaginative critique' of the source-text that open up the literalism and close-mindedness of Revelation's author and imply a more nuanced view of judgement than that contained in Revelation itself.[16] Brown and I are also in agreement regarding the importance of accessing the imaginative insights of the art inspired by Revelation via a range of examples. This range should encompass both more and less literal approaches to the text.[17] Interestingly, Brown also argues that the same work can contain a variety of approaches in terms of literality: 'Contrast ... the failed literalism of the Angers Tapestry's Beast from the Sea with its more imaginative treatment of the bleeding sea of the second trumpet.'[18] For Brown, then, some of the images in the Angers Tapestry have potential as 'imaginative critique', having been conceived along more metaphorical and less literal interpretative lines, while others do not. This is an interesting observation about a work that took around seven years to complete and may have been the product of several creative hands.[19] Where an art historian would point to the stylistic inconsistencies in which this resulted, Brown rightly finds the interpretative ones more thought-provoking. The extent to which Revelation is best served via literal or more metaphorical or imaginative interpretations is taken up in the following two sections.

Extension 1: Visualization as a Way of Understanding John's Visionary Experiences

Brown makes it clear he accepts the argument of those who see Revelation as a composite literary construct, and a rather poor one at that, complete with unworkable metaphors and a narrow-minded outlook.[20] It is beyond the scope of this contribution fully to rehearse the arguments on both sides of the debate regarding Revelation's nature as primarily a visionary or a literary text.[21] However, there are good arguments in favour of taking Revelation's claims to visionary inspiration seriously.[22] First, one can argue against the lengthy and contrived process of literary composition proposed by scholars such as David Aune and Elisabeth Schüssler Fiorenza on the basis of the evidence of Revelation itself. Aune's overarching argument is that Revelation's author has created a sophisticated frame narrative in the apocalyptic/prophetic genre into which he interpolated other earlier and disparate apocalyptic textual units.[23] His argument that this is both a sophisticated literary composition *and* a collection of obviously disparate apocalyptic narratives is flawed and has now been comprehensively discredited by Ian Paul, who argues in favour of viewing Revelation as a single composition.[24] Schüssler Fiorenza argues that Revelation is the product of a thoroughgoing attempt by John to make sense of his own situation and promote a particular world view via contemporary symbols drawn from Hebrew Scripture and Greco-Roman mythology.[25] Further evidence of the essentially literary nature of Revelation, 'in which images and symbols function more like words and sentences in a composition', is that the text cannot be successfully visualized.[26] While it is true that in some instances it is very hard to visualize Revelation 'as it is written', this hardly seems evidence that the text is a literary construct. It could just as well point to the fact that, as is the case with other texts inspired by 'visions', the text is an inadequate rendering of extraordinary experiences that John was unable to capture accurately in the diachronic medium of text.

In fact while Revelation does include evidence of later reflection and purposefully crafted material, which largely occurs at the beginning and end of the text (see 17.7–18; 1.1–6, 12b–3.22; 22.6–21), there are striking parallels between the main text and other 'vision reports, such as Jewish apocalyptic literature from the Exile to the first century CE, the *merkabah* mystics, Hildegard of Bingen (1098–1179), Bridget of Sweden (1303–73), Teresa of Avila (1515–82), William Blake (1757–1827), the visionary artist Cecil Collins (1908–89) and vision reports from Shamanistic and Inuit cultures.[27] Based on these examples, Johannes Lindblom compiled a list of criteria that authentic reports of visions must contain, including a dreamlike format, a concern for matters on an otherworldly plane, evidence of difficulty expressing the visionary experience in words, emotional side effects, and mention of the date and place of vision.[28] Revelation possesses all of these qualities. This in itself is not of course proof that the text is an authentic vision report but it is useful to see how it can be comfortably contextualized as part of the visionary genre.

If Revelation's claims to visionary inspiration are taken seriously, then readers/hearers should engage with the nature of the experiences John was attempting to evoke imperfectly with words. This is where Brown's argument about the deficiencies of viewing biblical texts as finite and final 'deposits' can be invoked. For although the text is punctuated with over 60 references to seeing, and John does claim to interact with angels and Christ (see especially 1.9–20; 4—5; 10; 11.1–2; 17.1–8; 21.5, 9–10; 22.8–9), he gives little detail regarding the nature of the visionary experiences themselves. Indeed, when John refers to the details of his own involvement in the visions, they fail to satisfy our need to understand the visionary process on a phenomenological level.[29] Are we to imagine, for instance, that John's visions were taking place externally to him and that he was being 'shown around' by an angel, as if in a heavenly art gallery? Or are visions hallucinations? This is where the role of the artist becomes integral to the task of interpreting Revelation, because in visualizing the text the artist must grapple with these issues. The most successful artistic interpretations help the viewer to a more profound understanding both of the visions and the nature of the visionary experience, precisely because they are able to 'conjure' this visual scene in a way words cannot.[30] They take us 'behind' *and* 'beyond' the text of Revelation in an imaginative sense. Although Revelation is the only formal 'apocalypse' in the New Testament, there are many other well-known apocalyptic passages that involve visions (e.g. Mark 13; Acts 9.3; 16.9; 18.9; 22.18; 27.23). Brown himself also makes a persuasive case for Jesus having experienced visions at the baptism and the temptation, which were embellished theologically by the Gospel writers.[31] Engaging with the concept of visionary experience is, therefore, a fundamental part of what it means to attempt to understand Christianity.

We shall now turn to three late-medieval and early modern visual examples that serve to illuminate different aspects of John's visionary experiences. The first is drawn from the Anglo-Norman Apocalypse manuscript tradition, which is explored by Brown in *Discipleship and Imagination*. Although it is not quite clear which series he is discussing, as he just refers to the Anglo-Norman 'archetype', it sounds very much like *The Lambeth Apocalypse*, c.1260.[32] This belongs to the so-called Berengaudus stem of Anglo-Norman illustrated Apocalypse manuscripts (of which there are 15 extant examples), which use commentary extracts from the eleventh-century Berengaudus commentary. The commentary is christological in focus, favours a predestined approach to the future, and is also stridently anti-Jewish.[33] Although the commentary extracts appear on every page, the *Lambeth* artists have not reflected the emphases of the commentary in their images of Revelation.[34]

All of the Anglo-Norman Apocalypse manuscripts follow a fairly rigid page layout, with an image (around 8 cm in height) at the top of each page, underneath which appear a few lines of text followed by an extract from the Berengaudus commentary. There are 78 images of Revelation in *The Lambeth Apocalypse*, and John appears in nearly all of them in various capacities as author, protagonist, voyeur and guide.[35] The result is an episodic approach to the text, in which the reader/viewer is taken on a 'tour' of Revelation by John, with a view to helping them internalize the text's narrative. The images, although beautiful, are literal, highly detailed and sometimes cluttered.

In terms of the nature of John's visionary experience, *The Lambeth Apocalypse* gives an impression of a vision that was experienced via some sort of sequential physical journey.[36] Thus we move from fo. 1, where John is asleep on Patmos being commanded by an angel to write whatever he sees in a book to send to the 'Seven Churches that are in Asia', via 78 images such as fo. 6 (the rider on the pale horse of Rev. 6.7–8), until finally we reach the last miniature in the Revelation series (fo. 39v), in which John has an unmediated vision of Christ. In all the images in which John appears, apart from the final one, he is clutching his book, noting what he sees as the visions unfold.

In addition to the artistic assertion that John received his visions via a physical heavenly journey punctuated by commands to record what he saw, the viewer of *The Lambeth Apocalypse* is also left with an impression of John as someone with whom we might identify, moving from incomprehension to understanding via the process of his participation. Within this framework, John's closed eyes in fo. 1 (see Rev. 1.1–12) are symbolic of his lack of understanding and his inability fully to engage with the first vision of the Son of Man. By the end of John's long visionary journey at fo. 39v (some 76 images later), he is alert and worshipful.[37]

Brown sees the images of *The Lambeth Apocalypse* as an 'invitation to personal pilgrimage' that takes the focus away from Revelation's emphasis on the faults of others and transforms it into 'a summons to continuing personal convergence and change'.[38] Although I would argue that *Lambeth* is perhaps not as 'unjudgemental' as Brown would have it, the idea of its acting as a catalyst for personal change is supported both by the manuscript itself and by what we know of how it was used.[39]

Memling's *Apocalypse Panel*, from his *St John Altarpiece* of around 200 years later (1474–9), in contrast, presents the visionary experience as something altogether different. This image presents the visionary experience as something internal and synchronic. The sheer size of the panel also gives the visions a far greater impact (176 cm × 79 cm).

The central panel of the altarpiece depicts the 'mystic marriage' of St Catherine and Christ, while the outer two panels of the triptych depict the life of St John the Baptist (left-hand panel) and the visions of St John the Evangelist (right-hand panel). The two Johns also appear in the central panel alongside Mary and the infant Christ (centre) and St Catherine and St Barbara. The *vitae* of the two Johns have been depicted in tiny scenes behind the central scene. Various suggestions have been put forward regarding the evocative power of this central panel, ranging from 'the afterlife', to the fusion of heaven and earth that takes place during the Eucharist, to the marriage of the bride (Israel) and the Lamb that takes place in Revelation 19.[40] If the latter is correct then the central panel constitutes the conclusion of the Revelation vision of the right-hand panel, which ends rather curiously at Revelation 13.

Like the *Isenheim Altarpiece* of 1515, which Brown argues stands at the apex of artistic representations of Christ's humanity, Memling's *Altarpiece* was also created for a hospital setting.[41] The overarching themes of the work relate to suffering and heavenly reward, which would have provided an apt focus for personal devotion for those suffering in the hospital and unlikely to return to the outside world.[42]

Focusing on the *Apocalypse Panel*, even the casual viewer notices that this panel adds 'body and colour' to our understanding of the narrative of Revelation.[43] For here, brought together in one visual plane, are the first 13 chapters of John's visions, providing the viewer with a 'snapshot' of the narrative. This style of 'simultaneous painting' was rare but not without precedent. Memling himself used this style in his 1471 *Scenes from the Passion*, and Giotto and the Bohemian Apocalypse frescoes had also used this style of painting to visualize Revelation in the fourteenth century.[44] Although the scenes from Revelation are depicted as occurring simultaneously, they are prioritized by virtue of their size and position in the image. John is the largest figure, followed by the heavenly throne room, which is enclosed in an eye-like roundel in the top left-hand corner of the image. The prioritization of the heavenly throne room (chs 4—5) presents it as the key to understanding the text (like many modern commentators).[45] It also evokes the notion of the 'Divine eye' looking down on the scene or, alternatively, the roundel could symbolize John's 'visionary' eye – his initiation into the divine secrets.

Also prominent in Memling's visualization of Revelation are the Four Horsemen, the Mighty Angel (ch. 10) and the Woman Clothed with the Sun (ch. 12). The last visible image depicts the Dragon handing over power to the Sea Beast on the horizon (13.1), although the implication is that the visions continue over the horizon.

In terms of how this image helps us understand the visionary experience, Memling's contribution is significant and seems to have influenced both Bosch (c.1489) and Velázquez (1618) in their versions of John receiving his visions on Patmos.[46] All of these artists focus primarily on John, who stares blankly into the middle distance, pen poised above his writing book.[47] While both Bosch and Velazquez 'summarize' the narrative of Revelation into a single vision of the Woman Clothed with the Sun in the top left-hand corners of their images, Memling paints the entire narrative of Revelation until chapter 13. However, unlike *The Lambeth Apocalypse*, which presents the visions as events to be physically experienced, the implication in all three of these images is that they exist only in John's mind and we, the viewer, are being given a 'window' into that reality. While Brown may prefer the metaphorical brilliance of the Velázquez to the literal nature of the Memling visions, Memling's image is a crucial addition to the reception history of Revelation. He was the first to grapple in one single image with the phenomenology of

John's visionary experience, and marks a distinct break from medieval conceptions of his visions.

While in some ways Dürer marks a return to a more episodic approach to the vision, in others his images are revolutionary. Dürer brought Renaissance values to the task of visualizing Revelation, introducing an element of frightening realism to the visual narrative.[48] In addition to this, in some of the images he places *himself* at the site of the visionary experiences, as a latter-day John.

What distinguishes Dürer from previous artists who had visualized Revelation is his degree of economic and artistic freedom. While I agree with Brown that we should not be too quick to dismiss the idea of a degree of artistic autonomy in the Medieval era, the fact remains that until the advent of the printing press around 1470, which enabled artists to mass-produce their work, artists had to work within the confines of patronage.[49] Now they could produce images to be printed themselves and even buy their own printing presses (like Dürer in 1497). Effectively, this ensured he could control every step of the process, from the design to the marketing of his woodcut images.[50] It is significant that he chose Revelation as the subject matter for his first major woodcut series in 1498.[51] For Dürer this text, and his visualization of it, represented both economic possibilities – the half millennium of 1500 had led to increased apocalyptic speculation – as well as personal fascination.[52] It is by now well known that Dürer had 'apocalyptic dreams' throughout his life and that these sometimes led to sketches and paintings of these visionary experiences (see the versos of *St Jerome in the Wilderness*, 1496 and *Christ as the Man of Sorrows*, c.1493 and the watercolour of his apocalyptic dream of 1525).[53] The extent of Dürer's immersion in his apocalyptic subject matter for the *Apocalypse Series* may even go as far as an identification with the figure of John.

Where the Medieval manuscript artists had 70 to 80 images to devote to Revelation, Dürer used only 15. Heavily influenced by the Koberger woodcut illustrations of 1483, Dürer found a certain power in this compressed visual narrative of Revelation. While artistically crude, the compression of the narrative into just eight images led to some interesting interpretative emphases. In the final image in the series, for example, which covers Revelation 17—22, the Whore of Babylon is introduced and then destroyed (symbolized by the burning of Babylon the city in the background), Satan is bound (Rev. 20.1-2) and the New Jerusalem hovers tantalizingly over the whole scene in the top right-hand corner.[54] Other compositional elements from the Koberger illustrations crop up frequently in the Dürer images. Interestingly, most of the compositional additions he makes to bring Koberger's eight images up to his fifteen are related to John.

In another sense, Dürer's images are without precedent. Unlike those of his artistic predecessors, his images were not inlaid into the text but appeared in transverse format on separate pages. The text of Revelation was set in columns on the verso of the images. The relationship between Dürer's Apocalypse images and the text of Revelation has been a matter of some debate.[55] Suffice it to say that the text plays a secondary role in the series. The text quality is inferior to the image quality and seems to have been hastily assembled, with the result that the images do not often appear next to the section of the text they are depicting. Even the additional captions that have been inserted into the text to direct the reader/viewer to the correct image are sometimes erroneous. As the text and images have been laid out, it is difficult to hold the textual and pictorial versions of Revelation in mind at the same time. Soon the images took on a life of their own. From the outset Dürer produced loose-leaf versions of the images for sale without the text, and ultimately the work was sold as a picture book, without text.[56]

Returning to the content of Dürer's *Apocalypse Series*, we find that he has integrated elements of heavenly/earthly dichotomy, synchronicity and self-identification with John into his images, elevating them beyond the individual images of the medieval manuscript versions of Revelation.

One of the key features of Dürer's visualization is his handling of compositional space. In nine of the images he has divided his composition into two realms, heavenly and earthly, thus evoking the contrasts between the two inherent in Revelation. This stands in marked contrast to earlier manuscript versions of Revelation where traditionally one realm was depicted at a time. In D3, for example (Dürer's throne-room scene), John has been subsumed into the heavenly throne room where God and Christ sit in the centre of the 'four living creatures' and the 'twenty-four elders' who are engaged in continuous worship.[57] The earthly realm presents a view of contemporary Nuremberg, which in its quotidian calmness seems entirely oblivious to the heavenly scene above. The way Dürer has constructed the throne room in this image brings to mind a courtroom in which God acts as the judge (cf. Rev. 20). This may evoke the 'judicial contest' that Bauckham argues runs through Revelation.[58] While Brown might view D3 as an overly literal visualization of Revelation, seeing Revelation visualized on two levels in this way offers the viewer an interpretative key to Revelation.

Even if Dürer's compositions are not entirely innovative, his representation of John surely is. Great prominence is given to John in D2 (the vision of the seven candlesticks), D3 (the throne-room scene), D9 (John devours the scroll) and D15 (New Jerusalem). In D3 and D9, John is the largest figure in the scene, and in D2 and D15 he is among the key figures. Frederick van der Meer argues persuasively that Dürer inserted his own likeness into the series four or five times (see D2, D3, D6, D9, D15), as well as into the 1511 frontispiece.[59] In all but one of these images (D6), it is the John figure who has been drawn in Dürer's likeness.[60] Interestingly D2, D9 and D15 also belong to what has been identified by Erwin Panofsky as the later group of images in terms of date of composition. These images are characterized by a greater focus on a few larger figures engaged in simpler actions.[61] I wonder, then, if Brown would allow that *some* of the later Dürer images in the series are less literal and more successful than others.[62]

Taking D9 as an example, we see John foregrounded in an unprecedented way.[63] Although this sequence (from Rev. 10) had been emphasized in earlier visualizations of Revelation, such as the *Angers Apocalypse Tapestry*, in these versions the focus is primarily on the mighty angel. Here the mighty angel is a shadowy figure, a few rays of light balanced on his shaky column-like legs. The eye is drawn away from the flimsy angel and towards the solid figure in the foreground, that of John, as he urgently devours the 'little book'. Two further observations about this image are worth raising. First, there are real similarities between the setting in this image and Dürer's 1496 *Landscape with a Woodland Pool*. Second, Dürer's monogram is very prominent. Although his famous 'AD' monogram appears in every image in the series (and indeed on every piece of work he produced), it ranges in size and intensity.[64] Was Dürer here emphasizing not only his authorship of the image but also the experience? Like many interpreters before and since, Dürer clearly saw Revelation 10 as a key turning point within the narrative, the time when John ceases to be a passive observer and is commanded to prophesy.[65] By locating himself at the scene of this intimate revelation, Dürer is effectively claiming great authority for his own visualization. He presents himself as an *alter Iohannis*, experiencing Revelation anew and just outside Nuremberg on the eve of the half millennium. An interesting consequence of this approach is that, unlike in the medieval manuscripts in which John appears in almost every scene, John is not an omnipresent figure. He appears only when he is invoked by the text. In this decision, Dürer locates his own representations, rather than John's experiences, at the locus of revelation. This move ultimately calls into question the status of the text. If Revelation is to be viewed as a series of words that engender pictures, a definitive rendition of that text, produced by an *alter Iohannis*, might render the text redundant.

It is hard not to find Brown's claim that Dürer's *Apocalypse Series* is evidence of Revelation's failure to work on a visual level somewhat baffling.[66] Admittedly, casual viewers of this series would not know that John has been drawn in the artist's image. However, as in the Memling image, they would be struck by the importance of the John figure as a visionary. They would also be struck by the clever compositions suggestive of the two distinct realms that govern the text itself. Most strikingly, anyone viewing the images next to a text of Revelation would surely question the ambiguity of the last image.[67] The previous image (D14) depicts the Whore in the foreground and the destruction of Babylon, and the appearance of the rider on the white horse of Revelation 19.11. This takes us up to the end of Revelation 19, but chapters 20—22 remain. Is this image therefore meant to depict the millennium, which follows the binding of Satan taking place in the foreground (Rev. 20.1-3), or the New Jerusalem itself? Indeed, this city looks more like an idealized version of Nuremberg than the New Jerusalem. Was Dürer here militating against the orthodox Augustinian interpretation of the millennium of Revelation 20.3 as already a present reality in the life of the Church, and suggesting that it was still a future event? The answers to these questions elude the viewer and we are left in a state of puzzlement.[68]

In these key ways Dürer's series is not the literal depiction that Brown argues it is. Furthermore the realism of the earthly settings and their resemblance to Northern European landscapes will also have a profound effect on the alert viewer. Dürer's series opens up the interpretative notion that John's visions can be experienced afresh in different times and places, whether that be in late-fifteenth-century Nuremberg or today. And while he does follow the narrative of Revelation fairly faithfully, closer attention to the images reveals efforts at synchronicity and 'editing', which suggests a sensitive understanding of the text. Portraying the destruction of Babylon in the background of the image depicting her in her prime (D14) has a very different exegetical effect from an image that just focuses on her. This synchronic presentation of the Babylon sequence (chs 17—18) introduces a note of ambiguity into the task of interpreting this figure. Is she as much a victim of the system of the 'Beast' as her own victims?[69] While some sections have been compressed or presented synchronically by Dürer, he positively lingers over other episodes, such as the war in heaven between St Michael and his angels and Satan and his army, devoting a whole image to a single verse of text (D11; Rev. 12.17).

The primacy of the images in the Dürer series, unprecedented in terms of apocalyptic imagery in book format, also suggests, for the first time, that the visions can be liberated from the text; that the text is an imperfect attempt to render 'what was seen'. Although this had also been suggested by Memling and was about to be by Botticelli in his *Mystic Nativity* of 1500, these were works with a comparatively tiny audience. Thus it could be said that Dürer introduced the idea that Revelation could be experienced primarily as a visual entity into the 'mainstream'.

Extension 2: An Exploration of Ambiguity in Images of Revelation's Beasts

Within his discussion of the development of Christian imagery surrounding hell and the afterlife, Brown examines the development of images of Revelation's Beasts. The iconography of these figures develops from a portrayal suggesting that they are unqualifiedly evil to more ambiguous presentations that allow for both critique (of the figures) and, more importantly, self-critique (of the viewer).[70] Brown suggests Botticelli's late-fifteenth-century *Mystic Crucifixion* and his *Mystic Nativity* as examples that take a more metaphorical approach to the interpretation of Revelation's Beasts, works in which it is implied that repentance can still bring about a different sort of world.[71]

I will analyse two images of Revelation's Beasts that present them as two-dimensional, wholly evil figures – it is helpful to understand the sorts of interpretations that do not 'advance the tradition' before moving on to those that do. This will be followed by a consideration of one of William Blake's visualizations of Revelation's Beasts, and a triptych by the contemporary Chicana artist Yolanda Lopez. Both artists introduce a degree of ambiguity to their interpretations that would appeal to Brown. For the purposes of this discussion I am taking 'Revelation's Beasts' to encompass the Satanic Trinity of the Dragon, the Sea Beast and the Earth Beast (chs 12–13), as well as the Whore of Babylon (ch. 17).

The *Master Bertram* or *Victoria and Albert Altarpiece* of c.1400 is a rare example of an Apocalypse altarpiece – Memling's *St John Altarpiece* and the Van Eycks' *Ghent Altarpiece* being the only others from this period – created by the German workshop of Master Bertram. The altarpiece, influenced by the thirteenth-century Alexander Minorita Apocalypse Commentary, visualizes the narrative of Revelation 1–16.[72] It is episodic and intended to be 'read' from left to right and line by line, rather like a manuscript. In one of the rectangular images towards the end of the altarpiece, the Earth Beast is portrayed as a bear with two heads.[73] The commentary text, which is included around the edge of each image, tells us that one head is the original Beast and the other is 'Mahomet' (Muhammad). His two horns represents his claim to wisdom and holiness, and the Fire descending from heaven is the Holy Scripture from which elements of the Qur'an were derived. Those killing the people refusing to worship the Sea Beast don the dress of Saracen soldiers. In line with Minorita's linear historical commentary, the Earth Beast is identified with Muhammad and his army with the Saracens, thus reflecting thirteenth-century medieval fears regarding 'the threat from the east'.[74] This is one of the purest examples of a 'decoding interpretation'.[75] No room is left for ambiguity or nuance, a way of interpreting texts that some will find comforting but most view as overly restrictive.

Lucas Cranach the Elder's Apocalypse images of 1522 are equally unambiguous. Wary of Revelation and the 'imaginative' readings to which it might give rise, Luther thought that accompanying the text – of his translation of Revelation, which was to appear in his first German New Testament of 1522 – with a set of very 'literal' interpretations would guide his readers to a 'correct' interpretation of the text.[76] The result is a series of images that are a simplified pastiche of the Dürer series with added polemical details. Cranach added six new images and amended details within images in order to reflect the text more faithfully, largely abolishing Dürer's 'two-tier' schema.[77]

However, in other instances Cranach added polemical details not found in the text, namely the addition of the papal triple tiara to three images (see C11, The Beast from the Abyss; C16, Angels with seven bowls; C17, Whore of Babylon). Cranach's earlier work, the *Passional Christi und Antichristi* of 1521, a pamphlet of woodcut illustrations and textual explanation by Philip Melanchthon, had already made the visual identification between the Pope and Antichrist. Given the exegetical links that had already been made between the Antichrist figure and Revelation's Beasts, it is not surprising that the latter wear the triple tiara in Cranach's Apocalypse images, provocative as it was. Interestingly, the papal tiaras were cut away in the December editions of Luther's New Testament, but the iconography was adopted by Holbein the Younger in his Apocalypse series of 1523, the first of many to promote the motif.[78]

Like the Bertram *Apocalypse Altarpiece*, this is a decoding interpretation of the Beast from the Abyss (Rev. 11.7), which allows for very little variety of interpretation. Contrarily, one could argue that Cranach is foregrounding Revelation's unsparing political critique of empire with his polemical reading, but it certainly lacks depth and ambiguity.[79] I wonder ultimately if it is the Cranach series rather than the Dürer series by whose legacy Brown feels frustrated. He argues that it is the influence of the Dürer series whose 'literal adherence to the text of the book of Revelation meant that the ability of the imagery to speak to viewers declined at the same rate as readers' capacity to find the biblical text meaningful in itself'.[80] While Dürer provided the template for Cranach, it was the Cranach series that stripped away the ambiguity and sense of synchronicity from the Dürer series.

This was not, however, an artistic legacy that impinged noticeably on William Blake, who returned to Revelation many times in his career. Blake went even further than Dürer in seeing himself as a visionary, linking his visions explicitly with those of John.[81] And while Benjamin Heath Malkin was correct to claim in 1806 that 'The book of Revelation, which may well be supposed to engross much of Mr Blake's study, seems to have directed him', Blake also 'resists' Revelation in the spirit that Brown praises.[82] Christopher Rowland writes of Blake:

> In one important respect, however, Blake's use of apocalyptic images differs significantly and decisively from that of Revelation. The fires of judgement turn out to be the cathartic water of life, and eternal judgement of the great white throne (Rev. 20) is forgiveness. Blake's apocalypse, unlike John's apocalypse, ends in the restoration of all things and universal forgiveness from which no-one is excluded ... The book is not viewed as a map to the end of the world, but a resources which can inspire and a language which will assist in the process.[83]

Thus in keeping with his rejection of binary oppositions, Blake's Beasts are not depicted as wholly evil. This can be seen particularly clearly in the series of four watercolours of the Dragon and the Beasts that Blake produced for his patron Thomas Butts. In this image, *The Great Red Dragon and the Woman Clothed with the Sun: The Devil is Come Down*, the second in the series, it is hard to see the Dragon, menacing as he is, as wholly evil.[84] He is flying with angel-like wings, and there is some suggestion that he may be a chrysalis on the road to a more perfect nature. And is the Woman's expression and gesture one of terror or of something else? She certainly seems more than a match for the Dragon, with her impressive wingspan. Her gesture of resistance via her outstretched arms mirrors the 'Dragon's' gesture of intimidation, suggesting that good and evil are far closer than Revelation, with its rigid systems of good and evil, heavenly and earthly, would have us believe. This suggestion will be seen as a welcome or unwelcome subversion of the 'literal' meaning of the text, depending on your viewpoint regarding where the essence of Revelation is to be found. If it is Revelation's absolute certainties that appeal, then the suggestion that good and evil are more fluid will not. If it is seen, however, as a call seriously to question the power structures of our own time, despite their superficial attraction, then Blake's image of the Woman and the Dragon resonate.[85]

Yolanda Lopez's *Virgen de Guadalupe* series (1978) is an updating of the famous Virgin of Guadalupe image, one of the most revered icons in Latin America. The vision that inspired the Virgin of Guadalupe iconography saw Mary appear to Mexican peasant Juan Diego in 1531 in the guise of the Woman Clothed with the Sun.[86] Her image was reportedly imprinted on his cloak, now housed in a nearby basilica. All her attributes are the same as the figure of the Woman Clothed with the Sun in Revelation 12, with the additional detail that the moon on which she stands is supported by a cherub. Lopez was troubled by the iconography of the Virgin of Guadalupe, the most famous version of which hangs in the Basilica de Guadalupe in Mexico City. She found her demure downcast gaze and perfect 'white' appearance at odds with the Chicana experience of religion.[87]

In Lopez's triptych the conventional image of the Virgin as a young white woman has been replaced with contemporary working-class Mexican women. Although the Virgin/Woman Clothed with the Sun is undoubtedly the central figure in these images, it is the portrayal of the Dragon (Rev. 12) that is our focus. The first image, *Portrait of the Artist as the Virgen of Guadalupe*, depicts the artist herself as an exuberant, muscular running Virgin, who clutches a snake around its neck. The snake appears to be alive but subdued and is completely subordinate to the young woman. The second image, *Margaret F. Stewart: Our Lady of Guadalupe*, shows the artist's mother at her sewing machine, bespectacled and unadorned.[88] She is sewing the blue cloak of the Woman Clothed with the Sun and stares out past the viewer in a rejection of the demure down-turned gaze of earlier images of the figure. The snake is now coiled tightly around the body of the sewing machine, part of the subject's sewing accessories, subdued by her labour. The third image is of the artist's grandmother, Victoria Franco, who is, according to Lopez, stoically and calmly waiting for death. The cessation of her earthly struggles is visually celebrated via the dead (skinned) snake that she holds.[89]

In contrast to earlier images of the Dragon and the Woman Clothed with the Sun in which the Dragon was very much the dominant figure (see the *Trinity Apocalypse* of c.1260), the Dragon is the minor character and the 'Woman' is the central figure. Lopez has self-consciously used a well-established Western European iconographic motif, reworking it in order to liberate the powerful figures of the Dragon and the Woman Clothed with the Sun from their ancient context, thereby forcing the viewer to reconsider how they should be interpreted today.

Conclusion

This contribution has offered an exploration of a selection of artistic responses to Revelation by way of engagement with Brown's central theses. Focusing on Revelation has allowed me also to engage with Brown's auxiliary arguments on Revelation and the art it has inspired. In particular, Brown reveals an enthusiasm for visual responses that introduce an element of ambiguity to Revelation's binary view of the world.

My first extension to Brown's work on the visual history of Revelation involved a selection of images from three works – *The Lambeth Apocalypse*, Memling's *Apocalypse Panel* and Dürer's *Apocalypse Series* of 1498 – that illuminate aspects of the visionary essence of Revelation.

I argued that while this visionary essence is a constant feature of the text of Revelation, the nature of John's visions and the form they took are left unarticulated. The original 'deposit' has limitations. It is visual interpretations, by virtue of their synchronic, figurative qualities, that illuminate this vital aspect of Revelation. While *Lambeth* presents the visionary experience as episodic, Memling presents the experience as internal, fluid and synchronic. Dispensing with the Anglo-Norman journey motif, Memling offers insight into John's mind at the moment of the visionary experience. Dürer, meanwhile, combines something of the two approaches while simultaneously adding a new element, situating himself at the site of the visionary experience. The fact that, in some versions, his images were produced from the start without text legitimates the idea that Dürer believed his images to have superseded the text.

The theme of ambiguity was taken up in the second set of images explored above, focusing on the theme of Revelation's Beasts. An example of two images that allow for very little ambiguity were presented as a benchmark by which other, more ambiguous interpretations could be judged. The *Bertram Apocalypse* and the Cranach Apocalypse series were created as polemic. While such images capture the unrelenting polemical aspect of Revelation, they reduce it to a set of two-dimensional symbols. William Blake and Yolanda Lopez's recastings of the Dragon of Revelation 12 were analysed as examples that could be added to Brown's list of works by Botticelli, Signorelli and Lotto, which he argues successfully reinterpret Revelation's binary approach to judgement and transform it into a call for self-critique. Both these images suggest that the Dragon is not what he seems, and call for a revaluation of the world view proposed in Revelation. Ultimately images, as opposed to textual interpretations, by virtue of their synchronic format afford more of the ambiguity Brown prizes as crucial in representations that help to advance 'the moving text' tradition.

I return therefore to the statement made towards the beginning of the piece on the importance of Brown's work for anyone engaged in biblical reception history, and particularly the *artistic* reception of the Bible. His contention that on some occasions, artistic representations of a biblical text can be 'both artistically and morally superior' and are therefore vital to finding one's way to a deeper understanding of that text (and of the very nature of Christian faith) is groundbreaking. Brown's thesis and the examples that he explores in support of it, alongside the examples I have presented, combine to suggest that more serious engagement with visual biblical reception history by the academy is urgently needed.

Notes

1 David Brown, *Tradition and Imagination: Revelation and Change* (Oxford: Oxford University Press, 1999), 62, 341.

2 Ibid., 107, 375.

3 See especially David Brown, *Discipleship and Imagination: Christian Tradition and Truth* (Oxford: Oxford University Press, 2000), 152–61.

4 See Brown, *Tradition and Imagination*, 74.

5 Ibid., 367.

6 See the following for other works by myself and others that follow a similar methodological approach to the task of analysis of the visual reception of a biblical text (namely, exploring a range of 'typical' examples from different time periods): Natasha F. H. O'Hear, *Contrasting Images of the Book of Revelation in Late Medieval and Early Modern Art: A Case Study in Visual Exegesis* (Oxford: Oxford University Press, 2011; Natasha O'Hear and Anthony O'Hear, *Picturing the Apocalypse: The Book of Revelation in the Arts over Two Millennia* (Oxford: Oxford University Press, 2015). See Brown, *Discipleship and Imagination*, 160, n. 169 for an endorsement of the importance of looking at a range of images from different eras.

7 Brown, *Tradition and Imagination*, 341.

8 Brown, *Discipleship and Imagination*, 102–62.

9 Ibid., 152. Of course there are those who still believe in the literal nature of hell.

10 Ibid., 158–9.

11 Ibid., 159–60

12 Ibid., 152–62.

13 Ibid., 154–5.

14 Ibid., 161.

15 See Christopher Rowland, *Revelation* (London: Epworth Press, 1993), 37–53; Wes Howard-Brook and Anthony Gwyther, *Unveiling Empire: Reading Revelation Then and Now* (New York: Orbis, 1999), xxiv; Ian Boxall, *Revelation: Vision and Insight* (London: SPCK, 2002); O'Hear and O'Hear, *Picturing the Apocalypse*, 18–27, 288–94; Judith Kovacs and Christopher Rowland, *Revelation: The Apocalypse of Jesus Christ* (Oxford: Blackwell, 2004), 147–59, 177–89.

16 Brown, *Discipleship and Imagination*, 157, 161.

17 See ibid., 160, n. 169.

18 See ibid.

19 See O'Hear, *Contrasting Images*, 49–51.

20 Ibid., 160, and Brown, *Tradition and Imagination*, 341.

21 See O'Hear, *Contrasting Images*, 243–53 for a fuller outline of these arguments. See also David Brown, *God and Mystery in Words: Experience through Metaphor and Drama* (Oxford: Oxford University Press, 2008), 9, 132–4, 137–8.

22 See Boxall, *Revelation*; idem, *The Revelation of St John* (London: A. & C. Black, 2006); Kovacs and Rowland, *Revelation*; Christopher Rowland, *The Open Heaven* (New York: Crossroads, 1982).

23 David E. Aune, *Revelation*, 3 vols (Nashville, TN: Thomas Nelson, 1997–99), 1.cxxxii–cxxxiv.

24 Ian Paul, 'Source, Structure and Composition in the Book of Revelation', *The Book of Revelation*, ed. G. V. Allen, I. Paul and S. P. Woodman (Tübingen: Mohr Siebeck, 2015), 41–54.

25 Elisabeth Schüssler Fiorenza, *Revelation: Vision of a Just World* (Edinburgh: T&T Clark, 1993), 26–7.

26 Ibid., 29.

27 On Jewish apocalyptic literature, see John J. Collins, *The Apocalyptic Imagination: An Introduction to Jewish Apocalyptic Literature* (Grand Rapids, MI: Eerdmans,

1998); Rowland, *The Open Heaven*. On *merkabah* mysticism, see I. Gruenwald, *Apocalyptic and Merkavah Mysticism* (Leiden: Brill, 1980); Christopher Rowland and Christopher R. A. Morray-Jones, *The Mystery of God: Early Jewish Mysticism and the New Testament*, CRINT, vol. 12 (Leiden: Brill, 2009). On Hildegard of Bingen, see St Hildegard, *Scivias: Hildegard of Bingen*, trans. C. Hart and J. Bishop (Mahwah, NJ: Paulist Press, 1990). On Bridget of Sweden, see Rosalyn Voaden, *God's Words, Women's Voices: The Discernment of Spirits in the Writing of Late-Medieval Women Visionaries* (York: York Medieval Press, 1999). On Teresa of Avila, see Rowan Williams, *Teresa of Avila* (London: Continuum, 2003). On Blake, see G. E. Bentley, *Blake Records* (London: Yale University Press, 1969); Martin Myrone, *The Blake Book* (London: Tate, 2007); Christopher Rowland, '*Wheels within Wheels*': William Blake and the Ezekiel's Merkabah in Text and Image* (Milwaukee, WI: Marquette University Press, 2007); Christopher Rowland, *Blake and the Bible* (London: Yale University Press, 2010). On Collins, see William Anderson, *Cecil Collins: The Quest for the Great Happiness* (London: Barrie & Jenkins, 1988); Nomi Rowe (ed.), *In Celebration of Cecil Collins: Visionary Artist and Educator* (London: Tate, 2009). On Shamanistic, Inuit and tribal visionaries, see Mircea Eliade, *Shamanism: Archaic Techniques of Ecstasy*, trans. W. R. Trask (London: Routledge & Kegan Paul, 1964); S. Niditch, 'The Visionary', in *Ideal Figures in Ancient Judaism: Profiles and Paradigms*, ed. J. J. Collins and G. W. E. Nickelsburg (Chico, CA: Scholars' Press, 1980), 153–79.

28 Johannes Lindblom, *Geschichte und Offenbarungen* (Lund: CWK Gleerup, 1968), 218.

29 He speaks of falling at the feet of the Son of Man 'as though dead' (1.17), of weeping over the failure to find anyone worthy to open the scroll (5.4), of finding the scroll given to him by the Mighty Angel both sweet and sour (10.10) and of being 'astonished' by the Whore of Babylon (17.6).

30 Christopher Rowland, 'British Interpretation of the Apocalypse', in *The Book of Revelation*, ed. Allen et al., 243.

31 Brown, *Tradition and Imagination*, 281–3.

32 Brown, *Discipleship and Imagination*, 152–3. The Lambeth Apocalypse measures 27.2 cm × 20.0 cm, making it a sizeable manuscript but not an unwieldy one.

33 See colour plates in O'Hear, *Contrasting Images*. For a summary of the Berengaudus commentary, see ibid., 16–22. For a more in-depth approach, see Suzanne Lewis, 'Exegesis and Illustration in Thirteenth Century English Apocalypses', in *The Apocalypse in the Middle Ages*, ed. R. Emmerson and B. McGinn (New York: Cornell University Press, 1992), 259–75; Derk Visser, *Apocalypse as Utopian Expectation (800–1500): The Apocalypse Commentary of Berengaudus of Ferrières and the Relationship between Exegesis, Liturgy and Iconography* (Leiden: Brill, 1996), 12–103.

34 Although the *vita* of John and the additional miniatures do include a fair amount of anti-Semitic imagery. See for instance the illustrated 'Life of Antichrist' that has been inserted into the margins around Revelation 10.11–11.8. These images depict Antichrist and his followers as Jews (identifiable by the fact that they are wearing pointed 'Jewish' hats). For more information on this, see O'Hear, *Contrasting Images*, 38–9. Note also that by the time of the *Gulbenkian* and *Abingdon Apocalypse Manuscripts* (*c.*1270), which pictorialized the commentary extracts as well as the text of Revelation, the anti-Jewish bias was much more obvious.

35 See colour plates in O'Hear, *Contrasting Images*. See also Nigel J. Morgan, *The Lambeth Apocalypse* (London: Harvey Miller, 1990). On John's role in the Lambeth miniatures, see Suzanne Lewis, *Reading Images: Narrative Discourse and Reception in the Thirteenth-Century Illuminated Apocalypse* (Cambridge: Cambridge University Press, 1995), pp. 19–39; O'Hear, *Contrasting Images*, 31–4. The prevalence of John indicates an interpretative decision on the part of the artists that is at odds with the presentation of John in the Berengaudus commentary, where he is the 'transparent

instrument through whom the vision is presented'. Barbara Nolan, *The Gothic Visionary Perspective* (Princeton, NJ: Princeton University Press, 1977), 12.

36 This notion reaches its apex in the monumental fourteenth-century *Angers Apocalypse Tapestry* in which the viewer literally has to walk alongside the sections of tapestry in order to view and comprehend the narrative (around 130 metres long and consisting of two tiers of tapestries each standing around 2 metres high). See O'Hear, *Contrasting Images*, 43–68.

37 This final miniature was a new and important addition to the Berengaudus cycles. Previous manuscripts had ended with an image of John and the angel and not of John and Christ (Rev. 22.8–9). See O'Hear, *Contrasting Images*, 29–30.

38 Brown, *Discipleship and Imagination*, 153.

39 See Lewis, *Reading Images*, 242–59 on the process of 'internalization' of the Revelation narrative, which she believes was facilitated by the Anglo-Apocalypse manuscripts.

40 See Dirk De Vos, *Hans Memling: The Complete Works* (London: Thames & Hudson, 1994), 151–6; Visser, *Apocalypse as Utopian Expectation (800–1500)*, 157–64.

41 It was commissioned by four ecclesiastics associated with St John's Hospital in Bruges (Jacob de Ceuninc, Antheunis Seghers, Agnes Casembrood and Clara van Hulsen) to hang above the new high altar in the hospital chapel. See Irène Smets, *The Memling Museum: St. John's Hospital Bruges* (Bruges: Ludion Guides, 2001), 35.

42 For discussion of hospitals in the Middle Ages and their relationship with the Church, see Roy Porter, *The Greatest Benefit to Mankind: A Medical History from Antiquity to the Present* (London: HarperCollins, 1997), 110–34.

43 Fig. 21 in O'Hear, *Contrasting Images*.

44 See Peter K. Klein, 'The Apocalypse in Medieval Art', in *The Apocalypse in the Middle Ages*, ed. Emmerson and McGinn, 193–96.

45 See Richard Bauckham, *The Theology of the Book of Revelation* (Cambridge: Cambridge University Press, 1993), 66–76.

46 See Hieronymus Bosch, *St John the Evangelist on Patmos* (c.1489 or later), Gemäldegallerie, Berlin, and Diego Velázquez, *St John the Evangelist on the Island of Patmos* (c.1618), London, National Gallery.

47 O'Hear, *Contrasting Images*, 96.

48 See Panofsky's famous quote to this effect: 'only when we behold a world evidently controlled by what is known as the laws of nature can we become aware of that temporary suspension of these laws which is the essence of a miracle'. Erwin Panofsky, *The Life and Art of Albrecht Dürer* (Princeton, NJ: Princeton University Press, 1955), 56.

49 See Brown, *Tradition and Imagination*, 324–5.

50 See Joseph Koerner, *The Moment of Self-Portraiture in German Renaissance Art* (Chicago, IL: University of Chicago Press, 1993), 203.

51 Dürer's Apocalypse books were loosely bound but had no cover and measured 39.4 cm × 28.3 cm.

52 On apocalyptic speculation in the 1490s, see Diarmaid MacCulloch, *Reformation Europe's House Divided 1490–1700* (London: Penguin, 2004), 53–7.

53 See J. M. Massing, 'Dürer's Dreams', *Journal of the Warburg and Courtauld Institutes* 49 (1986), 242–4; and Giulia Bartrum, *Albrecht Dürer and his Legacy* (London: British Museum Press, 2002), 115–6. For a summary, see O'Hear, *Contrasting Images*, 147–8.

54 For more on the Koberger Apocalypse illustration, see O'Hear, *Contrasting Images*, 150–4.

55 For an attempt to resolve the debate based on close analysis of the 1498 and 1511 versions of the book (the German and Latin versions respectively), see ibid., 154–8

56 Bartrum, *Albrecht Dürer*, 124.
57 Fig. 35 in O'Hear, *Contrasting Images*.
58 Bauckham, *The Theology of the Book of Revelation*, 73.
59 Frits van der Meer, *Apocalypse: Visions from the Book of Revelation in Western Art* (London: Thames & Hudson, 1978), 296, 298, 306.
60 See similarities with Dürer's *Self-Portrait with Landscape* of 1498.
61 Panofsky, *Life and Art of Albrecht Dürer*, 58–9.
62 For a summary of the Panofsky position on the order of composition and some suggested amendments, see O'Hear, *Contrasting Images*, 158–60.
63 Fig. 36 in O'Hear, *Contrasting Images*.
64 On Dürer's use of his monogram, see Panofsky, *Life and Art of Albrecht Dürer*, 46–7; Koerner, *The Moment of Self-Portraiture in German Renaissance Art*, 203–7; and Lisa Pon, *Raphael, Dürer and Marcantonio Raimondi: Copying and the Italian Renaissance Print* (London: Yale University Press, 2004), 39–41.
65 See Rowland, *The Open Heaven*, 420.
66 Brown, *Tradition and Imagination*, 341.
67 Fig. 33 in O'Hear, *Contrasting Images*.
68 See O'Hear, *Contrasting Images*, 169–170 for more on the Millennium/New Jerusalem debate.
69 See O'Hear and O'Hear, *Picturing the Apocalypse*, 166–8.
70 Brown, *Discipleship and Imagination*, 150–62.
71 For more on Botticelli's *Mystic Nativity*, see Rab Hatfield, 'Botticelli's *Mystic Nativity*, Savonarola and the Millennium', *Journal of the Warburg and Courtauld Institutes* 58 (1995), 89–114; and O'Hear, *Contrasting Images*, 105–33.
72 See Claus M. Kauffman, *An Altarpiece of the Book of Revelation from Master Bertram's Workshop in Hamburg* (London: Victoria and Albert Museum, 1968), 1–13. The visualization ends at Revelation 16 because that is where the commentary ends.
73 Fig. 6.5 in O'Hear and O'Hear, *Picturing the Apocalypse*.
74 See ibid., 144–5.
75 See Kovacs and Rowland, *Revelation*, 7–11.
76 See O'Hear, *Contrasting Images*, 186–8.
77 For a fuller discussion of the changes made by Cranach to the Dürer series, see ibid., 188–96.
78 On the afterlife of this motif, see O'Hear, *Contrasting Images*, 194.
79 On the political dimension of Cranach's interpretation of Revelation, see ibid., 195.
80 Brown, *Discipleship and Imagination*, 155.
81 See Rowland, 'British Interpretation of the Apocalypse', 234; Four Zoas 8.115 (E385).
82 Bentley, *Blake Records*, 567; quoted in Rowland, 'British Interpretation of the Apocalypse', 235.
83 Ibid.
84 Blakes's watercolour measures 40.8 cm × 33.7 cm. Fig. 5.7 in O'Hear and O'Hear, *Picturing the Apocalypse*.
85 On contrasting interpretations of the meaning of Revelation, see O'Hear and O'Hear, *Picturing the Apocalypse*, 288–94.
86 See Kovacs and Rowland, *Revelation*, 37; and Karen Mary Davalos, *Yolanda M. Lopez* (Los Angeles, CA: UCLA Chicano Studies Research Center Press, 2008), 87–8.
87 Ibid., 88.
88 Plate 53 in O'Hear and O'Hear, *Picturing the Apocalypse*.
89 Here the snake represents not so much evil as the cycle of life and death. See ibid., 93.

9

The Stained Glass *Biblia Pauperum* Windows of Steinfeld Abbey: Monastic Spirituality, Salvation History and the Theological Imagination

WILLIAM P. HYLAND

Scholars of Renaissance German stained glass consider the cloister windows of the former Premonstratensian abbey of Steinfeld to be among the best surviving examples of this medium. The abbey church was begun in 1142, and along with it, a Romanesque cloister. In the last years of the fifteenth century this Romanesque cloister was replaced by a new one built on its foundations. Part of a steady programme of renewal, this was envisaged and carried out by no fewer than six abbots of Steinfeld over half a century. The largest part of the new cloister was complete by 1517, and this would be the setting for the magnificent stained glass. The windows were commissioned from the workshop of the painter Gerhart Remisch, who may well have presided over the whole production. The first 21 windows were made between 1522 and 1542, while the remaining eight were completed between 1555 and 1558. The windows form an extensive typological cycle, essentially portraying the biblical narrative in glass, with some accompanying text. This method was inspired by the woodcut form known as *Biblia Pauperum* (Paupers' Bible), which since the mid fifteenth century had become an increasingly important devotional tool to enhance meditation on Scripture. The main register above includes scenes from the life of Christ, as well as scenes spanning from the Fall of the Rebel Angels to the Last Judgement. The lower register, however, contains not only portraits of patrons, which is to be expected, but also an extensive series of saints associated with the history of the Premonstratensian order and Steinfeld Abbey in particular.[1] This chapter will be the first attempt to analyse these windows from the perspective of Premonstratensian spirituality, and in doing so will utilize the work of David Brown stressing how artistic expression both reflects and shapes the reception of sacred narratives.

Imagination and Inspiration

The fact that the windows have survived the vicissitudes of history is a miracle in itself. The religious wars and other conflicts endemic to sixteenth- and seventeenth-century Germany resulted in the glass being removed from the cloisters for safe keeping on five occasions, the first in 1583. When Napoleon secularized Steinfeld Abbey in 1802, the glass disappeared, and for some time it was believed that the windows were lost for ever. But as was the case with many objects once belonging to secularized monasteries on the continent, the windows would have a new lease of life in Britain, and this due to the efforts of wealthy collectors and their agents in the early nineteenth century.[2]

The story of the Steinfeld glass making its way to Britain rivals the best detective fiction. While space does not permit the recounting of the entire story here, the main outline is as follows. Soon after the suppression of the abbey in 1802, the antique dealer Christian Geerling of Cologne probably acquired and restored the glass in his workshop. It made its way to England due to the efforts of John Christopher Hampp, a German immigrant who lived in Norwich and was known for buying large amounts of German, Flemish and French glass, and his partner William Stevenson. Panels ended up in 18 private collections and churches in the United Kingdom, and three in the United States. Lord Brownlow acquired and installed 38 panels in his chapel at Ashridge Park in Hertfordshire.[3] Eventually the Ashridge Park panels were auctioned off and purchased by Mr E. Cook, who subsequently donated them to the Victoria and Albert Museum. In subsequent years most of the Steinfeld glass has been located and identified, and with the help of a 1719 detailed description of the windows made by the canons of Steinfeld, scholars have made much progress in the recreation of the original plan and setting.[4]

The Victoria and Albert museum windows can be viewed in a tasteful and evocative setting, surrounded by period furnishings and helpful educational materials.[5] While this mode of display certainly does not of course perfectly recreate the original setting of the windows in the Steinfeld cloister, it does seem to reflect concerns, expressed so eloquently by Brown, to allow the public to encounter sacred objects in an environment conducive to contemplation and marked by sensitivity to the windows' original function and context.[6] The museum's website provides digital images and information about each window, making them more accessible to the public than at any time in their history. This allows the achievement of the artists and canons who supported them to live on, moving beyond education to fresh engagement.

But what of the windows' original purpose and their physical and sacral context within the cloister at Steinfeld Abbey? As interesting as the subsequent afterlife of the windows has been, following the secularization of the abbey in the early nineteenth century, their original function and symbolism remain of paramount importance. This chapter will next explore the context of humanism and ecclesiastical reform in which the windows came into being, and continued to play a part in the lives of the Premonstratensians and their supporters who lived in intimate proximity with them every day. More specifically, I will examine how the subject matter of several of the windows went beyond the conventions of the *Biblia Pauperum* to incorporate elements of Premonstratensian spirituality. For the canons of Steinfeld Abbey, the scenes portrayed in glass not only gave them the opportunity to visualize the scriptural text but also to insert themselves into the text, making it a living and a shared reality for the monastic community and its patrons. In so doing, the Premonstratensians extended the episodes of salvation history into the more recent past, reflecting on their own order's foundation in the twelfth century and its ongoing journey in their own time. This reception of the text is an excellent example of the process described by Brown, with art both reflecting and shaping the reception and understanding of sacred narratives. As Brown describes this phenomenon, artistic imagination and genius can help 'bridge the distance' between biblical and historical characters on the one hand and, on the other, those producing and experiencing art in later generations, in their own cultural contexts.[7] In fact he argues that 'the Christian artistic tradition drew its strength from its ability to innovate – its capacity to transmit the biblical story in ways which at times could speak more powerfully to contemporaries than the original deposit'.[8] Seen in this light, one can see how the windows of the Steinfeld cloister are manifestations of the canons' monastic spirituality and Christian humanist sensibilities. And beyond that, at the very time when the Scriptures in Germany were being used by the early Protestants to invalidate the foundational premises of both Catholic sacramental understanding and the religious orders, the Steinfeld windows can be seen as a theological and imaginative affirmation of Premonstratensian spirituality and of the ongoing place of the order in the narrative of salvation history.

Steinfeld Abbey: Humanism and Reform

The Premonstratensian order was founded by Norbert of Xanten (1080–1134) in the twelfth century, and its rapid spread throughout Latin Christendom represented one of the key elements in the articulation of the Gregorian reform of clerical and regular life. Norbert was a German nobleman, who pursued a careerist path as a cleric until his conversion at the age of 35. He gradually embraced a very austere life of penance, combining it with evangelical preaching, itinerancy and peacemaking. Norbert eventually founded a religious house at Prémontré in north-eastern France, and other houses quickly followed. As his influence spread all over Christendom, his new order was approved by the Pope in 1126. Norbert himself spent the last years of his life as Archbishop of Magdeburg, where he often served as a peacemaker between Pope and Emperor. He died in 1134, and would not be officially canonized until 1582.[9]

The Premonstratensians are also known as the Canons Regular of Prémontré, after their mother abbey, or the 'white canons', due to the colour of their habits. The Premonstratensian charism drew its inspiration from the *Rule of St Augustine*, and saw the mixed life of the regular canon as an ideal expression of the *vita apostolica*. This charism, expressed by twelfth-century canons with the phrase *docere verbo et exemplo* ('to teach by word and example'), was the basis of the involvement of the Premonstratensians in numerous apostolates, including parish life, missionary work, schools, hospice work, cathedral chapters and the episcopate, and of course the community life of their own abbeys. Among the larger Augustinian family of regular canons, one can single out the Norbertines for their emphasis on the communion of charity, the common good, mutual fraternal support, a strong liturgical life and Marian devotion.[10] Although there were Premonstratensian masters at the universities, most Premonstratensians who received a university education returned to their abbeys to undertake important leadership roles in the local community.[11]

This primary focus on the life of the local church was integral to Premonstratensian spirituality. Like the monastic orders, the Premonstratensians took a lifelong vow of stability; that is, to live in the monastery of their profession for their whole lives, in obedience to the abbot or abbess. Thus while Premonstratensians did belong to an international order, which was governed by an annual chapter and divided up into provinces known as circaries, their primary outlook was often coloured by the local environment in which they lived out their religious lives. Male Premonstratensian abbeys often had charge of many parishes in the area and were an integral part of local life over the generations and centuries. This included close and ongoing relations with important lay patrons of the abbey as well as other religious orders in the area.[12] Premonstratensian abbeys also tended to maintain close relations and ties of 'filiation' over time with their 'daughter houses'; that is, houses founded by canons from a particular abbey.

Studies of late-medieval Premonstratensian libraries indicate a marked conservatism and decided lack of trendiness. For example, beyond practical works of canon law, the emphasis was on patristics, the Victorines and writers such as Bonaventure, rather than on Ockham and the *via moderna*.[13] The evidence would seem to indicate that the late-medieval Premonstratensians, like the German Benedictines and Cistercians, preserved a spirituality based on *lectio divina* and couched in the rhythms of daily liturgical life.[14] One could speculate that, like many Benedictine and Cistercian abbeys in Germany, this would make the Premonstratensians very open to the humanistic currents of the sixteenth century, which was certainly the case at Steinfeld Abbey.

The former Premonstratensian abbey of Steinfeld is located in Kall, North Rhine-Westphalia, in a region known as the Eifel. The first monastic settlement at Steinfeld took place in about 1070, with regular canons from Springiersbach arriving in 1121. These canons put themselves under the Premonstratensian rule around 1130, within the lifetime of St Norbert himself. Steinfeld was raised to the status of an abbey in 1184. It became an important monastery in the German Empire and established a number of daughter houses across Europe in Ireland, the Netherlands, other regions of Germany and further east, including Strahov Abbey in Prague. The basilica, formerly the abbey church, was built between 1142 and 1150 by the Premonstratensians as one of the earliest vaulted churches in Germany. The present structure includes features representing a number of periods and styles, from the original Romanesque style through to the Gothic, Renaissance and Baroque. The basilica contains the tomb of St Hermann Joseph of Steinfeld, a popular Premonstratensian saint, mystic and poet of the thirteenth century. There would be an unbroken succession of 44 abbots until secularization in 1802. After its suppression by Napoleon the abbey was used for secular purposes, but since 1920 the abbey and church have been used by the Salvatorian religious order.[15]

In the later fifteenth century and through the middle decades of the sixteenth century the abbots of Steinfeld played an active role in the local affairs of the Premonstratensian order in their area of Germany. Steinfeld Abbey belonged to the important Westphalian circary of the order. This circary actually stretched over several different German territories, including those of the archbishopric of Cologne, the dukes of Westphalia, the town of Amsberg and the archdukes of Cleve-Mark and Julich-Berg, these latter two being joined into one in 1521. The circary included 50 Premonstratensian houses before the Reformation. Steinfeld was under the archbishops of Cologne. Besides its many daughter houses, Steinfeld also had the care of several female Premonstratensian houses in this area of Germany. The abbots of Steinfeld were often called on to formally visit and help reform neighbouring abbeys, involving the abbots in the intricate and complex world of local patronage and politics. This widespread reform activity attests to the high regard in which Steinfeld itself was held. Thus we have surviving records of the activities of many late-medieval abbots, such as Abbot John II Buschelman, Abbot John III and Abbot Reiner Hundt. The importance of the abbots of Steinfeld in this regard continued into the sixteenth century, and only intensified with the coming of the Lutheran reformation.[16]

The rise and spread of Protestantism threatened the elimination of all religious orders in those parts of Europe where it proved triumphant. Thus the Premonstratensian order by the mid-sixteenth century had completely disappeared in much of northern and central Germany, Scandinavia and England, with further losses on the horizon in Scotland, Ireland and parts of the Low Countries. In this rather grave situation, with the very existence of the order at stake, Nicholas Psaume, first abbot and then bishop of Verdun, followed by the vigorous abbot general John de Preutz, began the process, in the wider context of the first implementation of the Tridentine reforms, of essentially saving the order and guiding it towards what would become a significant era of reform, revival and renewal in the seventeenth century.[17]

As it lay within the lands of the prince archbishops of Cologne, Steinfeld Abbey was not suppressed at the Reformation. During this period of crisis it was guided by the able leadership of Jacob Panhausen, abbot of Steinfeld and vicar general of the Westphalian circary from 1540 to 1582, a reign initiated before the Council of Trent and symbolically ending the same year as the canonization of St Norbert. In Panhausen's writings we see the combination of zeal for monastic reform, humanistic learning and a strong sense of Premonstratensian identity that is also reflected in the Steinfeld stained glass, the final installation of which he oversaw.[18]

Jacob Panhausen was born near Liege to an important local family around 1500, educated there by the Brethren of the Common life, and completed his studies with the Brethren in Cologne. From them he would have absorbed the piety of the *Devotio Moderna*, as well as a humanist education, the model that would eventually influence the *ratio studiorum* of the Jesuits as well as schools in Protestant areas. He professed at Steinfeld and had several jobs there, including cellarer, which was a position of important responsibility in handling the economic affairs of an abbey. Panhausen's capability resulted in his being given many duties by Abbot Johann von Ahrweiler, who saw him as his natural successor. Despite Panhausen's popularity, when the abbot died he was seen as too young to be made abbot, so Fr Simon Diepenbach was put in charge. When Abbot Diepenbach succumbed to the plague shortly thereafter, Panhausen was elected abbot on 4 November 1540 and confirmed by the abbot general.

Abbot Panhausen was very involved in the life of the order, working closely with other prelates to preserve and reorganize the affairs of the Premonstratensians all over central Europe. As a young abbot in Steinfeld he reorganized the abbey school and expanded the library, determining that the lessons in philosophy and theology should occur on a daily basis. The great patristics scholar, jurist and philologist Laurentius Sifanus, professor at Ingolstadt, attested to Panhausen's intellectual reputation. In 1567 Sifanus fled Cologne because of the threat of plague and was given refuge at Steinfeld. The eminent humanist refers flatteringly, in a letter to a friend, to the erudition and piety of Abbot Panhausen. Panhausen's extensive spiritual writings show a deep immersion in the world of Christian humanism, with a strong focus on Scripture, on patristic writers such as St Augustine and on many classical Roman writers.[19] It is difficult not to see the humanistic style of the Steinfeld glass in the abbey cloisters as the perfect setting for, and indeed architectural expression of, the monastic humanism so evident in Panhausen's eloquent writings and orations.

The robust spiritual and reformist atmosphere at Steinfeld was paralleled, as previously mentioned, by the rebuilding of parts of the abbey in the early sixteenth century, including the stained glass windows in the new cloister. The choice of a *Biblia Pauperum* theme is not surprising in this context. The term *Biblia Pauperum* refers to a type of illustrated book popular in late-medieval northern Europe, including Germany and the Low Countries. The subject matter was not the whole Bible per se but scenes from the Old and New Testaments, often with a typological connection. The biblical scenes were generally accompanied by a short text or at least a few words, either in Latin or the vernacular, identifying the scene. With the invention of printing these began to be produced using woodcut illustrations. Despite their name, the books were not intended for the poor but were probably very popular in monasteries, where they served as tools for meditation. Many of the illustrations even incorporated smaller scenes in the background of the main picture, as well as architectural features such as church, cloister or houses. By the early sixteenth century in Germany, these books had become immensely popular, and important artists such as Albrecht Dürer were involved in their production.[20]

The last decades of the fifteenth century witnessed a happy confluence of three streams of creative endeavour, namely the flourishing *Biblia Pauperum* tradition; new and improved technologies in stained glass, allowing larger panels; and a high level of artistic achievement modelled on the imagery of Italian Renaissance painting, producing, as Susan Foister puts it, a 'subtle balance of painterly techniques and coloured glass, at its height in Germany in the early sixteenth century'.[21] These *Biblia Pauperum* in glass consisted of Old and New Testament scenes, along with donor panels. The images also include atmospheric backgrounds and the use of architectural details and perspective characteristic of the Renaissance. Important churches and abbeys commissioned and installed stained glass *Biblia Pauperum* of the highest quality; among them were the Cistercians at Mariawald and the Carthusians at St Barbara's charterhouse in Cologne.[22] These neighbouring abbeys undoubtedly served as an inspiration for the Premonstratensians at Steinfeld. The three monastic collections of glass, dispersed as they now are to various museums and churches, remain as a testament and final flowering of an artistic tradition that would come to an abrupt end with the Reformation. While much of northern Germany around them embraced Protestantism, and specifically rejected the monastic way of life and its perceived role and place in salvation history and contemporary society, these abbeys continued to thrive and contribute to the lasting reputation of Cologne as the 'citadel of Catholicism'.[23] Now we will turn to an analysis of windows from Steinfeld, and how they portrayed and embodied both key elements of Premonstratensian spirituality and specific aspects of Catholic theology in an age of upheaval and intense religious controversy.

Premonstratensian Images in the Steinfeld Stained Glass

More research needs to be done on the exact placement of the windows in the Steinfeld cloister. What does seem clear is that the typological biblical scenes were complemented by representations of donors to the abbey, as well as by events associated with the history of the abbey, and by an extensive series of accompanying saints, often with additional smaller scenes from their lives.[24] According to David King, there were a total of 272 scenes over 342 panels at Steinfeld. My reading of King's list indicates that there were at least 16 panels that include images of Premonstratensians or saints closely associated with the order. I will now consider the content and symbolism of six of the windows in which the Premonstratensians themselves are portrayed. How do these scenes correspond to Premonstratensian self-perception as expressed in the writings of Panhausen, and in light of a perceived continuity with the biblical events and their own role in salvation history? This spirituality is epitomized in the life of their founder St Norbert, by the commitment to the *Rule of St Augustine*, as well as by the sacred history of their own region and abbey.

The first window under consideration contains an image of St Augustine, a kneeling Premonstratensian and most likely St George in the background dressed as knight and holding a green dragon by the collar.[25] Augustine is dressed as a bishop with full episcopal regalia, and holds a crozier and open book. His heart is transfixed with arrows, a traditional iconographic symbol. Dated to 1530–2, this window originally sat in the Steinfeld cloister below typological images of Christ expelling merchants from the Temple and the rebuilding of the Temple. It is now found in South Wales, along with several other Steinfeld windows, in the church of St Cadoc, in Glynneath, Glamorgan.[26] The kneeling canon, although not identified, is almost certainly St Norbert himself. This is evident because the window clearly portrays a vision recounted in one of the earliest stories about Norbert, written down only a few years after the saint's death in 1134 in a collection known as *The Additions of the Brothers of Cappenberg*. The account begins with the supernatural source of Norbert's decision to adopt *The Rule of St Augustine* for his new community:

> I heard the same voice of orthodoxy (Norbert) go on to the chapter: 'I know a brother of our profession who was studiously examining our rule when the blessed Augustine himself appeared, not because of the brother's own merits but because of the prayers of his confreres. With his right hand Augustine held out a golden rule extending from his side. He revealed himself to the brother in glowing speech, saying, "I whom you see am Augustine, bishop of Hippo. Behold, you have before you the rule, which I wrote. If you confreres, my sons, serve faithfully under it, they will stand safely by Christ in the terror of the last judgement."' Norbert told these things humbly as if about another man, but I believe that this revelation was to him.[27]

This passage is clearly the one illustrated in the window, including even the golden colour of the Rule offered by Augustine to Norbert. The theme of standing steadfast at the final judgement is imaginatively portrayed by St George who, dressed as a faithful knight, confidently and reassuringly holds the Dragon in thrall. In the same Cappenberg collection, whose text and stories would be well known to the brothers of Steinfeld, an adjacent passage describes just what observance of the *Rule of St Augustine* meant to Norbert:

> It then pleased the Holy Spirit dwelling in Norbert, the messenger of truth, to raise a miraculous harvest from the Lord's fields, namely, that the brothers in the aforesaid communities should profess the Rule of Blessed Augustine. They observed the Rule more strictly than had been the general practice, abstaining from fatty meat and showing the rigor of their penance in rough attire, for the bridegroom's friend John ate of natural and woody food, not of delicacies, and was praised for the roughness of his garments by the Saviour himself before the crowds

who flocked to him in the desert. So our own way of life, divine mercy accompanying it, now stretches far and wide, and we may believe that it will extend much further in the future. So we know that it was both begun in the word of the Holy Spirit and made famous by God's ordination. For did not the Lord, the leader on the journey, carry the vine from Egypt in his arm, held high? And did he not cast out the robbers and criminals who lived in this place, planting the roots of the vine that now stretches its shoots to the sea and beyond, with the support of his heavenly hand?[28]

This passage from the brothers of Cappenberg is fascinating for several reasons. At the end it refers to how Cappenberg itself was founded, namely as a gift from the nobleman Godfrey of Cappenberg, who before his conversion to become a disciple of Norbert had participated in violence against the local archbishop. Godfrey became a disciple of Norbert and from his riches founded several abbeys, including Cappenberg. He became immediately regarded as a saint in the order. Godfrey regarded his donation of his lands and castles to Norbert as a restitution for what he and others perceived as his crimes.[29] In the context of this window, located underneath the story of Christ throwing the moneychangers out of the Temple, it would remind the Premonstratensian brothers of Steinfeld of their own foundations in Germany, when Christ, in the form of the repentant Godfrey, 'cast out the robbers and criminals who lived in this place'. This window then clearly places the foundation of the order in Germany within the wider and continuing action of the Holy Spirit in history. The text also brings up other aspects of Norbertine spirituality, such as living a life of austerity; that is, the rigour of penitence, in explicit imitation of and continuity with John the Baptist. The subsequent spread of the Premonstratensian order is evoked as a God-ordained prophecy, explicitly seeing the work of the order as a continuance of the story of the salvific work of God in the world.

Besides these familiar passages concerning the early days of the order, the images in this window would also affirm for the viewer the connection between the Premonstratensian order and the most eminent of the Latin Fathers of the Church, Augustine. At a time when many Protestant theologians were advancing interpretations of Augustine in favour of their own positions, this window clearly was meant to reassure the Premonstratensians that they, and not the new Protestant reformers, were not only faithful to the teachings of Augustine but also professed and lived the *religio Augustini*; that is, the religious life in community epitomized in his writings. It is not difficult to imagine Abbot Jacob Panhausen pondering this new window in the cloister before writing his lengthy and learned commentary on the Rule, as well as his many other writings that continually quote Augustine. This window, and the hagiographical texts it illustrated and made vividly present, were a daily reminder of the ideals Panhausen urged his canons to emulate. This pairing of Norbert and Augustine in iconography as the order's founders would later become standard in the churches and cloisters of Premonstratensian abbeys that flourished in the Baroque era.

Other Premonstratensian images illustrated aspects of the life of Norbert, while at the same time expressing the links of Steinfeld Abbey to the local and regional church. An example of this is a window showing a Premonstratensian canon, identified as Jacobus Scheuen, pastor in Bengen, kneeling in prayer next to a standing St Lambert.[30] In the background is an image of a simply dressed penitent in earnest prayer before a crucifix, with a church nearby on a hill. The image of St Lambert would have symbolized several important points for the Steinfeld Norbertines at this particular time in their history. Lambert was of a noble family of Maastricht, and served as a missionary and bishop until his martyrdom at the hand of a Frankish king in AD 700. Lambert was deeply venerated throughout the Rhineland and the Low Countries as a great pastor of souls and martyr; his most important shrine was in Liege cathedral. This window was created in 1542, two years after Jacob Panhausen became abbot of Steinfeld. As previously mentioned, Panhausen was born near Liege and educated there by the Brethren of the Common Life. The choice of Lambert could well be a homage and reaffirmation of his ties to his own family and to this large and powerful bishopric. St Lambert was also the patron of the church in Bengen, where the pictured Jacobus Scheuen was pastor. Furthermore, St Lambert was subject of an important cult in the nearby city of Münster. There was and still is an important annual festival and folk holiday in Münster during the two weeks leading up to his feast day of 17 September, the *Lambertusfest*. For the canons of Steinfeld, the city of Münster had also come to have very different connotations in recent years. From 1534 to 1535 the city had been taken over by radical Anabaptists, who had temporarily succeeded in overthrowing civic and ecclesiastical authority and indeed threatened to spread ideas of radical economic and social reform throughout Germany. For many, this episode seemed to fulfil all of the fears associated with radical Protestantism and rebellious social upheaval. When the city was recaptured after a long and grisly siege and the old order restored, the Anabaptist leaders were executed and hung in cages from the steeple of the church of St Lambert in the city. These events continued to haunt the imaginations and feed the fears of many in Germany, not least in Cologne.[31] This window, placed in the Steinfeld cloister under scenes of the resurrected Christ appearing to his disciples,[32] probably had a very particular meaning for those canons who paused to gaze upon it.

The background scene of the penitent prostrate before the crucifix, although not identified, almost certainly refers to an episode in the life of St Norbert. According to early hagiographers, Norbert spent years after his sudden conversion in heartfelt penance, including time at the abbey of Siegburg, whose name implies its mountainous setting. Norbert, like the figure in the painting, also wore a hair shirt, and divested himself of all his noble finery.[33] In Xanten itself there was a local tradition that Norbert at this time frequently prostrated himself before a crucifix, shedding tears and doing severe penance.[34] The spot in Xanten where Norbert practised the ascetical life after his conversion was a place of pilgrimage, undoubtedly well known to the Steinfeld Premonstratensians. Lambert's vestment in the painting is adorned by a large and prominent crucifix. Like Lambert the evangelist and martyr, Norbert also had given up all to pursue a way of life of simplicity and sacrifice. The connections between the two saints and their place in the spread and revival of Christianity in the Rhineland must have resonated with the canons in their own context of religious upheaval, the two crucifixes in the window an explicit rejection of the violent iconoclasm of the Münster Anabaptists.

Another link between local ecclesiastical history and Premonstratensian spirituality can be seen in the window, installed in 1525, commemorating the transfer of the relics of Sts Potentinus, Felix and Simplicius to Steinfeld Abbey.[35] St Potentinus, who was a Roman-era martyr and the patron saint of the abbey church, is also portrayed in other windows in the cloister. This particular scene shows an important event of the twelfth century, when the Premonstratensians were given Steinfeld and a new church was constructed. The important local nobleman who patronized and supported these events, Dietrich von Hochsteden, Count of Are, is shown prostrating himself before the relics carried in procession to the church. Next to this window was another one showing the Count's ancestor, Sibodo, the original founder of the first abbey in the year 920.[36] The relics of these early Roman martyrs had been transferred to the new abbey of Steinfeld in the tenth century, a gift of the archbishops of Cologne. The von Hochstedens continued to be a powerful family in the sixteenth century, and this window reaffirms the abbey's connection to the local nobility. Another scene of this same window reaffirms the abbey's close relationship with the archbishops of Cologne, portraying Archbishop Herman von Wied of Cologne (1515–47) kneeling before St Peter, who is wearing papal vestments.[37] Ironically, within only a few years of this window's installation, the archbishop would become a Lutheran and lead an ultimately unsuccessful attempt to introduce Lutheranism and secularize the archbishopric under his own rule.[38] As Premonstratensians walking in their cloister gazed upon this window during and after these tumultuous events, they must have reflected on the tenuous nature of their situation and way of life, despite its deep roots in the local life and history of the region.

Above these panels, in the upper registry of what is called Window II, were biblical scenes that provided a very specific context to the scenes from local history. One portrays the Old Testament King David, while another larger window shows the Virgin Mary as a young girl being presented for service in the Temple. The latter scene was very popular in late-medieval and Renaissance art. However, it was not strictly biblical, and instead was found in the important second-century apocryphal text, the *Protoevangelium of St James*.[39] This story, included among the scriptural stories of the *Biblia Pauperum*, is an excellent example of the willingness of the medieval Christian imagination to extend, quite happily, the sacred narrative beyond the boundaries of canonical texts in order to bring out the fullest possible interpretation of the events of salvation history.

The foundation and then 'restoration' of Steinfeld thus can be placed in the wider context of the salvific activity of God in human history, prefigured as it is by earlier events of sacred tradition. The image of the canons carrying the reliquary brings to mind Old Testament descriptions of the priests bearing the Ark of the Covenant, and Count Dietrich von Hochsteden's prostration before the procession clearly evokes images of King David reverencing the Ark of the Covenant (2 Sam. 6.14), which would eventually find its place in the newly constructed Temple. This Temple in turn would receive the service of the Virgin Mary as a young girl, and she herself was poised to become the Living Temple of God through her role in the Incarnation. The story continues into the coming of the Christian faith to Steinfeld and the enshrinement of the relics in another manifestation of the Temple, namely the Church. Thus these windows taken altogether represent a rich and powerful presentation of many aspects of Premonstratensian spirituality, as well as a reaffirmation of the cult of saints and relics just at the time when these aspects of traditional Christianity were being challenged and rejected by the Protestant reformers.

Finally, devotion to the Virgin Mary was another important aspect of Premonstratensian spirituality. From the twelfth century, along with the Cistercians they had played an important role in developing and propagating the *cultus* of the Virgin throughout Latin Christendom. Most of the early Premonstratensian foundations were dedicated to the Virgin. Marian devotion was reflected in the liturgical rites of the Norbertines, including special litanies and offices in honour of the Virgin, which marked the order down to modern times. The three most solemn feasts of Mary, namely the Purification (2 February), Annunciation (25 March) and Assumption (15 August), were days marked by very large amounts of almsgiving to the poor; indeed, much larger than the already considerable almsgiving that marked the normal course of the year among the Premonstratensians.[40] Thus it is not surprising that many of the Steinfeld windows contain images of Mary, both biblical scenes as well as those demonstrating conventional veneration, including one showing a Premonstratensian abbot kneeling in front of the Virgin and Infant Jesus.

But among these various windows with a Marian emphasis, one in particular links the Virgin to St Norbert and Premonstratensian tradition. In the bottom registry of the first window of the *Biblia Pauperum*, St Norbert is pictured in full archiepiscopal vestments, standing by a kneeling abbot, Johann von Ahrweiler. Von Ahrweiler was abbot of Steinfeld from 1517 to 1538, and was the main person responsible for the installation of the new windows and the continued vitality of Steinfeld. The abbot has placed his mitre on the altar, and behind kneels a lay brother holding the abbot's crozier. St Norbert wears an icon of the Holy Face, also known as Veronica's Veil, as part of his vestments. The ornate crozier of the abbot is crowned by an image of Madonna and Child. In the background is a scene from the life of St Norbert in which he receives the white habit of the order from an angel.[41]

The image of Norbert's vision is interesting for a number of reasons. First, it illustrates a story that is not in the twelfth-century *vitae* per se, but is perhaps implied when Norbert explains to his confreres that he has chosen white as their garment 'because the angels who witnessed the resurrection are said to have appeared in white'.[42] By the later sixteenth century, the oral tradition of Norbert receiving the white habit from an angel would be transformed into the idea that he received it from the Blessed Virgin herself.[43] In this window, with its strong Marian imagery along with the older tradition of the angelic visitation, we perhaps are offered a glimpse of an oral tradition in transformation.

The setting of these scenes in the lower registry of Window I reveals more aspects of their potential meaning for the viewer. The highest level has portraits of John the Baptist and John the Evangelist. In the middle level of the window are two other scenes. On the left, in the first window, is the Temptation and Fall of Adam and Eve. Next to that is the scene of the Fall of Lucifer, with the Archangel Michael driving Lucifer and the other wicked angels out of Heaven. Below the Adam and Eve window, Moses is pictured holding open the book of Genesis, of which he was considered to be the author. Next to him stands the Virgin Mary standing on a crescent moon, clothed in sunlight, holding the Infant Jesus. This image of the Virgin was seen as a portrayal of the woman described in the Apocalypse (Rev. 12.1).[44]

The setting of this scene with St Norbert and Abbot Johann von Ahrweiler thus takes on additional meaning for the Premonstratensian viewer. The kneeling abbot, mitre put aside, faces an open Bible on the altar, the joining of word and sacrament. On the side of the altar, facing the viewer, is an image of a tonsured head of a Premonstratensian in a simple white habit. He gazes on what symbolically is the whole Scripture, from the opening words of Genesis to the Apocalypse, embodied in the figures on the left. In Mary he contemplates the New Eve, and symbolically models for the viewer how they are to contemplate the integral unity of the two testaments in the Scripture, typologically presented in the stained glass *Biblia Pauperum*. Above him are pictured the two great episodes illustrating the ill effects of the Sin of Pride, traditionally associated with the Fall of both angels and humans. The angel giving the habit to Norbert seems almost to descend from the panel above, bringing to him a garment of simplicity and humility. Norbert himself, who according to tradition was highly ambivalent about being made a bishop and eschewed finery whenever possible, gazes almost admonishingly at the humble lay brother dressed in coarse woollen garments, as if to remind the abbot and the Premonstratensian viewer, surrounded by the beauty of their abbey and all its ecclesiastical trappings, that it is this humility that characterizes the religious life. Thus at the very beginning of the portrayal of the story of salvation, the stained glass windows of Steinfeld urge the Premonstratensians to see their own personal and corporate story in light of the central moral lessons of Scripture, and indeed as an extension of the sacred narrative.

Conclusion

Abbot Jacob Panhausen passed away in 1582, after over 40 years of pastoral leadership at Steinfeld. In that same year St Norbert was officially canonized, while the very next year saw the first of several dismantlements of the cloister windows due to the threats of religious warfare. But the windows came back, and Premonstratensians continued to thrive and Steinfeld Abbey remained a very important centre of Catholic culture. Some 200 years after the windows were completed, in 1754, a prominent German Premonstratensian of Roggenburg Abbey, Georg Lienhardt (1717–83), published a work entitled *Exhortator Domesticus*, in which he restated the essence of Premonstratensian spirituality in five characteristic emphases: *Laus Dei in choro* (liturgical prayer); *Zelus animarum* (zeal for the salvation of souls); *spiritus iugis penitentiae* (the spirit of habitual penance); *Cultus Eucharisticus* (devotion and veneration of the Eucharist); *Cultus Marianus* (a special devotion to the Virgin Mary).[45] The German canon Lienhardt must have seen the windows at Steinfeld on many occasions, and it is quite possible that they helped shape his ideas of Premonstratensian spirituality, expressing as they do in various ways all five points of his recapitulation. His synthesis was very influential, and continued to be normative for the order down to the middle of the twentieth century.

In the analysis of the Steinfeld glass we have seen 'the moving text' at work. In their initial setting at Steinfeld, as well as their afterlife at Ashridge Park, parish churches in England and Wales and museums such as the Victoria and Albert, the windows have continued to draw people under their spell. In a manner evoking and affirming the dynamic vision so eloquently articulated by Brown, there is little doubt that the Steinfeld glass will continue to inspire and contribute to the unfolding of the never-ending and always meaningful narrative, mediated by the theological imagination.

Notes

1 For the first systematic treatment of the windows, see Wilhelm Neuss (ed.), *Die Glasmalereien aus dem Steinfelder Kreuzgang* (Mönchengladbach: Kühlen, 1955). This must be supplemented by David J. King, 'The Steinfeld Cloister Glazing', in *Gesta* 37.2 (1998), 201–10; and David King's various pieces, including 'New Steinfeld Discoveries: Special Supplement', *Vidimus* 35 (June 2009). Online: http://vidimus.org/issues/issue-35/features. See also Ann Marsh, 'From Cloister to Museum', *Conservation Journal* 57 (2009). Online: www.vam.ac.uk/content/journals/conservation-journal/issue-57/from-cloister-to-museum; accessed 18 May 2018.

2 Paul Williamson, *Medieval and Renaissance Stained Glass in the Victoria and Albert Museum* (London: V&A Publications, 2003), 9–15.

3 For a drawing of how the chapel looked in 1823, see Williamson, *Medieval and Renaissance Stained Glass*, 13.

4 See King, 'The Steinfeld Cloister Glazing' for a full discussion of these issues, including the original plan and current locations of the windows. For a transcription of the 1719 manuscript, see Neuss, *Die Glasmalereien aus dem Steinfelder Kreuzgang*, 217–44.

5 For a photo of the display in the museum, see King, 'New Steinfeld Discoveries'.

6 David Brown, 'Context and Experiencing the Sacred', in *Philosophy and Museums: Ethics, Aesthetics and Ontology*, Royal Institute of Philosophy Supplement 79, ed. V. S. Harrison, A. Bergqvist and G. Kemp (Cambridge: Cambridge University Press, 2016), 117–32. See also I. Gaskell, 'Sacred to Profane and Back Again', in *Art and its Publics: Museum Studies at the Millennium*, ed. A. McClellan (Oxford: Blackwell, 2003), 149–62.

7 David Brown, *Discipleship and Imagination: Christian Tradition and Truth* (Oxford: Oxford University Press, 2000), 63ff.

8 David Brown, *Tradition and Imagination: Revelation and Change* (Oxford: Oxford University Press, 1999), 324.

9 For a recent biography of St Norbert, see Thomas Hangrätinger, O.Praem, *Der heilige Norbert, Erzbischof und Ordengründer* (Magdeburg: Norbertus Verlag, 2011).

10 Essential studies of Premonstratensian spirituality include Caroline Walker Bynum, 'The Spirituality of Regular Canons in the Twelfth Century', in *Jesus as*

Mother: *Studies in the Spirituality of the High Middle Ages* (Berkeley, CA: University of California Press, 1982), 22–58; Theodore J. Antry, O.Praem and Carol Neel, *Norbert and Early Norbertine Spirituality* (Mahwah, NJ: Paulist Press, 2007), 1–28; Bernard Ardura, *The Order of Prémontré: History and Spirituality*, trans. Edward Hagman (De Pere, WI: Paisa Publishing, 1995); Francois Petit, *The Spirituality of the Premonstratensians: The Twelfth and Thirteenth Centuries*, trans. Victor Szczurek (Collegeville, MN: Liturgical Press and Cistercian Publications, 2011).

11 James J. John, *A Repertoire of Students at the College of Prémontré in Medieval Paris* (MMedS thesis, University of Notre Dame, 1951), 67.

12 See the helpful remarks of Wolfgang Grassl, *Culture of Place: An Intellectual Profile of the Premonstratensian Order* (Nordhausen: Verlag Traugott Bautz, 2009), Part I, vol. 2, 419–544.

13 See Joseph A. Gribbin, *The Premonstratensian Order in Late Medieval England* (Woodbridge: Boydell Press, 2001), 132–73.

14 Franz Posset, *Renaissance Monks: Monastic Humanism in Six Biographical Sketches* (Leiden: Brill, 2005), 6.

15 Norbert Backmund, *Monasticon Praemonstratense*, 2nd edn (Berlin and New York: Walter de Gruyter, 1983), vol. 1, part 2, 251–6; J. Heinrich Schmidt, *Steinfeld: Die ehemalige Prämonstratenser Abtei* (Ratingen: Aloys Henn Verlag, 1951). For the abbey's history as well as the contemporary life and work of the Salvatorians at the abbey, see online: www.kloster-steinfeld.de; accessed 18 May 2018.

16 For an excellent discussion of Premonstratensian reform in this region of Germany and the role of various abbots of Steinfeld, see Johannes Meier, 'Die Nordwestdeutschen Prämonstratenser angesichts von Verfall und Reform des Ordens 1350–1550', *Analecta Praemonstratensia* 79 (2003), 25–56.

17 See Ardura, *Order of Prémontré*, 147–252.

18 Panhausen's writings remain for the most part unedited, and have not been translated from the Latin. For the first extended study of Panhausen's writings, with key texts, see my forthcoming volume, *Jacob Panhausen of Steinfeld: A Loving Exhortation to Prelates and their Subjects and Treatise on Monastic Life and Religious Vows* (Collegeville, MN: Cistercian Publications/Liturgical Press, forthcoming).

19 These biographical remarks on Panhausen are drawn from Jan Gerits, 'Jacob Panhuysen van Opoeteren, abt van Steinfeld: Een kloosterhervormer, ascetisch schrijver en humanist uit de 16de eeuw', *Tijdschrift Heemkunde Limburg* 2 (2006), 10–14; Ardura, *Order of Prémontré*, 198–201; Jean-Baptiste Valvekens, 'Abbatis I. Panhausen Commentaria in "Regulam" S. Augustini', *Analecta Praemonstratensia* 54.3-4 (1978), 144–65.

20 Avril Henry provides an excellent discussion of the genre with particular reference to the English context in *Biblia Pauperum: A Facsimile of the Forty-Page Block Book* (Aldershot: Scolar Press/Gower Publishing, 1987), 1–46. For German examples, see Gerhard Schmidt, *Die Armenbibeln des XIV. Jahrhunderts* (Graz: H. Bohlaus nachf. 1959) and Pfarrer Leib and Dr Schwarz, *Biblia Pauperum nach dem Original in der Lyceumsbibliothek zu Constanz* (Zürich: Leo Würl, 1867). Susan Foister, *Art of Light: German Renaissance Stained Glass* (London: The National Gallery, 2007), is excellent on every aspect mentioned here, including Dürer's influence on stained glass. For the specific influence of Dürer on the images found in the Steinfeld glass, see King, 'The Steinfeld Cloister Glazing', 203–5.

21 Foister, *Art of Light*, 12.

22 For excellent examples and bibliographies, see Foister, *Art of Light* and Williamson, *Medieval and Renaissance Stained Glass*.

23 For the importance of Cologne as a centre of Catholic faith and culture, see Sigrun Haude, *In the Shadow of 'Savage Wolves': Anabaptist Münster and the German Reformation during the 1530s* (Boston, MA: Humanities Press/Brill, 2000), 39–69.

24 King, 'The Steinfeld Cloister Glazing', 201.
25 For illustration, see Roger Rosewell and David King, 'The Recent Discoveries from Steinfeld Abbey'. Online: http://vidimus.org/issues/issue-35/features; accessed 18 May 2018, Fig. 4 (Window 1, panel 2a).
26 King, 'New Steinfeld Discoveries'.
27 Antry and Neel, *Norbert and Early Norbertine Spirituality*, 188.
28 Ibid., 187.
29 Ibid., 85–120.
30 For illustration and discussion, see online: http://collections.vam.ac.uk/item/O66104/premonstratensian-canon-jacobus-scheuen-with-panel-remisch-gerhard; accessed 18 May 2018,.
31 See Haude, *In the Shadow of 'Savage Wolves'*.
32 King, 'The Steinfeld Cloister Glazing', 206–7; Neuss (ed.), *Die Glasmalereien aus dem Steinfelder Kreuzgang*, 184–7, 238.
33 Antry and Neel, *Norbert and Early Norbertine Spirituality*, 126–9.
34 Cornelius James Kirkfleet, *History of Saint Norbert, Founder of the Norbertine (Premonstratensian) Order* (St Louis, MO: B. Herder, 1916), 14–15.
35 For illustration and discussion, see online: http://collections.vam.ac.uk/item/O65987/panel-remisch-gerhard; accessed 18 May 2018.
36 Neuss, *Die Glasmalereien aus dem Steinfelder Kreuzgang*, 102–5.
37 Ibid., p. 102.
38 For discussion of his attempts to introduce the Reformation, see Martin Greschat, *Martin Bucer: A Reformer and his Times*, trans. Stephen E. Buckwalter (Louisville, KY: Westminster/John Knox Press: 2004), 183–92.
39 For the relevant passages in the text, see Wilhelm Schneemelcher, *New Testament Apocrypha, Volume One: Gospels and Related Writings*, rev. edn, trans. R. McL. Wilson (Louisville, KY: Westminster/John Knox Press, 1991), 428–30.
40 See Francois Petit, *The Spirituality of the Premonstratensians: The Twelfth and Thirteenth Centuries*, 301–10; Ardura, *Order of Prémontré*, 31–2.
41 For illustration and discussion, see online: http://collections.vam.ac.uk/item/O65852/abbot-johann-von-ahrweiler-and-panel-unknown; accessed 18 May 2018.
42 Antry and Neel, *Norbert and Early Norbertine Spirituality*, 147
43 Kirkfleet, *History of Saint Norbert*, 68–9; Neuss, *Die Glasmalereien aus dem Steinfelder Kreuzgang*, 96
44 Ibid., 85–98.
45 Georg Lienhardt, *Exhortator domesticus* (Roggenburg: Augustae Vindelicorum, 1754), 21–31. On Lienhardt, see Grassl, *Culture of Place*, Part I, vol. 1, 363–8.

PART 3

The Literary Imagination

10

David Brown and the Virgin Mary: A Literary Perspective

THOMAS RIST

Disciplinary differences present challenges to a literary scholar responding to the work of David Brown. The historicist scholar of literature warms to the emphasis on imagination in *Discipleship and Imagination: Christian Tradition and Truth*, in which historical and artistic consciousness seems to produce, in general terms, 'a fertile path beyond the aridity of much systematic theology and modern biblical hermeneutics'.[1] For a scholar of early modern literature, this rapprochement of theology to the other humanities also offers an intriguing mirror-image to the context-seeking 'turn to religion' in early modern literary studies.[2]

Nevertheless, caveats apply. Literary study does not normally aim at Brown's conception of discipleship. While Brown views the humanities as a means of deepening biblical and Christian understanding, literary studies, whose origins lie in a perceived failure of Christianity to provide social coherence in the nineteenth century, rarely subjugates literature to religion. The early modern literary turn largely arose, notably, from concerns with historical rather than theological accuracy. Although theology has a place in what follows, therefore, this chapter considering literary presentations of the Virgin Mary in post-Reformation England prioritizes the historical over the theological – and the historical deserves comment.

A major inspiration of the religious turn in early modern studies has been the historical revision to the English Reformations that was first pioneered by G. R Elton and J. H. Plumb, and later by J. J. Scarisbrick, Eamon Duffy and Christopher Haigh. Demonstrating that a Protestant England, and so literature, could not be taken for granted after Elizabeth I's accession to the throne in 1558, these and following historians not only forced religion on the consciousness of early modern literary scholars but did so as a matter of the period. Rather than matters of discipleship and Christian continuity, then, the obligation of early modern literary scholars to religion concerns the increased fragmentation of Christianity of the period as it can be seen in literary texts, along with attendant questions of how complete or incomplete the fragmentation was.

Focusing on Mary in this chapter advances this project in two relevant ways. First, since venerating Mary was formally outlawed in Protestant practice after 1558, the presence of Mary in literary sources after that date illustrates the communal fragmentation.[3] Second, this emphasis on fragmentation offers a corrective to Brown's theological, interperiodic treatment of history in general and his treatment of the Reformation in particular.[4] Working through broad paradigms of 'Reformation' and 'Counter-Reformation', Brown cannot do justice to Mary's meaning as a figure of survival from 1558, whether as a sign of resistance in an England officially Reformed, or as sign of English continuity with its religious past. Yet since discipleship entails how people follow one another, these disjunctive dimensions of Mary in the era, and the disjunctive dimensions of the era itself, are especially germane to Brown's project – or ought to be.[5] We begin, therefore, with literary presentations of Mary as the Church, noticing how the fragmentation of the former entails the fragmentation of the latter. We turn, then, to two poets instancing this Christian fragmentation in more personal terms: Henry Constable and Ben Jonson's Marian poems to Elizabeth I and Queen Henrietta Maria. The chapter concludes with Jonson's Marian poem to his daughter. Here too the community of the faithful emerges as a form of Marian disarray.

Mary as the Church: Literary Representations

Originating in St Paul's designation of the Church as Christ's virgin bride (2 Cor. 11–12), the long-standing identification of Mary with the Church in Christian exegesis took material form in medieval England in the construction of a shrine to Mary in Walsingham in Norfolk.[6] Centred around an image of Mary in a 'Holy House' duplicating the locus of the Annunciation, the shrine became an Augustinian Priory in 1153, with further significant material developments in 1350 (the Slipper Chapel) and in the fifteenth century (the Priory Church). Walsingham was by now one of Europe's two leading cites of Marian devotion, presenting Mary as a matter of metonymy.[7] In celebrating the glory of the shrine, therefore, the sixteenth-century poem 'The Wracks of Walsingham' celebrates Mary metonymically; in mourning its destruction in 1538, when Mary's statue was taken to London and destroyed, the poem similarly mourns Mary's destruction.

> Level, level with the ground
> The towers do lie,

Which with their golden glittering tops
    Pierced once to the sky.
Where were gates no gates are now,
    The ways unknown
Where the press of peers did pass
    While her flame far was blown.[8]

These lines celebrate Mary's shrine by lamenting its destruction. The images of architectural towers, gates and the 'press of peers' evoke a vibrant Marian culture destroyed. The materials and persons, therefore, are themselves Marian metonyms, meaning that Mary herself is destroyed. The image of the flame 'blown' far and wide in Walsingham's heyday expresses the metonymic logic: Mary is simultaneously in Walsingham and elsewhere, in Walsingham's gates, towers and materials, and in Walsingham's persons.

The image of Marian destruction takes several forms. Beside the destruction of buildings is the destruction of the garden as a built environment:

Bitter was it, O, to view
The sacred vine
(While gardeners played all close)
Rooted up by the swine.
Bitter, bitter, O, to behold
The grass to grow
Where the walls of Walsingham
So stately did show.

This landscape is Marian in two ways: part of the larger site of Mary's material shrine, but also recollecting the enclosed garden of the Song of Songs, an established image of Mary before and after the poem.[9] The general use of metonymy as a principle of poetic organization extends to details: the 'swine' are the pigs left to roam the wasteland after the iconoclasm but also the iconoclasts who created it; the gardeners who 'played all close' are Walsingham's real gardeners, but also those who were charged generally with its cultivation.

In both of these, the Song of Songs is important. Its personal, amatory dimension develops and intensifies the personality present already in the metonymic idea that Walsingham is Mary, giving her an affective, touching and scriptural presence. It is the more shocking, therefore, that her presence is destroyed. Making its most explicit distinctions between good and evil, the poem focuses in on Mary's personal destruction:

> Weep, weep O Walsingham, Whose dayes are nightes,
> Blessing turned to blasphemies, Holy deedes to dispites
> Sinne is where our Ladye sate, Heaven turned to helle;
> Sathan sittes where our Lord did swaye, Walsingham oh, farewell.

Giving rise to several of Mary's metonymic meanings, it is not only the statue of our Lady that has gone, here, but rather our Lady herself: a figure who apparently 'sat' in Walsingham's heaven-on-earth. As Walsingham and as the Church it stands for, therefore, Mary is dead. As the local site of pilgrimage figuring the Christian pilgrimage, similarly, she is dead. In particular, as the 'way' of European pilgrims to come closer to the Christian heaven, with Walsingham acting as a locus for heaven and earth's interpenetration, Mary is dead.[10] The poem both endorses and throws into relief David Brown's argument for Mary:

> in our own pilgrimage of faith it is a matter of working gradually through the implications of Christ's life for our own, and if Mary can do this alongside us, she will be there in the narrative as fellow traveller and not merely as someone essentially beyond our own human struggles.[11]

It is a premise of 'The Wracks of Walsingham' that pilgrimage and fellow-travel towards heaven are, endorsing holiness and opposing sin, advantages of Mary; yet since she is the victim of historical iconoclasm giving rise to grief and waste, 'essentially beyond our own human struggles' is beside the point.

Maximizing Mary's suffering, though, is apposite. According to the contemporary, churchly trope showing 'rape as iconoclasm', the poem therefore presents the destruction of Walsingham as a rape.[12] Pre-figurations are in the personal and sexual dimensions of Mary as the enclosed garden of the Song of Songs, which echo both in general images of Mary – Mary the Rose and Mary the Lily, for example – and in the particular poetic focus on Walsingham's gardens. Yet these gardens being destroyed, the body of Mary is deflowered. The implications of the disturbing metaphor emerge in the lines quoted above. Focusing on where 'our Lady sate', the lines attend to Mary's 'seat': the source of Christ theologically and in contemporary poetry, and the more disturbing for it.[13] Theologically, the seat of Mary is necessary for Christ's Incarnation. Defiling the seat, the destruction of Walsingham evokes a rape not only personal and iconoclastic but with shattering connotations for humanity. The Incarnation having already taken place, the resulting wasteland is perhaps not for ever, but the damage is extreme. Applying to Mary as the Church, that damage extends to all features of the Christian community. The following considers two of the community's early modern subsections according to literary presentations.

Poets and Patrons: Constable and Jonson's poems to Mary

Henry Constable and Ben Jonson both wrote poems about Mary in court conditions entailing a poetic relationship between the poet and his patron. For Constable, the relationship was to Elizabeth I and for Jonson it was to Queen Henrietta Maria, wife of Charles I. The impacts of writing to these queens following the outlawing of Marian veneration are strikingly similar in outline but instructively different in detail. Both poets find the analogue between the earthly queen they address and the 'Queen of Heaven', Mary, productive in describing their social conditions and contentment, or (in Brown's phrase) how their 'pilgrimage of faith ... is a matter of working gradually through the implications of Christ's life for our own'.[14] Veneration of Mary being outlawed, both poets present the earthly and heavenly queens as rival patrons, with rival claims on loyalty. Loyalty being thus conflicted, fragmentation is a premise in the poetic representations of the self, the poems mirroring through personal representations what 'The Wracks of Walsingham' established as the bigger scheme.

Opening 'Why should I any love O queene but thee?', Constable's second poem, 'To Our Blessed Lady', forcefully evokes the challenge of loving rival queens. Its answer is equally explicit:

> An earthly sight doth onely please the eye,
> And breedes desire, but doth not satisfye:
> Thy sight, gives us possession of all ioye.[15]

Sight of the earthly queen, Elizabeth, is less joyful and satisfying than 'Thy' (Mary's) sight, the poem developing its illustration of incompatible loyalties and demands within the Christian community and so of Christian fragmentation. The fragmentation, moreover, extends to the individual. Squarely set against the proposal that the speaker might love differently and so gain different rewards, the poem ensures the attractions of Elizabethan loyalty are understood. 'Why should I any love O queene but thee?' shows not just that the speaker knows he must love Mary above Elizabeth, but that he does also love Elizabeth. The result is a picture of a speaker with divided loves, who fulfils his theological duty at a cost. That the duty is theological rather than just political (or perverse) is emphatic. Remembering that Mary's 'womb did bear ... breast my saviour feed' (line 3), this poem is like 'The Wracks of Walsingham' in illustrating Christian fragmentation in light of an Incarnation in which Mary was essential.

Jonson's Marian poem of 1630, 'An Epigram to the Queene, Then Lying In', similarly contrasts the queen of the day (now Henrietta Maria) with the Queen of Heaven, and since the topic is 'lying in', the Incarnation is again in view. The development of the analogue at the opening is extensive:

> HAile Mary, full of grace, it once was said,
> And by an Angell, to the blessed'st Maid,
> The Mother of our Lord; why may not I,
> (Without prophannesse) yet, a Poët, cry
> Haile Mary, full of Honours, to my Queene.[16]

As in Constable, contrasting the Queen of Heaven with a queen provides an opportunity for reflections on faith. A significant difference between the poets' evocations of patronage, though, concerns the different religions of the monarchs: while Elizabeth I was Protestant, Henrietta Maria was Roman Catholic. Unlike for Constable, therefore, parallels between the Virgin Mary and Henrietta Maria do not entail clashing demands of loyalty. Consistently praising the Catholic queen, Jonson develops the analogue between Henrietta Maria and the Virgin Mary without interruption, taking in not just the Incarnation and the Annunciation but, by extension, the idea that Henrietta Maria's son will be Christ-like for his kingdom:

> When was there seene
> (Except the joy that the first *Mary* brought,
> Whereby the safetie of Man-kind was wrought)
> So general a gladness to an Isle,
> To make the hearts of a whole Nation smile,
> As in this Prince?

By analogue to Henrietta Maria as the mother of England's saviour, the poem charts Mary's place in Scripture in the Annunciation, the Incarnation and as mother of Christ the Redeemer. As in each of the poems treated hitherto, Mary provides a means of reflecting on present concerns; but as in the deployment of Marian metonyms as a reservoir of meaning in 'The Wracks of Walsingham', Marian analogue in 'An Epigram to the Queene, Then Lying In' is able to encompass Jonson's entire trajectory of praise, from celebration of the queen, to celebrating her childbirth, to celebrating the future prospects of the kingdom. In this respect the poem is significantly different from the Marianism of

Constable, which immediately clashes with rival obligations to Elizabeth, disbarring Mary from Constable as a sufficient principle of reflection for his circumstance, and signalling his disjunction, as a recusant, from his court community. Presenting, in starkest contrast, a coherent, Christian community at court, Jonson's 'An Epigram to the Queene, Then Lying In' shows almost no fragmentation at all, either in the management of Henrietta Maria in relation to Mary, or in the poet's ability to serve two queens.

Yet in a juxtaposition of this court community with another there is fragmentation. It centres on what can be 'said' (line 1), what the poet can say loudly or 'cry' (line 4) and what kinds of 'compare' (line 12) are therefore permissible. This goes beyond the observed, general ban on Marian veneration in Christian practice in England from 1558, focusing on the particular Marian veneration of the Hail Mary prayer: developed by Christians from St Luke's Gospel but forbidden in England following the death of Mary I.[17] Juxtaposing what is 'lawful' (line 12) with 'Hail Mary' three times (lines 1, 5 and 13) evokes England's ban on the prayer forcefully, even as the opening 'HAile *Mary*, full of grace' evokes the gospel and the prayer together. Demanding 'let it [the Hail Mary prayer] be lawful' at line 12 as part of the poem's evocation of a newly emerging, happy, Christian 'Realme' (line 14) is therefore a positive way of requesting legal permission for the presently forbidden prayer.

Yet both focusing on the present restriction on expression, and juxtaposing this with a future of 'generall ... gladnesse' (line 9), pivots the poem – itself a series of 'Hail Mary' comparisons – on two ideas of English order: one allowing the Hail Mary and the other not. The orders reflecting England's Protestant and Catholic communities and divisions, in community and discipleship the poem displays fragmentation. Following the fragmentation of a church presenting the Church in 'The Wracks of Walsingham', which the poem blames both on iconoclasts and those who had the duty of care, Jonson and Constable's poems show the fragmentation impacting on personal relationships within the community. For Constable, this means dissociation from a court seemingly uniformly hostile under Elizabeth; for Jonson, it entails being part of a court coterie presided over by Henrietta Maria but at odds with English religious law. In the final poem of this chapter, these national and institutional divisions bearing both on persons and discipleship are at their most personal, as Jonson remembers his dead daughter in a domestic rather than patronage context.

'On My First Daughter': Mary in Domestic Life

There were various reasons for Protestant England's rejection of Mary. One, implicit in the throne- and also queen-imagery of each of the preceding poems, concerns her traditional status as Queen of Heaven and Queen of the Saints. Entailing intercession, and so in any traditional sense, in particular the latter of these made no sense in the world of double-predestination post-1558 England derived from Calvin.[18] A second reason, recurrent in this chapter and to which we shall return directly, concerns Mary's presentation of a female principle in Christian discipleship. The objections are linked, since Mary's queenship made her the principle. Yet distinguishing between sainthood and gender allows what was at stake in each category to become clearer. Designating Mary 'Queen of the Saints' would seem to suggest something otherworldly – 'essentially beyond our own human struggles', in Brown's phrase.

Yet saints might be people we know, the recently deceased, bringing us much closer to home and to our friends and relatives. This is the case when Jonson connects his daughter to Mary as Queen of the Saints in 'On My First Daughter', following his daughter's death around 1600:

> Here lyes to each her parents' ruth
> *Mary*, the daughter of their youth:
> Yet, all heaven's gifts, being heaven's due,
> It makes the father lesse to rue.
> At six monthes end, she parted hence
> With safetie of her innocence;
> Whose soule heaven's Queene (whose name she bears)
> In comfort of her mothers teares
> And placed amongst the virgin-traine:
> Where, while that sever'd doth remaine,
> This grave partakes the fleshly birth.
> Which cover lightly, gentle earth.[19]

The poem is a powerful expression of a father's grief, the more so for measuring itself against other versions of grief in the community.

As the manifestation of grief, then, the father's poem, neatly formed into 12 rhyming couplets of iambs and troches, contrasts with the 'mother's teares', opposing a verbal, written and above all controlled response with one synonymous with affect, according to grief's contemporary male and female distinctions.[20] Complementing the restraint is the poem's note that because heaven's gifts are 'due' to heaven, Jonson has the 'lesse to rue' at the loss of his child. The rationalization enforces distinctions between the father and the mother: being rational, his sadness is less than hers. Yet the argument that it is right to return to God what he gives us is not only a rationalization. It is the argument of the Church Fathers against excessive grief for the dead, which Reformers seeking the early Church against its medieval developments resuscitated.[21] Thus, the poem aligns itself with early Christianity, with Reformed Christianity, or with both these social groups at once, leaving the mother as an outsider.

Yet the mother beyond the pale both of early Church and Reformed receives support. Being Mary, the child is taken by the Virgin Mary, 'Heaven's Queen (whose name she bears)'. There is nothing 'beyond our own human struggles' either in this depiction of Mary's sainthood or in its presentation of her uses in the face of desolation.[22] Mary is 'alongside' the persons of the poem in several ways: sustaining Jonson in his grief; sustaining the mother in her isolation; and sustaining the identity of the girl, whose baptismal name comes imaginatively to define her salvation. Though each bears on 'discipleship', points regarding this Marian sanctity, gender and community arise.

First, this intervention of 'Heaven's Queen', the evocation of saints in her 'virgin-traine' and especially placing the girl within the saintly train, represent the beliefs of medieval England persisting in this period among recusants, church papists, waverers like Jonson, and on the continent, but made anathema by English Protestantism.[23] One thinks of Tina Beattie: 'Reading David Brown's *Discipleship and Imagination* rekindled memories of my experience of moving from an evangelical Presbyterian Church into the Roman Catholic Church in the 1980s.'[24] For Protestants seeking to utilize Mary as Jonson does, there is a circle to be squared.[25]

Second: the matter of gender. This saintly train of the Virgin, receiving the daughter, arises from and comforts the 'mother's tears'. The image establishes a line of communication between Mary, the mother and the daughter that is exclusively female. Sanctifying the mother's grief in contrast to the father's, Mary endorses their feminine mode: critiquing the masculine Jonson who would rise above his wife's affect, and turning the poem's rationality on its head. The observation stands for the feminine principles governing this chapter: in the Mary of Walsingham, in the contrasts of Mary, Elizabeth I and Henrietta Maria, and in this community of mother–daughter–Mary. Centring on Mary, each centres on the feminine. While existing in the poems and normally writing them, men therefore always exist in relation to the feminine: being never allowed to occlude that femininity and, thanks to Mary's sanctity, having to position themselves in deference towards it. Finally, authorizing female procedures, Mary allows female communities to form, both in contrast and relation to masculine principles, communities and persons. This is at its clearest in the intimate surrounds of 'On My First Daughter'; yet it is in Henrietta Maria's relation to Mary and their shared birth-giving in

Jonson's 'An Epigram to the Queene, Then Lying In'; it is in Constable's designation of two women, Mary and Elizabeth I, as the determinants of his religious and courtly life; and it is in Walsingham, where the 'press of peers' and other pilgrims certainly included women.

Third, there is the matter of communities. As we have seen, Jonson's 'On my first daughter' speaks to the responses to dying of early Christian, Reformed and Catholic communities, even as it guiltily suggests his rationality collaborates with the early Christian and Reformed against his better self. Reminding us that mourning is a communal action, this speech with communities is as important as their differentiation. For as much as Jonson, it is the Christian community fragmenting in this poem, one group isolating from another so that the daughter who has died is simultaneously the cause of disharmony and the victim of it. Presenting conflicting modes of mourning her, the poem implies that some of the mourning practices are inadequate, thereby also evoking obligations to the dead. Which mode of mourning fulfils those obligations? As we have seen, the suggestion is that rational modes including those of the poem are inadequate, but having obligations to the dead bears emphasis. John Bossy has called the medieval cult of the dead 'a cult of living friends in the service of dead ones', to which Lucy Wooding adds: '[p]rayers for the dead were one of the foremost obligations of the living, rooted in fundamental notions of compassion and friendship'.[26] By 1600, those bonds were sundered: 'on the Catholic side was the communal tradition of centuries coupled with the human instinct to do everything possible for family and friends', while 'to Protestants fell the parish community, and the obligation of sustaining communal ties through the correct observation of burial rites and the distribution of charity'.[27] In Jonson's poem the communal sundering emerges in a sundering of the self. While 'The Wracks of Walsingham' spoke evocatively of the institutional Church's rape, there is perhaps no more eloquent testimony to the pain of that social sundering in the individual.

Conclusion

This chapter has considered literary depictions of Mary as the material and institutional Church, within courtly relationships of Christian context, and in the domestic setting. From these, Mary emerges in many of the guises of interest to David Brown: as a model for independent women; as a female principle; in her instrumental role in the Incarnation; as a fellow-traveller in human spirituality; and so in her roles in discipleship, community and imagination.[28] Looking at Mary in a variety of early modern social spheres has also shown her significance for those spheres in the course of about 100 years following England's break with Rome. The chapter has thereby demonstrated Mary's agency across a spectrum of early modern social scenarios, showing her utility in personal, literary and also social practices. These uses pertain to social organization at a variety of levels: Christian community and the Church; the community of the court; and the community of family. Always divisive within these representations, Mary is instrumental in defining personal identities, affects, dilemmas and responses.

The analysis has been primarily qualitative rather than quantitative, inviting questions of how fully representative of early modern practice it is. I emphasize two, linked responses: theoretical and historical. Theoretically, then, while the Marian poems of this piece are either by Catholics or Catholic sympathizers, a putative examination of Protestant authors hostile to Marian veneration would not reveal contrary evidence, since contradicting responses to Mary, including hostile responses, are consistently part of the present literary evidence. At most, the putative examination would only reveal differences of degree regarding Mary's instrumentality. The historical evidence supports this. As Christine Peters observes, Protestants did not forget Mary, but rather reconfigured her into a model for emulation, 'primarily, but far from exclusively, for women'.[29] Though Mary's influence in Protestant communities narrowed prescriptively towards models for feminine behaviour, then, her influence and use in those communities remained. On the evidence of this chapter, we may add that Mary need not exist thus prescriptively, making David Brown's attempts to reverse the prescription welcome.[30]

The aims of David Brown return us squarely to *Discipleship and Imagination*: in terms of his priorities as a theologian regarding artistic – and for the purposes of this chapter, literary – representation; and in terms of historicism, which we have seen underpins literary approaches to early modern religion today. A historical implication of this chapter is that while Brown's argument for Mary in Christian discipleship is necessary, it underplays Mary's role *as* the Church in previous eras, and the fragmentation that occurred within the Church, as a body of disciples, once her unifying identity disappeared. Although there has presumably never been an entirely unitary Church, according to the evidence removing the identity of the Church with Mary in early modern England made discipleship as a singular proposition impossible. Only discipleships (plural) survived and survive. Far more directly than Brown, therefore, those interested in Christian unity must return to Mary.

The role of literary study in that project is unclear. Since the spur to religious criticism in the study was a re-evaluation of the English Reformation, the critical movement's reach would seem limited to the period. Outside the early modern, it seems likely that theologically orientated literary criticism will remain exceptional and fragmentary, the academy being no more governed by theology today than Christianity – in its various manifestations – is governed by Mary.[31] Still, since changes in the history of early modern religion led to transformations in early modern literary criticism, it is possible to envisage later literary periods – whose authors frequently drew on the early modern – experiencing revision in their turn. With a hopeful eye to the future, it is perhaps worth noting, therefore, that David Brown's latest professorship at St Andrew's University is at St Mary's College: a medieval foundation of and for scholarship commemorating Mary.[32] Brown's work does some duty to the foundation. It would be apposite if from it a more Marian, theological criticism arose.

Notes

1 David Brown, *Discipleship and Imagination: Christian Tradition and Truth* (Oxford: Oxford University Press, 2000); and Tina Beattie, 'From Ethics to Eschatology: The Continuing Validity of the New Eve for Christian Doctrine and Discipleship', in *Theology, Aesthetics, and Culture: Responses to the Work of David Brown*, ed. Robert MacSwain and Taylor Worley (Oxford: Oxford University Press, 2012), 65.

2 Ken Jackson and Arthur Marotti, 'The Turn to Religion in Early Modern Literary Studies', *Criticism*, 46.1 (2004), 167–90.

3 On the outlawing of Marian veneration in Protestant practice, see Christine Peters, *Patterns of Piety: Women, Gender and Religion in Late Medieval and Reformation England* (Cambridge: Cambridge University Press, 2003), 228.

4 Brown, *Discipleship and Imagination*, 257–60.

5 Observing Brown is 'too cautious about offending his more Protestant readers in his engagement with Catholic art and devotion', Beattie sees an 'unresolved tension' in Brown's desire to argue for the value of religious traditions and his Protestant (originally Lutheran) adherence to Scripture. The tension is particularly evident in the exceptionally 'cautious' way Brown writes about Mary. See Beattie, 'From Ethics to Eschatology', 64, 65, 68.

6 For Mary as the Church, see Miri Rubin, *Mother of God: A History of the Virgin Mary* (London: Allen Lane, 2009), 168; and Beattie, 'From Ethics to Eschatology', 67. For a wide-ranging cultural history of Walsingham, see *Walsingham in Literature and Culture from the Middle Ages to Modernity*, ed. Dominic Janes and Gary Waller (Farnham: Ashgate, 2010).

7 Indeed, as 'Mary's dower' – a term especially associated with Walsingham – England presented this metonymic meaning.

8 Anonymous, 'The Ruins of Walsingham', in *The New Oxford Book of Sixteenth-Century Verse*, ed. Emrys Jones (Oxford: Oxford University Press, 2002), 550. Since this name of the poem is imputed, however, I call it 'The Wracks of Walsingham', reflecting its opening line.

9 For Mary as the Song of Songs in contemporary literature, see Stanley Stewart, *The Enclosed Garden: The Tradition and the Image in Seventeenth-Century Poetry* (Madison, WI: University of Wisconsin Press, 1966); and Thomas Rist, 'Mary of Recusants and Reform: Literary Memory and Defloration', in *Biblical Women in Early*

Modern Literary Culture, 1550–1700, ed. Victoria Brownlee and Laura Gallagher (Manchester: Manchester University Press, 2015), 163–79.

10 In the culture of Walsingham, Mary became known as the 'milky way'. See Michael Caroll, 'Pilgrimage at Walsingham on the Eve of the Reformation: Speculations on a "Splendid Diversity" only Dimly Perceived', in *Walsingham in Literature and Culture*, ed. Janes and Waller, 34–48 (43). Images of Mary as an 'approach to the sacred' are standard in the period: Rist, 'Mary of Recusants and Reform', 169–70.

11 David Brown, 'Mary's Discipleship and the Artistic Imagination', in *Say Yes to God: Mary and the Revealing of the Word Made Flesh*, ed. Martin Warner (London: Tufton Books, 1999), 80.

12 The phrase derives from Anna Swärdh, *Rape and Religion in English Renaissance Literature: A Topical Study of Four Texts by Shakespeare, Drayton and Middleton* (Upsalla: University of Uppsala Press, 2003), 223. I show its still wider currency in the period in Rist, 'Mary of Recusants and Reform', 170–5

13 On the contemporary poetry, see ibid., 170–2.

14 Brown, 'Mary's Discipleship and the Artistic Imagination', 80.

15 *The Poems of Henry Constable*, ed. J. Grundy (Liverpool: Liverpool University Press, 1960). All following citations of Constable are from this edition.

16 Ben Johnson, *The Complete Poetry of Ben Jonson*, ed. William Hunter, The Stuart Editions (New York: New York University Press, 1963), 219–20. All following quotations of this poem are from this edition.

17 Diarmaid MacCulloch, 'Mary and Sixteenth-Century Protestants', in *The Church and Mary*, ed. R. N. Swanson (Woodbridge: Boydell, 2004), 214.

18 Peter Marshall, *Beliefs and the Dead in Reformation England* (Oxford: Oxford University Press, 2002), 195.

19 Johnson, *The Complete Poetry of Ben Jonson*, ed. Hunter, 11–12.

20 On grief's contemporary male and female distinctions, see Patricia Phillippy, *Women, Death and Literature in Post-Reformation England* (Cambridge: Cambridge University Press, 2002), 9.

21 St John Chrysostom, for example, strongly associates excessive mourning with women (Phillippy, *Women, Death and Literature in Post-Reformation England*, 15). In this he follows stoic and other contemporary norms. According to Stephen Barton, St Paul defied these norms, making 'no distinction (of the kind evident in pagan sources …) … between expectations for men and expectations for women'. See Barton, 'Eschatology and the Emotions in Early Christianity', *Journal of Biblical Literature* 130.3 (2011), 571–91 (590). This suggests Jonson – and early modern women – were closer to St Paul than either Chrysostom or the Reformers; and that regarding grief, Chrysostom and the Reformers took more from paganism, and less from Scripture, than the medieval Church.

22 For this and the following quotation, see Brown, *Discipleship and Imagination*, 80.

23 For further discussion of Mary as Queen of Heaven, see Rist, 'Mary of Recusants and Reform', 163–79; for 'church papists', see Alexandra Walsham, *Church Papists: Catholicism, Conformity and Confessional Polemic in Early Modern England* (Woodbridge: Boydell, 1999).

24 Beattie, 'From Ethics to Eschatology', 64.

25 In view of her claim to have had theological activity restricted by the Congregation for the Doctrine of the Faith (Tina Beattie, 'Sex, Marriage and the Catholic Church', *The Guardian*, 8 October 2014), the circle may not have been entirely squared by Beattie herself.

26 John Bossy, 'The Mass as a Social Institution', in *Past and Present*, 100.1 (1983), 29–61. For Wooding's claim, responding directly to Bossy, see Lucy Wooding, 'Remembrance in the Eucharist', in *The Arts of Remembrance in Early Modern England:*

Memorial Cultures of the Post Reformation, ed. by Andrew Gordon and Thomas Rist (Farnham and Burlington, VT: Ashgate, 2013), 19–36 (19).

27 Wooding, 'Remembrance in the Eucharist', 36.

28 Brown, *Discipleship and Imagination*, 226–88,

29 Peters, *Patterns of Piety*, 243.

30 Brown is not alone in seeking this reversal. See Eamon Duffy, 'May Thoughts on Mary', in *Faith of our Fathers: Reflections on Catholic Tradition* (London and New York: Continuum: 2004), 29–38.

31 In general in the medieval academy, theology was the prime discipline to which other disciplines were subsidiary. Evidently this has changed. See Alasdair MacIntyre, *God, Philosophy, Universities: A History of the Catholic Philosophical Tradition* (New York and London: Continuum, 2009), 64 and as a whole. Presenting a detailed correlation between the transformation of the academy and the early modern fragmentation of Marian Christianity is beyond the scope of this chapter, but the general correlation – and the point about academia below – is notable.

32 The full and original title of the College is the 'New College of the Assumption of the Blessed Virgin Mary'. See 'Records of St Mary's College', 1413–1953 (Muniments of the University of St Andrews, 1215), University of St Andrews Archive Catalogue; https://pacific.st-andrews.ac.uk/DServe/dserve.exe?dsqIni=Dserve.ini&dsqApp=Archive&dsqDb=Catalog&dsqCmd=show.tcl&dsqSearch=(RefNo=='UMUN%2F4'); accessed 4 December 2016.

11

Intertextuality, Tradition and Finding Theology in Unexpected Places: Reading *Frankenstein* with the Help of David Brown

JON GREENAWAY

Rather than respond to the work of David Brown in terms of a critique or criticism of his considerable and impressive oeuvre, this chapter will seek to offer a response by way of *application*. Brown's work has been hugely productive and challenging in the fields of theology and philosophy, raising provocative questions about the interrelated status of aesthetics, human experience and revelation.[1] It would seem to be in keeping with Brown's admirable commitment to 'widening the conversation' to continue this work in a direction Brown has not yet engaged in any sustained fashion. The aim here is to explore how both imagination and tradition – whether this be theological or literary in nature – generate fresh theological insights in the most surprising of places. My own area of specialism is the determinedly lowbrow form of Gothic and horror literature that, through its transgressive and often shocking writing, performs vital cultural work in reflecting the anxieties and fears of a given historical moment. It is a writing with a 'unique ability to explore human nature and consciousness', revealing to us 'our most sublime terrors'.[2] Here I choose to focus on *Frankenstein*, from 1818 – partly due to its landmark status as a Gothic text as well as its overwhelming popularity as a pop-culture icon. Given the ways *Frankenstein*, particularly the creature, has been transmitted and adapted throughout culture and across forms, it seems that a reading of the original text through the insights of David Brown's work is not only seriously overdue but also carries with it the potential to bring to light the theological potential of large swathes of popular culture that might be all too easily dismissed as lowbrow, kitsch or immoral. However, before turning to *Frankenstein* and the issue of textual analysis, a few brief – and necessarily general –

remarks about the terms of the wider debate between Gothic literature and theology are necessary.

In an era of disciplinary speciality, examination of an intersection between theology and Gothic literature[3] may initially seem something of an exercise in reconciling two incompatible forces. Theology, the 'queen of the sciences', appears to have little to do with a body of literature that Coleridge memorably dismissed as the trash of the circulating libraries.[4] While an understandable response from the high-minded Coleridge, this dismissal neatly ignores the oblique yet ever-present engagement with religious iconography, theological language of hell, damnation and salvation throughout Gothic texts. Even in a modern context with a greater focus on interdisciplinary research, the Gothic is for many theologians at best a distraction and at worse something with the potential to cause actual spiritual harm.[5] On the other side of the scholastic divide, the Gothic scholar trained in the hermeneutics of suspicion views theology as a diversion from issues of cultural history or concealing other ideological or psychoanalytic readings.[6] Happily, this generalization seems to be on the wane as Gothic studies begins to open itself to greater dialogue between its own specific concerns and theological or religious discourse.[7] What follows is an attempt at reading *Frankenstein* in terms that are sensitive to Brown's central insight in *Tradition and Imagination*, namely that the Christian story has, can and indeed must acquire new insights or reinterpretations – rereadings – through fresh stimuli, even if it comes from unexpected sources such as the Gothic. As Brown articulates it, 'it will be a matter of the dynamic of an inherited past interacting with fresh stimuli ... from the wider surrounding culture'.[8] The challenge presented by Brown's work for the theologically minded literary critic is to take seriously the possibility that even in cultural forms that seem to have little to offer, challenging theological insights may be present and God's grace still active.

Mary Shelley's *Frankenstein* and John Milton's *Paradise Lost*: The Theological Connection

Mary Shelley's *Frankenstein* is deeply embedded in the textual canon of the Gothic,[9] yet for a text that deals so closely with the 'theological consequences of creation',[10] criticism on the theological elements of the text is somewhat lacking. Shelley's representation of Victor Frankenstein and his creature presents a practical theology of personhood which shows that, for all the interest in the transcendent and poetic potential of creativity developed within the Romantic era,[11] creation alone may have disastrous consequences. Through Shelley's imaginative retelling of the Miltonic narrative (the disobedience of man, the knowledge of good and evil and the need for salvation), the strengths of the theological tradition of which Milton is a part are rearticulated while at the same time the flaws of the Romantic view of a singular isolated monster – and genius – are trenchantly critiqued. The figure of the monster is only superficially monstrous, as Shelley presents a being, who, like us all, is seeking a connection to the divine power that brought it into being. In short, therefore, *Frankenstein* details the narrative of a created individual seeking a theology.

Such a search for a theological perspective is clear from the very beginning of Shelley's novel – the opening of *Frankenstein* quotes from one of the definitive examples of theological literature, *Paradise Lost*, using as the novel's epigraph: 'Did I request thee, Maker, To mould Me man? Did I solicit thee From darkness to promote me?'[12] This epigraph and the monster's own speech and thought are linked, as the monster repeatedly echoes biblical language: 'I ought to be thy Adam, but I am rather the fallen angel whom thy drivest from joy for no misdeed.'[13] Despite this shared language, some critics claim that within *Frankenstein* 'the universe is emptied of God and of theistic assumptions of "good" and "evil"'.[14] This argument fails completely, as the extent to which theological language recurs throughout the novel is impossible to ignore. The theological significance of the novel's language culminates with 'the rationalist [Victor] who ... ends up excoriating his Creature as a fiend and a devil'.[15] Shelley goes so far as to link Frankenstein's monster to a tradition of theodicy that extends as far back as the book of Job.[16] Once the theological dimensions of Shelley's text are considered, it comes to be seen as participating within a tradition of texts that attempt a theodicy without claiming to be a full theology.[17] This reimagining of theodicy takes place in a variety of ways across shifting historical contexts – forming an ongoing retelling of a theological concern brought about through new stimuli. Literary texts such as *Frankenstein* that reimagine theological concerns can be understood as expressing the 'capacity of the Christian faith for renewal, reform and even revolution',[18] allowing for the articulation of theological truth about God in decidedly non-orthodox venues such as Gothic horror.

However, theological revelation represented in the literary form is always mediated through various textual forms and always subject to a degree of interpretation. At stake within *Frankenstein* is the mediation of competing texts (be these letters, journals, diaries or even Victor's laboratory notes) and the status that the act of creation (be that literary or otherwise) is given because of this. The novel is a complex palimpsest of texts exhibiting a multiplicity of characters and voices. The narrative is a combination of different forms – letters, diaries, journals and even personal testimony – that work to destabilize the idea of any kind of singular narrative authority, shifting the reader's conception of authority from a singular source towards a greater awareness of the polyvocal character of textual authority. Given the emergence of the novel form in the eighteenth century and the accompanying debates about 'realism', *Frankenstein* is tied not only to the issue of the epistemology of novel writing[19] but also to a deeply held theological concern, namely the need to express theological certainty through language that is always inevitably riven by metaphor and analogy. As Brown writes:

> in trying to conceptualize God, words must necessarily resort to images and metaphors that in the nature of the case draw unexpected connections between different aspects of reality, and indeed derive much of their power precisely from the fact that they are unexpected.[20]

Literature, specifically non-realist forms such as the Gothic, 'reaches out towards mystery, towards a reality that is our final concern but which eludes empirical investigation and bursts rational concepts'.[21] This holds true even if the format – in the case of *Frankenstein*, letters, journals and other writings – is one that seems to lend itself to empirical understanding. Frankenstein's story 'reaches out' beyond the verisimilitude of testimony narratives in terms of its form through the novel's content. *Frankenstein*, as a heavily influenced theological text articulating an imaginative theodicy, participates within a tradition of 'searching for something of ultimate concern', framing this search by 'taking as [its] theme the telling of a story'.[22] The framing device in the form of a series of conversations between Walton and Frankenstein ensures that the character of Frankenstein can only make sense of his life in the act of narration – his existence can only be understood in retrospect. As Walton articulates it, 'strange and harrowing must be his story, frightful the storm which embraced the gallant vessel on its course and wrecked it – thus!'[23] Victor himself seems to recognize this as, towards the end of his life, he frames his struggle as one ordained by spiritual forces: 'you may give up your purpose, but mine is assigned to me by heaven'.[24] By framing his own experience through the wider idea of Christian teleology, Frankenstein is given access to 'a pattern by which he can find *himself* in what would otherwise be a meaningless end to his journey'.[25] Thus the displacement of the narrative voice of the text is not simply a result of the multiplicity of forms that it employs but the means by which the novel contributes to the theological quest for a larger narrative or grander 'story' that gives sense to one's existence.[26]

Milton and Polyvocal Creation: Creation and Transcendence

This shift to a more polyvocal understanding of storytelling ties *Frankenstein* to *Paradise Lost*, as Milton's poem also makes space for a creation of multiplicity – 'a multivocality at the heart of creation'.[27] Yet human participation in creation can affirm difference, but the line between individual freedom as part of some harmonious vision of creation and free participation that strays into Miltonic pandemonium seems perilously fine. In both *Paradise Lost* and *Frankenstein*, human participation in the act of creation is seen as highly dangerous. Consequently there is a common critical position that perceives God in *Paradise Lost* as a tyrant – a creator who maintains his control by allowing there to be only one set of possibilities for the whole of existence to function within. C. S. Lewis decries Milton's presentation of God as 'unsatisfactory' as it '[gives] us a cold, merciless or tyrannical Deity'.[28] William Empson alights upon such divine disparagement as part of the poem's appeal, arguing that the 'reason that the poem is so good is that it makes God so bad'.[29] Such a critical strain perceives in Milton's poem a creation placed under the tyranny of the divine, with any action controlled through God.[30] While the criticism of God as a removed absolute ruler has proved remarkably consistent within a certain school of Miltonic criticism,[31] it ignores a theological issue of Christology as it is only in Christ that creation can continue to exist in the first place.[32] On a textual level Milton resolves this apparent theological tension between his Puritan leanings and more orthodox doctrine by ensuring the continuation between the new life of Eden and the pre-existence of God, and thus by implication Christ too. This echoes the opening of the book of Genesis, which 'focuses on how God forms this world out of pre-existing materials, thereby opening up space for human beings to continue to participate in its development'.[33] The creative act in Milton's work is one that is ongoing and one in which all participants are said to be in a 'charming symphony ... [m]elodious in their harmony'.[34] Adam and Eve are participants within this ongoing process – to quote from Book 4: 'God hath set Labour and rest as day and night to man ... man hath his daily work of body or mind / Appointed which declares his dignity.'[35] Thus *Paradise Lost* does not depict the 'cosmic creation as a privileged beginning, a single event occurred once-upon-a-time and for all time'.[36] Rather, creation in *Paradise Lost* is, like textual creation itself, a polyvocal and ongoing exchange. As Adam says, 'millions of spiritual creatures walk the earth ... sole or responsive to each other's notes, Singing their great Creator'.[37]

By contrast, Victor Frankenstein, in claiming that 'life and death appeared to me ideal bounds, which I should first break through, and pour a torrent of light into our dark world',[38] is arguing for his own revelatory act of *creation ex nihilo* with the expressed aim of bringing about a reality over which he has complete unmediated control. Whereas within *Paradise Lost* the work and involvement of God allows for the flourishing of creation, Frankenstein seeks instead to explain and restrict his own creation. In the character of Victor we see this combination of exploration of the physical world, representative of the new rise of science and discovery, coupled with a semi-religious and imaginative 'rapture'. Whereas his cousin Elizabeth continues the Miltonic exegesis and description of the world (in her upbringing she spends her time 'contemplating the magnificent appearance of things'[39]), Victor seeks mastery over the created, material world. Specifically, Victor seeks the imaginative and 'Christ-like capacity of redemption and reconciliation, one which mimes God's own creative power'.[40] It is no longer in Christ that creation is held together but in the mind of the singular genius who can, like the Christ he has replaced, resurrect the dead and create life. The 'new man' of Romanticism does not just describe and explore creation – as Milton's retelling of the creation story does – but actively participates in the process of bringing new elements of creation into being. Victor Frankenstein has no patience for participation within the continuing harmonious work of God's creation but seeks a new and entirely separate realm of creativity. Victor figures as a type of the Romantic ideology as throughout the period poets, writers and philosophers sought to go beyond the material into the realm of imaginative transcendence.[41]

Creator and Creation: Textual Tradition and Theological Insight

Victor refers to himself as the creator and source of a new species: 'no father could claim the gratitude of his child so completely as I should deserve theirs'.[42] Despite his stated desire to create from nothing he admits that this is not the case; rather, he is visiting the charnel houses to piece together his 'dark materials', disturbing the 'secrets of the human frame' with his own 'profane fingers', and assembling his monster in a 'workshop of filthy creation'.[43] His successful acquisition of the ability to create life ignores the reality that life is dependent on its coexistence with other forms. As such, scientific revelation within the novel leads only to solitude and undeniable catastrophe. For this we need only see Frankenstein's inability to accept his responsibilities for his creation, his vituperation towards the unfortunate creature and his complete failure to grasp how his invention might bring others killed during the novel back to life. All of these examples reinforce the view that knowledge outside the social milieu is, at best, dangerous and that dogmatic certainties, of whatever system, should be viewed with suspicion. Victor thus embodies the very essence of imaginative engagement but without the stabilizing influence of tradition. His imaginative excesses wreak terrible and frequently bloody consequences. However, there is one character, Victor's own creation, who the novel takes pains to show engaging with an intellectual and literary tradition as well as an awareness of the mediated quality of existence.

Whereas Victor is the embodiment of the so-called Romantic 'great man' who thrives on solitary revelation, Frankenstein's creature is the direct opposite. Abandoned by his creator, the creature is motivated by a desire for not just a sense of community or companionship but a need to understand himself as a created being-in-the-world: 'I had never yet seen a being resembling me, or who claimed intercourse with me. What was I?'[44] It is this desire that leads him to forge his own textual canon – first finding Frankenstein's journal notes, then moving on to Volney's *Ruins of Empires*, then Goethe's *Sorrows of Young Werther*, Plutarch's *Lives* and most importantly, Milton's *Paradise Lost*. The choice of texts is striking, as Frankenstein's creature uses them to ground his being in the historical, social and cultural contexts of the time. From Volney, his being is placed within a historical context as he learns of 'the manners, governments and different religions of the earth ... the strange system of human society was explained to me'.[45] Moving from the historic, the creature's engagement with Goethe's *The Sorrows of Young Werther* allows for a more personal articulation of subjectivity: 'The gentle and domestic manners it described, combined with lofty sentiments and feelings, which had for their object something out of self, accorded well with my experiences ... and the wants alive in my own bosom.'[46] Here Goethe's novel not only allows the creature some degree of expression in regards to subjectivity but serves as a powerful reminder of the potential of imaginative forms to validate and confirm the legitimacy of private experience. From this engagement with the subjective comes an interest in the theological. Milton's *Paradise Lost* allows the creature to frame his position in theological terms, as both created and abandoned by his creator. These encounters with traditional texts are vital. From an understanding of this textual canon the creature comes to recognition of himself as well as the vital responsibilities of that Frankenstein as a creator has abandoned. The engagement with tradition gives insight to his own condition but little comfort, as he compares his state with Milton's Adam:

> Like Adam, I was apparently united by no link to any other being in existence; but his state was far different from mine in every other respect. He had come forth from the hands of God a perfect creature,

happy and prosperous, guarded by the especial care of his Creator ... but I was wretched, helpless and alone ... the bitter gall of envy rose within me.[47]

This sense of exile from God is reinforced when Frankenstein and the creature come face to face for the first time. The envy the creature feels in regards to Adam's relationship to God serves only to underscore the extent to which Frankenstein has forsaken his creature. The first conversation between the creature and Frankenstein reveals this sense of envy and confusion. Drawing from Job 23, the creature's language reverses the power dynamics established by the more disingenuous Frankenstein. Job, forsaken by his creator and suffering for reasons that seem not only vague but also unfair, wishes for an audience with God to put forward his case and seek justice. As Job says:

> I would lay my case before him, and fill my mouth with arguments. I would learn what he would answer me, and understand what he would say to me. Would he contend with me in the greatness of his power? No; but he would give heed to me. There an upright person could reason with him, and I should be acquitted for ever by my judge.[48]

The language of Job presupposes the duty of care of the creator towards the created and simultaneously the possibility of a kind of rational communication between the two. These elements are interdependent, for without the possibility of rational conversation between the two, Job cannot be acquitted in the sight of his judge. Frankenstein's creature shares this desire, asking, 'let your compassion be moved, Listen to my tale when you have heard that, abandon or commiserate me, as you shall judge that I deserve. But hear me ... listen to me, Frankenstein!'[49] Here the creature combines appeals to justice, wisely noting that 'even the guilty are allowed, by human laws, bloody as they are to speak in their own defence',[50] with an awareness of the theological nature of the relationship between himself and Victor – 'if you can and if you will, destroy the work of your hands'.[51]

In the conversation between the two the creature takes on the role of the rationalist, the subject aware of his own nature and his position in relation to divine power, whereas Victor, ostensibly the novel's hero, becomes an extremist. Victor's language takes on theological and apocalyptic tones as he lambasts his creation as a 'Devil' and 'a vile insect'.[52] Victor goes beyond the use of theological invective and instead seeks to use divine power to undo his own creative act: 'Cursed be the day, abhorred devil, in which you first saw light! Cursed (although I curse myself) be the hands that formed you!'[53] Unknowingly or not, Victor's outburst articulates a vital theological point – as a fallen individual in creation, the hands that formed the creature are not the perfect hands of the divine presence that Milton details but are cursed by the stain of original sin. As a created being in the world, Victor is literally incapable of creating in any other way, despite his imaginative reach. Furthermore, Victor is bound up within the network of human relationships that always carry with it the potential for failure, hurt and sin. Because of this theologically inflected vitriol, the conversation between Frankenstein's creature and Victor is not the rational exchange between man and God that the creature (and Job) desired. Rather, the reader sees rational, created man encounter the terrible genius of the Romantic Imagination. The awful 'Other' in the novel is not the creature but rather Victor himself: 'You my creator, detest and spurn me ... You purpose to kill me! How dare you sport thus with life?'[54] Victor assumes the role of the divine presence speaking out of the whirlwind at the end of the book of Job. However, his commitment to his revelatory act of creation denies him any grounding in tradition to allow him to make sense of what he has done. Furthermore, as his creature understands, Victor lacks an awareness of the duties and responsibilities that creation carries with it. Creation is not merely a revelatory act of science but a theologically inflected act, laden with responsibility.

The Duty of Creation: Frankenstein and the Question of Personhood

From here attention must turn to a closer examination of the theology of creation that *Frankenstein* puts forth. Once more Milton forms not only a vital poetic influence but also an often-missed theological influence. On his arrival into Paradise in Book 4 of *Paradise Lost*, Satan sees Adam and Eve for the first time: 'into our room of bliss, thus high advanced creatures of other mould, earth borne ... yet to Heav'nly spirits bright'.[55] The created Adam and Eve are both earth borne or fully material and yet theologically aware, bright to the 'Heav'nly spirits'. Milton's Devil goes on to note how 'lively shines in them divine resemblance, and such grace the hand that formed them on their shape hath poured'.[56] The physical appearance of Adam and Eve is entirely bound up in the grace used by the hand that created them – in short, their physical appearance is a reflection of their spiritual condition. In contrast to Milton, Frankenstein deliberately problematizes this relationship as the link between physical appearance and spiritual nature is shown in a more complex light:

> It was on a dreary night of November that I beheld the accomplishment of my toils ... I saw the dull yellow eyes open; it breathed hard, and a convulsive motion agitated its limbs ... Oh! No mortal could support the horror of that countenance ... had gazed upon him while unfinished; he was ugly then; but when those muscles and joints were rendered capable of motion it became a thing such as even Dante could not have conceived.[57]

This passage, a Gothic echo of the creation of man in Genesis 1, repeatedly links aesthetics with theology. The inability of mortal man to cope with the horror of the creature's appearance and the reference to Dante creates a theologically inflected aesthetics – the creature transforms from a scientific object of curiosity and becomes a 'demonical corpse'.[58] Whereas the creation of Adam and Eve in *Paradise Lost* forms a smaller part within the melodious harmony of the ongoing act of divine creation, Victor's creative act reveals his lack of awareness about the theological realities at play. Victor's creature reflects no 'divine resemblance' or 'grace the hand that formed them on their shape hath poured'.[59] Simply put, creation for Victor Frankenstein is a singular event – a great revelatory act of insight; yet as Milton understands, the act of creation depends on a continued involvement with that which has already been brought into being. Within *Paradise Lost*, God does not create Paradise for Adam and Eve and then leave; rather, the Garden, their involvement with it and the relationship between the human subject and the divine are assiduously maintained. God goes so far as to send angels to warn his creation that their enemy is at hand[60] – the reason given for this intervention in the world is, as Milton writes, 'to fulfil all justice'.[61] The idea of the Romantic man as a lone figure of genius is, via Milton, held up as being guilty of moral failure and dramatized through the figure of Victor.

Victor's moral failure is well noted by the creature in their first face-to-face encounter; 'do your duty towards me ... I am thy creature, and I will be even mild and docile to my natural lord and king, *if thou wilt also perform thy part, the which thou owest me.*'[62] At a later stage the creature adds: 'but on you only had I any claim for pity and redress'.[63] What is owed to Frankenstein's creature is, first, the involvement of the creator with creation and, second, a degree of ontological recognition from a source external and prior to the self. Frankenstein's creature has, by this point in the narrative, begun to engage with the textual tradition of his day but comes to his creator seeking the recognition of his personhood from an external source. His request for Victor to create for him a companion is not simply to fulfil a desire for companionship but a subtle awareness that companionship carries with it the possibility of personhood. Through identification, through sympathy and through the intimacy relationships afford, the Other can be brought from the status of the monstrous to a member within human society. As the creature explains, 'everywhere I see bliss, from which I alone am irrevocably excluded ... am I not alone, miserably alone? You, my creator, abhor me; what hope can I gather from your fellow-creatures who owe me nothing?'[64]

The status of the Other as Other is therefore dependent on first, the abandonment of the created by his creator and second, a refusal to acknowledge the figure of the Other as possessing a degree of personhood. The comparison once more comes from Milton as Shelley draws a contrast between the monster's own awakening to self-awareness and the earliest memories and self-recognition of Eve in *Paradise Lost*. Eve awakens and comes to consciousness 'under a shade of flowers ... not distance far from thence a murmuring sound of waters issued from a cave', and like Frankenstein's creature she is 'much wond'ring where / And what I was'.[65] From there she comes to recognize herself and experience the joy of self-recognition: 'A shape within the wat'ry gleam appeared ... pleased I soon returned.'[66] In contrast, while Frankenstein's creature also comes to and gains consciousness by a brook, the creature comes to no such understanding: 'I was a poor, helpless, miserable wretch; I knew and could distinguish, nothing; but feeling pain invade me on all sides, I sat down and wept.'[67] Frankenstein's creature has a moment of self-regarding, catching sight of his reflection, but in contrast to Eve, who is drawn towards the pleasing shape: 'I was terrified when I viewed myself ... when I became fully convinced that I was in reality the monster that I am, I was filled with the bitterest sensations of despondency and mortification.'[68] However, simply to describe the creature as monstrous based solely on appearance is far too reductive and fails to appreciate the significance of the contexts within which both Eve and the creature are placed. Eve is drawn away from her own reflection and told by the divine voice to 'follow me and I will bring thee where no shadow stays thy coming and thy soft embraces'.[69] By her creator she is placed within relationship with Adam, and here Milton makes clear that the relationship they share is not simply a degree of biological necessity or even romance but something bound up with their theological status:

Whom fli'st thou? Whom thou fli'st, of him thou art,
His flesh, his bone. To give thee being I lent
Out of my side to thee, nearest my heart,
Substantial life to have thee by my side
Henceforth an individual solace dear
Part of my soul I seek thee and thee claim
My other half.[70]

Adam and Eve share a physical connection, a recognition of their sameness, but this recognition goes beyond the material into the spiritual. The physical connection and similarity they share is merely the visible sign of the non-material connection. They are brought together through the active involvement of their creator and through relationship that in itself reflects the ongoing act of divine creation; they find in each other the other part of their souls and, as a result, an answer to the question Frankenstein's creature is unable to resolve: 'What was I?' This desire for ontological certainty informs Frankenstein's creature's own desire for a companion. The creature's request for a mate does not simply show a need for the satisfaction of a physical desire; rather, the creature's request is framed as a need to 'become linked to the chain of existence and events from which I am now excluded'.[71] Frankenstein's creature seeks a visible reflection of the link between God and his creation that is ongoing and participatory, and that allows for the affirmation of the individual's personhood within it. The relationship he asks Frankenstein to provide is something Frankenstein is incapable of granting as Frankenstein refuses to recognize that his creation requires his ongoing involvement and that the relationship that the creature desires reflects this ongoing process.

Frankenstein's creature is made monstrous not through his material creation or through being stitched together from the filthy fragments of the earth but rather through the complete failure of his creator to recognize either the significance of what he has made or the act of creation more generally. Materiality is something shared by all but it is the inclusion of the individual within relationship that seems key to the establishing of personhood. An awareness of the 'various relationships which bind one human being to another in mutual bonds' is absolutely vital for the development of personal subjectivity and the establishing of healthy and supportive community.[72] The closest Frankenstein's creature gets to this state is through the observations of the De Lacy family – the creature even goes so far as to hope that they may 'become acquitted with my admiration of their virtues, they would compassionate me, and overlook my personal deformity'.[73] The desire for a relationship is touchingly conveyed: could they 'turn from their door one, however monstrous, who solicited their compassion and friendship?'[74] As the narrative progresses, the link between the Miltonic understanding of personhood as dependent on the acknowledgement of another becomes more clear – 'the more I saw of them the greater became my desire to claim their protection and their kindness ... my heart yearned to be known and loved by these amiable creatures'.[75] Crucially there is also a sense of this reciprocity being deserved – as a created being the creature seems aware of the intrinsic value he possesses: 'I required kindness and sympathy; but I did not believe myself unworthy of it.'[76]

However, the equivocation of moral quality with aesthetic appearance that repulsed the theologically naïve Victor proves to be sadly irresistible to the De Lacys. The creature flees this potential reciprocal relationship in a fit of violence, physically driven from the brink of humanity back to its outer limits. Strikingly, the creature never lays blame at the feet of the De Lacys exclusively, admitting that he 'could with pleasure have destroyed the cottage'. However, he does not do so until the De Lacy family is safely out of harm's way. Immediately following his violent expulsion from their midst, the creature turns his attention to the source of his unrecognized humanity – his creator. 'Cursed, cursed creator! Why did I live?'[77] Forcibly expelled from the boundaries of the human world of identification and relationship, the creature's humanity is neglected: 'I was like a wild beast that had broken the toils, destroying the objects that obstructed me and ranging through the woods with a stag-like swiftness.'[78] Denied the acknowledgement of his personhood by his fellow men and entirely ignored by the force that brought him into being, Frankenstein's creature truly appears as monstrous for the first time.

Radical Evil and the Creature

Frankenstein himself clearly believes his creature to be evil, but as discussed above, the link between appearance and moral status serves only to indict Victor's failings as a creator, presenting him as a metaphysically absent Father. It is not enough to consider evil as a category of behaviour or a set of actions one performs. This is shown within the novel as Victor positions his creature as evil before the creature has any ability to do anything, good or not. Rather, as Eagleton claims, 'evil is a condition of being' as well as 'a category of behaviour'.[79] Victor's argument lends itself to circular logic, for 'if some people really are born evil ... they are no more responsible for this condition that being born with cystic fibrosis. The condition which is supposed to damn them succeeds only in redeeming them.'[80] To hold Frankenstein's monster as morally responsible requires evil to be something freely chosen, and if Frankenstein has created the monster evil then the monster is rendered incapable of being anything else. To label the monster evil requires an understanding of evil as something willed into action, a series of actions carried out for their own sake, frequently labelled as 'radical evil'.[81] Ewan Fernie calls this understanding of evil 'a form of existence founded upon destruction',[82] where actions are the result of evil beings rather than any kind of external factors. The attraction of such a position is clear but reductive – often radical evil is used as an ideological means of ensuring that those who have committed acts that are met with disapproval cannot be excused by appeal to circumstance, mistakenly conflating explanation with absolution. Evil actions are performed by evil persons because they are evil persons is an unsatisfying conclusion and gets no closer to the ontological reality of Frankenstein's creature. Frankenstein's creation shows himself to be little interested in negation or the annihilation of being; his aims and actions are mundane and everyday. The creature's concerns are with satiating hunger and thirst, with shelter and rest, and ultimately with companionship. Even when the creature experiences negative emotions, they are contextualized in such a way as to make the creature more sympathetic:

> I continued for the remainder of the day in my hovel in a state of utter and stupid despair. My protectors had departed, and had broken the only link that held me to the world. For the first time the feelings of revenge and hatred filled my bosom, and I did not strive to control them; but allowing myself to be borne away by the stream, I bent my mind towards injury and death. When I thought of my friends, of the mild voice of De Lacy. The gentle eyes of Agatha ... these thoughts vanished ... but again when I reflected that they had spurned and deserted me, anger returned, a rage of anger.[83]

Here, alongside a confessional tone that further links Frankenstein's creature to the lamentations of Job, we see the perilous emotional trauma tied up in the expulsion of the subject from any kind of community. The anger and thoughts that bend towards injury and death become understandable if not justifiable. While these actions are wrong, it seems extreme to label them as evil for they do not come from the creature but from multiple causes, including the great network of relationships and peoples that the creature has been introduced to by the very act of being created. Frankenstein's creature is *made* monstrous, and the narrative neatly highlights both the interrelated nature of the self with the Other and the dangerous trauma and violence that emerges when the personhood of the Other is ignored. Frankenstein's creature is evil in as much as we all are morally responsible and morally compromised through the very notion of acting in the world. Furthermore, the novel emphasizes the vital role of community in the recognition of the ontological status of the individual, and the high cost of equating aesthetics with morality or ontology.

Conclusion

Understood as a theological text, *Frankenstein* becomes more than simply part of the canonical Gothic but presents an imaginative theology, declaring the value, worth and personhood of Frankenstein's creature. The Gothic is not simply concerned with expressing the cultural fears of a social or historical moment but is a literary form that can participate within the theological narrative between the divine and humanity. However, theological criticism such as this must not seek to assert a new closure – Brown warns against this in *God and Mystery in Words*, challenging the assumption that metaphor is redundant 'once we have got the point'.[84] So the conclusion should not be that *Frankenstein* is 'truly' a theological text underneath it all. Rather, what I have sought to argue is that within the Gothic the interaction between theology and literature is highly productive and that Brown's work allows for a fruitful engagement with literary forms usually excluded from theological analysis. In the horror and violence of *Frankenstein* the monstrous comes to illuminate much that is theologically provocative, around the status of the Other and the relationship between created and creator. Through its symbolism and connection to other theological writing, *Frankenstein* shows that 'thinking does not always proceed by logical inference but sometimes develops imaginatively, simply through symbolic images being put to new uses'.[85] The challenge with which I close is to ask what further theological reimaginings may be found in the trash of the circulating libraries.

Notes

1 See David Brown, *Tradition and Imagination: Revelation and Change* (Oxford: Oxford University Press, 1999).

2 Carol Margaret Davison, *Gothic Literature 1764–1824* (Cardiff: University of Wales Press, 2009), 225.

3 The typical definition of Gothic is assumed to be referring to a period of literature from 1764 (with the publication of Horace Walpole's *Castle of Otranto*) onwards. The contested nature of the Gothic as a historical genre is too complex to be fully outlined here, but the Gothic is also treated as not just a period of literary history but also as an aesthetics, discourse and epistemology. For more, see David Punter, *The Literature of Terror*, 2 vols (London: Routledge, 1996) as well as Fred Botting, *Gothic: The New Critical Idiom* (London: Routledge, 2013).

4 Samuel Taylor Coleridge, Review of Matthew G. Lewis's *The Monk*, *The Critical Review* (February 1797), 194–200.

5 Despite growth in the fields of imaginative apologetics and literature and theology, the Gothic and horror are often marginalized as literature, and theology as a field has chosen to focus on areas that seem to lend themselves immediately to theological

analysis. One only need see the breadth of material available on Romanticism or the Inklings, for example. David Brown's own *God in Mystery and Words* makes mention of Romanticism (David Brown, *God and Mystery in Words: Experience through Metaphor and Drama* [Oxford: Oxford University Press, 2008], 89, 262–3) but not Radcliffe – P. B. Shelley (65) but not Mary Shelley. While God may be found in words, that search may not have been carried as far as the Gothic as yet.

6 For an exemplary piece of work in this vein, see Diane Hoeveler, *The Gothic Ideology: Religious Hysteria and Anti-Catholicism in British Popular Fiction, 1780–1880* (Cardiff: University of Wales Press, 2015).

7 See Victor Sage, *Horror Fiction in the Protestant Tradition* (London: St Martin's Press, 1988) as well as Zoë Lehmann Imfeld, *The Victorian Ghost Story and Theology: From La Fanu to James* (London: Palgrave Macmillan, 2016).

8 Brown, *Tradition and Imagination*, 25.

9 The book has been a recurrent part of Gothic scholarship for at least 50 years. See *Mary Shelley*, ed. Harold Bloom (London: Modern Critical Voices, 1985).

10 Mark Knight, *An Introduction to Religion and Literature* (London: Continuum, 2009), 9.

11 See Gavin Hopps and Jane Stabler, *Romanticism and Religion from William Cowper to Wallace Stevens* (London: Routledge, 2006).

12 John Milton, *Paradise Lost*, ed. Gordon Teskey (London: Norton Critical Editions, 2005).

13 Mary Shelley, *Frankenstein* (London: Penguin Classics, 2012), 98.

14 Joyce Carol Oates, 'Frankenstein's Fallen Angel', *Critical Inquiry* 10.3 (1984), 550.

15 Nora Crook, 'Mary Shelley, Author of Frankenstein', in *A Companion to the Gothic*, ed. David Punter (London: Blackwell, 2000), 6.

16 For a more detailed exploration of the notion of theodicy, see *Problems in Theology: Evil – A Reader*, ed. Jeff Astley, David Brown and Ann Loades (London: Continuum, 2003) as well as Joseph F. Kelly, *The Problem of Evil in the Western Tradition: From the Book of Job to Modern Genetics* (Collegeville, MN: Liturgical Press, 2001).

17 Much of the Gothic could be argued to fit in with this tradition, from the early controversy of Matthew Lewis's *The Monk* (Oxford: Oxford University Press, 2016), first published in 1798, to the modern Catholic theodicy explored in William Peter Blatty's *The Exorcist* (London: Corgi, 2011).

18 Mark Knight and Emma Mason, *Nineteenth-Century Literature and Religion: An Introduction* (Oxford: Oxford University Press, 2006), 5.

19 See Ian Watt, *The Rise of the Novel* (London: Hogarth Press, 1987).

20 Brown, *God in Mystery and Words*, 20.

21 Paul Fiddes, *Freedom and Limit: A Dialogue Between Literature and Christian Doctrine* (London: Palgrave, 1991), 11.

22 Ibid., 8.

23 Shelley, *Frankenstein*, 22.

24 Ibid., 223.

25 Fiddes, *Freedom and Limit*, 8.

26 Here *Frankenstein* is connected to not only John Milton's *Paradise Lost* (1667) but also *The Pilgrim's Progress* by John Bunyan (1678). Furthermore, this idea of finding some purpose within a larger narrative idea links *Frankenstein* to the early epistolary novels, wherein the ethical problem of their 'fictionality' was solved through the potential virtue of the story in informing a larger ethical narrative. See Samuel Richardson's book (and its telling subtitle), *Pamela: Or Virtue Rewarded* (1740).

27 Mark Knight, *Introduction to Literature and Religion* (London: Continuum, 2009), 13.

28 C. S. Lewis, 'A Preface to Paradise Lost', in *Paradise Lost*, ed. Gordon Teskey (London: Norton Critical Editions, 2005), 92.

29 William Empson, 'Milton's God', in *Paradise Lost*, ed. Teskey, 439.

30 See Stanley Fish, 'The Milk of the Pure Word', in *Surprised by Sin: The Reader in Paradise Lost* (Cambridge, MA: Harvard University Press, 1998), 12–92; Northrop Frye, 'The Garden Within', in *The Return of Eden: Five Essays on Milton's Epics* (Toronto: University of Toronto Press, 1965), 60–72.

31 Tying in to broader debates about how and where encounter with the Divine may occur and the changes in how and where this divide or presentation of God as somehow 'over there' has developed. For a useful summary of this, see David Brown, 'Response: Experience, Symbol and Revelation', in *Theology, Aesthetics, and Culture: Responses to the Work of David Brown*, ed. Robert MacSwain and Taylor Worley (Oxford: Oxford University Press, 2012), 266.

32 For the biblical justification for this belief, see Colossians 1.15–19 (esp. 16). For theological exegesis on this point, see Marilyn McCord Adams, *Christ and Horrors: The Coherence of Christology* (Cambridge: Cambridge University Press, 2008).

33 Knight, *Introduction to Literature and Religion*, 15.

34 Milton, *Paradise Lost*, 379–80

35 Ibid., 94

36 Regina Schwartz, *Remembering and Repeating: Biblical Creation in Paradise Lost* (Cambridge: Cambridge University Press, 1988), 1.

37 Milton, *Paradise Lost*, 96.

38 Shelley, *Frankenstein*, 47.

39 Ibid., 28.

40 Terry Eagleton, *Culture and the Death of God* (London: Yale University Press, 2014), 101.

41 This is dealt with in detail by M. H. Abrams, *Natural Supernaturalism* (London: Norton, 1971), 21–32, 97–117.

42 Shelley, *Frankenstein*, 47.

43 Ibid., 48.

44 Ibid., 120.

45 Ibid., 119–20

46 Ibid., 128.

47 Ibid., 129.

48 Job 23.4–7 (NRSV).

49 Shelley, *Frankenstein*, 99.

50 Ibid.

51 Ibid.

52 Ibid., 97.

53 Ibid., 99.

54 Ibid., 97.

55 Milton, *Paradise Lost*, 88.

56 Ibid.

57 Shelley, *Frankenstein*, 50–1.

58 Ibid., 51.

59 Milton, *Paradise Lost*, 89.

60 Ibid., 106.

61 See Christ's speech in Book 3, 62–3.

62 Shelley, *Frankenstein*, 98; emphasis provided.

63 Ibid., 108.

64 Ibid., 98.

65 Milton, *Paradise Lost*, 90.

66 Ibid.

67 Shelley, *Frankenstein*, 102.
68 Ibid., 113.
69 Milton, *Paradise Lost*, 91.
70 Ibid., 91.
71 Shelley, *Frankenstein*, 148.
72 Ibid., 120.
73 Ibid., 130.
74 Ibid.
75 Ibid., 131.
76 Ibid., 132.
77 Ibid.
78 Ibid., 136.
79 Terry Eagleton, *On Evil* (New Haven, CT: Yale University Press, 2008), 152.
80 Ibid., 5.
81 See Immanuel Kant, *Religion within the Bounds of Reason Alone* (1793). For a more modern summary of the philosophical underpinnings of Radical Evil and the theoretical implications, see *Radical Evil*, ed. Joan Copjec (London: Verso, 1996).
82 Ewan Fernie, *The Demonic: Literature and Experience* (London, Routledge, 2013), 10.
83 Shelley, *Frankenstein*, 138.
84 Brown, *God and Mystery in Words*, 6.
85 David Brown, *Discipleship and Imagination: Christian Tradition and Truth* (Oxford: Oxford University Press, 2000), 176.

12

The Forms of Faith in Contemporary American Fiction

DENNIS F. KINLAW III

In a December 2012 piece published by the *New York Times*, the writer and editor Paul Elie offers the kind of inquiry that seems to revel in its capacity to precipitate panic: 'Has Fiction Lost its Faith?' Looking mournfully across the last half-century of American literature as a series of false starts and second-rate attempts to come to grips with a religious sensibility that seems to have dissolved, Elie abandons the contemporary novelist in the shadowlands of Christian faith's past masters, such as Flannery O'Connor, Walker Percy and even John Updike. 'If any patch of our culture can be said to be post-Christian', he notes, 'it is literature.' While the struggle for belief and the maintenance of faith once figured prominently in the pages of some of the best and most serious American fiction, today such explorations appear like some 'dead language' as the depth and drama of religious yearning is replaced by the enervating forces of secularism.[1] The apparent demise of religiously engaged fiction would seem to be in full bloom by Elie's time, for as early as 1989 George Steiner was opening his work *Real Presences* with the observation that '[w]here God clings to our culture, to our routines of discourse, He is a phantom of grammar'.[2] Accordingly, the collective cry for the contemporary 'novel of belief' discloses a more general cultural estrangement from the Christian faith as well as its narrative foundation: Scripture.

If fiction once offered an arena in which the story of Christ could be imaginatively advanced, it would seem our inability to hear the message of Scripture clearly today impairs any attempt to 'improve upon' its content within the realm of literature.[3] Such a dilemma seemingly deters at the outset David Brown's elevation of the aesthetic as a valuable and revelatory extension of the story of Christ as told in Scripture. Brown's suggestion that the salvific story of Christ needs to be 'mediated through other narratives that bear more directly on the sort of life situation faced by the contemporary Christian' assumes a cultural setting in which belief and biblical narrative remain foundational frameworks capable of being drawn upon and revised for productive purposes.[4] However, it is precisely the foundational status of such frameworks that is called into question in a 'post-Christian' era. As a result, the possibility for fiction to participate within the 'imaginative mediation of Christ's life' seems to be constrained by a narrative form that has 'lost' its faith.[5] Yet even if we accept the effects of secularism and so recognize the relationship between fiction and faith in the twenty-first century to reflect something like a 'broken estate',[6] in what manner might this fragmented period offer the contemporary novelist a fresh canvas on which to perceive the presence of the divine?

The constructive enterprise set before the 'post-Christian' novelist is that of reframing the drama of meaning and belief within an era in which the foundations for belief have been called into question. In this way the task of the novelist mirrors that of the theologian in the wake of biblical criticism. Both confront a Christian tradition no longer grounded within a 'static' text but subjected to a 'gradualism in perception', as David Brown suggests, and therefore are challenged to adopt a certain flexibility in their approach to narrative in order to attend to the 'needs and aspirations of the community' more effectively.[7] Consequently, the narrative frame through which the Christian story is conveyed is no longer perceived as 'firmly set' but open to critique, reconsideration and reformulation.[8] As such, the destabilization of the 'fixed text' of Scripture by biblical criticism,[9] as well as the loss of religious belief as a 'fixture' within American fiction,[10] represents less of an absolute exile from Christian tradition than the exposure of that tradition's evolving narrative makeup. 'The life of any literary text, including the Bible, is greater than simply its original setting', Brown writes, and writers and readers seeking to engage that tradition must be willing to approach it not as 'something static' but as 'always on the move'.[11] Viewed from a perspective that permits this movement to unfold rather than enforcing an enclosure of sorts on divine disclosure, the vitality of Christian tradition remains intact even as it evolves in significant ways across time. The 'Christian faith is richer for that new story', as Brown notes of belief in the aftermath of biblical criticism, 'not the poorer'.[12] Contemporary considerations of the 'decline' or 'loss' of the Christian tradition today, therefore, seemingly fail to discern the possibility that disbelief itself signals only a 'stage' in the continued unfolding of that tradition.[13] Any backward-glancing appeal to an era in which the Christian narrative remained unquestioned, as evinced in Elie's lament, betrays an impoverished view of the flexibility of the Christian tradition; furthermore, by dwelling on the apparent deterioration of faith in contemporary fiction, critics like Elie ignore the capacity for critique to invigorate new forms of its narrative expression.[14] Conversely, Brown's contention that 'tradition itself needs first to be undermined before it can acquire a capacity for further development' provides a valuable framework from which the presence of these more oblique forms of faith may be glimpsed in contemporary American fiction.[15] Recognizing at once the importance of maintaining 'consistency with the historical narrative' in our approach to Scripture without ignoring 'how [God's] presence and influence can be appropriated in the here and now', Brown points to the possibility of that presence remaining active beyond Scripture and amid disbelief.[16] The capacity for fiction to mediate that presence, however, requires a writer capable of countenancing the reality of disbelief as well as the instability of narrative meaning in a post-foundational era. It is the work of late American novelist David Foster Wallace (1962–2008), this chapter suggests, that best addresses these dilemmas within contemporary American fiction.

As an author attuned to the fragmentation of religious tradition within contemporary literature and American culture more generally, Wallace provides a critically neglected counterpoint to the type of facile assessment that consigns contemporary fiction to the dustbin of 'post-Christian' anomie. Writing the bulk of his fiction in the secular twilight between Steiner and Elie's respective critiques, Wallace confronts the contemporary crisis of meaning and belief in a manner that accounts for the deconstruction of Christianity as a fixed narrative framework while remaining attentive to the ways tradition – both religious and literary – provide the necessary resources for repurposing more suitable frames of reference. At once convinced of faith's relevance for fiction today even as that faith becomes increasingly hard to communicate on the far side of postmodernity, Wallace opens his work to the critique of Scripture as kind of 'leximancical fraud'[17] while exploring alternative approaches to expressing its continued vitality nevertheless. The productive inquiry into the vitality of religious belief, however, requires one to recognize the extent to which such belief has dissipated in a post-religious era. As Wallace explains in an interview:

> America is one big experiment in what happens when you're a wealthy, privileged culture that's pretty much lost religion or spirituality as a real informing presence. It's still a verbal presence – it's part of the etiquette that our leaders use, but it's not inside us anymore.[18]

Here Elie's reduction of religion to a 'dead language' is seemingly echoed in Wallace's assessment. In contrast to the sense of resignation that shapes Elie's perspective, however, is Wallace's sensitivity to the force of faith that exceeds language itself. As Wallace notes, 'the stuff that's truly interesting about religion is inarticulable'.[19] By opening his fiction to the exploration of this 'inarticulable' dimension of religious belief, Wallace fashions a type of 'post-secular' fiction that accounts for the fragmentation of religious tradition in the contemporary setting without assuming such fragmentation signals the dissolution of the religious altogether.[20] It is within this fractured and fluid narrative framework that a 'fresh discernment of things spiritual' is made possible once again in contemporary American fiction.[21] But in what manner does contemporary fiction's ability to address issues of meaning and belief on the other side of postmodernity inform our assessment of Scripture as a story open to the provocations of the present yet rooted in historical fact? And how might the fiction of David Foster Wallace – and particularly his emphasis on the self-opening and transfigurative aspects of literature – present a 'weakened'[22] form of Scripture's restorative message and so in some manner operate as a revelatory medium in which the 'divine dialogue' between God and humanity may be seen to take place?[23] By attending to these questions in light of David Brown's understanding of the Christian tradition as a 'process',[24] as well drawing on his appreciation for fiction's capacity to illuminate our place within the story of Scripture, I hope to bring into view a more comprehensive awareness of the relations between faith and fiction in the contemporary American setting.

The Place of Tradition in Contemporary Literature

In assessing the ways faith presents itself in contemporary American fiction, one must confront more squarely the contemporary novelist's tenuous relation to literary tradition. Paul Elie's critique of contemporary fiction as representing a kind of narrative 'hangover' from more direct religious engagements by writers like Flannery O'Connor fails to exhibit any critical sensitivity to the effectiveness of certain narrative forms in relation to the cultural context in which they are employed.[25] The potential for 'new contexts' to provide a 'necessary spur to new ways of thinking' as well as writing about faith, as noted by Brown, demands an attentiveness to the ways cultural conditions provide 'fresh stimuli' for the development of Christian tradition.[26] Reflecting briefly on just a few of the experiential transitions that have arisen since the narratives of Scripture were composed – of which 'the rise of individualism, the emergence of capitalism, and the changes in human self-understanding wrought by science' are mentioned – Brown concludes that 'it would seem scarcely credible that the last significant change that required a fresh imaginative application of the tradition occurred in the first century of our era'.[27] While Brown's critique is aimed at biblical critics seeking to fix Scripture within an 'unaltered' framework, his sensitivity to the interdependence between narrative tradition and cultural context offers a helpful approach for considering the role of faith in contemporary literature as well.[28] While the fragmentation of fixed narrative frames might complicate the writer's effort to convey certain truths narratively, the possibility that such narrative flexibility provides an opening for the development of more culturally appropriate narrative forms remains. Or as Wallace's fictionalized Lyndon Baines Johnson remarks: 'This is not a change in purpose. It is a change in what we believe that purpose requires.'[29] Reflecting on her fiction as a contemporary extension of Henry James's suggestion that great fiction should make us 'finely aware so as to become richly responsible', the novelist Zadie Smith admits her work is able to precipitate this awareness within her reader only by countenancing her shifting cultural context. Like Brown, Smith perceives amid the ascent of individualism, capitalism and even the 'ubiquity of television', the importance of reconsidering the role of narrative tradition in order to connect affectively to readers.[30] The communication of meaning across time comes to be seen then as an event of continual renewal rather than an unending effort to isolate a fixed script from the scribbles of later scribes.

The work of Wallace reflects a similar sensitivity to the importance of maintaining a flexible approach to narrative form as a means of addressing more traditional issues in a contemporary context. The instability of cultural perspectives, Wallace argues, demands a narrative form capable of grappling with such instability in relevant ways. Wallace explains:

> Every two or three generations the world gets vastly different and the context in which you have to learn how to be a human being, or to have good relationships, or decide whether or not there is a God, or decide whether there's such a thing as love, and whether it's redemptive, become vastly different.[31]

In addition to acknowledging the importance of context as an energizing element in the refashioning of fiction for a contemporary age, Wallace finds himself tasked with finding new forms in which these fundamental areas of experience may be best addressed. As Wallace notes, 'the structures with which you can communicate these dilemmas or have characters struggle with them seem to become appropriate and then inappropriate again and so on'.[32] While the notion of 'appropriateness' might seem an underdeveloped principle on which to base one's aesthetic agenda, Wallace's sensitivity to the cultural setting within which he finds himself writing enables him to address 'very old traditional human verities that have to do with spirituality and emotion and community' without ostracizing his reader.[33] It is precisely this type of interpretative dynamism that Brown challenges the Church to develop today. Indeed, Brown's contention that the narratives of Scripture must 'engage the imagination' in a way that relates to 'the readers' own life situations and dilemmas' suggests an almost mirrored enterprise between those interested in renewing Christian tradition and Wallace's own effort to address 'traditional' values in a seemingly irreligious era.[34] More problematic still is postmodern theory's impact on the appeal to tradition carried out by the contemporary theologian and novelist alike.

If the ascent of secularism sidetracks certain narrative approaches to religious expression and so renders some of the more memorable figures of faith in fiction anachronistic, it is postmodern theory's rupture from the past that seems further to impair literature's capacity to speak freely when it comes to faith. By calling into question language's capacity to reflect reality in any reliable manner, postmodern theory grants the contemporary novelist an unprecedented licence to exploit narrative recursion as a means of exposing fiction's own instability. It is within this overexposed and unstable narrative landscape that meaning and belief must be reassembled by writers. Yet as the link to literary tradition grows increasingly tenuous (nineteenth-century 'big-R Realism'[35] now considered naïve and the innovative techniques of the modernist masters seemingly spent), contemporary novelists find themselves marooned amid exhausted forms. As Wallace writes in his first published article, 'Fictional Futures and the Conspicuously Young' (1988): 'We seem, now, to see our literary innocence taken from us without anything substantial to replace it.'[36] Convinced the only option left for literature in the wake of reference was the ironization of literature's claim to meaning, postmodern authors devote themselves to exposing the 'used-upness of certain forms' and illustrating 'the felt exhaustion of certain possibilities' left for literature itself.[37] Indeed, John Barth, author of the metafictional *Sot-Weed Factor* (1960) and *Life in the Funhouse* (1968), decried as early as 1967 that the state of narrative was perhaps best described as a 'Literature of Exhaustion'. In addition to challenging fiction's capacity to progress in the face of theoretical crisis, postmodern authors like Barth saw themselves as carrying out the necessary task of severing its connection to the past – tradition now a burden to slough rather than an inheritance to reimagine within theoretically fraught times. Like the Russian Futurists of the 1930s, many postmodernists viewed themselves as part of a movement set out to destroy the past – only this time there would be no eschatological hope hanging on literature's horizon. 'We live in a moment that is, paradoxically, both emptied of intrinsic meaning or end and quite literally *eternal*', Wallace reflects.[38] And so with the lineaments of language shot through with an unprecedented self-awareness and any connection to tradition seemingly lost, the novelist finds their most elementary task of communicating to the reader – let alone expressing something of religious significance – challenged.

While the crises introduced by postmodern theory may seem an overly fraught arena in which to address the dilemma of faith and contemporary narrative forms, I would argue that it is precisely in literature and theology's capacity to countenance such crises that their effectiveness in the contemporary sphere is determined. Far from simply exhausting certain narrative structures or exposing the illusion of correspondence models of reference, postmodern theory illuminates as well 'the relations between literary artist, literary language, and literary artifact' as vastly 'more complex and powerful than has been realized hitherto'.[39] Such an appreciation for the serviceability of postmodern insights into language for the reclamation of more nuanced modes of meaning can be found across the work of Brown as well as Wallace. In *Continental Philosophy and Modern Theology*, Brown celebrates Jacques Derrida's emphasis on the irreducible nature of language as instrumental in countering the theological tendency to 'tie down' biblical language too soon.[40] Here the biblical critic's desire for a singular foundation on which to ground his interpretation of Scripture is undone by a newfound appreciation for the open-endedness of narrative. But even as Brown emphasizes the extent to which 'the thought of New Testament writers' tends to be 'more complex than we commonly like to admit', he refrains from embracing an interpretative relativism or adopting a posture of rigid foundationalism and establishes instead a middle way in which a more nuanced model of meaning may be maintained.[41] In *God and Mystery in Words*, Brown develops his sensitivity to language's capacity to 'access ... something more' by exploring some of the ways Scriptural imagery, symbolism, and metaphor convey a mode of meaning which exceeds historical correspondence.[42] It is in this text that Brown presents his revisionary approach to reference in light of postmodern theory – a charitable both/and approach to the modern–postmodern debate over correspondence that offers both the biblical critic and contemporary novelist an avenue beyond the theoretical impasse: 'Words can of course be used purely instrumentally', he writes, 'they can even be used as a form of play merely to refer internally to one another ... But their power is surely at their greatest when they act neither purely referentially nor as some form of internal play' but instead '[help] us grasp the totality of whatever reality it is with which we wish to engage'.[43] By adopting a pragmatic approach to language that at once recognizes the imprecision of its capacity to map reality while nevertheless remaining capable of pointing us towards truths whose significance is experiential as much as it is referential, Brown improves on our own understanding of the potential for language to remain meaningful after postmodernity. As such, he serves as an ideal dialogue partner in our own consideration of contemporary fiction's attempt to engage issues of meaning and belief today.

David Foster Wallace's Post-Foundational Faith

Like Brown, Wallace employs language's referential instability productively as a means of creating a fiction that more effectively incorporates its reader within the reading experience. Convinced that 'the contemporary artist can simply no longer afford to regard the work of critics or theorists or philosophers ... as divorced from his own', Wallace challenges the contemporary novelist to confront rather than reject the narrative instabilities exposed in postmodernity. Far from signalling the end of a transfigurative form of narrative exchange, Wallace's reading of postmodern theory suggests that 'it is precisely in those tangled relations that a forward-looking, fertile literary value may well reside'.[44] Committed to creating compelling narratives that 'make you feel something' you have otherwise forgotten without in any way being 'manipulative or old-fashioned or falsely naïve about the way language can stretch [the] world in which [we] live', Wallace advances a thoroughly contemporary approach to language while emphasizing its continued capacity to affect us in significant ways.[45] According to Wallace, it is through a theoretically informed and culturally sensitive approach to reference that narrative enables us to 'enter into relationships with ideas and with characters that are not permitted within the cinctures of ordinary verbal intercourse'.[46] Yet if the imprint of deconstruction on fiction offers more than a reflexive awareness of its own referential imprecision and represents instead a certain appreciation for the manner in which meaning persists outside of correspondence, the challenge of meaningfully engaging issues of religious significance within a 'post-Christian' era remains.

Postmodern theory falls noticeably short, however, in providing anything like a workable framework by which the religious may assert itself once more in fiction. Terry Eagleton argues as much in *After Theory*, writing that theory 'has been shamefaced about morality and metaphysics, embarrassed about religion ... and dogmatic about essences', a critical slight that abandons 'a rather large slice of human existence'.[47] For Wallace, a more sustainable path for the contemporary novelist seeking to address issues of meaning and belief today commences with a reconsideration of religious writers within literary tradition itself. Thus unlike the generation of writers before him who tended to view tradition as an obstacle to overcome, Wallace *returns* to tradition as a resource from which the exigencies of his own time may at least be measured if not mapped directly. In addition to his reverence for the religious poets Richard Crashaw, John Donne and Gerard Manley Hopkins (a poetic tradition one would assume to be beyond recovering in the wake of writers like John Barth), Wallace finds himself drawn to novelists who situate religious crisis at the centre of their texts. Fyodor Dostoevsky looms large here. Echoing Rowan Williams's reflection that 'so many of the anxieties that we think of as being quintessentially features of the early twenty-first century are pretty well omnipresent in the work of Dostoevsky', Wallace turns to Dostoevsky as a kind of litmus test for the state of religiously engaged fiction today.[48] 'What exactly [is it] that makes many of the novelists of our own place and time look so thematically shallow and lightweight', Wallace asks, 'so morally impoverished' once placed alongside Dostoevsky? How is it that he 'appears to possess degrees of passion, conviction, and engagement with deep moral issues' that American writers today seem incapable of mustering?[49] And more important for Wallace's own project:

> Why [do] we seem to require of our art an ironic distance from deep convictions or desperate questions, so that contemporary writers have to either make jokes of them or else try to work them in under cover of some formal trick like intertextual quotation or incongruous juxtaposition, sticking the really urgent stuff inside asterisks as part of some multivalent defamiliarization-flourish or some such shit?[50]

The irony here is that it is precisely through these more oblique means of narrative approach that Wallace introduces the idea of faith in his fiction and non-fiction. Situated abruptly between paragraphs of his own critical engagement with Dostoevsky's work, Wallace inserts the type of asterisk-framed inquiries he bemoans within the same piece. '**What exactly does "faith" mean?**', we are asked in the middle of a lengthy aside on the challenge of balancing criticism with biography.

> **Does this guy Jesus Christ's life have something to teach me even if I don't, or can't, believe he was divine? Did he know he could have broken the cross with just a word? Did he know that death would just be temporary ...?

On one level such inquiries accede to the very narrative bind Wallace bemoans as a result of our cultural estrangement from tradition, while on another level they offer the kind of honest – even if unconventional – engagement with issues of belief that remain largely absent in literature today. Indeed, if we are in fact in the midst of a 'post-Christian' period, as Wallace seems to concede to some extent, the more pressing task for the novelist would seem to be that of anticipating the post-Christian perspective within their work while pressing into the resources of religious and literary tradition all the while. This seems to be a key reason Wallace is even drawn to Dostoevsky, for while Dostoevsky advanced the 'unfashionable stuff in which he believed' within 'unfriendly cultural circumstances', he did this not by ignoring such circumstances but 'by confronting them' and 'engaging them'.[51]

Wallace's fiction similarly seeks to engage our contemporary 'post-Christian' ambience of unbelief through its appreciation for language's capacity to connect us to spiritual truths in ways that exceed reference while remaining guided by those literary predecessors whose fiction speaks convincingly of faith. As a result, Wallace's work enacts the type of imaginative recontextualization of religious tradition that Brown encourages us to remain attentive to as readers. No matter how 'confused the present situation may be', as Brown writes in *Tradition and Imagination*, 'there are also considerable signs of hope, with some artists at least trying to root themselves in ways that develop artistic insights of previous generations.'[52] The work of Wallace offers one such sign of hope.

Notes

1 Paul Elie, 'Has Fiction Lost its Faith?', *New York Times*, 19 December 2012. Online: www.nytimes.com/2012/12/23/books/review/has-fiction-lost-its-faith.html; accessed 27 September 2017.

2 George Steiner, *Real Presences* (Chicago: University of Chicago Press, 1989), 3.

3 David Brown, *Tradition and Imagination: Revelation and Change* (Oxford: Oxford University Press, 1999), 329.

4 David Brown, 'In the beginning was the Image', a paper delivered at the Society for the Study of Theology, 2010.

5 Brown, *Tradition and Imagination*, 373.

6 James Wood, *The Broken Estate: Essays on Literature and Belief* (New York: Picador, 1999), xv–xxii.

7 Brown, *God and Mystery in Words: Experience through Metaphor and Drama* (Oxford: Oxford University Press, 2008), 10.

8 Brown, *God and Mystery in Words*, 10.

9 Brown, *Tradition and Imagination*, 273.

10 Elie, 'Has Fiction Lost its Faith?'

11 Brown, *The Divine Trinity* (London: Duckworth; LaSalle, IL: Open Court, 1985), 86–7.

12 Brown, *God and Mystery in Words*, 10.

13 Brown, *Tradition and Imagination*, 51.

14 See Gregory Wolfe, 'Whispers of Faith in a Postmodern World', *Wall Street Journal*, 10 January 2013. Online: www.wsj.com/articles/SB10001424127887324081704578231634123976600; accessed 27 September 2017.

15 Brown, *Tradition and Imagination*, 51.
16 Ibid., 25.
17 David Foster Wallace, 'Westward the Course of Empire Takes its Way', in *Girl With Curious Hair* (New York: W. W. Norton, 1989), 263. This critique is levelled by D. L. Eberhardt, a character 'who is postmodern, and so atheist'.
18 Patrick Arden, 'David Foster Wallace Warms Up', in *Conversations with David Foster Wallace*, ed. Stephen J. Burn (Jackson, MS: University Press of Mississippi, 2012), 99–100.
19 Wallace, 'Quo Vadis', *Review of Contemporary Fiction* 16.1 (1996), 7.
20 See John McClure, *Partial Faiths: Postsecular Fiction in the Age of Pynchon and Morrison* (Atlanta, GA: University of Georgia Press, 2007).
21 Giles Gunn, *The Interpretation of Otherness: Literature, Religion, and the American Imagination* (Oxford: Oxford University Press, 1979), 224.
22 McClure, *Partial Faiths*, 6.
23 Brown, *The Divine Trinity*, 70.
24 Brown, *Tradition and the Imagination*, 57.
25 Elie, 'Has Fiction Lost its Faith?'
26 Brown, *Tradition and the Imagination*, 374, 25.
27 Ibid., 58.
28 Ibid.
29 Wallace, 'Lyndon', in *Girl With Curious Hair*, 103.
30 Zadie Smith, 'Brief Interviews With Hideous Men: The Difficult Gifts of David Foster Wallace', in *Changing My Mind: Occasional Essays* (New York: Penguin, 2010), 266.
31 Hugh Kennedy and Jeffrey Polk, 'Looking for a Garde of Which to be Avant: An Interview with David Foster Wallace', in *Conversations with David Foster Wallace*, 18.
32 Ibid.
33 Dazzle Communication, 'Le Conversazioni 2006', Filmed May 2007, YouTube video, 1:17 (Posted May 2007), www.youtube.com/watch?v=MsziSppMUS4; accessed 27 September 2017.
34 Brown, *Tradition and Imagination*, 59.
35 Larry McCaffery, 'An Expanded Interview with David Foster Wallace', in *Conversations with David Foster Wallace*, 34.
36 Wallace, 'Fictional Futures and the Conspicuously Young', in *Both Flesh and Not* (Boston, MA: Little, Brown & Co., 2012), 66.
37 John Barth, 'The Literature of Exhaustion', in *The Friday Book: Essays and Other Non-Fiction* (London: Johns Hopkins University Press, 1984), 63–4.
38 Wallace, 'Fictional Futures', 50–1.
39 Ibid., 63–4.
40 Brown, *Continental Philosophy and Modern Theology* (London: Blackwell, 1987), 36.
41 Ibid.
42 Brown, *God and Mystery in Words*, 51.
43 Ibid., 45–6.
44 Wallace, 'Fictional Futures', 62.
45 David Wiley, 'Transcript of the David Foster Wallace Interview', *Minnesota Daily*, 27 February 1997. Online: www.badgerinternet.com/~bobkat/jestwiley2.html; accessed 27 September 2017.
46 Kennedy and Polk, 'Looking for a Garde', 18.
47 Terry Eagleton, *After Theory* (London: Allen Tate, 2003), 101–2.
48 Rowan Williams, *Dostoevsky: Language, Faith and Fiction* (London: Continuum, 2011), 1.

49 Wallace, 'Joseph Frank's Dostoevsky', in *Consider the Lobster* (New York: Back Bay Books, 2006), 271.
50 Ibid.
51 Ibid., 272.
52 Brown, *Tradition and Imagination*, 39.

The Moving Text – A Reply*

DAVID BROWN

I feel deeply honoured by the care and insight with which contributors to this volume have discussed my ideas as they might apply to their own particular specialities, whether these be in biblical studies or textual criticism, in theology and its historical development, or in the visual arts and English literature. All have been so unfailingly polite and generous in consideration of the possibilities that in an ideal world it would have been good to respond to each chapter in order. But that would have resulted in a somewhat disjointed reply. So instead I will take major themes from each of the three parts of the volume in turn, interweaving my response to individual contributions with an attempt to develop a little further the book's overarching notion, my proposal that divine revelation is best conceived in terms of a moving text. In what follows, Part I therefore deals with the biblical text itself, while Parts II and III then focus on how two key agents of such development – the visual and the literary – can best be seen to operate both within the canon and beyond.

Part 1: The Biblical Text

Given that my general reasons for speaking of a moving text have been so well delineated in the Editor's Introduction and in subsequent chapters, there is no need for repetition here. Instead, I may therefore use this as an opportunity to indicate why since writing *Tradition and Imagination* (1999) and its companion volume, *Discipleship and Imagination* (2000), further reflection has brought an increase in conviction, not its diminution. One source for such confidence comes from the increasingly important discipline of textual criticism (considered at the end of this section), but I shall begin with the world, as it were, before the currently established text.

---

* I am grateful to Christopher R. Brewer and Robert MacSwain for helpful comments on the text of this chapter and its style.

In composing those earlier works, although fully aware that neither the Jewish nor Christian canon were fixed at the time of any individual work's composition or for that matter its constituent parts (where these exist), my assumption still tended to be of a developing tradition that operated within clear lines of written development, with one canon of assumptions in due course giving place to a new set or group. Now, however, it seems to me that I must concede a more pluralist tradition in which a number of competing developments were tried at the same time, with sometimes only one slowly emerging as the triumphant perspective, or else on occasion a number of competing positions being allowed to stand more or less permanently alongside each other in creative tension. Perhaps the easiest place to indicate the difference in perspective is to consider how Jesus' own contribution is best understood. Although fully acknowledging some key points where Christian interpretation differed significantly from the more obvious meaning of the Hebrew text,[1] I still tended to envisage a scenario in which Jesus could be viewed as responding to an agreed literary heritage whereas it now seems to me that a much more complex creative process must be supposed, in which he interacted with various competing visions for the future direction of religious belief before either choosing between them or else weaving aspects of them all into a coherent whole. So while direct interaction with that more distant past remained integral, also relevant were several reinterpretations of that past now competing for attention in the present. One might thus, for example, envisage Jesus borrowing heavily from the kind of literature found at Qumran from 1947 onwards for some of his key imagery, such as messiah or apocalyptic,[2] as well as perhaps being challenged by the Pharisees into conceding such a large role to resurrection,[3] or even developing a more open approach to other races in part as a response to the Sadducees.[4]

That analysis need not of itself suggest that these other groups should themselves be seen as recipients of revelation. They could still be viewed as similar to other external triggers to changes in perspective. Yet it is surely not without significance that at Qumran some key works, such as the book of Jubilees, seem to have been effectively treated as already part of the canon of Jewish Scripture,[5] while some others that enshrine aspects of imagery also found in Jesus' teaching – such as 1 Enoch – were subsequently included within the Christian canon by some ancient branches of the church.[6] I mention that openness partly as a way of introducing the need for a parallel degree of openness in considering the earlier history of Judaism. While the so-called Copenhagen school's notion of the stories of the patriarchs, Exodus and united kingdom only emerging in the post-exilic period seems an absurd overreaction,[7] there can be no doubt that more recent archaeological research has successfully challenged the self-assurance of an earlier generation that had assumed clear confirmation of a history securely embedded in the times for which it laid claim. Instead, we seem to have a people and creed that only gradually emerged as fully set apart from the surrounding cultures.[8]

Factual exaggeration as a way of securing significance for Jewish history in face of larger surrounding nations would seem scarcely contestable. The mocking tone of Bishop Colenso on the impossible numbers involved in the Exodus has been with us for well over a century,[9] while the continuing absence of any archaeological evidence for the alleged great empire of David makes it now much more likely that the text has elaborated on some minor successes of a relatively insignificant chieftain.[10] However, while such historical inaccuracies are usually conceded with ease, Jews and Christians often worry that any parallel admission of competitive interaction with the surrounding culture with regard to the text's theological content would inevitably undermine its status as revelation. But why should this be so? Here, as in the case of Jesus, it is possible to view the external influences as stimulants or triggers to further thought, which may or may not then be used to argue for divine involvement also with those surrounding cultures. Nor need the same answer be given in each case. So if on the one hand the Canaanite and Babylonian creation stories are transformed almost out of all recognition, on the other, borrowings from the Egyptian Wisdom of Amenemhaet in Proverbs remain almost unchanged.[11] The Church's notion of a closed canon with a single dominant perspective has gradually yielded among biblical scholars to one in which various competing positions have been found, whether in the earlier contrast between prophet, priest and scribe, or more recent contestations.[12] But why should this pluralism not also include relations with the theology of the surrounding culture? One might then allow the possibility that the kind of covenant theology found on Moab's Mesha stela at the very least emerged from a similar background to Israel's own (perhaps implicitly acknowledged in the book of Ruth),[13] or again that Yahweh's universal rule came fully to expression partly because of the rise of Persian power (with Second Isaiah perhaps conceding as much in his insistence in treating Cyrus as God's anointed).[14]

These are of course hugely complex issues. I mention them here partly because, as already mentioned, thinking of a non-static or moving text helps to make better sense of the ever more complex story that is emerging about the origins of Jewish and Christian belief but also because it strongly suggests a similar analysis for what has happened since the apparent closure of the biblical canon. Even though further development was now apparently excluded, the external triggers of social factors or rediscovered neglected internal aspects continued to pressure towards changes in how these texts were appropriated. Had the text really been closed, a maximal reading would have been the obvious approach to adopt; that is, with every passage and verse declared relevant. But what history actually discloses is at various points of challenge certain passages being deliberately demoted, as for example in attitudes to war or sexual equality.

Yet, surprisingly, attempts to wrestle with that complexity are for the most part absent from contemporary systematic and philosophical theology. Indeed, in the latter case there seems almost a nostalgic longing for the simplest version of each detail of the complete text being itself revelatory, something that can easily be illustrated from two major writers in the analytic tradition, Eleonore Stump and Richard Swinburne.[15] It is, therefore, of particular interest to note the contrasts Robert MacSwain makes in his contribution between my own approach and Stump's in cases where the possibility of direct comparison is available. Since the issue will emerge once more in the next section, I propose setting to one side here his main concern with my approach, which is that I fail to pay sufficient attention to how the text should be read in the present. Instead, let me expand on his implicit critique of Stump, which is that however perceptive her suggested interpretations are as a response to moral issues, she sits so loose to historical context that it is hard to see her proposals as simply inspired by the text in its own right. A conspicuous example is the way she builds into her reading of the book of Job a divine concern for Satan's welfare. It is an interpretation unparalleled in the long history of the book's interpretation, just as her distinctive take on divine endorsement of the *herem* in the book of Samuel and elsewhere departs radically from what the text actually says.[16] The discovery of divine truth is thus more like a more developed – and ingenious – imposition of a truth already known rather than serious wrestling with the essential otherness of a work coming to us from a quite different historical context.

Nor is much systematic theology any better in attending to the original settings of revelation. Consider a major figure in the field like my erstwhile colleague, the late British theologian John Webster. John saw his role as the ordering and interrelating of the various doctrines derived from Scripture without regarding it as also his task to interact with the often complex way biblical scholars now suggested these ideas had come into being. There is therefore parallel artificiality in his observations about what those texts really mean, though admittedly it is often matched by the failure of biblical scholars to meet such colleagues halfway.[17] Thus sadly few of those who study reception history seem prepared to ask the further question of how, if at all, later alterations once spoke to the community of faith, far less whether they might continue to speak to us today.[18] It is precisely the way Ian Boxall departs from that norm in his own chapter that makes it for me such an exciting contribution.

Of course, one way the various subdisciplines can come together more easily is if the more conservative conclusions urged by some New Testament scholars were to prove true, for obviously there would not then be so great a gap to be bridged. Two of the most distinguished of these scholars are, like myself, associated with the University of St Andrews, Richard Bauckham and N. T. Wright. Probably the most influential of the former's writings is *Jesus and the Eyewitnesses*, which has recently appeared in a second edition.[19] In the book Bauckham argues against the assumption of form critics of an oral transmission predating the Gospels, according to which Jesus' original words were adapted to various contexts in which they were received, and then in turn modified by the Gospel writers themselves. Instead he uses the frequency of the language of witness ('see' etc.) to suggest that most is based on actual eyewitness testament carefully sought out by the evangelists, although at the same time he does not hesitate to concede that modifications have indeed occurred to suit the theological purposes of the evangelists (for example, the creation of a Sermon on the Mount in Matthew to parallel Sinai).[20] The most appropriate ancient parallel, Bauckham therefore argues, is not religious imaginative literature of the time but rather the practice of ancient historians.

A short single-paragraph reply to a work of more than 600 pages would scarcely be fair. At most I can say that its arguments do deserve careful consideration. Nonetheless, my own inclinations do move in a somewhat different direction, one of the major reasons for which is fortunately provided in Stephen Barton's chapter in this volume. There he provides excellent grounds for thinking quite differently, specifically on the question of memory. Taking the way the cleansing of the temple is described in John, he notes how John ties the story to the question of memory, but not in order to challenge the historical record offered by Matthew and Luke, who understand the incident quite differently, but to explain how its significance should now be read in the light of subsequent Christian understanding of both Jewish Scriptures and the significance of Jesus' resurrection.[21] This may have involved putting directly into Jesus' mouth words ascribed by his enemies to him (though in a somewhat different context), almost certainly in the process thereby generating literal falsehood that is, nonetheless, at the same time appropriately seen as falling under a wider overarching, symbolic truth.[22] Bauckham is willing to concede retrospectively interpreted memory but insists this must always have remained subject to strictly historical considerations.[23] But why? If the setting of Jesus' teaching and the meaning of his cleansing of the temple could be changed, should not then a much larger role be assigned to the creative imagination in conveying Jesus' significance, as Barton proposes?

Such an approach has of course the potential for more general applicability in reconciling the discourses of Jesus in John with the short pithy way he teaches in the synoptics: although never delivered, they are nonetheless true reflections of who Jesus really was, having been developed as imaginative expansions of images already present in his teaching as recorded in the synoptics.[24] Such an observation might seem to take us very far away from the topic of memory, but I am not so sure. Even in our own everyday lives memory is seldom a flat record. Instead it is continually shifting as our own interpretation of our life's past itself changes: for instance, now one incident and now quite another being used to shape our memory of how a relationship with some significant other has changed or developed.[25]

But while the majority of New Testament scholars would be quite prepared to acknowledge such backward influences on the writing of the Gospels, far fewer are willing to take seriously forward projections of the kind endorsed by Ian Boxall and which are scattered throughout my own writings. Probably the principal reason is a worry that it seems to produce an open text with no fixed boundaries, but most modern sermons are in fact engaged in a not dissimilar exercise as the meaning of the text is commonly pulled well beyond what can safely be inferred as being entirely inherent within the text itself. In the particular case he considers, Boxall can claim some support from a major contemporary expert on Matthew's Gospel, who suggests that Pilate and his wife were probably already intended by the evangelist as a suitable model for a Gentile appropriation of Jesus.[26] If so, while later narratives go considerably further, even to the extent of canonizing Pilate and his wife, it cannot be said that the motivation is then fundamentally different from Matthew's, in seeking to identify figures from within Jesus' story that help generate an appropriate response. Nor will it then do to treat an objection on grounds of historicity as itself decisive, if Matthew has already set a precedent. Of course, central to Christian claims is the contention that God became incarnate at a specific moment in history, but as I have tried to indicate above, from this it by no means follows that the only way of appropriating such good news must therefore always be purely historical. If story and poetry can contribute in other contexts, why not through adaptation of the gospel story itself? Indeed, one might argue that in resorting to a simpler version of the nativity story or of the life of Mary Magdalene, all that has happened within the contemporary Church is a move from one form of illuminating fiction to another. So, for example, can we really be sure that in honouring Mary Magdalene as the first witness to the resurrection we are not distorting the evidence from Paul and the other Gospels, even as we attempt to honour women in a new way?[27]

And so finally for this section to Garrick Allen on textual criticism. As Allen persuasively contends, the new more complex way of understanding how textual variants arise is much more suited to interpretation in terms of my account of a moving text than is the pattern once firmly established by earlier scholarship as represented by Westcott and Hort, according to which any uncertainties stemming from the *Textus Receptus* had at last been replaced by the security of the so-called Neutral Text based on the two major codices Sinaiticus and Vaticanus.[28] All that changed, however, with the discovery of important early papyri and other manuscripts during the course of the twentieth century, with various complex relations between them that are still being explored in a process that is hoped will lead eventually to a major new critical edition.[29]

Not that this new situation is evaluated by all in the same way. Some still hope for a new original text with all later additions demoted. A conspicuous example of such an attitude is Bart Ehrman's *The Orthodox Corruption of Scripture*, whose conclusions I briefly discussed in *Tradition and Imagination*.[30] But whether the changes were orthodox or otherwise, 'corruption' seemed to me simply the wrong way of looking at such matters. There was a freedom in seeking to clarify what was said that might pull now in one direction, now in another. Of course, sometimes no deeper motive may have been at play than conscious or otherwise assimilation of the text to other remembered parallels. But for more profound motives one might consider the opening of Mark as an example. To add 'son of God' may on the one hand seem too early a disclosure of Jesus' significance and moreover undermine the notion of a messianic secret gradually revealed over the course of the Gospel, but on the other hand it does anticipate well what many would see as the culmination of Mark's narrative in the centurion's profession of faith at the foot of the cross: 'Truly this was the son of God.' So it would be more appropriate to speak of two methods of achieving the same purpose rather than one scribal tradition more concerned with fact than the other.

While, at the time of writing that earlier book, I was fully aware of new versions of biblical stories being written, I had not appreciated that a similar freedom was also applied to the copying of texts, as has emerged clearly from Hebrew texts at Qumran but also from variants in the Greek Septuagint.[31] Although some texts can be used to argue that the Greek translation is more likely to be closer to the original, in other cases it looks as though extraordinary liberties were taken, in one case even turning the meaning of a particular verse on its head.[32] Whereas the Masoretic text eventually gave a fixed form to the Hebrew that thereafter rarely varied,[33] Christian scribes appear to have followed earlier Hebrew and Septuagint practice in seeing their role as also an interpretative one, in clarifying the meaning and indeed sometimes the literary quality of the text.[34]

One criticism that Allen rightly makes of my earlier account was my failure to make use of the writings of the British scholar David Parker in my response to Ehrman. Parker is the leading scholar in the field in Britain, who as well as more technical contributions has produced two general introductions to the significance of this changed perspective. In both works he not only rejects the notion of ever recovering an 'original' text but also any suggestion that what succeeds the earliest recoverable is necessarily therefore inferior.[35] Instead, in the earlier book he insists that 'manuscripts do not carry a tradition. They are that tradition', while in the later work he criticizes more conventional New Testament scholars for still being too tied to the notion of a set printed text whereas what the reader is in fact responding to is 'a process', 'the result of two thousand years of development'.[36] In particular he urges us to think of a 'living text', the Gospel authors having probably expected later editors to adopt a similar freedom to their own.[37] Among the helpful examples he gives is how the full version of the Lord's Prayer can still be seen as a legitimate expansion of earlier material, or the Matthean exception on divorce be misunderstood so long as it is treated as an original piece of legislation rather than an attempt to clarify.[38] Parker reminds us that even in more recent times authors such as Shakespeare and Wordsworth have not always felt bound to a single version of their creation, which contrasts nicely with Ehrman's rather naïve insistence that all that matters is the historical original.[39]

Part 2: The Visual Imagination

Two of the contributions to this section (O'Hear and Hyland) deal mainly with the question of appropriate application of artistic images to the history of reception of the biblical text, while three (Brewer, Rosen and Worley) choose to focus instead on the potential role of contemporary art. Of these, Christopher Brewer's chosen example (Jacob's ladder) can serve nicely here as an introduction to why I see the arts – and visual art in particular – as so important for the possibility of revelation. This is because, as Brewer observes, whether it be the specific allusion of past images or the more generalized notion of contemporary art, the fundamental implication remains the same: that it mediates the possibility of a connection with transcendental reality, nowhere more effectively illustrated than in Brewer's account of his own moment of revelation in a London art gallery. In other words, what makes the arts so important for theology is that their images and symbols characteristically seek to move their viewers or readers to a different place and, although this is usually only to a different, still this-worldly location, the principle is at least established of moves towards relations with the alternative realities that lie at the root of all religion.[40]

The standard objection within the three western monotheisms to including art as a way of opening up such a possibility is to raise the issue of idolatry, but idolatry of the word is in fact no less a danger for religion than that of the visual image.[41] Indeed, the sheer variety and multitude of imagery in a religion like Hinduism could be argued to be a more effective foil to such a danger than these monotheisms' attempts to define the meaning of their sacred texts very precisely. But another, equally legitimate way of questioning western orthodoxies on this matter would be to challenge how the evolution of these religions has conventionally been told. As I indicated earlier in this chapter, their history is now seen to have been considerably more fluid than was once believed, and with that has come the possibility of recognizing a larger role for the visual in that story.

It would be easy to mock the ceremonies deployed in the ancient Middle East to make pagan imagery come alive and the subsequent cult of feeding such statues, washing and clothing them and so forth,[42] even though elements in those traditions continued into modern Hinduism and indeed into some aspects of the treatment of icons within Eastern Orthodoxy.[43] Although it is hard to prove subtlety in worshippers' interpretation of such practices, it is perhaps significant that we now know that Israel's use of aniconic imagery was by no means unique in the ancient world. Thus in ancient Greece a non-representational *xoanon* long antedated Pheidias' famous anthropomorphic statue of the goddess Athene, just as Shiva's *lingam* is much older than, for example, him as the cosmic dancer.[44] Equally, ancient Celtic imagery that gave divine figures extra heads or horns was surely intended to imply a deity that is more than simply a more powerful version of human beings. So it seems not implausible to suggest that it was not just the form of the temple at Jerusalem that was borrowed from surrounding culture but also that even the resistance to anthropomorphic imagery may have been in part derived from other ancient ways of thinking about divinity. At the same time the eventual introduction of anthropomorphic imagery by other peoples needs to be recontextualized in view of their earlier non-iconic practices. Might the change have indicated overconfidence that such images would not be misunderstood, rather than simply idolatry and nothing more?

It is perhaps against such a more complex set of ideas that hints of attention to visual imagery within the pages of Scripture can then be fitted. It is not that through fear of idolatry its writers only ever thought in verbal terms but that sometimes, at least, what biblical scholars have insisted on treating as merely literary metaphors may well have begun life as visual images.[45] This is surely one possible way to read some of the striking images in the prophets or the psalms: God delivering through religious experience words of comfort or direction that involved seeing the way ahead, internally or externally.[46] Indeed, in *Tradition and Imagination* I had already suggested that this is the best way of understanding some elements of Jesus' own experience, such as the temptations in the wilderness or his baptism.[47] One also notes Paul's encounter on the Damascus Road and his being caught up into the third heaven – scarcely identifiable unless accompanied by some visual element.[48] Responses to art in subsequent Christian history would then not be something wholly new but rather in continuity with such experience. Again, although the different approach of the Renaissance could conceivably have put an end to such encounters, it seems to me that claims to massive change – in how religious vision operated at this time – are much exaggerated.[49] As William Hyland's chapter successfully argues, even that form of art that is most commonly viewed as merely illustrative – stained glass – could function as very much more, even at the height of the Renaissance. At Steinfeld Abbey the stained glass there was deliberately designed, as Hyland notes, not just to give the monks 'the opportunity to visualize the scriptural text but also to insert themselves into the text'; indeed, to see their own lives as 'an extension of the sacred narrative', thanks to elements and juxtapositions that allowed clear applications to be drawn from their own native Premonstratensian spirituality.

However, another chapter in Part II does argue that my own attempts to provide a foundation for such visual spirituality have still not gone far enough. In particular Natasha O'Hear contends that I have hitherto failed to take the visual dimensions of the book of Revelation and its artistic inheritance with sufficient seriousness. Certainly, if the work is more visual than literary, this would strengthen my claim that Christianity was founded no less on a visual heritage as on a literary. It was partly the complexity of its images that persuaded me in my earlier writings to follow Farrer and Schüssler Fiorenza in supposing the work to be an artificial literary creation, and partly what turns out to have been too narrow a focus on a limited number of subsequent artistic attempts to recreate these images.[50] As O'Hear observes, I was perhaps too willing to condemn all of the Angers tapestry on the basis of a few defective attempts by others' hands, or again Dürer's own possibly direct visual experience through failing to attend too closely to its metamorphosis in the less accomplished hands of Lucas Cranach the Elder.

These are of course large issues. Usually it is a mistake to introduce a personal dimension into academic essays but I think that on this issue it may possibly help. Despite the extensive discussion of apocalyptic literature over the course of my own lifetime, I have continued to find its reception exceedingly difficult. Partly this may be due to a deep-seated antipathy to fantasy literature of all kinds (including science fiction), but also relevant is its tendency to see its world in terms that are starkly black and white, with only two extremes: oppressed and oppressor. As an example of the kind of problem I experience may be mentioned the story of how one of my New Testament colleagues at St Andrews offered me a platform to consider the theology of 1 Enoch at an international conference, only for me to withdraw in exasperated puzzlement about what I could possibly say.[51] Here of great help has been O'Hear's willingness to develop with further examples my own suggestion that such literature does eventually generate its own critique. So perhaps a two-stage process might be envisaged: the first in which because of the urgency of the situation the poor and marginalized are simply provided with assurance that God is on their side; then, second, the eventual emergence of a more nuanced account in which a more complex message can now be heard that admits evil is seldom, if ever, wholly on one side. Sustained experience of the motives and actions of oneself and other close allies has forced a rather different perception.

If apocalyptic is one area in which I struggled to find meaning, another is contemporary art. In defence of its relative absence from most of my earlier work, I could easily plead that in advancing a new way of understanding revelation it behoved me to consider principally instances where there might be general agreement that the art in question reflected the apparent direction in which revelation seemed already to be tending. In other words, my main task was to demonstrate how the model could provide a plausible way of reading the past, not to attempt the more difficult role of detecting particular pointers for future developments, and thus, as it were, act the prophet. But the truth is that I was also reticent to comment for another, more deep-seated reason: wariness of the way so much contemporary art operates, in a manner quite unlike most of the modern art of the earlier twentieth century, in seeking to free itself from antecedent traditions of interpretation, and thus stand alone.[52] Whereas I saw progress in understanding coming through pursuit, however subversive, of potential trajectories from past tradition, contemporary art seemed to suppose not only that one could stand free from such a past but also that this was the best way of engaging viewers.

While continuing to question whether such engagement without presuppositions is possible (on my view they are not apparent only because they have become more deep-seated),[53] it would seem to me quite wrong to suppose that the current climate of suspicion of religion has therefore made contemporary art a desert terrain, essentially inimical to religious belief, or for that matter that it could not continue, as in the past, to offer challenges to how that belief is most appropriately interpreted.[54] Sadly, I continue to detect my own earlier suspicions reflected in the writings of many Christians who are impressively well informed about the history of Christian art but remain nonetheless deeply suspicious of the possibility of any truth to be found in the contemporary art world. If Calvin Seerveld represents continuity with the suspicions first voiced by fellow Calvinists such as H. R. Rookmaaker,[55] somewhat surprising to find in this group is David Lyle Jeffrey's recent work, *In the Beauty of Holiness*.[56] While in an earlier work on literature he made an outstanding contribution to our understanding of the interrelation between the Bible and the subsequent history of English literature,[57] this volume dismisses almost all art from the nineteenth century onwards, even where the intention was explicitly religious, as in the work of the Pre-Raphaelites.[58] Only three later artists are reserved for unqualified praise: Georges Rouault, Marc Chagall and Arcabas (Jean-Marie Pirot). But just as God in times past chose to speak through pagan rulers or even writings that almost never mention the divine name,[59] so in the contemporary world it is not unreasonable to find not just uncertain agnostics but even ardent opponents unconsciously acting as media for divine disclosure, a disclosure that might not otherwise be heard because of the inherent tendency of much religion towards conservatism. That is why I have not hesitated in more recent writings to identify many contemporary agnostic artists as having something important to say to the Church but also even some who have declared themselves unqualifiedly hostile, such as Francis Bacon or Damien Hirst.[60] It is for this reason that I therefore positively welcome the contributions made to this volume by Brewer, Rosen and Worley. As Christopher Brewer's work has already been deployed to indicate the general reasons for the importance of art to any theological project – its ability to move viewers in a different direction and so, potentially at least, towards transcendent notions – I shall only consider Aaron Rosen and Taylor Worley here. While Worley illustrates nicely the ability of contemporary art to revise even the most traditional of biblical insights, Rosen presents a powerful challenge that merits both positive response and some resistance.

Worley suggests that because interpretation of the Genesis story has been so heavily corrupted by false labels such as 'the mark of Cain' or 'curse of Ham', in order to counter racism it is not enough to propose simply a colour-blind reading of the story of Adam and Eve. Instead, black readings like those of Kerry James Marshall and Chris Ofili need to become the Church's own. Undoubtedly, one could argue that the visual portrayals of earlier ages are already serious distortions, inasmuch as an Arab ethic identity would seem a more natural choice for the story's original setting in the Tigris/Euphrates valley than either the European or Jew who is usually found in visual representations.[61] But were one to appeal to the long march of history, a better case could indeed be made for black faces, given that human ancestry is now commonly traced to the African continent. Yet such considerations would be secondary to Worley's main point, which is that the two artists concerned are seeking something rather more than historical accuracy: nothing less than the restoration of black dignity – hence the emphasis in the two paintings on the restoration of paradise. As such, Worley draws our attention to the power of contemporary art to perform an important new role. Instead of, as in past artistic practice, envisaging the basic requirement of religious art to be the necessity of drawing a distant biblical narrative into the particulars of the viewers' own situation, the fundamental challenge in this case is to hear that universal original take on the particulars of a group the majority continue to marginalize. Of course, in acknowledging as much it is just as important to note that this problem was primarily a phenomenon of more recent Christianity, not a general fault in its religious history as such.[62]

Much of Rosen's chapter explores how the sacrifice of Isaac has been treated in the history of the three monotheisms. While basically endorsing my own account, there are quite a number of useful expansions, as well as the occasional critique. On the question of the contest between Ghiberti and Brunelleschi, I must admit to standing corrected: the later work of Ghiberti entirely fails to back my claim that the Renaissance in general continued to support the earlier tradition of Isaac as a willing sacrificial victim. However, on Rembrandt I am much less willing to concede Rosen's interpretation, according to which in the Hermitage version of 1635 only a determined Abraham can be detected. Even Simon Schama, who wants to escape any reference to 'abstruse confessional iconography', admits that the hand over Isaac's face is 'at once a gesture of tenderness and suffocating brutality', though another commentator notes why even that appearance of brutality might nonetheless also be a sign of tenderness, given that the head needed to be forced back in order to ensure a single clean cut.[63] But in my view it is Susanna Partsch who provides the best overall account. She observes how, although Abraham looks in surprise at the angel, the angel looks not towards him but at the true focus of the painting: at Isaac, who is in any case a 'youth' and not 'a child'.[64] Again, although 'forcing his son's face to the ground', his motives include a desire 'to spare him the ghastly sight of his father laying hands on him'. Rembrandt, I would therefore argue, continues in the historic tradition. Yet that particular issue is a matter of no great moment in terms of Rosen's overall argument.

Rather, his central concern is to address how the story is being interpreted in contemporary art, especially Jewish and Palestinian. Here the focus has moved back once more to the behaviour of Abraham and as such is intended to provide a critique either of God or of religion, or of both. For Rosen, such current readings represent a summons to believers in all three monotheisms to reflect seriously on their own particular religion's problematic roots. Given his recent outstanding survey of contemporary art and religion,[65] one naturally expects from Rosen well-founded knowledge on this issue, and indeed there seems no reason to question his estimate of the situation. Nonetheless, it does seem to me a real tragedy that contemporary art of this kind has chosen to set itself free from any wider religious reflection on the incident. Thus while accepting the need for religion to dialogue with the implications of such art, I would contend deeper religious reflection should continue to be focused elsewhere, on the profound mystery of all three religions in their developing traditions having reached the same point in identifying the revelatory potential of the story: in the self-sacrificial action offered by the son.

In other words, these modern art works not only return us to a rightly rejected past but force consideration of difference where none need exist, on the question of the intrinsic superiority of self-sacrifice. None of these observations, though, is intended to deny the need for each of these religions to face problematic aspects of their past. However, I would prefer such questions to be focused on where no other reading is possible, and indeed where the passages in question have been used to justify further horrendous acts in their turn, such as the *herem* passages in the Hebrew canon, the anti-Jewish verses of the New Testament, or sections from the Qur'an that might on their own be taken to imply an unqualified jihad.[66] The reinterpretation of the Isaac story could then be allowed to continue to function as a standing reminder of how texts can themselves generate their own critique but in a way that goes well beyond purely negative observations.

Part 3: The Literary Imagination

Here too the responses are of somewhat different kinds, with that from Thomas Rist markedly different from the other two. Indeed, unless I have radically misunderstood his intentions, Rist seems the least sympathetic of all the chapters in this volume to my project. Starting from the more positive descriptions of the place of Catholic piety in late English medieval society that has come from historians in more recent years, his characterization of what followed is of a regrettable 'fragmentation', in particular the loss of any real role for the Virgin Mary except in those still conscious of the loss, such as the poets Henry Constable (d. 1613) and Ben Johnson (d. 1637). While not denying the essential correctness of these new assessments of medieval piety, my contention would remain that these were bought at too high a price, in an exaggerated role for Mary, partly devised to counter a distorted image of a less forgiving, more wrathful son.[67]

However, rather than repeating that analysis here, it will be more useful to make two key alternative points. The first is that, in contrast to Rist's implicit model of smooth progress in a developing revelation, as earlier parts of this chapter will have already indicated, difference and disagreement within the community of faith do not seem to me necessarily a bad thing. Deeper understandings often emerge through the clear presentation of alternative positions, neither side remaining entirely unchanged by such encounters. Thus arguably Judaism was enriched by the three streams of prophet, priest and scribe being all eventually included within the canon. Indeed, the point might even apply to forces coming from outside the Church, as with the Enlightenment – which it should not be forgotten was also to transform Christian understanding as well. There is not the space to pursue that question in any detail here, but that the claim is not nearly as contentious as is often supposed is well indicated by the number of books now emerging to challenge the conventional story of how the movement marked the beginning of the divorce between progressive ideas and religious belief.[68]

But there is also another important point that needs to be made, namely that it was not at all the case, as Rist asserts, that the veneration of the Virgin Mary was effectively banned in 1558, and so she retreated entirely from Protestant consciousness. The Prayer Book in fact required Mary's nativity song the *Magnificat* to be recited each evening, while the Collect for Christmas Day introduced a reference to the Saviour being 'born of a pure Virgin' that had not existed in the earlier Sarum rite. Then 1561 – only three years after Elizabeth's accession – witnesses the reintroduction into the Protestant calendar of Mary's conception, nativity and visitation, as well as a conclusion to the Advent antiphons, 'O Virgin of Virgins'. So it is perhaps not altogether surprising that in such a climate Bishop Lancelot Andrewes (d. 1626) included in his *Preces Privatae* the phrase 'commemorating the all-holy, immaculate, more than blessed mother of God and ever-virgin Mary',[69] or that John Donne (Dean of St Paul's, d.1631) presented in one of his poems a request for Mary's prayers,[70] or again that Archbishop William Laud (d. 1645) arranged for a fine statue of her to be erected outside the University Church in Oxford. Admittedly, the Assumption was not among the feasts that were restored in 1561, and reference to Mary as Queen of Heaven, though not unknown, is exceedingly rare among Protestants.[71] Yet the more important point to observe is surely that exploration in respect of what might or might not be appropriate continued. Indeed, just as some pre-Reformation Catholics found some aspects of Marian piety distasteful,[72] so in later centuries Paul VI was to suggest (in 1964) that veneration of Mary as Mother of the Church was perhaps the most fitting tribute we could ever pay to her. In other words, the power of the tradition lay in its ability to respond to changing needs and experience rather than in any requirement for uniformity or a single line of development.

In the eyes of some, one of the greatest achievements of modern literature, the reinvention of the novel, should be seen, as with Rist's view of the Reformation or Peter Gay's of the Enlightenment, as yet another move towards fragmentation, to the decline of religion overall. Congruent with that view has been a whole spate of books that has interpreted the work of novelists like George Eliot and Thomas Hardy as simply marking loss of faith. But significantly, both novelists refused to allow themselves to be classified as non-believers.[73] So it is in fact quite plausible to maintain that their aim was not at all the wholesale rejection of Christianity but rather a search in changed circumstances for an alternative, more easily defensible account of what might generate belief.[74] Accordingly, although absolute authority for the biblical text had gone, in its place came the search for a means of legitimating spiritual belief in a more experiential setting.

It is perhaps into this context that we could then set Jon Greenaway's discussion of Mary Shelley's *Frankenstein* (1818). It was never intended just as a chilling or even amusing tale but rather, whatever its undoubted merits at such levels, as also a serious discussion of what might be meant by creativity more generally, divine no less than human. Every schoolchild knows that her brother the poet P. B. Shelley was sent down from Oxford for 'atheism', but the term appropriately characterizes neither brother nor sister. They had detected the inadequacy of the then current expressions of religious belief and sought another alternative, more consonant with Romantic presuppositions. As such they can be seen as engaging in a task not essentially different from the work of one of the greatest theologians of the nineteenth century, Friedrich Schleiermacher, whose *Speeches to Religion's Cultured Despisers* (1799) was intended to prove that Christianity was after all appropriately grounded in experience. Sadly, as with the visual arts, academic theologians view the novel and literature more generally as peripheral to their concerns, but Jon Greenaway seems to me quite right that rather more was at stake: the continued embedding of religion within a particular culture, continued examples of which we may detect from the twentieth century in the works of novelists such as Anthony Burgess, William Golding, Graham Greene, Flannery O'Connor, John Updike and Patrick White or, to change the medium to film, in the work of, among others, Terrence Malick, Martin Scorsese and Andrei Tarkovsky.[75]

This is not of course to claim that all these various figures were after all orthodox Christians, only that, fleeing too absolutist claims for the biblical text, they nonetheless saw possibilities for continued belief in God that demonstrated continuity by borrowing extensively from the ideas and images in that text. Sadly, though, consideration of the potential implications for Christian theology of such work tends only to be marginally represented, if at all, in the halls of more academic theology. This is perhaps scarcely surprising given that theology continues to view itself as a self-contained discipline that need not give much heed to what happens beyond its 'inspired' contours. Whether this is due to an integrity that is, appropriately, resolutely loyal to the revelation that was once definitively given or is symptomatic of either a certain laziness or self-satisfaction that refuses to consider what God might be saying elsewhere, is too large a question to embark on here. All I can do here is observe that for better or worse, theology is influenced by the culture in which it is set, and so finds itself confronted by the same sort of dilemmas as were taken up by sympathetic, creative artists such as those mentioned. Of course, this is not to say that they will have come up with the right answers, but it is to suggest that possible options were explored and that similar emphases are sometimes eventually adopted even by those who see themselves at the heart of orthodoxy.[76]

In his consideration of the novels of David Foster Wallace, however, Dennis Kinlaw sets me a different sort of challenge: how to view writers who provide a profound analysis of contemporary culture but who do so in a way that does not draw directly on the Christian inheritance, as nineteenth-century novelists usually did.[77] In his short life Wallace produced two major novels, *Infinite Jest* (1996) and *The Pale King* (2011).[78] Wallace made much of the corrupting influence of television and prescription and other drugs on modern society, and this is reflected in *Infinite Jest*, where a future North America has turned into a capitalist dystopia in which a film of the same name has compelling power to reduce viewers to addictive watching. The intention is to satirize a totally self-absorbed society in which television is symptomatic of the way people's fear of being ridiculed has deprived them of the ability to express any deeper emotions that involve sentiment or commitment. By contrast, *The Pale King* is set in the past, in a tax office in Peoria, Illinois in 1985. Here the analysis is in terms of the boredom and loneliness that each of the characters experiences, with their longing for something to fill the hole but totally unaware of what it is they might be looking for. These are absurdly brief summaries of very complex plots that even include a large number of endnotes, but if offering anything approaching an analysis of present society's malaise, then this is very far removed from any starting point in the Bible or the history of the Christian tradition.

Yet the important point for the idea of revelation as a developing tradition is that David Foster Wallace did attempt to make connections. In a much-quoted commencement speech given at Kenyon College in 2005 (entitled *This is Water*), he argued that the default position of human beings is self-centredness and that this can only be overcome by sustained attention, discipline and effort.[79] It is a process in which Wallace suggested any form of religion might help in directing our thoughts away from ourselves, whereas most forms of reverence will merely seek to augment our own self-esteem and thus fail ever to satisfy completely.[80] Although the speech was never intended as a specific endorsement of Christianity, it does help to indicate how his novels – and any like them – could potentially be seen as part of a revelatory process: in disclosing the void at the heart of contemporary society, with which Christianity could then connect but only if it were willing to face the need for a radical re-expression of its message were it successfully to bridge the divide. In other words, to allow the possibility of dialogue over such ideas as addiction, boredom and fear of commitment, much more substantial adjustments would be required than was the case with the nineteenth-century novelists we considered earlier.

No doubt for some readers the degree of disjoint between historical Christianity and society's present ills as presented by David Foster Wallace will appear as nothing less than an absurd exaggeration. They will probably suggest that a more balanced view is to be found in the writings of the individual who is widely regarded as today's most influential Christian novelist, Marilynne Robinson (b. 1943). Her four major novels, *Housekeeping* (1980) and the trilogy *Gilead* (2004), *Home* (2008) and *Lila* (2014), widely praised by religious and secular critics alike, may be read as a summons to return to the root values of the Christian culture of America's Midwest.[81] Yet there are least two criticisms that might be made of so simple a presentation. The first is that the sort of Christianity offered in Robinson's novels cannot really be described as no more than a return to some ideal historical past, inasmuch as, for example, more emphasis is to be found on forgiveness and less on sin than might have been expected from a purely historical reconstruction of Calvinism, or again there is less emphasis on transcendence and more on the immanence of the divine in the everyday.[82] In other words, Robinson's novels can be seen to constitute already some degree of adaptation to the contemporary American situation. Second, and perhaps more fundamentally, there is no doubt that the various collections of essays Robinson has also produced are intended, as with Wallace, to offer a profound critique of much of present American culture.[83] Thus although, unlike Wallace, she still wants to find hope in the America of today,[84] she is nonetheless adamant about the degree to which things have gone badly wrong. America has, for instance, forgotten the extent to which responsibility for others was actually embedded in its past thinking, or again how deep suspicion of others actually represents a manufactured distrust.[85] It is also a critique that she turns against the churches themselves, in her insistence on the extent to which, whatever their undoubted faults, both the Old Testament and Calvinism required social responsibility and kindness towards allegedly hostile neighbours of a kind that the contemporary Church seems to have forgotten.[86]

Nonetheless, there remains a considerable difference of degree. So it remains possible to give quite different estimates of how extensive the required revisions are in order to enable Christianity to re-engage with contemporary culture. As previously noted, personally I feel more confident in analysing past developments than in prophesying future directions, and so it scarcely becomes me at the end of this chapter to take sides. Suffice it to say that even Robinson, as the more conservative of our two writers, concedes the need for change.[87] So the issue is not whether to change at all but where, in the world of imaginative literature or the arts more generally, the Church is to find the most appropriate guides for interacting, as accelerating social change challenges Christianity to adapt the creative dynamic of its traditions without endangering the essence of its historical roots. At times that might seem an impossible task but then, as I have maintained throughout, the task remains undergirded not only by imaginations that can reach out to God but also by a divine reality that never ceases to reach out in turn to its human creation.

Notes

1 E.g. justification by faithfulness versus justification by faith; see further my *Tradition and Imagination: Revelation and Change* (Oxford: Oxford University Press, 1999), esp. 218–19.

2 For an excellent overall survey, see Philip R. Davies, George J. Brooke and Phillip R. Callaway (eds), *The Complete World of the Dead Sea Scrolls* (London: Thames & Hudson, 2002), esp. 200–3. For specifically on the issue of the expectation of a messiah (one or two), see the commentary on relevant texts in Michael A. Knibb, *The Qumran Community* (Cambridge: Cambridge University Press, 1987), 49–50, 60–1, 116, 139–40, 145, 153–5; Joseph A. Fitzmyer, *The Dead Sea Scrolls and Christian Origins* (Grand Rapids, MI: Eerdmans, 2000), esp. 73–110.

3 The largely hostile portrayal of the Pharisees in the Gospels has long been superseded by more nuanced accounts, e.g. E. P. Sanders, *Judaism: Practice and Belief 63BCE–66CE* (London: SCM Press, 1992), 380–451.

4 Their doctrinal conservatism on resurrection and other issues was balanced by both political realism and a willingness to see some merits in classical culture. As such

they offered Jesus an alternative perspective in a largely hostile native population, though no doubt other encounters also played their part: e.g. Mark 7.24–30.

5 For a brief summary of the evidence, see James C. VanderKam, *The Dead Sea Scrolls Today* (London: SPCK, 1994), 150–8; for a more extended discussion but heavily weighted towards conservative conclusions, see Lawrence H. Schiffman, *Reclaiming the Dead Sea Scrolls* (New York: Doubleday, 1994), 159–241. More willing to accept an evolving story is Eugene Ulrich, *The Dead Sea Scrolls and the Origins of the Bible* (Grand Rapids, MI: Eerdmans, 1999).

6 For example, the Ethiopian canon includes both Jubilees and 1 Enoch.

7 Although Philip R. Davies of Sheffield inaugurated this sceptical approach in 1992, the group acquired the nickname because of the university at which others worked, including Thomas L. Thompson, author of *The Bible in History: How Writers Create a Past* (London: Jonathan Cape, 1999).

8 For a helpful survey of the current archaeological evidence, see Amy Dockser Marcus, *Rewriting the Bible: How Archaeology is Reshaping History* (London: Little, Brown & Co., 2000).

9 *The Pentateuch and the Book of Joshua Critically Examined* appeared in parts between 1862 and 1879, the battle over his continuing role as a bishop already beginning in 1863. Sadly, simple defences of the text are still attempted, e.g. Clive Anderson and Brian Edwards, *Evidence for the Bible* (Leominster: DayOne, 2014), 21, 196.

10 Despite the biblical references to a great empire, only one reference to David has so far emerged, from a piece of basalt stone at Dan. For the issues more generally, see Marcus, *Rewriting the Bible*, 105–28.

11 Ancient parallels are most easily pursued through J. B. Prichard (ed.), *Ancient Near Eastern Texts Relating to the Old Testament*, 3rd edn (Princeton, NJ: Princeton University Press, 1969). Also helpful is Kenton L. Sparks, *Ancient Texts for the Study of the Hebrew Bible: A Guide to the Background Literature* (Peabody, MA: Hendrickson, 2005).

12 An earlier approach of contrasting prophet, priest and scribe has now been superseded by a more complex dynamic of conflict: e.g. Walter Brueggemann, *Theology of the Old Testament: Testimony, Dispute, Advocacy* (Minneapolis, MN: Fortress Press, 1997).

13 It envisages their own god Chemosh guiding the Moabites in relation to neighbouring King Ahab. The book of Ruth posits Ruth the Moabite as one of David's ancestors.

14 In the famous Cyrus Cylinder, now in the British Museum, King Cyrus of Persia ascribes his success to the Babylonian neglect of their gods, and the consequent need for him to respect all gods, including that of the Jews. However, the Persians saw the sway of their own god as universal, and Second Isaiah finds Yahweh so acting in choosing Cyrus as his anointed (Isa. 45.1).

15 For my critique of their similar positions, see *God in a Single Vision: Integrating Philosophy and Theology*, ed. Christopher R. Brewer and Robert MacSwain (London and New York: Routledge, 2016), 73–86, esp. 78–83.

16 Ibid., 81; 1 Samuel 15.2–3. See also Stump, 'The Problem of Evil and the History of Peoples', in *Divine Evil? The Moral Character of the God of Abraham*, ed. Michael Bergmann, Michael J. Murray and Michael C. Rea (New York: Oxford University Press, 2011), 179–97.

17 The great exception was of course Brevard Childs (1923–2007) with his notion of canonical criticism, with its idea that earlier versions of the text were all successfully incorporated into a reconciled, final version: cf. B. S. Childs, *Introduction to the Old Testament as Scripture* (Philadelphia, PA: Fortress Press, 1979). While impressively argued, it still proved too simplistic in relation to the evidence: cf. James Barr, *Holy Scripture: Canon, Authority, Criticism* (Oxford: Oxford University Press, 1983), 49–104.

18 This is not to deny exceptions, such as the commentary by Paul M. Joyce

and Diana Lipton on Lamentations: see my *God in a Single Vision*, ed. Brewer and MacSwain, 81–3.

19 Richard Bauckham, *Jesus and the Eyewitnesses: The Gospels as Eyewitness Testimony*, 2nd edn (Grand Rapids, MI: Eerdmans, 2017).

20 Acknowledged during the promotional lecture at St Andrews (3 November 2017) rather than in the text itself.

21 In describing the cleansing of the temple, remembrance is used: first, to account for appeal to a different OT text (John 2.17; Zech. 14.20–21) and then, second, to link Jesus' general connection of the temple and his body specifically with this incident (John 2.22; Mark 14.58 and 15.29).

22 In other words, such pronouncements as Mark 14.58 and 15.29 have been retrojected into an earlier stage of the ministry.

23 Quoting Ricoeur, he suggests that we cannot have 'the prophetic moment' without also having 'the historical moment': Bauckham, *Jesus and the Eyewitnesses*, 508.

24 As in the suggestion of Larry W. Hurtado, quoted with approval in Barton's chapter 'Remembering and Revelation: The Historic and Glorified Jesus in the Gospel of John', in *Israel's God and Rebecca's Children: Christology and Community in Early Judaism and Christianity*, ed. David Capes et al. (Waco, TX: Baylor University Press, 2007), 195–213, esp. 206–7.

25 One may note the repeated theme in Sartre's philosophy that the past is not something wholly beyond our control but rather continually being reshaped as the present reality that is memory: see, for example, his novel *Nausea* (1938) or *Being and Nothingness* (London: Methuen, 1958), 107–20.

26 'In a preview of wholesale conversion among all the nations, Pilate's wife and Pilate himself become Gentile disciples of Jesus'. Robert H. Grundy, *Matthew: A Commentary*, 2nd edn (Grand Rapids, MI: Eerdmans, 1994), 562.

27 Paul does not mention her at all in his list of appearances (1 Cor. 15.4–8), while Luke also seems to imply a first appearance to Peter (24.34). For a defence of later church treatments of Mary Magdalene, see my *Discipleship and Imagination: Christian Tradition and Truth* (Oxford: Oxford University Press, 2000), 31–61.

28 B. F. Westcott and F. J. A. Hart (eds), *The New Testament in the Original Greek*, 2 vols (London: Macmillan, 1881). They relied heavily on Tischendorff's discovery earlier that century of the fourth-century Codex Sinaiticus.

29 Important new papyri discoveries included Chester Beatty (1930s), Bodmer (1950s and 1960s) and Oxyrhynchus (from 1898 onwards). Using digitalized technology, a new *Editio critica maior* is due to be completed by 2030.

30 Bart D. Ehrman, *The Orthodox Corruption of Scripture* (New York: Oxford University Press, 1993); Brown, *Tradition and Imagination*, 300–2. There I briefly defended both the opening of Mark and the addition of Jesus dropping blood in Gethsemane (Luke 22.43–44).

31 For defences of the value of the text followed by the Greek and adopted by New Testament writers, see M. Müller, *The First Bible of the Church: A Plea for the Septuagint* (Sheffield: Sheffield Academic Press, 1996); T. M. Law, *When God Spoke Greek: The Septuagint and the Making of the Christian Bible* (Oxford: Oxford University Press, 2013).

32 Whereas in the Hebrew, Exodus 15.3 reads 'the Lord is a warrior, the Lord is his name', in the Greek we find 'the Lord, when he shatters wars, the Lord is his name.'

33 Produced by Jewish grammarians between the sixth and tenth centuries AD. As well as introducing vowel points and accents to indicate how the words should be pronounced, marginal notes indicated where potential problems existed.

34 For the influence of 'Atticizing' on Mark's text, see the summary of G. D. Kilpatrick's approach in D. C. Parker, *New Testament Manuscripts and their Texts* (Cambridge: Cambridge University Press, 2008), 343–5.

35 D. C. Parker, *The Living Text of the Gospels* (Cambridge: Cambridge University Press, 1997), 182, 204; Parker, *Textual Scholarship and the Making of the New Testament* (Oxford: Oxford University Press, 2012), 24.

36 Parker, *The Living Text*, 209–10; *Textual Scholarship*, 146–7, cf. 19.

37 Parker, *The Living Text*, 213; *Textual Scholarship*, 24.

38 Parker, *The Living Text*, 49–94.

39 *King Lear* went through different versions, while Wordsworth's *Prelude* of 1850 is quite different in texture from that of 1805. Ehrman seems to me naïve on two grounds: first, he ignores how often in unrelated contexts, such as the aftermath of the First World War, much later assessment of events are more accurate than contemporary; second, he is far too ready to describe as 'historical' what is in fact just one perspective, namely his own! So, for example, on the latter point, how can he claim that 'early Christianity was extremely diverse' when all we can know for certain is that diverse groups existed, not their relative numbers: B. D. Ehrman, *The New Testament: A Historical Introduction*, 6th edn (New York: Oxford University Press, 2016), 1.

40 For this type of argument explored in more detail, see my *Divine Generosity and Human Creativity: Theology through Symbol, Painting and Architecture*, ed. Christopher R. Brewer and Robert MacSwain (London and New York: Routledge, 2017), 23–36, esp. 24–6.

41 Ibid., 7–22, 157.

42 Called 'the opening of the mouth', the Old Babylonian ritual sounds suspiciously like turning something inanimate into a living reality: Zainab Bahrani, *Mesopotamia: Ancient Art and Architecture* (London: Thames & Hudson, 2017), 217.

43 For an attempt at an extended comparison, see Christine Mangala Frost, *The Human Icon: A Comparative Study of Hindu and Orthodox Christian Beliefs* (Cambridge: James Clarke, 2017).

44 Athena's *xoanon* was a faceless pillar that was believed to have miraculously fallen to earth. Although in origin a phallic symbol, the *lingam* was clearly non-representational and indeed is now conceived in essentially mystical terms. By contrast, the much later image of Shiva as Nataraja or cosmic dancer is undoubtedly anthropomorphic in design.

45 See further my chapter and the Editor's Introduction in Robert MacSwain (ed.), *Scripture, Metaphysics and Poetry: Austin Farrer's* The Glass of Vision *With Critical Commentary* (Farnham: Ashgate, 2013).

46 Johannes Lindblom, *Prophecy in Ancient Israel* (Oxford: Blackwell, 1962), esp. 122–47, in which various types of visions are distinguished; William P. Brown, *Seeing the Psalms: A Theology of Metaphor* (Louisville, KY: Westminster John Knox Press, 2002), in which the origin of many of the psalms' key metaphors is argued to be visual.

47 Brown, *Tradition and Imagination*, 282. Cf. also Christopher Rowland, *The Open Heaven* (New York: Crossroads, 1982), 358–60; Joel Marcus, 'Jesus' baptismal vision', *New Testament Studies* 41.4 (1995), 512–21.

48 Although some interpret 2 Corinthians 12 as Paul's demotion of visions, the passage has also been used to argue that Paul was part of the *merkabah* tradition of visionary mysticism: see e.g. C. R. A. Morrey-Jones, 'Paradise Revisited: The Jewish Mystical Background of Paul's Apostolate', *Harvard Theological Review* 86.2 (1993), 177–217, 265–92.

49 The existence of a marked change from the icon as image of veneration to assessment as a work of art is most emphasized in Hans Belting, *Likeness and Presence: A History of the Image before the Era of Art* (Chicago, IL: University of Chicago Press, 1994). But although some religious images were no doubt treated as purely illustrative, the desire of viewers to use them as a means of engaging with the divine also continued.

50 Austin Farrer, *The Revelation of St John the Divine* (Oxford: Clarendon Press, 1964), esp. 23–9; Elisabeth Schüssler Fiorenza, *Revelation: Vision of a Just World* (Edinburgh: T&T Clark, 1993), esp. 26–9. As in my sermon in this volume, 240–4.

51 The colleague in question was Philip Esler, now Portland Chair in New Testament Studies at the University of Gloucestershire.

52 Rather than a totally fresh start, modern art can be seen to draw powerfully on early traditions. So, for example, Pablo Picasso was much influenced by the Romanesque art of his native Catalonia, Henry Moore by the monumentality of African, Mexican and Oceanic art, and so on.

53 It is impossible to escape entirely conditioning from the culture in which one is set. So attempting to float free from the past in reality merely allows the underlying prejudices of the present age more power.

54 For an extended discussion on my part of the relevance to theology of one movement in modern art (abstract art), see my *God and Enchantment of Place: Reclaiming Human Experience* (Oxford: Oxford University Press, 2004), 136–50.

55 H. R. Rookmaaker, *Modern Art and the Death of a Culture* (Downers Grove, IL: Intervarsity Press, 1970) set the pattern for a generation. Although Seerveld in *Bearing Fresh Olives Leaves* (Carlisle: Piquant, 2000) is more moderate and his specific objections deserve a response, the presupposition of something essentially wrong remains.

56 David Lyle Jeffrey, *In the Beauty of Holiness: Art and the Bible in Western Culture* (Grand Rapids, MI: Eerdmans, 2017).

57 David Lyle Jeffrey, *A Dictionary of Biblical Tradition in English Literature* (Grand Rapids, MI: Eerdmans, 1992).

58 The two key chapters are entitled 'God after Belief' and 'God against Belief': Jeffrey, *In the Beauty of Holiness*, 253–315.

59 The treatment of Cyrus as the Lord's anointed (Isa. 45.1) is one case in point, as is the absence of God's name from Esther or the extreme pessimism of the book of Ecclesiastes.

60 For some examples, see 'Learning from Pagans' in my *Divine Generosity and Human Creativity*, ed. Brewer and MacSwain, 37–48, esp. 41-2, 46. One might contrast what I say there on Max Ernst's painting, *Virgin Mary Spanking the Infant Jesus Before Three Witnesses* (41, 110) with Jeffrey's comments (Jeffrey, *In the Beauty of Holiness*, 304–5).

61 Although the other two rivers in Genesis 2.11–14 are sometimes used to argue for a location elsewhere (e.g. by Gerhard von Rad), the last two known rivers suggest Mesopotamia.

62 Thus, to give two examples, one of the three wise men became black (Balthasar), while it was the black St Maurice who defended Europe against the pagan Slavs. Equally, the pagan ancient world was mixed in its attitudes, Egyptians being much more negative in their treatment of those of black race than were the Romans. For the full history, see Ladislas Bugner (ed.), *The Image of the Black in Western Art*, 4 vols (Cambridge, MA: Harvard University Press, 1976).

63 Simon Schama, *Rembrandt's Eyes* (London: Allen Lane, 1999), 410–11; Christopher Brown, Jan Kelch and Pieter van Tiel (eds), *Rembrandt: The Master and his Workshop* (New Haven, CT: Yale University Press, 1991), 181–3.

64 Susanna Partsch, *Rembrandt* (London: Weidenfeld & Nicolson, 1991), 109–10, esp. 109. Contrast Schama's 'the helpless boy'.

65 Aaron Rosen, *Art + Religion in the 21st Century* (London: Thames & Hudson, 2015).

66 As candidates for possible inclusion, consider Deuteronomy 20.16-20, Matthew 27.25 and Qur'an 5.33 or 8.67.

67 Brown, *Discipleship and Imagination*, 226–87, esp. 250–70.

68 The classic position is presented in Peter Gay, *The Enlightenment: An Interpretation – The Rise of Modern Paganism* (New York: Knopf, 1966). It has been challenged by, among others, S. J. Barnett, *The Enlightenment of Religion: The Myths of Modernity* (Manchester: Manchester University Press, 2003); David Sorkin, *The Religious*

Enlightenment (Princeton, NJ: Princeton University Press, 2008); Ulrich L. Lehner, *The Catholic Enlightenment* (New York: Oxford University Press, 2016).

69 L. Andrews, *Preces Privatae*, trans. F. E. Brightman (London: Methuen, 1903), 85.

70 *The Litanie* (lines 37–45), in which he places Mary fourth in order after the Trinity and before the angels or any other saints. Donne was a convert from Rome to Anglicanism.

71 For an exception, see Mark Frank (d. 1664), Second Christmas Sermon, in *Sermons of Mark Frank* (Oxford, 1849), I, 79–80.

72 Such as St Thomas More. See the article on Anglicanism in Michael O'Carroll, *Theotokos: A Theological Encyclopedia of the Blessed Virgin Mary* (Dublin: Dominican Publications, 1982), 27–9.

73 Rosemary Ashton, *George Eliot: A Life* (London: Hamish Hamilton, 1996), 82; Claire Tomalin, *Thomas Hardy: The Time-Worn Man* (London: Viking, 2006), 223. Hardy's poem 'The Darling Thrush', written in response to the song of a thrush in winter, perhaps best indicates that his pessimism was not total: it suggests 'some blessed Hope whereof he knew / And I was unaware.'

74 Cf. Norman Vance, *Bible and Novel: Narrative Authority and the Death of God* (Oxford: Oxford University Press, 2013), e.g. viii. A similar claim is made for Dickens in Keith Hooper, *Charles Dickens: Faith, Angels, and the Poor* (London: Lion, 2017).

75 With the novelists I have listed three Roman Catholics, two Anglicans and one Presbyterian. Because of the huge success of Stanley Kubrick's adaptation in the film *A Clockwork Orange*, Anthony Burgess's work is often misunderstood but in fact his novel has a final, more hopeful Christian chapter that the film lacks. Graham Greene makes his position clear in his distinction between 'novels' and 'entertainment'. Golding's best religious novel is *Lord of the Flies*, White's *Riders in the Chariot*. Of the film-makers one might select Malick's *Tree of Life*, Scorsese's *Silence* and Tarkovsky's *The Sacrifice*.

76 So, for example, although not usually denying them as such, twentieth-century theology also witnessed a decline in appeal to the more miraculous aspects of the Gospel accounts.

77 Kinlaw also notes 'the contemporary novelist's tenuous relation to literary tradition', though in Wallace's case there are a considerable number of allusions of various kinds.

78 After a long period of clinical depression, he committed suicide in 2008 at the age of 46.

79 The speech was subsequently published in 2013.

80 'There is no such thing as not worshipping ... The only choice we get is what to worship.'

81 Among many other awards, she won the Pulitzer Prize in 2005 and the Library of Congress Prize for American Fiction in 2016.

82 She talks about 'the resurrection of the everyday', while invoking divine presence in unspectacular landscape, such as pools of water.

83 These include *The Death of Adam* (1998), *Absence of Mind* (2010) and *The Givenness of Things* (2015).

84 E.g. *When I was a Child I Read Books* (London: Virago, 2012), 26, 137.

85 For the former, *When I was a Child*, 50, 93–4; for the latter, her defence of Soviet suspicions of America, 39–44.

86 On Calvinism, 59–83; on Bible, 95–124. In particular, she draws attention to verses where the Old Testament urges concern for enemies, 104, 116 (Deut. 2.4–11; 23.7).

87 She mentions more than once her pride in the fact that her own denomination (Congregationalism) long anticipated the rest of the Church in ordaining women and in allowing blessings of same-sex unions.

APPENDIX

The Moving Text in the Life of the Church

Introduction

GARRICK V. ALLEN, CHRISTOPHER R. BREWER AND DENNIS F. KINLAW III

Brown ended his 'Reply' by observing that he felt more confident in analysing the past history of the Church rather than in attempting the role of prophet, and thus searching for future directions to which the moving text of Scripture might lead. But we wonder if he was being quite fair on himself. Having been given access to many of his past sermons, quite a few strike us as having in effect been engaged in just this sort of task. Indeed, preachers often see this as their role, but in the case of Brown it is sometimes possible to hear wider academic concerns rumbling just beneath the surface in what could be seen as a healthy interaction between the world of academia and Christian life and witness.

To illustrate various aspects of that dynamic, we have selected four sermons for inclusion here. The first, 'Ladder between Heaven and Earth' (in addition to obvious connections with Chapter 7), illustrates Brown's belief that understanding biblical texts properly is sometimes itself a fully imaginative exercise, as the preacher and reader jointly seek to recover the allusions and images beneath the surface of the text, as a way of trying to allow it to continue to speak to us today. The second sermon, 'Rachel and Leah', observes how the same text can be put to widely differing usage at different historical periods but yet each have their own appropriate validity. The third, 'Food Offered to Idols and Idolatry in Word and Image', is then found urging listeners and readers to face the fact that the Bible is not a flat unity but embraces conflicting positions that mean we need not always wholly agree with any one particular passage. Indeed, idolatry is precisely the unwillingness to step outside such fixed boxes and so be open to God's future. Finally, 'Emotion and the Tears of Peter' reminds any who think that on this model past interpretations are now in danger of losing any permanent significance that it is precisely within the power of any text to recover its original force and speak anew to the contemporary world.

The Ladder between Heaven and Earth: John 1.43–51

DAVID BROWN

Many of the dialogues in the Gospel narratives are quite easy to follow but today's Gospel reading is an obvious exception, with the exchange between Nathaniel and Christ apparently consisting of a series of non-sequiturs; that is, no obvious connection between one sentence and the next. So this morning let me first expand the story for you, to make it more readily intelligible, before then drawing some practical implications for our own life of faith.

First, the name of the central figure, Nathaniel. Nathaniel is only mentioned in John's Gospel as one of the twelve apostles. In the other three the person linked with Philip is called Bartholomew, not as big a contradiction as you might suppose since Bartholomew is a patronymic, indicating that the individual was Bar-Tholmai, son of Tholmai. So it is quite reasonable to suppose that Nathaniel's full name was Nathaniel Bar-Tholmai, just as Jesus' full name was Joshua ben Joseph. The next thing to note is the place of encounter, Bethsaida, a large Gentile city on the north-east side of the Sea of Galilee, the place that Philip the tetrarch has established as his capital. There was, however, also a significant Jewish population, among which was the apostle Philip, who summons Nathaniel to come and hear Jesus. But Nathaniel is none too pleased, and asks, 'Can any good thing come out of Nazareth?' Nowhere else in Scripture do we find negative comments on Jesus' home town; so why such a negative response from Nathaniel? Well, elsewhere in John (21.2) we learn that he was not himself from Bethsaida but from Cana on the opposite side of the Lake, and only a few miles distant from Nazareth. So a common speculation has been that the remark is based on rivalry between the two neighbouring places, much as I'm told similar remarks are made here in St Andrews about children from the nearby village of Tayport: they are far too wild and likely to be up to no good. It doesn't bode too well for people like me who actually live there!

Still, Philip does persuade Nathaniel after all to come and hear Jesus, and again we have a surprising response, this time on the side of Jesus. He says: 'Behold an Israelite indeed, in whom is no guile.' Here you need to know that the Israelites believed their name to be derived from the new name (Israel) given in Genesis to Jacob as their founding father; and Jacob, as I'm sure you know, had begun his adult life with a notorious piece of guile or trickery. Together with his mother he had conspired to deprive his older brother Esau of his birthright. So in effect Jesus is declaring Nathaniel to be superior to Jacob in his absolute integrity. Not surprisingly, Nathaniel is bowled over by the compliment but, puzzled, asks, 'How do you know me?' It is an enigmatic response that he gets from Jesus: 'I saw you under the fig tree.' Here once more a little background knowledge is needed. 'Sitting under a fig tree' is a common prophetic image of the messianic age, when swords will have been beaten into ploughshares (cf. Mic. 4.1–4). Presumably Jesus had seen Nathaniel praying and meditating under a fig tree, and presumes a similar connection in Nathaniel's mind as the image has in his own. So, not surprisingly perhaps, Nathaniel, like Philip, does not hesitate to identify Jesus as that very Messiah for whom he has been longing.

But once more Jesus springs a surprise on him, and tells Nathaniel not to be content with just that thought, for greater things are possible. 'He will see the heavens open and the angels of God ascending and descending upon the Son of Man.' On first hearing it may sound like a promise of some strange future visionary experience, but I do not think that this is what Jesus, or for that matter John as the author of this passage, has primarily in mind at just this moment. For recall the earlier reference to Jacob. One of the best-known incidents in his life was his dream at Bethel when he saw a ladder with angels ascending and descending from heaven (Gen. 28.10ff.), an incident of course particularly dear to all Scots since Jacob's stone pillow that night was allegedly eventually brought to Scotland to form the Stone of Destiny upon which ever since Scottish kings and British monarchs have been crowned. But here a much greater claim is made, that Christ himself will be the ladder that opens the heavens for Nathaniel, and thus is able to unite heaven and earth.

Certainly that was true for Nathaniel (or Bartholomew as we may also call him), since he was one of the disciples who saw the resurrected Christ (John 21.1–2), and eventually brought similar perceptions to others, as he preached, it is believed, in far-off India. But what of ourselves? Is there not a message for each and every one of us in this progressive exchange between Christ and Nathaniel here? It is relatively easy for us to rest content with the conviction that God knows and loves us. But what of us sitting, as it were, under our own particular contemporary fig tree? Can we too not dream of something more? Why should each of us not have our own particular Bethels, moments when the heavens open and we see that bit more of God's purpose for ourselves and for his world? It may be here at Communion, or it may be in a walk in the countryside, or while listening to a particular moving piece of music. The possibilities are endless but unless we are open to them, the heavens will remain closed. Indeed, it is worth remembering that God is in the mundane and ordinary, no less than in the luminous sunset: in your friends, in your routine housework, in the bustle of a great city. So with that thought in mind, let me end with part of a famous poem by the English nineteenth-century poet, Francis Thompson. You may need to know that Gennesareth is another name for the Sea of Galilee, and Charing Cross a busy junction in the centre of London.

'Tis ye, 'tis your estrangèd faces,
That miss the many-splendoured thing.

But (when so sad thou canst not sadder)
Cry, – and upon thy sore loss
Shall shine the traffic of Jacob's ladder
Pitched betwixt Heaven and Charing Cross.

Yea, in the night, my Soul, my daughter,
Cry – clinging Heaven by the hems,
And lo, Christ walking on the water
Not of Gennesareth, but Thames.

All Saints', St Andrews

Rachel and Leah: Genesis 29.15–28

DAVID BROWN

For reasons that will become apparent in due course, I thought that I would subject you to no less than four sermons this morning, all on the text of our first reading from Genesis. But don't worry! Even when combined they will be no longer than the usual Sunday morning offering.

So, first then to Jericho and a sermon from the local rabbi at the time of the reign of King Herod the Great. Try to envisage me wearing a yarmulka, or Jewish skull cap. So here goes:

In the story read from our Scriptures a few moments ago you heard how Jacob had to serve Laban 14 years in all before he was allowed to have as his wife Rachel, the woman he really loved, and not her elder sister, Leah. Yet Jacob was of course father of us all, for it was his other name, Israel, that was eventually given to the people we now are. But if God could treat the father of his people like that, what hope, you might say, is there for any of us? How can we ever expect to escape a tyrant like the one we are now living under, or still worse the threat of the Romans themselves taking over and governing us directly? Certainly, none of us can predict the future, and for all we know the Messiah may come on the morrow. But what we do know is that God is just, and so there was always a reason why one thing happens rather than another. And so take those 14 years that Jacob laboured to get Rachel. Do you not see how Jacob is really getting back some of his own medicine? Just recall how earlier in his life he had cheated his own elder brother, Esau, of his birthright by disguising himself in front of his elderly father Isaac, taking on the semblance of Esau – the same hair and smells as his brother. Now here Leah, Rachel's elder sister, plays a similar trick on him on their wedding night, substituting her veils for Rachel's in the midnight gloom. So if even the father of the nation must bear the consequences of his wrongful acts, so too must we.

Let's now speed through time and join the congregation at a monastic house in twelfth-century Paris. You will observe my skull cap has now gone, and been replaced by monastic tonsure, and so very little of my hair is left.

Brothers, you all know the story of how it was Mary Magdalene who sat at Jesus' feet and listened to his teaching while Martha busied herself with household chores. Yet when Martha complains, it is she whom Jesus reprimands, and not Mary. In fact he tells Martha that it is Mary who has chosen the better way. It is to that way that you also have been called as monks, as you meditate daily on Christ's words in your cells and in this chapel. But to what point, you may sometimes say to yourselves? Blessed Augustine gave us the answer when he reflected on the very passage you have just heard. For is Leah not a bit like Martha, and Rachel like Mary Magdalene? Leah gave Jacob the immediate satisfaction of sexual desire but it was the more distant prospect, Rachel, that provided Jacob with the greater reward. As Scripture tells us, 'Jacob served seven years for Rachel, and they seemed to him but a few days because of the love he had for her' (v. 20). And so it should be with us. We need to cultivate daily the virtue of patience, as like Rachel and Jacob we see in the far distance our heavenly union with God, knowing it is still a long way off but at the same time certain that it will indeed come and with a glory and magnificence that will make all this world has to offer pale into relative insignificance.

And now with an even bigger effort of imagination, turn me into a woman with long hair teaching at Harvard Divinity School in the 1980s. My preaching engagement today is in downtown Boston.

Sisters – and any brothers willing to listen – to read the Scriptures properly you need to open your eyes and ears, and just see and hear how biased the surface meaning always has been in favour of men. Just reflect for a moment on today's reading from Genesis. The depth of Jacob's love for Rachel is constantly held up for our admiration, but who gives a thought for Rachel? Certainly not the author of this story, who doesn't even bother to mention how Rachel felt about the impending marriage, or about having to wait so long for it to come to pass. Given that we are told how beautiful she was (typical of the male gaze!), she probably had plenty of admirers, any one of whom she could have obtained with much less effort. And, then, what of her elder sister, Leah? The story is told in such a way as to imply that she ought to have been grateful to her father for having been saved from otherwise being permanently left on the shelf, totally neglected by men. But possibly she might actually have been happier that way, living independently, or at any rate with no man exercising total control over her, as marriage in those days entailed. In short, let's pay heed to the subversive power of our Scriptures, and stop reading them as though all they do is support male authority and superiority. Instead, hidden just under the text God offers us a way out from all those male delusions of power, summoning us to liberate any

Leah or Rachel in downtown Boston or elsewhere suffering under the heel of tyrannical or indifferent men.

Finally, back to the real me, preaching in All Saints' church, this July 2014.

All three sermons you have heard were based on actual texts of the time. What may have most struck you is their extraordinary diversity, and perhaps their very variety seems so bewildering to you that it calls into question whether God could be speaking through the preacher in each case at all. If so, I would beg to differ. What it really demonstrates, I would suggest on the contrary, is the great richness of Scripture, and so the importance of always reading and listening with care, not assuming that we already know what a particular passage means long before we have heard it. God may have something new to say to us precisely through that very passage.

But there is also a second lesson to learn, and that is that God is no respecter of persons. He speaks to each and every one of us, and that has nothing at all to do with how important or how good we are. Rachel and Leah were very different, but God was concerned for both alike. Again, read the story of Jacob and you will find that he is a trickster and scoundrel through and through, and not just in his treatment of his brother; yet he it was, we are told, that God chose as his instrument for the founding of his chosen people, Israel.

So likewise then with ourselves. Don't pretend to an importance you don't have. But equally, don't turn any alleged lack of gifts, inadequacies, your sins or even your doubts into excuses for holding back. For lying behind these apparently trivial tales from Scripture, and even within something as small as a tiny wafer, is God, the very God who wants you and no other.

All Saints', St Andrews

Food Offered to Idols and Idolatry in Word and Image: Revelation 2.12–17

DAVID BROWN

This morning we heard as our second reading the third of John's seven letters to the churches of Asia Minor (present-day south-west Turkey). In it he takes up once more his earlier image of Christ wielding a two-edged sword (1.16; 2.12; 2.16) to indict the people of Pergamon, the province's administrative capital, with the sin of idolatry. In their readiness to eat meat offered in sacrifice in the imperial and other cults, John suggests, such temporizing Christians (called Nicolaitans in the text) are really like the Israelites of old who succumbed to the wiles of the pagan prophet Balaam, as described in the book of Numbers in the Old Testament (chs 22—25). For according to John, the idolatry that follows Balaam's prophecy was entirely Balaam's fault.

The plot seems simple enough, but is it? For most of its history, our faith has assumed that idols meant artistic objects – statues and so forth – and that these are the greatest dangers to belief. Hence John's worry about food offered in association with statues and their exclusion from Christian worship. By comparison, words have in effect been seen as the natural and safe medium, with music almost as welcome. Yet are matters really quite that simple? Might not words – even biblical words – sometimes be potentially just as idolatrous, and the visual actually sometimes be much less dangerous, much less subject to corruption of the spirit? Let me use the rest of my time to explore that possibility, and what it might mean both in respect of what John actually says here and more generally with regard to the book of Revelation as a whole.

But hold on, you may say. Isn't John interested in the visual as well? Are you sure? Take that initial image of the two-edged sword in Christ's mouth. Now try to visualize it. As the average such sword in the ancient world was between sixteen inches and three feet, no human mouth could easily bear its weight. The result is that your attempt to visualize Christ in this way will almost certainly have resulted in a problem. Respect for our Lord will have made you hesitate, but the result, however much you try, I suspect, will have tended towards the comic, and that is what I suggest in general happens with John's imagery in this work. The two most famous examples of attempts to visualize the book's message as a whole – the late-medieval Angers tapestry and Dürer's sixteenth-century woodcuts – are both, I suggest, magnificent failures. The more you study them the less inclined you are to believe in John's version of the end of all things. And that seems confirmed even if you confine yourself to what are today the most generally acceptable elements in John's work, his vision of the heavenly Jerusalem. Attend to the details in chapters 21—22, and you find a city dwarfing Manhattan at 1,500 miles high, but with surrounding walls of only 140 feet; again, a great tree arching over its solitary street that has a river flowing through its middle but yet able to sustain the tree's roots on either side. No wonder modern translations, rather than confronting us with the absurdity of the project, in general keep the obscurity of the original – measurements in stadia and cubits and so forth!

There is of course a way out, and that is to concede, as many commentators do, that John after all lacks a visual imagination. What he is really doing is drawing metaphors from the Old Testament and reapplying them, somewhat indiscriminately, to the new dispensation. So the two-edged sword is no more intended to be visualized than is the reference to Balaam, or for that matter the new city of Jerusalem. The two-edged sword is John's way of referring us back to his own version of Daniel's vision (10.4–5) of God and his entourage in judgement in the previous chapter; and his allusion to the story of Balaam of Numbers 22—25 is his way of ensuring that what his opponents are up to is taken with maximum seriousness. Again, the dimensions of tree and city do not really matter. It is just John's way of making sure that we revisit the story of the Garden of Eden and the new Jerusalem promised by the prophets: the new future, we are being told, will reverse the fate of the former and fulfil the promise of the latter.

Now in a religion suspicious of art, all this might be thought to be an advantage. But is it? What in effect we have found in John is a narrowing of our options. The meaning of his images is in fact not yielded through our own explorations but rather by their literary relationship to the Old Testament. They are thus, as it were, controlled and controlling metaphors, means of dictating to us how we should read the community of faith's past and future. And what is idolatry if not the assigning of absolute significance to what is merely provisional, replacing the one absolute God by what is created and subordinate? Now of course John's metaphors may not have been intended in this absolute way, but the fact that they are more like rules for reading than images for exploration does suggest that he is not as far distant from idolatry as one might initially suppose.

I want to pursue that thought a little further in a moment, but let's think first about how such reflections might apply more generally to art and music. Are these media more or less constrictive than words, more or less subject to the temptation of absolutes? Certainly, art is sometimes just as constrictive. Since we are still in the season of Easter, think how the resurrection is commonly portrayed. The familiar image of Christ standing on the open tomb is surely as pedantic an absolute as you can get – all very literal, and very unbelievable. Calvin was surely right to protest that whatever Easter's message is, it was not this, and so the more extreme Reformation's reluctance to see such imagery as a part of faith becomes quite understandable. But need art be so literalistic? Of course not. Go to the National Gallery in London and you will see Titian's great painting of the appearance of Christ to Mary Magdalene in the garden. Admittedly, Titian was tempted initially to literalism. In the painting's first version he gave Christ the gardener's hat to which John's Gospel alludes. But his final version is quite otherwise. If I can put it like this, you have to work at seeing to see the meaning, but eventually it does emerge. Mary is kneeling at Christ's feet. If you allow your eye to follow the arch of her back, it takes you up to Christ and then through him to a tree that stands between them both, and then on heavenwards. Our salvation, we are being told, comes like Mary's through penitence and a longing to follow Christ wheresoever he may lead. It is one of the great paintings of European art. It achieves its effect, however, not by force but by invitation and exploration: the provisional, the open uncertainty, eventually leading us on to the transcendent and absolute.

Turn now to music. There are quite a few references in John to music in the worship of heaven. Christianity has on the whole tended to see music as less inherently dangerous than art, but I cannot help wondering whether Plato was not after all right in thinking music the more potentially seductive of the two, for its inevitably temporal sequence means that it normally has to chose to direct us along one path rather than another. As an example, consider the ending of Bach's *St John Passion*. In John's Gospel there is a delicate balance struck between Christ's two concluding utterances, the human cry of 'I thirst' and the divine 'It is finished' (perhaps better translated as 'All is now accomplished'). Reading, one has time to stop and reflect, moving back and forth between the one verse and the other, but of course the music cannot do this. Bach had to lead us in one direction and not another. Intriguingly, his choice is to play down the triumph in 'It is finished'. We hear that phrase no less than three times before it is given a more confident note. This has led some – such as Karl Barth – to pronounce his interpretation of John a failure, but of course what his strategy does allow us is to absorb fully the death before we look to the triumph. Either way, though, Bach is directing our emotions: not simply allowing them free sway, the space to explore, as in the written version of the Gospels or in many a painting where divinity and humanity are set side by side on the cross but viewers left to themselves as to how and when either is appropriated.

I say this not to decry music. Sometimes the direction it leads is exactly the right one. Sometimes too alternatives are opened up, as for instance in rival interpretations of the same musical text or in opera singers singing simultaneously, expressing at the one and the same time opposing emotions and potential directions for the plot. All I am trying to get across is that there is no inevitability about the ranking of the three media and their degree of exposure to idolatry. One can be seduced by the sensuality of Wagner's *Tristan und Isolde* no less than Pygmalion was by the statue he created, by apparently ethereal words no less than by a Venus de Milo.

And so finally back to John in this passage. John was not one for compromise. As already mentioned, those eating meat offered to idols are unequivocally condemned and compared to those once seduced by the pagan prophet Balaam in the Old Testament. In such an estimate he is much less generous than Paul in 1 Corinthians 8, who found nothing wrong with such conduct. He is also much less generous to Balaam than was many another contemporary Jew for whom Balaam was not only an honourable pagan but also something of an honorary Jew (cf. *Sifre* on Deut. 34.10). Indeed, even to this day his words are part of the morning service in the Jewish synagogue.

And what of Pergamon itself? Apart from the imperial temple there was also a magnificent one to Zeus on the top of Pergamon's main hill and another, a great centre of pilgrimage, at its foot, the temple of Asclepius where many sought cures for their illnesses. The former's fine carvings are preserved in Berlin, the latter's are no more. No doubt for John the fact that Asclepius' sign was a serpent was already grounds enough for condemnation, and that is why the allusion to Satan is introduced in our passage. But whatever the explanation, there seems little doubt that cures were effected at the shrine. Pergamon was also the birthplace of one of the great doctors of the ancient word, Galen. The city, though, produced something still more famous: parchment, the word itself derived from the city's name, Pergamon. So writing is itself intimately connected with this city, a supreme irony in that John uses his writing to attack the very basis of the city in its visual beauty, one of the great ordered and planned cities of the ancient world, with careful zoning practised as one ascended the hill to Zeus' great temple on top.

John seems unaware of all of this. Could it be that he only ever saw one side of the argument in the early Church's attempt to form some estimate of the Roman Empire, and that we must turn to Paul if we are to obtain a more rounded view? If that is so, perhaps the most dangerous form of idolatry lay not after all in the statues in the temples of Zeus or Asclepius or of the emperor, but actually in his own writings, in absolutizing his own view of the world and assigning all who disagreed with him to perdition? We today – in the Church at least – now generally live in a much more gentle world, but the danger is surely still there. God is the only acceptable absolute. Failing to listen to the views of those with whom we differ, imposing perspectives, is already halfway on the road to the worst idolatry of all: that of words – the most insidious precisely because, unlike statues, it is hidden, trapping us when we are least aware of it. May God protect us from that evil in our own day.

Durham Cathedral

Emotion and the Tears of Peter: Mark 8.31–38

DAVID BROWN

The men in the congregation who are my age or older will no doubt recall as children being told that 'boys don't cry'. Indeed, in my case that lesson was heavily reinforced at boarding school where, thanks to Thomas Arnold, the father of the poet Matthew, the idea of 'muscular Christianity' continued to exercise considerable influence. As you may recall, it was under Arnold's headmastership of Rugby School in the early nineteenth century that that particular pattern was established. But there are of course alternative ways of thinking about education, not least as one reflects on the life of St Peter, one incident from which we heard as this morning's Gospel reading.

Hearing of Jesus' commitment to the way of the cross, Peter impetuously bursts in to protest, only to be reprimanded by his Lord for offering a dangerous and seductively appealing alternative path; hence Jesus' words, 'Get behind me Satan'. It was of course much the same emotional impulsiveness that also lay behind some of the major other incidents familiar to us from Peter's life: for example, early on in Jesus' ministry, his attempt to walk on water towards Jesus, only to sink (Matt. 14.22–33); or again, after Jesus' arrest his promising to remain for ever loyal, only to buckle at the first challenges he receives when some servants accuse him of having a northern accent and so an obvious connection with Jesus (Mark 14.70). It was this last incident, of course, that generated those tears of repentance when he heard the cock crow.

But intriguingly, these were not at all the scenes most frequently recalled in the centuries that followed. Because Peter was reputedly the first bishop of Rome, it was Jesus symbolically giving him the promised keys of the kingdom (Matt. 16.19) that appears repeatedly in art, making him thus a figure of authority and power and not one of emotional impulsiveness or occasional weakness. Indeed, the relevant passage – which only appears in Mathew's Gospel – came to be given a quite different interpretation from the one it had originally, for example in Saint Augustine. 'Thou art Peter and on this rock I will found my church' (Matt. 16.18) was interpreted as referring primarily to Peter himself and not to the confession 'Thou art the Christ', which had first elicited Jesus' response – Augustine's interpretation. Admittedly, at first sight it may seem odd to give Simon Peter such a nickname (the Rock), and refer this not to his character but to something he had said, but if you think for a moment of the genesis of the nicknames of some of your friends, you will soon note how various and unusual the ways are in which such nicknames originate.

What that change of interpretation – from a focus on the implication of the words to Peter himself – indicates is just how reluctant the papacy was to take the emotional character of Peter seriously, and not just the papacy but male clergy more generally. Indeed, it was not until the time of the Counter-Reformation that imagery of Peter crying becomes common, and that for two reasons. First, biblical scholars of the time had begun to attack Pope Gregory the Great's equation of Mary Magdalene with the sinful woman who had washed Jesus' feet with her hair, and so a substitute figure to represent penitence was required. But a more powerful influence still was the desire of the new religious orders, especially the Jesuits, to get men more deeply committed to their faith and in particular to the religious upbringing of their children: remember that Peter was married (Matt. 8.14). The result was a penitent and crying Peter, found in numerous images from the sixteenth and seventeenth centuries, among them a very famous one by El Greco. Even so, this image of male tears was oddly accompanied by a new resistance to women crying, and in particular the Virgin Mary at the foot of the Cross, the argument being that if she truly knew her son would rise again, how could she possibly be subject to such extremes of emotion, and so faint or swoon as she saw him die in agony?

So much, then, for your history lesson! I mention such facts from the past to draw two conclusions for our life of faith in the present. First, there is the need to acknowledge that, whatever the eventual outcome, emotions are part of who it is that we are, and it takes time for them to work themselves through, at their own appropriate speed. You may think this an obvious point but it is amazing how often Christians forgot the fact. I recall once attending a funeral in Oxford for a student who had died very suddenly and tragically, and was astonished to hear the curate declare that there was no need to mourn, as his devout faith guaranteed that he was now with Jesus in heaven. What that sermon ignored was the need for parents and friends to pass through grief before any such greater reality could be recognized. Indeed, we can see the same process at work in Jesus himself. As I'm sure you all know, the shortest verse in the New Testament is 'Jesus wept' (John 11.35). He wept because whatever the longer term might bring, he foresaw what would happen to Jerusalem in the immediate short term. Again, on the cross he utters the cry of dereliction, 'My God, My God, why have you forsaken me?' (Mark 15.34) before he can work through to the more confident ending of the psalm from which he quotes this opening verse (Ps. 22). And indeed, this is precisely what we find reflected in other words attributed to Jesus on the cross: the commending of his spirit to his Father in Luke (23.46) and the declaration that all has now been accomplished in John (19.30).

But there is also a second and deeper reason why emotions matter. Christianity teaches the resurrection of the body and not the immortality of the soul. By such resurrection it does not mean that our present bodies will one day be reconstituted from the same matter that they now have; as Paul observes, our new bodies will be as different from the old as seed is from the final crop (1 Cor. 15.37). Rather, something much more profound is promised: that the totality of ourselves, everything that makes us who we are, will be redeemed in God's new creation. So it is not just a matter of our intellects, of what we believe, it is equally a matter of where our bodies feel most deeply. Peter was hardly as great an intellect as St Paul but he can still show us one important way of following Christ, and that is learning what that entails through our emotions, and their development. And as one might expect of a man of emotion, he was also to bring his life to an end in one great symbolic bodily gesture, in his insistence on being crucified upside down – at one level a pointless act but at another profound, since it demonstrated that to the last his body was Christ's no less than his mind.

All Saints', St Andrews

Bibliography

Abdessemed, Adel, and Pier Luigi Tazzi, *Adel Abdessemed Conversation with Pier Luigi Tazzi*, Arles: Actes Sud, 2012.
Abraham, William J., *Canon and Criterion in Christian Theology: From the Fathers to Feminism*, Oxford: Oxford University Press, 1998.
——'Scripture, Tradition, and Revelation: An Appreciative Critique of David Brown', in *Theology, Aesthetics, and Culture: Responses to the Work of David Brown*, edited by Robert MacSwain and Taylor Worley, 13–28, Oxford: Oxford University Press, 2012.
Abrams, M. H., *Natural Supernaturalism*, London: Norton, 1971.
Adams, Marilyn McCord, *Christ and Horrors: The Coherence of Christology*, Cambridge: Cambridge University Press, 2008.
Agati, M. L., *La Minuscola 'Bouletée'*, LA 9,1, Vatican City: Scuola Vaticana di Paleografica, Diplomatica e Archivistica, 1992.
Aland, B., et al., eds, *Novum Testamentum Graecum: Editio Critica Maior VI/1-2 Catholic Letters*, 2nd edition, Stuttgart: Deutsche Bibelgesellschaft, 2013.
Aland, K., 'Novi Testamenti Graeci Edition Critica Maior: Der Gegenwärtige Stand der Arbeit an einer neuen grossen kritischen Ausgabe des Neuen Testamentes', *New Testament Studies* (1970), 163–77.
Allen, Garrick V., Ian Paul and Simon P. Woodman, eds, *The Book of Revelation: Currents in British Research on the Apocalypse*, Tübingen: Mohr Siebeck, 2015.
Allen, Garrick V., 'Image, Memory, and Allusion in the Textual History of the Apocalypse: GA 2028 and Visual Exegesis', in *Studien zum Text der Apokalypse II*, edited by M. Sigismund and D. Müller, 435–54, Berlin: De Gruyter, 2017.
—— 'The Reception of Scripture and Exegetical Resources in the *Scholia in Apocalypsin* (GA 2351)', in *Commentaries, Catenae and Biblical Tradition*, edited by H. A. G. Houghton, 141–163, Piscataway: Gorgias, 2016.
Alter, Robert, *The Five Books of Moses: A Translation with Commentary*, New York and London: W. W. Norton & Company, 2004.
Amichai, Yehuda, *The Selected Poetry of Yehuda Amichai*, translated by Chana Bloch and Stephen Mitchell, Berkeley, CA: University of California Press, 2013.
Anderson, Clive, and Brian Edwards, *Evidence for the Bible*, Leonminster: DayOne, 2014.
Anderson, William, *Cecil Collins: The Quest for the Great Happiness*, London: Barrie and Jenkins, 1988.
Andrews, Julian, *The Sculpture of David Nash*, Berkeley, CA: University of California Press, 1996.
Andrews, L., *Preces Privatae*, translated by F. E. Brightman, London: Methuen, 1903.
Ankori, Gannit, *Palestinian Art*, London: Reaktion Books, 2006.
Anonymous, *The Bible in Art: Miniatures, Paintings, Drawings and Sculptures Inspired by the Old Testament*, London: Phaidon, 1956.
—— 'The Ruins of Walsingham', in *The New Oxford Book of Sixteenth-Century Verse*, edited by Emrys Jones, 550, Oxford: Oxford University Press, 2002.

BIBLIOGRAPHY

—— Whitechapel Gallery, Winter 2014 (gallery brochure).

Antry, Theodore J., O. Praem, and Carol Neel, *Norbert and Early Norbertine Spirituality*, Mahwah: Paulist, 2007.

Arden, Patrick, 'David Foster Wallace Warms Up', in *Conversations with David Foster Wallace*, edited by Stephen J. Burn, 94–100, Jackson, MS: University Press of Mississippi, 2012.

Ardura, Bernard, *The Order of Prémontré: History and Spirituality*, translated by Edward Hagman, De Pere, WI: Paisa, 1995.

Ashton, Rosemary, *George Eliot: A Life*, London: Hamish Hamilton, 1996.

Astley, Jeff, *Ordinary Theology: Looking, Listening and Learning in Theology*, Aldershot: Ashgate, 2002.

Attia, Kader, *Continuum of Repair: The Light of Jacob's Ladder*, London: Whitechapel Gallery, 2013.

—— *The Repair: From Occident to Extra-Occidental Cultures*, Berlin: Green Box, 2014.

Auerbach, Erich, *Mimesis: The Representation of Reality in Western Literature*, translated by Willard Trask, Princeton, NJ: Princeton University Press, 2003.

Augustine, *Concerning the City of God against the Pagans*, translated by Henry Bettenson, London: Penguin, 2003.

Aune, David E., *Prophecy in Early Christianity and the Ancient Mediterranean World*, Grand Rapids, MI: Eerdmans, 1983.

—— *Revelation*, 3 volumes, Nashville, TN: Thomas Nelson, 1997–99.

Austen, Ben, 'Chicago After Laquan McDonald', *New York Times Magazine*, (20 April 2016), online: www.nytimes.com/2016/04/24/magazine/chicago-after-laquan-mcdonald.html?mcubz=1; accessed 27 August 2017.

Backmund, Norbert, *Monasticon Praemonstratense*, 2nd edition, De Gruyter: Berlin, 1983.

Bahrani, Zainab, *Mesopotamia: Ancient Art and Architecture*, London: Thames & Hudson, 2017.

Barnett, S. J., *The Enlightenment of Religion: The Myths of Modernity*, Manchester: Manchester University Press, 2003.

Barrett, C. K., *The Gospel According to John*, London: SPCK, 1978.

Barr, James, *Holy Scripture: Canon, Authority, Criticism*, Oxford: Oxford University Press, 1983.

—— *Biblical Faith and Natural Theology: The Gifford Lectures for 1991 Delivered in the University of Edinburgh*, Oxford: Clarendon, 1993.

—— *The Concept of Biblical Theology: An Old Testament Perspective*, Minneapolis, MN: Augsburg Fortress, 1999.

—— *Bible and Interpretation: The Collected Essays of James Barr*, Volume 1: Interpretation and Theology, edited by John Barton, Oxford: Oxford University Press, 2013.

Barth, John, *The Friday Book: Essays and Other Non-Fiction*, London: Johns Hopkins University Press, 1984.

Barton, Stephen, 'Remembering and Revelation: The Historic and Glorified Jesus in the Gospel of John', in *Israel's God and Rebecca's Children: Christology and Community in Early Judaism and Christianity*, edited by David Capes, April D. DeConick, Helen K. Bond and Troy A. Miller, 195–213, Waco, TX: Baylor University Press, 2007.

—— 'Eschatology and the Emotions in Early Christianity', *Journal of Biblical Literature* 130.3 (2011), 571–91.

Barton, Stephen C. et al., eds, *Memory in the Bible and Antiquity*, Tübingen: Mohr Siebeck, 2007.

Bartrum, Giulia, *Albrecht Dürer and His Legacy*, London: British Museum Press, 2002.

Baskind, Samantha, *Encyclopedia of Jewish American Artists*, s.v. 'Jonathan Borofsky', Westport, CT: Greenwood, 2007.
Bauckham, Richard, *The Theology of the Book of Revelation*, Cambridge: Cambridge University Press, 1993.
—— *Jesus and the Eyewitnesses: The Gospels as Eyewitness Testimony*, 2nd edition, Grand Rapids, MI: Eerdmans, 2017.
Baudoin, Anne-Catherine, 'La femme de Pilate dans les *Actes de Pilate*, recension grecque A (II, 1)', *Apocrypha* 21 (2010), 133–49.
Beattie, Tina, 'From Ethics to Eschatology: The Continuing Validity of the New Eve for Christian Doctrine and Discipleship', in *Theology, Aesthetics and Culture: Responses to the Work of David Brown*, edited by Robert MacSwain and Taylor Worley, 64–78, Oxford: Oxford University Press, 2012.
—— 'Sex, Marriage and the Catholic Church', *The Guardian*, 8 October 2014.
Belting, Hans, *Likeness and Presence: A History of the Image before the Era of Art*, Chicago, IL: University of Chicago Press, 1994.
Bengel, J. A., *New Testament Word Studies*, Volume 1: *Matthew–Acts*, translated by Charlton T. Lewis and Marvien R. Vincent. Grand Rapids, MI: Kregel, 1971.
Bentley, G. E., *Blake Records*, London: Yale University Press, 1969.
Bergmann, Michael, Michael J. Murray and Michael C. Rea, *Divine Evil?: The Moral Character of the God of Abraham*, Oxford: Oxford University Press, 2011.
Blatty, William Peter, *The Exorcist*, London: Corgi, 2011.
Bloom, Harold, ed., *Mary Shelley*, London: Modern Critical Voices, 1985.
Boeve, Lieven, *Interrupting Tradition: An Essay on Christian Faith in a Postmodern Context*, Louvain Theological and Pastoral Monographs 30, Leuven: Peeters, 2003.
Boring, M. Eugene, *The Continuing Voice of Jesus: Christian Prophecy and the Gospel Tradition*, Louisville, KY: Westminster John Knox, 1991.
Borysewicz, Alfonse, 'Naked Grace', *Image* 32 (2001), 24–34.
Bossy, John, 'The Mass as a Social Institution', *Past and Present* 100 (1983), 29–61.
Botting, Fred, *Gothic: The New Critical Idiom*, London: Routledge, 2013.
Bouyer, Louis, *Liturgical Piety*, Notre Dame: University of Notre Dame Press, 1954.
Boxall, Ian, *Revelation: Vision and Insight*, London: SPCK, 2002.
—— *Patmos in the Reception History of the Apocalypse*, Oxford: Oxford University Press, 2013.
Brewer, Christopher R., 'Rolling With Release Into the Future: William Desmond's Donation to a Natural Theology of the Arts', in *William Desmond and Contemporary Theology*, edited by Christopher Ben Simpson and Brendan Thomas Sammon, 217–37, Notre Dame, IN: University of Notre Dame Press, 2017.
—— ed., *Christian Theology and the Transformation of Natural Religion: From Incarnation to Sacramentality—Essays in Honour of David Brown*, Leuven: Peeters, 2018.
Brinks, C, L. 'On Nail Scissors and Toothbrushes: Responding to the Philosophers' Critiques of Historical Biblical Criticism', *Religious Studies* 49 (2013), 357–76.
Broadie, Thomas L., *Genesis as Dialogue: A Literary, Historical, and Theological Commentary*, New York: Oxford University Press, 2001.
Brontë, Charlotte, Emily Brontë and Anne Brontë, *Poems by Currer, Ellis, and Acton Bell*, London: Aylott and Jones, 1846.
Brown, Christopher, Jan Kelch, and Pieter van Tiel, eds, *Rembrandt: The Master and his Workshop*, New Haven, CT: Yale University Press, 1991.
Brown, David, *Choices: Ethics and the Christian*, Oxford: Basil Blackwell, 1983.
—— *The Divine Trinity*, London: Duckworth, 1985.
—— 'Wittgenstein Against the "Wittgensteinians": A Reply to Kenneth Surin on *The Divine Trinity*', *Modern Theology* 2 (1986), 257–76.

BIBLIOGRAPHY

—— *Continental Philosophy and Modern Theology: An Engagement*, Oxford: Blackwell, 1987.

—— *Invitation to Theology*, Oxford: Basil Blackwell, 1989.

—— 'God and Symbolic Action', in *Divine Action: Studies Inspired by the Philosophical Theology of Austin Farrer*, edited by Brian Hebblethwaite and Edward Henderson, 103–22, Edinburgh: T&T Clark, 1990; republished in *Scripture, Metaphysics, and Poetry: Austin Farrer's* The Glass of Vision *with Critical Commentary*, edited by Robert MacSwain, 133–47, Farnham: Ashgate, 2013.

—— 'Did Revelation Cease?' in *Reason and the Christian Religion: Essays in Honour of Richard Swinburne*, edited by Alan G. Padgett, 121–41, Oxford: Clarendon, 1994.

—— *The Word to Set You Free: Living Faith and Biblical Criticism*, London: SPCK, 1995.

—— 'Revelation through Art', in *Where Shall We Find God?: Lincoln Lectures in Theology 1997*, 41–51, Lincoln Cathedral: Lincoln Cathedral Publications, 1998.

—— *Tradition and Imagination: Revelation and Change*, Oxford: Oxford University Press, 1999.

—— 'Mary's Discipleship and the Artistic Imagination', in *Say 'Yes' to God: Mary and the Revealing of the Word Made Flesh*, edited by Martin Warner, 69–82, London: Tufton Books, 1999.

—— 'The Trinity in Art', in *The Trinity: An Interdisciplinary Symposium on the Trinity*, edited by Stephen T. Davis, Daniel Kendall and Gerald O'Collins, 329–56, New York: Oxford University Press, 1999; republished as 'Artists on the Trinity', in David Brown, *Divine Generosity and Human Creativity: Theology through Symbol, Painting and Architecture*, edited by Christopher R. Brewer and Robert MacSwain, 130–49, London: Routledge, 2017.

—— *Discipleship and Imagination: Christian Tradition and Truth*, Oxford: Oxford University Press, 2000.

—— 'The Incarnation in Twentieth-Century Art', in *The Incarnation: An Interdisciplinary Symposium on the Incarnation of the Son of God*, edited by Stephen T. Davis, Daniel Kendall and Gerald O'Collins, 332–72, New York: Oxford University Press, 2002.

—— *God and Enchantment of Place: Reclaiming Human Experience*, Oxford: Oxford University Press, 2004.

—— 'Images of Redemption in Art and Music', in *The Redemption: An Interdisciplinary Symposium on Christ as Redeemer*, edited by Stephen T. David, Daniel Kendall and Gerald O'Collins, 295–319, New York: Oxford University Press, 2004.

—— 'The Glory of God Revealed in Art and Music: Learning from Pagans', in *Celebrating Creation: Affirming Catholicism and the Revelation of God's Glory*, edited by Mark Chapman, 43–56, London: Darton, Longman and Todd, 2004; republished as 'Learning from Pagans', in *Divine Generosity and Human Creativity: Theology through Symbol, Painting and Architecture*, edited by Christopher R. Brewer and Robert MacSwain, 37–48, London: Routledge, 2017.

—— *God and Mystery in Words: Experience through Metaphor and Drama*, Oxford: Oxford University Press, 2008.

—— 'Sinai in Art and Architecture', in *The Significance of Sinai: Traditions about Sinai and Divine Revelation in Judaism and Christianity*, edited by George J. Brooke, Hindy Najman, and Loren T. Stuckenbruck, 313–31, Leiden: Brill, 2008.

—— 'Science and Religion in Nineteenth- and Twentieth-Century Landscape Art', in *Reading Genesis After Darwin*, eds, Stephen Barton and David Wilkinson, 111–24, New York: Oxford University Press, 2009.

—— *Divine Humanity: Kenosis Explored and Defended*, London: SCM, 2011; and with an alternate subtitle – *Kenosis and the Construction of Christian Theology* – Waco, TX: Baylor University Press, 2011.

——— 'Human Sacrifice and Two Imaginative Worlds, Aztec and Christian: Finding God in Evil', in *Sacrifice and Modern Thought*, edited by Julia Meszaros and Johannes Zachhuber, 180–96, Oxford: Oxford University Press, 2013.

——— *God in a Single Vision: Integrating Philosophy and Theology*, edited by Christopher R. Brewer and Robert MacSwain, London: Routledge, 2016.

——— 'The Bible and Wider Culture: Animals as a Test Case', in *In the Fullness of Time: Essays on Christology, Creation, and Eschatology in Honor of Richard Bauckham*, edited by Daniel M. Gurtner, Grant Macaskill, and Jonathan T. Pennington, 65–81, Grand Rapids, MI: Eerdmans, 2016.

——— 'Context and Experiencing the Sacred', in *Philosophy and Museums: Essays on the Philosophy of Museums*, Royal Institute of Philosophy Supplement 79, edited by Victoria S. Harrison, Anna Berquist and Gary Kemp, 117–32, Cambridge: Cambridge University Press, 2016.

——— *Divine Generosity and Human Creativity: Theology through Symbol, Painting and Architecture*, edited by Christopher R. Brewer and Robert MacSwain, London: Routledge, 2017.

Brown, David, and Gavin Hopps, *The Extravagance of Music*, New York: Palgrave Macmillan, forthcoming.

Brown, Raymond E., *The Community of the Beloved Disciple*, London: Geoffrey Chapman, 1979.

——— *The Birth of the Messiah*, new updated edition, London: Geoffrey Chapman, 1993.

——— *The Death of the Messiah: From Gethsemane to the Grave*, New York: Doubleday, 1994.

Brown, William P., *Seeing the Psalms: A Theology of Metaphor*, Louisville, KY: Westminster John Knox, 2002.

Brueggemann, Walter, *Theology of the Old Testament: Testimony, Dispute, Advocacy*, Minneapolis, MN: Fortress, 1997.

Bugner, Ladislas, ed., *The Image of the Black in Western Art*, 4 volumes, Cambridge, MA: Harvard University Press, 1976.

Burge, Gary M., *The Anointed Community: The Holy Spirit in the Johannine Tradition*, Grand Rapids, MI: Eerdmans, 1987.

Bynum, Caroline Walker, *Jesus as Mother: Studies in the Spirituality of the High Middle Ages*, Berkeley: University of California Press, 1982.

Callon, Callie, 'Pilate the Villain: An Alternative Reading of Matthew's Portrayal of Pilate', *Biblical Theology Bulletin* 36 (2006), 62–71.

Carruthers, Mary, *The Book of Memory: A Study of Memory in Medieval Culture*, Cambridge: Cambridge University Press, 1990.

Carter, Warren, *Matthew and the Margins*, Maryknoll: Orbis, 2000.

——— *Matthew and Empire: Initial Explorations*, Harrisburg: Trinity, 2001.

Cerulli, E., *Tiberius and Pontius Pilate in Ethiopian Tradition and Poetry*, proceedings of the British Academy LIX, London: Oxford University Press, 1973.

Chagall, Marc, *The Biblical Message of Marc Chagall*, New York: Tudor, 1973.

Charlesworth, James H., *The Old Testament Pseudepigrapha: Expansions of the 'Old Testament' and Legends, Wisdom and Philosophical Literature, Prayers, Psalms and Odes, Fragments of Lost Judeo-Hellenistic Works*, Volume 2, New Haven, CT: Yale University Press, 1983.

Childs, B. S., *Introduction to the Old Testament as Scripture*, Philadelphia, PA: Fortress, 1979.

Choon, Angela, Klaus Kertess, Chris Ofili and Cameron Shaw, *Chris Ofili: Devil's Pie*, New York: Steidl/David Zwirner Gallery, 2008.

BIBLIOGRAPHY

Cixous, Hélène, *Insurrection de la poussiere: Adel Abdessemed*, translated by Eric Prenowitz, Paris: Galilée, 2014.

Clough, W. O., ed., *Gesta Pilati; or the Reports, Letters and Acts of Pontius Pilate*, Indianapolis: Robert Douglass, 1880.

Coleman, Janet, *Ancient and Medieval Memories: Studies in the Reconstruction of the Past*, Cambridge: Cambridge University Press, 1992.

Collins, John J., *The Apocalyptic Imagination: An Introduction to Jewish Apocalyptic Literature*, Grand Rapids, MI: Eerdmans, 1998.

Collins, John J. and George W. E. Nickelsburg, eds, *Ideal Figures in Ancient Judaism: Profiles and Paradigms*, Chico, CA: Scholars Press, 1980.

Constantinou, E. S., ed., *Andrew of Caesarea: Commentary on the Apocalypse*, Fathers of the Church 123, Washington, DC: Catholic University of America Press, 2011.

—— *Guiding to a Blessed End: Andrew of Caesarea and his Apocalypse Commentary in the Ancient Church*, Washington, DC: Catholic University Press of America, 2013.

Cosentino, Donald J., 'Hip-Hop Assemblage: The Chris Ofili Affair', *African Arts* 33, n.1 (2000), 40–51, 95–6.

—— 'Cosentino Replies', *African Arts*, 34, n.1 (2001), 10.

Crook, Nora, 'Mary Shelley, Author of Frankenstein', in *A Companion to the Gothic*, edited by David Punter, 110–22, London: Blackwell, 2000.

Crutchfield, Margo A., *Martin Puryear*, Richmond: Virginia Museum of Fine Arts, 2001.

Cumming, Laura, 'Kader Attia: Continuum of Repair: The Light of Jacob's Ladder – review', *The Guardian*, 15 December 2013, online: www.theguardian.com/artand design/2013/dec/15/kader-attia-jacobs-ladder-review-whitechapel; accessed 2 March 2017.

Dacos, Nicole, *The Loggia of Raphael: A Vatican Art Treasure*, translated by Josephine Bacon, New York: Abbeville, 2008.

Dahl, Nils A., *Jesus in the Memory of the Church*, Minneapolis, MN: Augsburg, 1976.

Davalos, Karen Mary, *Yolanda M. Lopez*, Los Angeles, CA: UCLA Chicano Studies Research Center Press, 2008.

Davies, Philip R., George J. Brooke, and Phillip R. Callaway, eds, *The Complete World of the Dead Sea Scrolls*, London: Thames and Hudson, 2002.

Davies, W. D. and Dale C. Allison, *A Critical and Exegetical Commentary on the Gospel according to Saint Matthew*, Volume 3, Edinburgh: T&T Clark, 1997.

Davison, Carol Margaret, *Gothic Literature 1764–1824*, Cardiff: University of Wales Press, 2009.

de Groote, Marc, *Oecumenii Commentarius in Apocalypsin*, Leuven: Peeters, 1999.

De Vos, Dirk, *Hans Memling: The Complete Works*, London: Thames and Hudson, 1994.

Derrett, J. Duncan M., '"Have Nothing to Do With That Just Man!" (Matt 27, 19), Haggadah and the Account of the Passion', *Downside Review* 97 (1979), 308–15.

Derrida, Jacques, *The Gift of Death*, translated by David Wills, Chicago, IL: University of Chicago, 1995.

Dery, Mark, 'Black to the Future: Interviews with Samuel R. Delaney, Greg Tate, and Tricia Rose', in *Flame Wars: The Discourse of Cyberculture*, edited by Mark Dery, 179–222, Durham, NC: Duke University Press, 1994.

Desmond, William, *Art and the Absolute: A Study of Hegel's Aesthetics*, Albany: State University of New York Press, 1986.

—— *God and the Between*, Oxford: Blackwell, 2008.

Dickinson, Emily, *The Complete Poems of Emily Dickinson*, edited by Thomas Johnson, Boston, MA: Back Bay Books, 1960.

Dillenberger, Jane, *Secular Art with Sacred Themes*, Nashville, TN: Abingdon, 1969.

Dillenberger, John, 'Introduction', in Paul Tillich, *On Art and Architecture*, edited by John Dillenberger and Jane Dillenberger, ix–xxviii, New York: Crossroad, 1987.

Dillon, Sarah, 'Reinscribing De Quincey's Palimpsest: The Significance of the Palimpsest in Contemporary Literary and Cultural Studies', *Textual Practice* 19 (2005), 243–63.

Dodwell, C. R., *The Great Lambeth Bible*, London: Faber and Faber, 1959.

Dodson, Derek S., 'Dreams, the Ancient Novels, and the Gospel of Matthew: An Intertextual Study', *Perspectives in Religious Studies* 29 (2002), 39–52.

—— 'Dream Magic: The Dream of Pilate's Wife and the Accusation of Magic in the Acts of Pilate', in *Gelitten, Gestorben, Auferstanden, Passions- und Ostertraditionen im antiken Christentum*, edited by Tobias Nicklas, Andreas Merkt and Joseph Verheyden, 21–30, Tübingen: Mohr Siebeck, 2010.

Duffy, Eamon, *Faith of our Fathers: Reflections on Catholic Tradition*, London: Continuum: 2004.

Dunn, James D. G., *Jesus Remembered*, Grand Rapids, MI: Eerdmans, 2003.

—— *New Testament Theology: An Introduction*, Nashville, TN: Abingdon, 2009.

Eagleton, Terry, *After Theory*, London: Allen Tate, 2003.

—— *On Evil*, New Haven, CT: Yale University Press, 2008.

—— *Culture and the Death of God*, London: Yale University Press, 2014.

Ehrman, Bart D, *The Orthodox Corruption of Scripture*, New York: Oxford University Press, 1993.

—— *The New Testament: A Historical Introduction*, 6th edition, New York: Oxford University Press, 2016.

Elderfield, John, ed., *Martin Puryear*, New York: Museum of Modern Art, 2007.

Eliade, Mircea, *Shamanism: Archaic Techniques of Ecstasy,* translated by W. R. Trask, London: Routledge & Keagan Paul, 1964.

Elie, Paul, 'Has Fiction Lost its Faith?' *New York Times*, 19 December 2012.

Elkins, James, *On the Strange Place of Religion in Contemporary Art*, London: Routledge, 2004.

Elliott, J. K., ed., *The Apocryphal New Testament*, Oxford: Clarendon, 1993.

Emmerson, Richard K. and Bernard McGinn, eds, *The Book of Revelation in the Middle Ages*, New York: Cornell University Press, 1992.

England, Emma, and William John Lyons, eds, *Reception History and Biblical Studies: Theory and Practice*, London: Bloomsbury, 2015.

Eshun, Kodwo, 'Further Considerations on Afrofuturism', *CR: The New Centennial Review* 3.2 (2003), 287–302.

Farrer, Austin, *The Revelation of St John the Divine*, Oxford: Clarendon Press, 1964.

Fascher, Eric, *Das Weib des Pilatus (Matthäus 27, 19); Die Auferweckung der Heiligen (Matthäus 27, 51–53), Zwei Studien zur Geschichte der Schriftauslegung*, Hallische Monographien 20, Halle: Max Niemeyer, 1951.

Feldman, Yael, *Glory and Agony: Isaac's Sacrifice and National Narrative*, Stanford, CA: Stanford University Press, 2010.

Fentress, J. and C. Wickham., *Social Memory: New Perspectives on the Past*, Oxford: Blackwell, 1992.

Fernie, Ewan, *The Demonic: Literature and Experience*, London, Routledge, 2013.

Fiddes, Paul, *Freedom and Limit: A Dialogue Between Literature and Christian Doctrine*, London: Palgrave, 1991.

Finney, Paul Corby, ed., *The Eerdmans Encyclopedia of Early Christian Art and Archaeology*, Volume 1, Grand Rapids, MI: Eerdmans, 2017.

Fiorenza, Elisabeth Schüssler, *Revelation: Vision of a Just World*, Edinburgh: T&T Clark, 1993.

Firestone, Reuven, *Journeys in Holy Lands: The Evolution of the Abraham-Ishmael Legends in Islamic Exegesis*, Albany, NY: State University of New York Press, 1990.
Fish, Stanley, *Surprised by Sin: The Reader in Paradise Lost*, Cambridge, MA: Harvard University Press, 1998.
Fitzmyer, Joseph A., *The Dead Sea Scrolls and Christian Origins*, Grand Rapids, MI: Eerdmans, 2000.
Foister, Susan, *Art of Light: German Renaissance Stained Glass*, London: The National Gallery, 2007.
Fonzo, Kimberly, 'Procula's Civic Body and Pilate's Masculinity Crisis in the York Cycle's "Christ Before Pilate 1: The Dream of Pilate's Wife"', *Early Theatre* 16 no 2 (2013), 11–32.
Ford, David F. and C. C. Pecknold, eds, *The Promise of Scriptural Reasoning*, Oxford: Blackwell, 2006.
Frank, Mark, *Sermons of Mark Frank*, Oxford, 1849.
Frost, Christine Mangala, *The Human Icon: A Comparative Study of Hindu and Orthodox Christian Beliefs*, Cambridge: James Clarke, 2017.
Frye, Northrop, *The Return of Eden: Five Essays on Milton's Epics*, Toronto: University of Toronto Press, 1965.

Gadamer, Hans-Georg, *Truth and Method*, London: Sheed and Ward, 1979.
Gallagher, Ann, and Molly Donovan, eds, *Rachel Whiteread*, London: Tate, 2017.
Gamble, Harry Y., *Books and Readers in the Early Church: A History of Early Christian Texts*, London: Yale University Press, 1995.
Gamwell, Lynn, ed., *Dreams 1900–2000: Science, Art, and the Unconscious Mind*, Ithaca, NY: Cornell University Press, 2000.
Garcia, Cathy Rose A., 'Walk to the Sky With Jonathan Borofsky', *The Korea Times*, 31 October 2008, Online: www.koreatimes.co.kr/www/news/art/2009/07/148_33617.html; accessed 2 March 2017.
Gaskell, I. 'Sacred to Profane and Back Again', in *Art and its Publics: Museum Studies at the Millennium*, edited by A. McClellan, 149–62, Oxford: Blackwell, 2003.
Gay, Peter, *The Enlightenment, an Interpretation: The Rise of Modern Paganism*, New York: Knopf, 1966.
Geerard, M., *Clavis apocryphorum Novi Testamenti*, CCCA 62, Turnhout: Brepols, 1992.
Gerdts, William H. and Theodore E. Stebbins, Jr., '*A Man of Genius': The Art of Washington Allston (1779–1843)*, Boston, MA: Museum of Fine Arts Boston, 1979.
Gerits, Jan, 'Jacob Panhuysen van Opoeteren, abt van Steinfeld: Een kloosterhervormer, ascetisch schrijver en humanist uit de 16de eeuw', *Tijdschrift Heemkunde Limburg* 2 (2006), 10–14.
Getty-Sullivan, M. A., *Women in the New Testament*, Collegeville, MN: Liturgical, 2001.
Gillman, Florence M., 'The Wife of Pilate (Matthew 27:19)', *Louvain Studies* 17 (1992), 152–65.
Giorgi, Rosa, *Saints in Art*, edited by Stefano Zuffi, translated by Thomas Michael Hartmann, Los Angeles, CA: Getty, 2003.
Gnilka, Joachim, *Das Matthäusevangelium II, Teil F*, Basel: Herder, 1988.
Gnuse, Robert, 'Dream Genre in the Matthean Infancy Narratives', *Novum Testamentum* 32 no 2 (1990), 97–120.
Goetz, Oswald, *The Rembrandt Bible: A Selection from the Master's Graphic Work*, New York: Greystone, 1941.
Goldenberg, David M., *The Curse of Ham: Race and Slavery in Early Judaism, Christianity, and Islam*, Princeton, NJ: Princeton University Press, 2005.
Grassl, Wolfgang, *Culture of Place: An Intellectual Profile of the Premonstratensian Order*, Volume 2, Nordhausen: Verlag Traugott Bautz, 2009.

Greschat, Martin, *Martin Bucer: A Reformer and His Times*, translated by Stephen E. Buckwalter, Louisville, KY: Westminster John Knox, 2004.

Gribbin, Joseph A., *The Premonstratensian Order in Late Medieval England*, Woodbridge: Boydell, 2001.

Gruenwald, Ithamar, *Apocalyptic and Merkavah Mysticism*, Leiden: Brill, 1980.

Grundy, J., ed., *The Poems of Henry Constable*, Liverpool: Liverpool University Press, 1960.

Gundry, Robert H., *Matthew: A Commentary*, 2nd edition, Grand Rapids, MI: Eerdmans, 1994.

Gunn, Giles, *The Interpretation of Otherness: Literature, Religion, and the American Imagination*, Oxford: Oxford University Press, 1979.

Haines-Eitzen, Kim, *Guardians of Letters: Literacy, Power, and the Transmitters of Early Christian Literature*, Oxford: Oxford University Press, 2000.

Halbwachs, M., *On Collective Memory*, edited and translated by Lewis A. Coser, Chicago, IL: University of Chicago Press, 1992.

Hangrätinger, Thomas, and O. Praem, *Der heilige Norbert, Erzbischof und Ordengründer*, Magdeburg: Norbertus Verlag, 2011.

Harrington, Daniel J., *The Gospel of Matthew*, Collegeville, MN: Liturgical, 1992.

Harris, Markham, trans., *The Cornish Ordinalia: A Medieval Dramatic Trilogy*, Washington, DC: Catholic University of America Press, 1969,

Hatch, W. H. P., *Facsimiles and Descriptions of Minuscule Manuscripts of the New Testament*, Cambridge, MA: Harvard University Press, 1951.

Hatfield, Rab, 'Botticelli's *Mystic Nativity*, Savonarola and the Millennium', *Journal of the Warburg and Courtauld Institutes* 58 (1995), 89–114.

Haude, Sigrun, *In the Shadow of "Savage Wolves": Anabaptist Münster and the German Reformation during the 1530's*, Boston, MA: Brill, 2000.

Haynes, Stephen R., *Noah's Curse: The Biblical Justification of American Slavery*, Oxford: Oxford University Press, 2007.

Hays, Richard, 'Reading Scripture in Light of the Resurrection', in *The Art of Reading Scripture*, edited by Ellen F. Davis and Richard B. Hays, 216–238, Grand Rapids, MI: Eerdmans, 2003.

Heartney, Eleanor, *Postmodern Heretics: Catholic Imagination in Contemporary Art*, New York: Midmarch Arts, 2004.

Hengel, Martin, *The Johannine Question*, London: SCM, 1989.

Henry, Avril, *Biblia Pauperum: A Facsimile of the Forty Page Block Book*, Aldershot: Scolar, 1987.

Herbert, Máire, and Martin McNamara, *Irish Biblical Apocrypha: Selected Texts in Translation*, Edinburgh: T&T Clark, 1989.

Hildegard, *Scivias: Hildegard of Bingen*, translated by C. Hart and J. Bishop, Mahwah: Paulist, 1990.

Hoeveler, Diane, *The Gothic Ideology: Religious Hysteria and Anti-Catholicism in British Popular Fiction, 1780–1880*, Cardiff: University of Wales Press, 2015.

Hooker, Morna D., 'Traditions about the Temple in the Sayings of Jesus', *Bulletin of the John Rylands Library* 70 (1988), 7–20.

Hooper, Keith, *Charles Dickens: Faith, Angels, and the Poor*, London: Lion, 2017.

Hopps, Gavin, and Jane Stabler, *Romanticism and Religion from William Cowper to Wallace Stevens*, London: Routledge, 2006.

Houtman, C., 'What Did Jacob See in his Dream at Bethel?', *Vetus Testamentum* 27 (1977), 337–51.

Howard-Brook, Wes, and Anthony Gwyther, *Unveiling Empire: Reading Revelation Then and Now*, New York: Orbis, 1999.

BIBLIOGRAPHY

Hurtado, Larry W., 'Remembering and Revelation: The Historic and Glorified Jesus in the Gospel of John', in *Israel's God and Rebecca's Children: Christology and Community in Early Judaism and Christianity*, edited by David Capes et al., 195–213, Waco, TX: Baylor University Press, 2007.

Hyland, William P., *Jacob Panhausen of Steinfeld: A Loving Exhortation to Prelates and their Subjects & Treatise on Monastic Life and Religious Vows*, Collegeville, MN: Liturgical, 2018.

Hynes, Nancy, 'Africanizing Chris Ofili?', *African Arts* 34 no. 1 (2001), 9–10.

Imfeld, Zoë Lehmann, *The Victorian Ghost Story and Theology: From La Fanu to James*, London: Palgrave Macmillan, 2016.

Izydorczyk, Zbigniew, ed., *The Medieval Gospel of Nicodemus: Texts, Intertexts, and Contexts in Western Europe*, Tempe, AZ: Arizona State University, 1997.

Jackson, Ken, and Arthur Marotti, 'The Turn to Religion in Early Modern Literary Studies', *Criticism* 46 (2004), 167–90.

James, Montague R., *The Apocryphal New Testament*, Oxford: Oxford University Press, 1966.

Janes, Dominic and Gary Waller, eds, *Walsingham in Literature and Culture from the Middle Ages to Modernity*, Farnham: Ashgate, 2010.

Jeffrey, David Lyle, *A Dictionary of Biblical Tradition in English Literature*, Grand Rapids, MI: Eerdmans, 1992.

——— *In the Beauty of Holiness: Art and the Bible in Western Culture*, Grand Rapids, MI: Eerdmans, 2017.

John, James J., 'A Repertoire of Students at the College of Prémontré in Medieval Paris', M.Med.S. thesis, University of Notre Dame, 1951.

Johnson, Ben, *The Complete Poetry of Ben Jonson*, edited by William Hunter, New York: New York University Press, 1963.

Jones, Jonathan, 'Paradise Reclaimed', *The Guardian Weekend*, June 15, 2002, Online: www.theguardian.com/artanddesign/2002/jun/15/artsfeatures; accessed 5 July 2017.

Joslin, Mary Coker, and Carolyn Coker Joslin Watson, *The Egerton Genesis*, Toronto: University of Toronto Press, 2001.

Kafka, Franz, *Parables and Paradoxes*, New York: Schocken, 1974.

Kany, Roland, 'Die Frau des Pilatus und ihr Name: Ein Kapitel aus der Gesehichte neutestamentlicher Wissenschaft', *ZNW* 86 (1995), 104–10.

Karrer, Martin, 'Der Text der Johannesoffenbarung—Varianten und Theologie', *Neotestamentica* 42 no 2 (2009), 373–398.

——— 'The Angels of the Congregations in Revelation—Textual History and Interpretation', *Journal of Early Christian History* 1 no 1 (2011), 57–84.

——— 'Der Text der Johannesapokalypse', in *Die Johannesapokalypse: Kontexte—Konzepte—Rezeption*, edited by J. Frey, J. A. Kelhoffer and F. Tóth, 43–78, Tübingen: Mohr Siebeck, 2012.

——— 'Die neue Edition der Johannesapokalypse: Ein Arbeitsbericht', in *Studien zum Text der Apokalypse*, edited by M. Sigismund, M. Karrer and U. Schmid, 3–14, Berlin: De Gruyter, 2015.

Kasfir, Sidney, 'Assigning Identity: Cosentino's 'Hip-Hop Assemblage: The Chris Ofili Affair', *African Arts* 34 no 1 (2001), 9.

Kauffman, Claus M., *An Altarpiece of the Book of Revelation from Master Bertram's Workshop in Hamburg*, London: Victoria and Albert Museum, 1968.

Kelly, Joseph F, *The Problem of Evil in the Western Tradition: From the Book of Job to Modern Genetics*, Collegeville, MN: Liturgical, 2001.

Kerr, Alan R., *The Temple of Jesus' Body: The Temple Theme in the Gospel of John*, Sheffield: Sheffield Academic Press, 2002.
Kierkegaard, Søren, *Fear and Trembling*, translated by Sylvia Walsh, Cambridge: Cambridge University Press, 2008.
Kilgore, De Witt Douglas, 'Afrofuturism', in *The Oxford Handbook of Science Fiction*, edited by Rob Latham, 561–72, Oxford: Oxford University Press, 2014.
King, David J., 'The Steinfeld Cloister Glazing', *Gesta*, 37 (1998), 201–10.
—— 'New Steinfeld Discoveries: Special Supplement', *Vidimus* 35 (2009), Online: http://vidimus.org/issues/issue-35/features/; accessed 21 December 2017.
Kirk, Alan and Tom Thatcher, eds, *Memory, Tradition, and Text: Uses of the Past in Early Christianity*, Leiden: Brill, 2005.
Kirkfleet, Cornelius James, *History of Saint Norbert, Founder of the Norbertine (Premonstratensian) Order*, St Louis, MO: B. Herder, 1916.
Knibb, Michael A., *The Qumran Community*, Cambridge: Cambridge University Press, 1987.
Knight, Mark, and Emma Mason, *Nineteenth Century Literature and Religion: An Introduction*, Oxford: Oxford University Press, 2006.
Knight, Mark, *An Introduction to Religion and Literature*, London: Continuum, 2009.
Koerner, Joseph, *The Moment of Self-Portraiture in German Renaissance Art*, Chicago, IL: University of Chicago Press, 1993.
Kosky, Jeffery L., *Arts of Wonder: Enchanting Secularity—Walter DeMaria, Diller + Scofidio, James Turrell, Andy Goldsworthy*, Chicago, IL: University of Chicago Press, 2013.
Kovacs, Judith, and Christopher Rowland, *Revelation: The Apocalypse of Jesus Christ*, Oxford: Blackwell, 2004.
Kresten, Otto, 'Der Schreiber und Handschrifthändler Andreas Darmarios', *Mariahilfer Gymnasium, Jahresbericht* (1967), 6–11.
Kugel, James L., *The Ladder of Jacob: Ancient Interpretations of the Biblical Story of Jacob and His Children*, Princeton, NJ: Princeton University Press, 2006.
Kysar, Robert, 'The Whence and Whither of the Johannine Community', in *Life in Abundance: Studies in John's Gospel in Tribute to Raymond E. Brown, S.S*, edited by John R. Donahue, 65–81, Collegeville, MN: Liturgical, 2005.

Lange, Christy, 'In Search of the Real Me: Interview with Chris Ofili', *TATE ETC*, 18 (2010), online: www.tate.org.uk/context-comment/articles/search-real-me; accessed 19 December 2017.
Law, T. M., *When God Spoke Greek: The Septuagint and the Making of the Christian Bible*, Oxford: Oxford University Press, 2013.
Le Gendre, Armelle, in *Illuminations from the Wildenstein Collection*, edited by Bernard Wooding, translated by David Wharry, Paris: Musée Marmottan Monet, 2010.
Lehner, Ulrich L., *The Catholic Enlightenment*, New York: Oxford University Press, 2016.
Leib, Pfarrer, and Dr Schwarz, *Biblia Pauperum nach dem Original in der Lyceumsbiblitek zu Constanz*, Zürich: Leo Würl, 1867.
Lembke, Markus, 'Beobachtungen zu den Handschriften der Apokalypse des Johannes', in *Die Johannesoffenbarung: Ihr Text und ihre Auslegung*, edited by M. Labahn and M. Karrer, 19–69, Leipzig: Evangelische Verlagsanstalt, 2012.
Lembke, Markus, et al., eds, *Text und Textwert der griechischen Handschrifen des Neuen Testaments VI, Die Apokalypse: Teststellenkollation und Auswertungen*, Berlin: De Gruyter, 2017.
Levenson, Jon D., *The Death and Resurrection of the Beloved Son: The Transformation of Child Sacrifice in Judaism and Christianity*, New Haven, CT: Yale University Press, 1993.

BIBLIOGRAPHY

———. *Inheriting Abraham: The Legacy of the Patriarch in Judaism, Christianity, and Islam*, Princeton, NJ: Princeton University Press, 2012.

Levine, Amy Jill and Marianne Blickenstaff, eds, *A Feminist Companion to Matthew*, Sheffield: Sheffield Academic Press, 2001.

Lewis, Matthew, *The Monk*, Oxford: Oxford University Press, 2016.

Lewis, Suzanne, *Reading Images: Narrative Discourse and Reception in the Thirteenth-Century Illuminated Book of Revelation*, Cambridge: Cambridge University Press, 1995.

Lienhardt, Georg, *Exhortator domesticus*, Roggenburg: Augustae Vindelicorum, 1754.

Lincoln, Andrew T., *Truth on Trial: The Lawsuit Motif in the Fourth Gospel*, Peabody, MA: Hendrickson, 2000.

——— *The Gospel According to St John*, London: Continuum, 2005.

Lindblom, Johannes, *Prophecy in Ancient Israel*, Oxford: Basil Blackwell, 1962.

——— *Geschichte und Offenbarungen*, Lund: CWK Gleerup, 1968.

Llewellyn, Sacha, and Paul Liss, eds, *Evelyn Dunbar (1906–1960): The Lost Works*, Chichester: Pallant House Gallery, 2015. Published in conjunction with the exhibition of the same name, shown at Pallant House Gallery, Chichester.

Love, Stuart L., *Jesus and Marginal Women: The Gospel of Matthew in Social-Scientific Perspective*, Cambridge: James Clarke, 2009.

Luz, Ulrich, *Matthew in History: Interpretation, Influence, and Effects*, Minneapolis, MN: Fortress, 1994.

——— *Matthew 21–28*, Hermeneia, Minneapolis, MN: Fortress, 2005.

Lynes, Barbara Buhler, *Georgia O'Keeffe: Catalogue Raisonné*, Volume 2, London: Yale University Press, 1999.

MacCulloch, Diarmaid, *Reformation Europe's House Divided 1490–1700*, London: Penguin, 2004.

——— 'Mary and Sixteenth Century Protestants', in *The Church and Mary*, edited by R. N. Swanson, 191–217, Woodbridge: Boydell, 2004.

MacIntyre, Alasdair, *God, Philosophy, Universities: A History of the Catholic Philosophical Tradition*, London: Continuum, 2009.

Macquarrie, John, Review of David Brown, *Discipleship and Imagination: Christian Tradition and Truth*, The Journal of Theological Studies 52 no 2 (2001): 980–82.

MacSwain, Robert, ed., *Scripture, Metaphysics and Poetry: Austin Farrer's* The Glass of Vision *With Critical Commentary*, Farnham: Ashgate, 2013.

MacSwain, Robert, 'Introduction: Theology, Aesthetics, and Culture', in *Theology, Aesthetics, and Culture: Responses to the Work of David Brown*, edited by Robert MacSwain and Taylor Worley, 1–10, Oxford: Oxford University Press, 2012.

——— *Solved by Sacrifice: Austin Farrer, Fideism, and the Evidence of Faith*, Leuven: Peeters, 2013.

MacSwain, Robert, and Taylor Worley, eds, *Theology, Aesthetics, and Culture: Responses to the Work of David Brown*, Oxford: Oxford University Press, 2012.

Marcus, Amy Dockser, *Rewriting the Bible: How Archaeology is Reshaping History*, London: Little, Brown and Company, 2000.

Marsh, Ann, 'From Cloister to Museum', *Conservation Journal* 57 (2009), online: www.vam.ac.uk/content/journals/conservation-journal/issue-57/from-cloister-to-museum/; accessed 18 May 2018.

Marsh-Edwards, J. C., 'The Magi in Tradition and Art', *Irish Ecclesiastical Record* series 5 (1956), 1–9.

Marshall, Peter, *Beliefs and the Dead in Reformation England*, Oxford: Oxford University Press, 2002.

Marta, Karen, and Massimiliano Gioni, eds., *Chris Ofili: 2000 Words*, New York: Artbook | D.A.P., 2015.

Martyn, J. Louis, *History and Theology in the Fourth Gospel*, Nashville, TN: Abingdon, 1979.
Mason, Wyatt, 'Kerry James Marshall Is Shifting the Color of Art History', *The New York Times Style Magazine*, 17 October 2016. Online: www.nytimes.com/2016/10/17/t-magazine/kerry-james-marshall-artist.html?_r=1; accessed 31 March 2017.
Massing, Jean Michel, 'Dürer's Dreams', *Journal of the Warburg and Courtauld Institutes* 49 (1986), 238-44.
McClure, John, *Partial Faiths: Postsecular Fiction in the Age of Pynchon and Morrison*, Atlanta, GA: University of Georgia Press, 2007.
Meier, Johannes, 'Die Nordwestdeutschen Prämonstratenser angesichts von Verfall und Reform des Ordens 1350-1550', *Analecta Praemonstratensia* 79 (2003), 25-56.
Mendels, Doron, *Memory in Jewish, Pagan and Christian Societies of the Graeco-Roman World*, London: T&T Clark, 2004.
Merian, Matthäus, *Iconum Biblicarum*, Wenatchee, WA: AVB, 1981.
Michaud, Philippe-Alain, 'Funambule', *Adel Abdessemed*, translated by Deke Dusinberre, Paris: Manuella Editions, 2016.
Miller, Alice, *The Untouched Key: Tracing Childhood Trauma in Creativity and Destructiveness*, translated by Hildegarde Hunter Hannum, New York: Doubleday, 1991.
Milton, John, *Paradise Lost*, edited by Gordon Teskey, London: Norton Critical Editions, 2005.
Mink, Gerd, 'Eine umfassende Genealogie der neutestamentlichen Überlieferung', *New Testament Studies* 39 (1993), 481-99.
—— 'Contamination, Coherence, and Coincidence in Textual Transmission: The Coherence-Based Genealogical Method (CBGM) as a Complement and Corrective to Existing Approaches', in *The Textual History of the Greek New Testament: Changing Views in Contemporary Research*, edited by K. Wachtel and M. W. Holmes, 141-216, Atlanta, GA: SBL, 2011.
Molesworth, Helen, ed., *Kerry James Marshall: Mastry*, New York: Skira Rizzoli, 2016.
Morgan, Stuart, 'The Elephant Man', *Frieze* 15 (1994), 40-3.
Morrey-Jones, C. R. A., 'Paradise Revisited: The Jewish Mystical Background of Paul's Apostolate', *Harvard Theological Review* 86 (1993), 177-217, 265-92.
Müller, M., *The First Bible of the Church: A Plea for the Septuagint*, Sheffield: Sheffield Academic Press, 1996.
Murray, Peter, Linda Murray, and Tom Devonshire Jones, eds, *The Oxford Dictionary of Christian Art and Architecture*, 2nd edition, Oxford: Oxford University Press, 2013.
Myers, Terry R., 'Chris Ofili: Power Man', *Art/Text* 58 (1997), 36-9.
Myrone, Martin, *The Blake Book*, London: Tate, 2007.

Neuss, Wilhelm, ed., *Die Glasmalereien aus dem Steinfelder Kreuzgang*, M. Gladbach: B. Kühlen, 1955.
Nolan, Barbara, *The Gothic Visionary Perspective*, Princeton, NJ: Princeton University Press, 1977.
Nolland, John, *The Gospel of Matthew*, NIGTC, Grand Rapids, MI: Eerdmans, 2005.

O'Carroll, Michael, *Theotokos: A Theological Encyclopedia of the Blessed Virgin Mary*, Dublin: Dominican Publications, 1982.
O'Connor, Flannery, 'Revelation', in *The Complete Stories*, New York: Farrar, Straus and Giroux, 1971.
O'Gorman, Richard, 'The *Gospel of Nicodemus* in the Vernacular Literature of Medieval France', in *The Medieval Gospel of Nicodemus: Texts, Intertexts, and Contexts*

in Western Europe, edited by Zbigniew Izydorczyk, 103-32, Tempe, AZ: Arizona State University, 1997.

O'Hear, Natasha F. H., *Contrasting Images of the Book of Revelation in Late Medieval and Early Modern Art*, Oxford: Oxford University Press, 2011.

O'Hear, Natasha, and Anthony O'Hear, *Picturing the Apocalypse: The Book of Revelation in the Arts over Two Millennia*, Oxford: Oxford University Press, 2015.

Oates, Joyce Carol, 'Frankenstein's Fallen Angel', *Critical Inquiry* 10 (1984), 543-54.

Oberhuber, Konrad, *Raphael: The Paintings*, Munich, London and New York: Prestel Verlag, 1999.

Ofili, Chris, et al., *Chris Ofili*, New York: Rizzoli, 2009.

Oliver, Gordon, *Holy Bible, Human Bible: Questions Pastoral Practice Must Ask*, Grand Rapids, MI: Eerdmans, 2006.

Owen, Wilfred, *The Collected Poems of Wilfred Owen*, New York: New Directions, 1965.

Panofsky, Erwin, *The Life and Art of Albrecht Dürer*, Princeton, NJ: Princeton University Press, 1955.

Parker, David C., 'Scripture is Tradition', *Theology* XCIV (1991), 11-17.

———— *Codex Bezae: An Early Christian Manuscript and its Text*, Cambridge: Cambridge University Press, 1992.

———— *The Living Text of the Gospels*, Cambridge: Cambridge University Press, 1997.

———— 'Textual Criticism and Theology', *Expository Times* 118 no 12 (2007), 583-89.

———— *New Testament Manuscripts and their Texts*, Cambridge: Cambridge University Press, 2008.

———— *Textual Scholarship and the Making of the New Testament*, Oxford: Oxford University Press, 2012.

Parris, David P., *Reception Theory and Biblical Hermeneutics*, Eugene, OR: Pickwick, 2009.

Partsch, Susanna, *Rembrandt*, London: Weidenfeld and Nicolson, 1991.

Pearson, Sara L., 'Charlotte Brontë's Poetics: A Study of 'Pilate's Wife's Dream'', *Brontë Studies* 37 no 3 (2012), 194-207.

Peleg, Yitzhak (Itzik), 'What Do Jacob's Ladder, the Tower of Babel, and the Babylonian Ziggurat Have in Common?', in *Bethsaida in Archaeology, History and Ancient Culture: A Festschrift in Honor of John T. Greene*, edited by J. Harold Ellens, 330-59, Newcastle upon Tyne: Cambridge Scholars, 2014.

———— *Going Up and Going Down: A Key to Interpreting Jacob's Dream (Genesis 28:10-22)*, translated by Betty Rozen, London: Bloomsbury, 2015.

Pennington, Richard, *A Descriptive Catalogue of the Etched Work of Wenceslaus Hollar 1607-1677*, Cambridge: Cambridge University Press, 1982.

Peppard, Michael, *The World's Oldest Church: Bible, Art, and Ritual at Dura-Europos, Syria*, New Haven, CT: Yale University Press, 2016.

Peters, Christine, *Patterns of Piety: Women, Gender and Religion in Late Medieval and Reformation England*, Cambridge: Cambridge University Press, 2003.

Petit, Francois, *The Spirituality of the Premonstratensians: The Twelfth and Thirteenth Centuries*, translated by Victor Szczurek, Collegeville, MN: Liturgical, 2011.

Phillippy, Patricia, *Women, Death and Literature in Post-Reformation England*, Cambridge: Cambridge University Press, 2002.

Pickthall, Marmaduke, trans., *The Glorious Koran*, London: Everyman's Library, 1992.

Pon, Lisa, *Raphael, Dürer and Marcantonio Raimondi: Copying and the Italian Renaissance Print*, London: Yale University Press, 2004.

Porter, Roy, *The Greatest Benefit to Mankind: A Medical History from Antiquity to the Present*, London: Harper Collins, 1997.

Posset, Franz, *Renaissance Monks: Monastic Humanism in Six Biographical Sketches*, Leiden: Brill, 2005.
Powell, Mark A., 'The Magi as Kings: An Adventure in Reader-Response Criticism', *Catholic Biblical Quarterly* 46 (2000), 1–20.
Prichard, J. B., ed., *Ancient Near Eastern Texts Relating to the Old Testament*, 3rd edition, Princeton, NJ: Princeton University Press, 1969.
Provan, Iain, *Discovering Genesis: Content, Interpretation, Reception*, Grand Rapids, MI: Eerdmans, 2016.
Punter, David, *The Literature of Terror*, 2 volumes, London: Routledge, 1996.

Quash, Ben, *Found Theology: History, Imagination and the Holy Spirit*, London: T&T Clark, 2013.

Rist, Thomas, 'Mary of Recusants and Reform: Literary Memory and Defloration', in *Biblical Women in Early Modern Literary Culture, 1550–1700*, edited by Victoria Brownlee and Laura Gallagher, 163–179, Manchester: Manchester University Press, 2015.
Robinson, Marilynne, *The Death of Adam: Essays on Modern Thought*, New York: Picador, 1998.
―――― *Absence of Mind: The Dispelling of Inwardness from the Modern Myth of the Self*, New Haven, CT: Yale University Press, 2010.
―――― *When I was a Child I Read Books: Essays*, London: Virago, 2012.
―――― *The Givenness of Things: Essays*, New York: Picador, 2015.
Rookmaaker, H. R., *Modern Art and the Death of a Culture*, Downers Grove, IL: IVP, 1970.
Root, Howard E., *Theological Radicalism and Tradition: 'The Limits of Radicalism' with Appendices*, edited by Christopher R. Brewer, London: Routledge, 2018.
Rosen, Aaron, *Imagining Jewish Art: Encounters with the Masters in Chagall, Guston, and Kitaj*, Studies in Comparative Literature 16, Oxford: Legenda, 2009.
―――― 'Re-visions of Sacrifice: Abraham in Art and Interfaith Dialogue', *Jewish Quarterly* 61 no 2 (2014), 10–15.
―――― *Art and Religion in the 21st Century*, London: Thames & Hudson, 2015.
―――― 'The Sacrifices of Adel Abdessemed', in *Adel Abdessemed: Bristow*, edited by Hans Ulrich Obrist, Hannah Barry, and Donatien Grau, 134–47, London: Bold Tendencies, 2017.
Rose, Barbara, *Frankenthaler*, New York: Harry N. Abrams, 1970.
Ross, Leslie, in *Medieval Art: A Topical Dictionary*, London: Greenwood, 1996.
Rowe, Nomi, ed., *In Celebration of Cecil Collins: Visionary Artist and Educator*, London: Tate, 2009.
Rowland, Christopher, *The Open Heaven: A Study of Apocalyptic in Judaism and Early Christianity*, New York: Crossroad, 1982.
―――― *Revelation*, London: Epworth, 1993.
―――― *'Wheels within Wheels': William Blake and the Ezekiel's Merkabah in Text and Image*, Milwaukee, WI: Marquette University Press, 2007.
―――― *Blake and the Bible*, London: Yale University Press, 2010.
Rowland, Christopher, and Christopher R. A. Morray-Jones, *The Mystery of God: Early Jewish Mysticism and the New Testament*, Leiden: Brill, 2009.
Rubin, Miri, *Mother of God: A History of the Virgin Mary*, London: Allen Lane, 2009.

Sage, Victor, *Horror Fiction in the Protestant Tradition*, London: St. Martin's Press, 1988.
Saltz, Jerry, 'The Painting that Jerry Saltz Can't Stop Thinking About', *Vulture* 3 November 2016, online: www.vulture.com/2016/11/kerry-james-marshall-mastry.html; accessed 7 July 2017.

BIBLIOGRAPHY

Sanders, E. P., *Judaism: Practice and Belief 63BCE–66CE*, London: SCM, 1992.

Sartre, Jean-Paul, *Nausea*, 1938; New York: New Directions, 1969.

——— *Being and Nothingness*, London: Methuen, 1958.

Schama, Simon, *Rembrandt's Eyes*, London: Allen Lane, 1999.

Scheidgen, A., *Die Gestalt des Pontius Pilatus in Legende, Bibelauslegung und Geschichtsdichtung vom Mittelalter bis in die frühe Neuzeit: Literaturgeschichte einer umstrittenen Figur*, Frankfurt am Main: Lang, 2002.

Schiffman, Lawrence H., *Reclaiming the Dead Sea Scrolls*, New York: Doubleday, 1994.

Schmidt, Gerhard, *Die Armenbibeln des XIV: Jahrhunderts*, Graz: H. Bohlaus nachf. 1959.

Schmidt, J. Heinrich, *Steinfeld: Die Ehemalige Prämonstratenser Abtei*, Ratingen: Aloys Henn Verlag, 1951.

Schnackenburg, Rudolf, *The Gospel of Matthew*, Grand Rapids, MI: Eerdmans, 2002.

Schneemelcher, Wilhelm, *New Testament Apocrypha, Volume One: Gospels and Related Writings*, translated by R. McL. Wilson, revised edition, Louisville, KY: WJK, 1991.

Schapiro, Meyer, *Late Antique, Early Christian and Mediaeval Art: Selected Papers*, New York: George Braziller, 1979.

Schmid, J., *Studien zur Geschichte des griechischen Apokalypse-Textes*, 3 volumes, Munich: Karl Zink, 1955.

Schwartz, Regina, *Remembering and Repeating: Biblical Creation In Paradise Lost*, Cambridge: Cambridge University Press, 1988.

Seerveld, Calvin, *Bearing Fresh Olives Leaves*, Carlisle: Piquant, 2000.

Senior, Donald P., *The Passion Narrative According to Matthew*, Leuven: Leuven University Press, 1975.

Shackelford, George T. M., *Paul Gauguin: Where Do We Come From? What Are We? Where Are We Going?* Boston, MA: MFA Publications, 2013.

Shelley, Mary, *Frankenstein*, London: Penguin Classics, 2012.

Sievers, Ann H., with Linda Meuhlig, and Nancy Rich, *Master Drawings from the Smith College Museum of Art*, New York: Hudson Hills, 2000.

Sigismund, Marcus, 'Die neue Edition der Johannesapokalypse: Stand der Arbeiten', in *Studien zum Text der Apokalypse II*, edited by M. Sigismund and D. Müller, 3–15. Berlin: De Gruyter, 2017.

Siker, Jeffrey, *Disinheriting the Jews: Abraham in Early Christian Controversy*, Louisville, KY: WJK, 1991.

Simonetti, Manilo, ed., *Matthew 14–28*, Ancient Christian Commentary on Scripture: New Testament 1b, Downers Grove, IL: IVP, 2002.

Smets, Irène, *The Memling Museum: St. John's Hospital Bruges*, Bruges: Ludion Guides, 2001.

Smith, Raoul N., 'The Ladder of Divine Ascent–A Codex and an Icon', online: www.museumofrussianicons.org/wp-content/uploads/2016/09/LadderOfDivineAscent FINAL2013Opt.pdf; accessed 28 June 2017.

Smith, Terry, *What is Contemporary Art?* Chicago, IL: University of Chicago Press, 2009.

Smith, Zadie, *Changing My Mind: Occasional Essays*, New York: Penguin Press, 2010.

Sommer, Benjamin D., *Revelation and Authority: Sinai in Jewish Scripture and Tradition*, New Haven, CT: Yale University Press, 2015.

Sorkin, David, *The Religious Enlightenment*, Princeton, NJ: Princeton University Press, 2008.

Soskice, David, 'Foreword', *Crossing Paths: Interdisciplinary Institutions, Careers, Education and Applications*, London: The British Academy, 2016, online: www.britac.ac.uk/sites/default/files/Crossing%20Paths%20-%20Full%20Report.pdf; accessed 30 April 2017.

Sparks, Kenton L., *Ancient Texts for the Study of the Hebrew Bible: A Guide to the Background Literature*, Peabody, MA: Hendrickson, 2005.
Spiegel, Shalom, *The Last Trial: On the Legends and Lore of the Command to Abraham to Offer Isaac as a Sacrifice*, translated by Judah Goldin, Woodstock, VT: Jewish Lights Publishing, 2007.
Stamberg, Susan, 'Kerry James Marshall: A Black Presence in the Art World is "Not Negotiable"', *NPR: Morning Edition,* 28 March, 2017, online: www.npr.org/2017/03/28/521683667/kerry-james-marshall-a-black-presence-in-the-art-world-is-not-negotiable; accessed 10 August 2017.
Steiner, George, *Real Presences*, Chicago, IL: University of Chicago Press, 1989.
Stewart, David James, 'The Fulfillment of a Polanyian Vision of Heuristic Theology: David Brown's Reframing of Revelation, Tradition, and Imagination', *Tradition & Discovery: The Polanyi Society Periodical* 41 no 3 (2015), 4–19.
Steward, Stanley, *The Enclosed Garden: The Tradition and the Image in Seventeenth-Century Poetry*, Madison, WI: University of Wisconsin Press, 1966.
Stock, Augustine, *The Method and Message of Matthew*, Collegeville, MN: Michael Glazier, 1994.
Strutwolf, H. et al., eds, *Novum Testamentum Graecum: Editio Critica Maior III The Acts of the Apostles*, Stuttgart: Deutsche Bibelgesellschaft, 2017.
Stuhlmacher, Peter, 'Spiritual Remembering: John 14:26', in *The Holy Spirit and Christian Origins*, edited by Graham N. Stanton, et al., 55–68, Grand Rapids, MI: Eerdmans, 2004.
Stump, Eleonore, 'Modern Biblical Scholarship, Philosophy of Religion, and Traditional Christianity', *Aletheia* 1 (1985), 75–80.
——— 'Visits to the Sepulcher and Biblical Exegesis', *Faith and Philosophy* 6 (1989), 353–77.
——— 'Biblical Commentary and Philosophy', in *The Cambridge Companion to Aquinas*, edited by Norman Kretzmann and Eleonore Stump, 252–68, Cambridge: Cambridge University Press, 1993.
——— 'Aquinas on the Sufferings of Job', in *Reasoned Faith: Essays in Philosophical Theology in Honor of Norman Kretzmann*, edited by Eleonore Stump, 328–57, Ithaca: Cornell University Press, 1993.
——— 'Revelation and Biblical Exegesis: Augustine, Aquinas, and Swinburne', in *Reason and the Christian Religion: Essays in Honour of Richard Swinburne*, edited by Alan G. Padgett, 161–97, Oxford: Clarendon Press, 1994.
——— *Wandering in Darkness: Narrative and the Problem of Suffering*, Oxford: Oxford University Press, 2010.
——— 'The Problem of Evil and the History of Peoples', in *Divine Evil? The Moral Character of the God of Abraham*, edited by Michael Bergmann, Michael J. Murray and Michael C. Rea, 179–97, New York: Oxford University Press, 2011.
Stump, Eleonore and Thomas P. Flint, eds, *Hermes and Athena: Biblical Exegesis and Philosophical Theology*, Notre Dame, IN: University of Notre Dame Press, 1993.
Subash, William J., *The Dreams of Matthew 1:18–2:23 Tradition, Form, and Theological Investigation*, New York: Lang, 2012.
Swärdh, Anna, *Rape and Religion in English Renaissance Literature: A Topical Study of Four Texts by Shakespeare, Drayton and Middleton*, Uppsala: University of Uppsala Press, 2003.

Taylor, Charles, *A Secular Age*, London: Belknap, 2007.
Thatcher, Tom, ed., *Memory and Identity in Ancient Judaism and Early Christianity: A Conversation with Barry Schwartz*, Atlanta, GA: SBL, 2014.
Thompson, Thomas L., *The Bible in History: How Writers Create a Past*, London: Jonathan Cape, 1999.

BIBLIOGRAPHY

Tomalin, Claire, *Thomas Hardy: The Time-Worn Man*, London: Viking, 2006.
Tradigo, Alfredo, *Icons and Saints of the Eastern Orthodox Church*, translated by Stephen Sartorelli, Los Angeles, CA: Getty, 2006.
Trilling, Wolfgang, *Das Wahre Israel: Studien zur Theologie des Matthäusevangeliums*, Leipzig: St Benno-Verlag, 1959.
Tronzo, William, *The Via Latina Catacomb: Imitation and Discontinuity in Fourth-Century Roman Painting*, London: Pennsylvania State University Press, 1986.
Tzamalikos, P., *An Ancient Commentary on the Book of Revelation: A Critical Edition of the Scholia in Apocalypsin*, Cambridge: Cambridge University Press, 2013.

Ulrich, Eugene, *The Dead Sea Scrolls and the Origins of the Bible*, Grand Rapids, MI: Eerdmans, 1999.

Valvekens, Jean-Baptiste, 'Abbatis I. Panhausen Commentaria', *Analecta Praemonstratensia* 54 (1978), 144–65.
Vance, Norman, *Bible and Novel: Narrative Authority and the Death of God*, Oxford: Oxford University Press, 2013.
van der Bergh, Ronald H., 'The Reception of Matthew 27:19b (Pilate's Wife's Dream) in the Early Church', *Journal of Early Christian History* 2 no 1 (2012), 70–85.
van der Meer, Frits, *Book of Revelation: Visions from the Book of Revelation in Western Art*, London: Thames and Hudson, 1978.
VanderKam, James C., *The Dead Sea Scrolls Today*, London: SPCK, 1994.
Vasari, Giorgio, *The Lives of Artists*, translated by Julia Conaway Bondanella, Oxford: Oxford University Press, 1991.
Visser, Derk, *Apocalypse as Utopian Expectation (800–1500): The Apocalypse Commentary of Berengaudus of Ferrières and the Relationship between Exegesis, Liturgy, and Iconography*, Leiden: Brill, 1996.
Voaden, Rosalyn, *God's Words, Women's Voices: The Discernment of Spirits in the Writing of Late-Medieval Women Visionaries*, York: York Medieval Press 1999.
von le Fort, Gertrude, *The Wife of Pilate and Other Stories*, translated by M. J. Miller, San Francisco, CA: Ignatius, 2015.
von Tischendorf, Constantin, ed., *Evangelia Apocrypha*, Hildesheim: Georg Olms, 1966.

Wachtel, Klaus, 'The Coherence-Based Genealogical Method: A New Way to Reconstruct the Text of the Greek New Testament', in *Editing the Bible: Assessing the Task Past and Present*, edited by J. S. Kloppenborg and J. H. Newman, 123–38, Atlanta: SBL, 2012.
Wallace, David Foster, *Girl With Curious Hair*, New York: W. W. Norton & Company, 1989.
—— 'Quo Vadis', *Review of Contemporary Fiction* 16 no1 (1996), 7–8.
—— *Consider the Lobster*, New York: Back Bay Books, 2006.
—— *Both Flesh and Not*, Boston, MA: Little, Brown and Company, 2012.
Walsham, Alexandra, *Church Papists: Catholicism, Conformity and Confessional Polemic in Early Modern England*, Woodbridge: Boydell, 1999.
Waltke, Bruce K., *Genesis: A Commentary*, Grand Rapids, MI: Zondervan, 2001.
Wasserman, Tommy and Peter J. Gurry, *A New Approach to Textual Criticism: An Introduction to the Coherence-Based Genealogical Method*, Atlanta, GA: SBL, 2017.
Watt, Ian, *The Rise of the Novel*, London: Hogarth Press, 1987.
Weaver, Dorothy Jean, '"Thus You Will Know Them By Their Fruits": The Roman Characters of the Gospel of Matthew', in *The Gospel of Matthew in its Roman Imperial Context*, edited by John Riches and David C. Sim, 102–27, New York: T&T Clark, 2005.

—— '"Wherever This Good News Is Proclaimed": Women and God in the Gospel of Matthew', *Interpretation* 64 no 4 (2010), 390–401.

Wedderburn, Alexander J. M., 'Jesus' Action in the Temple: A Key or a Puzzle?', *ZNW* 97 (2006), 1–22.

Weitzmann, Kurt, and Herbert L. Kessler, *The Frescoes of the Dura Synagogue and Christian Art*, Washington, DC: Dumbarton Oaks Research Library and Collection, 1990.

Westcott, B. F., and F. J. A. Hart, eds, *The New Testament in the Original Greek*, 2 volumes, London: Macmillan, 1881.

Westermann, Claus, *Genesis 12–36: A Commentary*, translated by John J. Scullion S.J, London: SPCK, 1985.

Whitford, David M., *The Curse of Ham in the Early Modern Era: The Bible and the Justifications for Slavery*, London: Routledge, 2016.

Williams, Catrin H., 'Unveiling Revelation: The Spirit-Paraclete and Apocalyptic Disclosure in the Gospel of John', in *John's Gospel and Intimations of Apocalyptic*, edited by Catrin H. Williams and Christopher Rowland, 104–27, London: Bloomsbury, 2013.

Williams, Rowan, *Teresa of Avila*, London: Continuum, 2003.

—— *Dostoevsky: Language, Faith, and Fiction*, London: Continuum, 2011.

Williamson, Paul, *Medieval and Renaissance Stained Glass in the Victoria and Albert Museum*, London: V&A Publications, 2003.

Wolfe, Gregory, 'Whispers of Faith in a Postmodern World', *Wall Street Journal*, 10 January 2013.

Womack, Catherine, 'Kerry James Marshall Brings Blackness to the White Walls of a White Space', *LA Weekly*, 21 March 2017, online: www.laweekly.com/arts/kerry-james-marshalls-moca-retrospective-mastry-brings-blackness-to-a-traditionally-white-space-8045004; accessed 1 June 2017.

Wood, James, *The Broken Estate: Essays on Literature and Belief*, New York: Picador Press, 1999.

Wooding, Lucy, 'Remembrance in the Eucharist', in *The Arts of Remembrance in Early Modern England: Memorial Cultures of the Post Reformation*, edited by Andrew Gordon and Thomas Rist, 19–36, Burlington, VT: Ashgate, 2013.

Woods, Susanne, ed., *The Poems of Aemilia Lanyer: Salve Deus Rex Judaeorum*, New York: Oxford University Press, 1993.

Worsdale, Godfrey, ed., *Chris Ofili*, London: Serpentine Gallery, 1998.

Young, Frances, *Biblical Exegesis and the Formation of Christian Culture*, Cambridge: Cambridge University Press, 1997.

Zanger, Anat, 'Hole in the Moon or Zionism and the Binding (Ha-Ak'eda) Myth in Israeli Cinema', *Shofar: An Interdisciplinary Journal of Jewish Studies* 22 no 1 (2003), 95–109.

Index of Scripture References

Genesis	
1–11	74
2.7	17
2.9	78
3.11	73
21	94
22	58, Ch. 6 passim
28.10–17	Ch. 7 passim
29.15–28	237–9

Exodus	
19.16–19	10

Deuteronomy	
21.1–9	25
34.10	243

Job	
1.6–12	95
23	184

Psalms	
22	247
69.9	42, 44

Isaiah	
35.4	45
56.7	42

Jeremiah	
7.11	42

Zechariah	
9.9	45
14.20–21	42

4 Maccabees	
13.12	95

Matthew	
1–2	17
1.1–6	126
1.6	21
1.12b–3.22	126
1.19	19
1.20	19, 21, 28
1.20–21	28
1.24	21
2.1–12	17, 23
2.12	19, 28
2.13	19, 28
2.19	19, 28
2.20	28
2.22	28
3.15	19
5.6	19
8.5–13	19, 23
8.11	18, 32
8.14	246
8.31	20
10.5	20
10.16	20
10.16–23	20
10.40	20
11.10	20
13.41	20
14.3	21
14.22–33	245
15.21–28	19, 23
15.24	20
16.18	246
16.19	245
16.21	20
17.7–18	126
17.12	20
18.25	21
20.2	20
21.1	20
21.5	45
21.10–17	40
21.34	20
21.36	20
21.37	20
22.3	20
22.4	20
22.6–21	126
22.24	21
22.25	21
22.28	21
23.34	20
23.34–35	20
23.37	20
24.9–22	20
24.31	20
26.28	30
27	25, 27–8
27.19	18–20, 31
27.20	19
27.24	19

Mark	
8.31–38	245–7
10.17–18	43
11.15–19	40
11.17	42
13	127
14.58	42–3
15.29	43
15.30	42
15.34	247

Luke	
7	63
19.45–48	40
23.40–43	21
23.46	247

John	
1.14	41

1.34	41	**Acts**		11.1–2	126
1.43–51	234–6	9.3	127	11.7	135
1.49	41	16.9	127	12	11, 124, 129, 136–7
1.51	41	18.9	127		
2	44–5, 47	22.18	127	12–13	134
2.1–11	41	27.23	127	12.1	156
2.11	42			12.3	11
2.12	42	**1 Corinthians**		12.3–4	11
2.13–17	42	8 243		12.9	11
2.13–22	40, 45	12	47	12.17	133
2.13a	41	14	47	13	124, 128–9
2.16b	42	15.37	247	13.1	11, 129
2.17	42, 44			13.11	11
2.18–22	42–3	**Galatians**		16.17	10
2.19	43–4	3.28	54	16.17–21	10
2.21	42, 44			16.18	10
2.22	42, 44, 46	**2 Timothy**		17	124, 134
2.23a	41	4.21	22	17–18	133
2.23b	41			17–22	130
3.1–12	43	**Hebrews**		17.1–3	11
7.37–39	45	11.19	58	17.1–8	126
9	46			17.3	11
11.12	63	**James**		19	128, 133
11.35	246	2.21–2	96	19.11	133
12.12–19	45			20	131, 136
12.16	45	**Revelation**		20–22	133
14.1	46	1–16	134	20.1–2	130
14.8	46	1.1–12	128	20.1–3	133
14.16	45	1.9–20	126	20.3	133
14.16–17	41	1.10–11	47	21.5	126
14.25–26	46	2–3	124	21.9–10	126
14.26	41, 45	2.12–17	240–4	22.2	79
16.7–11	47	4–5	126	22.8–9	126
16.12–15	47	6.7–8	128		
16.13	17	10	126, 129, 132		
19.30	17, 247				
20.22	17	11	123		

268

Index of Names and Subjects

Abdessemed, Adel 101-2
Abraham xvi, 18, 32, 39, 53, 55, 57, 58-9, 61, 63, Ch. 6 *passim*, 111, 219-20
Accuser *see* Satan
Acts of Pilate 21-4, 29, 31
Adam 21, 73, 74, 80, 86, 156, 179, 181, 183-8, 218
Afrofuturism 74-6, 80-2, 86
After Theory 202
Ahrweiler, Johann von 148, 156
Akedah 12, 58, 93, 95, 100
Aland, Kurt 4
Allston, Washington 111
Ambrose of Milan 27, 29
Amichai, Yehuda 99
Andreas Darmarios 11
Andrew of Caesarea 5, 9-11
Andrewes, Bishop Lancelot 221
Angers Apocalypse Tapestry 124-5, 132
Aquinas, Thomas 60-1
Arethas 9
art
  installation Ch. 7 *passim*; Celtic 215; Hindu 215; Islamic 102; modern Ch. 6 *passim*; contemporary 73-121, 217-20; sculpture Ch. 7 *passim*; stained glass Ch. 9 *passim*, visual 38, Ch. 5 *passim*, Ch. 8 *passim*
atonement 95-6
Attavante 112
Attia, Kader 113, 115-16
Auerbach, Erich 97
Augustine 23-4, 30, 32, 96, 146, 149, 150-3, 238, 246
Aune, David 125-6
Ausgangstext 8

authorial intent, intention 2, 8-9, 54

Bach, John Sebastian 242
Bacon, Francis 218
Barabbas 19
Barr, James ix-x
Barth, John 200, 203
Barth, Karl 242
Baskind, Samantha 114
Bath Abbey 111
Bauckham, Richard 131, 211
Beattie, Tina 171
Berger, Peter 116
Bible
  correction/critique of 74, 75, 207-214; fallibility of x-xii, 51; interpretation of Ch. 4 *passim*
Biblia Pauperum see Paupers' Bible
Blake, William 60, 61, 64, 111, 123, 126, 134-6, 138, 140
Boeve, Lieven xiii
Bol, Ferdinand 111
Bonaventure 147
Book of Adam and Eve 21
Borofsky, Jonathan 113-15
Borysewicz, Alfonse 108
Botticelli, Sandro 124, 133-4, 138
Brewer, Christopher R. 51, 122, 214-15, 218
Bridget of Sweden 126
Brinson, Katherine 83-4
Brontë, Charlotte 27, 31
Brunelleschi, Filippo 98, 219
Bruno of Segni 29
Burgess, Anthony 222
Butts, Thomas 136

Cain, the mark of 73, 74, 86
Callon, Callie 25

Calpurnia 19, 24
Calvin, John 29, 60, 170
Calvinism 224–5
Calvinists 218
canon, canonical xi–xii, xiv, 7, 8, 17, 38, 54, 58, 60, 65, 79, 86, 155, 207–9, 220–1
  art historical 76; textual 178, 183, 191
Caravaggio 98, 101
Carracci, Ludovico 111
Chagall, Marc 98–9, 100, 111, 218
Christian of Stavelot 29
Chronicle of Pseudo-Dexter 22
Cigoli, Ludovico 111
Cione, Nardo di 112
Climacus, John 113
Coherence-Based Genealogical Method 5–6
Colenso, Bishop 209
Coleridge, Samuel Taylor 178
Collins, Cecil 126
commentary 9–11, 127, 134
Constable, Henry 164, 167–9, 172, 220
Corrin, Lisa 81
Cranach, Lucas (Elder) 123, 135, 138, 216
Crashaw, Richard 203
criteria xi–xii
critical edition Ch. 1 *passim*
Crutchfield, Margo A. 114

David (King) 155
DeMille, Cecil B. 22
Derrida, Jacques 100, 201
Dery, Mark 74
Desmond, William xiii
Diego, Juan 136
Dillenberger, Jane 113
Dionysius bar-Salibi 22
Donne, John 203, 221
Dostoevsky, Fyodor 203–4
Dream (vision), 24–5, 97, 126
  Jacob's Ch. 7 *passim*
  Pilate's Wife's Ch. 2 *passim*
Drury, John 91
Dunbar, Evelyn 111
Dura-Europos 107
Dürer, Albrecht 74, 123–5, 130–3, 135, 137–8, 149, 216, 241

Eagleton, Terry 202
Eden, 23, Garden of Ch. 5 *passim*, 95, 181, 241
Editio Critica Maior Ch. 1 *passim*
Edmondson, William 73
Ehrman, Bart 213–14
Elie, Paul 195–8
Eliot, George 222
Elizabeth I 164, 167–9, 170–2, 221
Ellison, Ralph 75–6
emotion(s), emotional 84, 126, 190, 199, 243, 245–7
Empson, William 181
Enwezor, Okwui 83
Ephrem the Syrian 29
eschatology 10, 41–2
Eshun, Kodwo 75, 82
Eve 86, 156
evil, problem of 60

Farrer, Austin 216
Feti, Domenico 111
fiction 54, 56, Ch. 11 *passim*, Ch. 12 *passim*
Fiorenza, Elisabeth Schüssler 125–6, 216
Fonzo, Kimberly 30
Ford, David 39
Frankenstein Ch. 11 *passim*

Gadamer, Hans-Georg 54
Garvey, Marcus 83
Gauguin, Paul 114
Gay, Peter 222
gentile Ch. 2 *passim*
George (Saint) 150–1
Gershuni, Moshe 99
Ghiberti, Lorenzo 98, 219
Gibson, Mel 22
Gillman, Florence 19
Glossa ordinaria 29
Gnilka, Joachim 18
Goethe, Johann Wolfgang von 183
Golding, William 222
Gospel of Nicodemus 22, 29–30
Gothic literature Ch. 11 *passim*
Goupy, Joseph 111
Gregory the Great 60–1, 63, 246
Greene, Graham 222
Gundry, Robert 25

Hagar 59, 99, 100

INDEX OF NAMES AND SUBJECTS

Ham, the curse of 73, 74, 86
Hardy, Thomas 222
Harries, Richard 91
Hengel, Martin 45
Hilary of Poitiers 23–4, 26
Hildegard of Bingen 126
hip-hop 81–2
Hirst, Damien 218
history, historical x, xii, 3, 21, 53–4, 56, 84, 91, 107, 164, 174, 208–10, 212, 215–16, 219, 224, 233, 240, 246
 art 81, 85, 91, 97, 218; cultural 178; Jewish 209; salvation Ch. 9 passim; textual 4, 12; visual Ch. 8 passim
Hollar, Wenceslaus 111
Holocaust 95–6, 99
Holy Spirit 51, 152
Hopkins, Gerard Manley 203
Hurtado, Larry 46–7

iconoclast 92, 165, 166, 169
icons 112–13, 136, 215
 cultural 82
idols 240–4
Ignatius of Antioch 29
imagination 17, 37–8, 47, 55, 57, 81, 84, 85–7, 99, 109, 155, 163, 172, 177, 200, 211, 238
 Literary Pt 3 passim; theological Ch. 9 passim; Romantic 185; Visual Pt 2 passim, 241
imaginative fit 109
immanence 115–6, 224
Incarnation, incarnational x, 37, 51, 91–2, 155, 166, 168, 172
Infinite Jest 223
interdisciplinary ix, 12, 52, 55, 178
interfaith/interreligious dialogue Ch. 6 passim
Isaac 18, 32, 39, 58–9, Ch. 6 passim, 219–20, 237
Isenheim Altarpiece 128
Ishmael 58–9, 94, 97, 99, 100, 102
Islam Ch. 6 passim

Jacob 19, 32, Ch. 7 passim, 214, 235–6, 237–9
Jeffrey, David Lyle 218
Jerome 26
Job xvi, 53, 55, 57, 60–2, 63, 64, 95, 179, 184, 185, 190, 210

John Chrysostom 27, 29
John the Baptist 152, 156
John the Evangelist 156
Jones, Jonathan 84
Jonson, Ben 164, 167–9, 170–2, 221
Joseph novella 12
Josephus 19–20, 24, 58
Joyce, Paul M. xiv
Julius Caesar 19

Kadishman, Menashe 99, 100
Kertess, Klaus 82
Kierkegaard, Søren 58–9, 96, 101
Kilgore, De Witt Douglas 75
Koine text 5

Lambert 153–4
Lambeth Apocalypse (manuscripts) 127–8, 137–8
Lambeth Apocalypse Tapestry 123
Lambeth Bible 111
Lange, Christy 84
Lanyer, Aemilia 27
Laor, Yitzhak 99
Laud, William 221
Lawrence, Jacob 74
lectionary 5
Lewis, C. S. 181
Lindblom, Johannes 126
Lipton, Diana xiv
Lloyd-Webber, Andrew 22
Lopez, Yolanda 123, 134, 136–8
Lot 59
Lotto, Lorenzo 124, 138
Luther Bible 111
Luther, Martin 135
Lutheran, Lutheranism 148, 154

Macquarrie, John ix
Madonna *see* Mary (Virgin)
Magi 18–19, 28, 31–2
majority text 5
Malick, Terrence 223
Malkin, Benjamin Heath 135
Mansour, Sliman 100
manuscripts Ch. 1 passim
Marshall, Kerry James Ch. 5 passim, 218
Martha 63, 238
Martin, John 124
Mary (Virgin) Ch. 10 passim, 155–6, 220–2, 246

Mary Magdalene/Mary of Bethany 55–6, 57, 62–4, 246
Master Bertram Apocalypse Altarpiece 123, 134–5, 138
math 64
Meeks, Wayne A. 52
Melanchthon, Philip 135
Memling, Hans 123, 128–9, 132–4, 137–8
memory Ch. 3 *passim*, 97, 211–12
Merian, Matthäus 111
metaphor, metaphorical 9, 54, 112, 124–5, 129, 134, 166, 180, 191, 201, 216, 241
metaphysics, metaphysical 108, 110, 111, 202
metatext 10
Michaud, Philippe-Alain 101
Milton, John Ch. 11 *passim*
modernism 53, 63, 85
monastic, monasticism Ch. 9 *passim*, 237
Monty Python 22
morality 112–13, 190
Morgan, Stuart 82
Mors Pilati 27
Moses 156
Muhammad 100, 134
multiculturalism 84
Murillo 111

narrative(s) 54, 55–61, 64–5
Nero 19, 24–5
neuroscience 56–7
Newman, John Henry x, xv
New Testament Virtual Manuscript Room 5
Nicene Creed 22
Norbert of Xanten Ch. 9 *passim*
Nuremberg Chronicle 111

O'Connor, Flannery 195, 198, 222
O'Keeffe, Georgia 114
Ockham 147
Ofek, Avraham 99
Ofili, Chris Ch. 5 *passim*, 218
ontology 190
open tradition xiii
Origen 23
Orion, Ezra 111
The Orthodox Corruption of Scripture 213

Panhausen, Jacob 148–9, 153
papyrus 7
Paradise Lost see Milton, John
Paradosis Pilati 22, 26
paratexts Ch. 1 *passim*
Parker, David xiv, Ch. 1 *passim*, 214
Partsch, Susanna 219
Passio Christi 29
Passion des jongleurs 29
patronage 92, 147
Pattison, George 91
Paupers' Bible Ch. 8 *passim*
Peleg, Yitzhak (Itzik) 107
Pentecost 17
Percy, Walker 195
personhood 185–9
Peter 154, 245–7
Peters, Christine 173
Philo 58–9
Piers Plowman 22, 29
Pilate, wife of Ch. 2 *passim*
  Claudia Procula 22, 32
  Longina 22
  Prokla/Procula 22, 26, 30
Pirot, Jean-Marie 218
Plutarch 183
Pontius Pilate Ch. 2 *passim*
postmodernism 53–4, 63, 200–4
post-Christian Ch. 12 *passim*
preaching 12, 233–47
Preces Privatae 221
Premonstratensian Ch. 9 *passim*
Puryear, Martin 113–14

Quash, Ben 91
Queen Henrietta Maria 164, 167–9, 170–2,

Raphael 110, 111
reception
  exegesis xiv, 57, 65; history 8, 10, 17, 20–1, 37, Ch. 8 *passim*, 214
  relevance xiii, xvii, 12, 197
religious experience x, xii, 52, 216
Rembrandt 98, 101, 219
rewriting Ch. 3 *passim*
  pneumatic 45–7
Ribera, José de 111
Rice, Tim 22
Robinson, Marilynne 224–5
Romuald 110, 112

INDEX OF NAMES AND SUBJECTS

Rookmaaker, H. R. 218
Root, Howard E. xiii
Rosa, Salvator 111
Rouault, Georges 218
Rowland, Christopher 136
Rubens, Peter Paul 74

Saltz, Jerry 76
Samson 55
Sarah 58, 59, 95, 99–100
Satan, Satanic 11, 61–2, 95, 97, 130, 133, 134, 185, 210, 243, 245
Schama, Simon 219
Schapiro, Meyer 98
Schleiermacher, Friedrich 222
Schmid, Josef 9
Scorsese, Martin 223
scribe(s)/scribal habits Ch. 1 *passim*
sculpture *see* art
Second Temple Period 12
secular 109–10, 113–16
Seerveld, Calvin 218
Senior, Donald 19
Shelley, Mary Ch. 11 *passim*, 222
Signorelli, Luca 124, 138
Smith, Raoul N. 113
Smith, Zadie 199
Sommer, Benjamin D. xv
Steiner, George 195, 197
Steinfeld Abbey Ch. 8 *passim*
Stump, Eleonore Ch. 4 *passim* 210
suffering 20, 22, 24, 28, 31, 60–1, 64, 129, 166, 184, 239
Swinburne, Richard 210
symbol(s), symbolic, symbolism 11, 23, 29, 41, 42, 45, 63, 77, 79, 86, 96, 100, 110, 112, 114, 126, 128, 129, 130, 138, 145, 150, 151, 153, 157, 191, 201, 211, 214, 245, 247

Tarkovsky, Andrei 223
Teresa of Avila 126
Tertullian 26
Testament of Job 60–1
textual criticism Ch. 1 *passim*
theodicy 52
theology ix, 3, 8, 12, 13, 64, 91, 92, 110, 149, 150, 163, 174, Ch. 11 *passim*, 201, 207, 209, 210, 214, 217, 223
  biblical x, contemporary 51–2;
  historical 8; natural xii; ordinary 38; participatory xv; revealed xii; systematic 17, 163, 210
Theophylact 29
This is Water 224
Thompson, Francis 236
Tiberius 26
Tintoretto 111
Tischendorf, Constantin 3–4, 22
Titian 242
Topçuoglu, Nazif 101
transcendence 109, 114, 115, 116, 181–2, 224
Traylor, Bill 73
tree
  of the knowledge of good and evil 78; of life 78;
truth(s) xii, 17, 18, 23, 30, 31, 38–9, 40, 41, 43, 45–6, 47, 54, 109, 199, 201, 204, 210, 211, 217, 218
triggers xi, 208, 209

Updike, John 195, 222
un-visibility 75–6

van der Meer, Fritz 131
van Eyck, Jan 134
Vasari, Giorgio 110–11
Veronica's Veil 156
Vesely, Alec 112
Victoria and Albert museum 144
visual art *see* art
visual exegesis 11
Volney, comte de 183
von le Fort, Gertrude 22
von Soden, Hermann 4

Wallace, David Foster 197–204, 223–5
Webster, John 210
Westcott and Hort 3, 213
Westermann, Claus 116
White, Patrick 222
Whore of Babylon 11, 130, 133–5
Williams, Rowan 203
wisdom literature 209
Womack, Caterine 75–6
Worsdale, Godfrey 82
Wright, N. T. 211

Yehoshua, A.B. 99

www.ingramcontent.com/pod-product-compliance
Lightning Source LLC
Chambersburg PA
CBHW021937290426
44108CB00012B/874